AUDEN'S O

Auden's O

The Loss of One's Sovereignty
in the Making of Nothing

ANDREW W. HASS

STATE UNIVESITY OF NEW YORK PRESS

Published by
STATE UNIVERSITY OF NEW YORK PRESS, ALBANY

© 2013 State University of New York

For information, contact
State University of New York Press, Albany, NY
www.sunypress.edu

Production, Laurie Searl
Marketing, Anne M. Valentine

Library of Congress Cataloging-in-Publication Data

Hass, Andrew.
    Auden's O : the loss of one's sovereignty in the making of nothing / Andrew W. Hass.
        pages cm
    Includes bibliographical references and index.
    ISBN 978-1-4384-4831-2 (hc : alk. paper) 978-1-4384-4832-9 (pbk : alk. paper)
    1. Nothing (Philosophy) in literature.   2. Hermeneutics—Philosophy.   3. Postmodernism.
4. Nothing (Philosophy)   I. Title.

    PN56.N69H37 2013
    809'.9338—dc23   2012045469

10 9 8 7 6 5 4 3 2 1

CONTENTS

ACKNOWLEDGMENTS   ix

EPICYCLE   xi
   "Nothing will come of nothing"   xi
   Falsetto   xiii
   Auden's Circumlocution   xv

CHAPTER O
INTRODUCTION   1
   Giotto's O   1
   The Binary   3
   The Binary Code   5
   The Binary Code Cracked   6
   The Paradigm   13
   The Paradigm Shift   13
   The Paradigm Rift   16
   The Modern   17
   The Modern Crisis   18

PART ONE
FROM RELIGION AND PHILOSOPHY TO ARTIFICE

CHAPTER ONE
THE SOVEREIGNTY OF ONE   25
   One's Punch Line   25
   From the Many, One: The Hebrews   29
   The Nature of One: The Presocratics   32
   The Metaphysics of One: Plato, Aristotle   35
   The Wholly, Plenary One: Plotinus   44
   The Christian One: Paul   48
   The Paradigms of One   52
   One's Retreat   65

CHAPTER TWO
THE REVOLUTIONS OF O   67
    The Romeo Effect   67
    Zero and its History   69
    Ground Zero   74
    Mirror/Speculum/Eye   77
    The Artificer's Circle   82
    The Hermeneutical Circle   88
    I The Author's O   93
    Eternal Recurrence   97

PART TWO
POESIS' FIGURE—THE MAKING OF O

CHAPTER THREE
SHAKESPEARE'S EYE OF THE STORM   105
    Lear's Tragic O   105
    Shakespeare's Specular O   109
    Caliban's Negating O   115

CHAPTER FOUR
REFLECTIONS OF AUDEN   121
    W. H. Auden   121
    The Sea and the Mirror   124

CHAPTER FIVE
THE EMPTY MIDDLE   159
    Originating O (Blanchot)   159
    Historicizing O   166
    Alternate Os of the Middle   168
    The O of Auden   183
    The Erotics of O   188
    Simone de Beauvoir   191

PART III
LOOKING AFTER O

CHAPTER SIX
THE REMAKING OF PHILOSOPHY AND RELIGION   199
    Philosophy and Religion: Inside the Perimeter   199
    Negation's Triumvirate: Hegel, Nietzsche, Heidegger   201
    Before the Postmodern: Sartre   214

Through the Postmodern: Derrida, Irigaray   220
Out of the Postmodern: Badiou   235
gOd—Postmortem Theology   243

CHAPTER SEVEN
THE FUTURE OF O?   253
  Auden's Brecht   254
  The Parabolic Within   256
  Pontius Pilate in the Creed   259
  The Other Rogue   261
  The Rogue Within   263

ANOTHER EPICYCLE   267
  The Truest O is the Most Feigning   267
  "Signifying Nothing"   268

NOTES   271

BIBLIOGRAPHY OF CITED WORKS   301

INDEX   311

ACKNOWLEDGMENTS

A book of this ambition and breadth does not come together—if it comes together at all—without the thoughts, input, and support of a great number of people. Many names are now lost to the process of thinking on so many different levels and over such a length of time. But some continue to stand out, with feedback that had direct impact on the content of the text: Tom Altizer, Pamela Sue Anderson, Andrew Cutrofello, Bettina Bergo, Ward Blanton, Val Cunningham, David Jasper, Werner Jeanrond, David Klemm, Ben Morgan, Dan Price, Robert Sherwood, and Heather Walton. Of course the more formative influence of these and others could never be captured, though my gratitude for such influence is as great if not greater. I am also deeply indebted to the anonymous reviewers of this manuscript, who drew my attention to the pockmarks and seams still present in the argument of the final draft. I also owe much thanks to the tremendous support of my colleagues at the University of Stirling, especially those in Critical Religion—Tim Fitzgerald, Alison Jasper, Michael Marten, Richard Roberts—who keep the inspiration for such interdisciplinary interrogations, amid the intensities of daily academic life, very much alive. But I owe my greatest gratitude to the love and support of my partner, Jennifer Davidson, whose indefatigable belief, even during the most arduous of times, and when our own children entered our lives, sustained me beyond my own belief, and in ways I cannot say. Thank you.

EPICYCLE

"NOTHING WILL COME OF NOTHING"

Parmenides, the Eleatic philosopher predating Socrates, handed this famous circularity to the West. From nothing comes nothing. Or as Parmenides said more tautologically, nothing is not. This seems patently clear, at least in terms of basic logic. But the idea keeps returning, keeps haunting us, as if there remains something unresolved in it, something more than pure tautology. Philosophers and theologians, ever since Parmenides, have continued to grapple with it, whether Aristotle in his *Physics*, or the Scholastics in its Latin form (*nihil ex nihil fit*), or Leibniz's altered version, "Nothing is without reason"(*nihil est sine ratione*). Most people today, however, know the saying from a source other than philosophy: from the injudicious Lear, who says to his youngest and favored daughter Cordelia in the opening scene of Shakespeare's tragedy: "Nothing will come of nothing. Speak again." In response to her father's solicitations, Cordelia has said nothing. Literally, "Nothing." "Nothing?," Lear asks dumbfoundedly. "Nothing." But nothing can possibly come from nothing, says Lear, summoning the many great minds before him. Or, might Lear be overlooking something?

Aristotle himself wondered this, and agreed with the statement only after some qualification. Few remember the philosopher's qualifications. But many remember the plight of Lear. For Lear is himself reduced to nothing. And only then does he see that Cordelia's "nothing" was in fact the fullest, the most meaningful response of all the daughters. According to the playwright, then, something might indeed come of nothing. Or nothing is a place where things of a deep nature might come to be known.

By tending to concepts, the philosopher and theologian focus on the substantive nature of the subject and its predicate, in this case "nothing." By attending to drama, the playwright focuses on the action of the verb, "will come." Substantively, nothing is . . . nothing. Actively, something *will come*, even if it is nothing. Parmenides says nothing is not possible, so let us not speak about it. Shakespeare says nothing will come, even from nothing, so let us speak again. And so the "nothing" of Cordelia speaks again and again throughout the play, until it ripens in its nothing as "something." This coming to ripeness is what the following pages will explore.

The primary question in this movement, this ripening, is about sovereignty. Who has the better claim, the higher authority, on nothing? Conceptually, and traditionally, it has been the philosopher/theologian. And he—it has almost exclusively been a *he*—has exercised that claim and authority by trying to rid us of nothing. The poet, on the other hand, has always seen the profound irony in that gesture: if nothing is truly nothing, there is nothing to rid. So let it be, and make nothing of it. But how, puzzles the philosopher, can you *make nothing be*? By *making* nothing of nothing, responds the poet. But how, asks the theologian, can you *make* nothing, and make it from nothing, without encroaching upon the divine office (*creatio ex nihilo*)? By letting go of sovereignty, says the poet. And both philosopher and theologian here have the poet banished.

Let us tell a story of a banished king. This king makes a poor initial choice in dividing up his kingdom between two ingratiating children. His blatant folly lies in inviting the ingratiation as a measure and pageantry of his reward. A third child says nothing. The first two, over the course of time, strip their father of his sovereignty. The third maintains her love and loyalty, but the king cannot see this until he is stripped down to the barest of beings, in a nakedness that is at once physical, mental, psychological, existential, spiritual. By then it is too late—events have overtaken the possibility of regaining any of his loss, and he dies with nothing, neither his beloved third child, nor his other two children, nor his restored kingdom and sovereignty. But something arises from this nothing: the recognition, the tragic recognition, that his third child said volumes in her nothing. That her nothing bore love, bore devotion, bore the honor due a sovereign. The paradox is that this honor, nothing's honor, reaches its height only when sovereignty has slid from its place.

What if we used this story as an allegory of the history of nothing itself? Parmenides would tell us that nothing cannot have a history. The poet would tell us to invent such a history. The poet would translate the philosopher's claim into "everything must have a history," and this would include nothing. So we must give it a history. But nothing would have to be figured somehow, figured in such a way that brings its history alive, out of its bare nothingness. Lear might be some such figure.

The problem, however, is twofold. On the one hand, Lear himself has his own history, dramatically, aesthetically, critically, and therefore is not the bare nothingness from which something might emerge, as nothing. On the other hand, if we take Lear's allegorical role seriously enough, if we embrace the import of his negative symbolism in a thoroughgoing manner, his nothingness is all too bare. This the Fool has poignantly revealed when the sovereign crown of the king has been dashed on the ground: "Now thou art an O without a figure. I am better than thou art now: I am a fool, thou art nothing" (I.iv.183–85).[1] If the Fool is right, there is absolutely nothing here to go on. How do we make something without a figure?

But of course there is a figure, drawn by the Fool. An O. It is without an accompanying figure, or cardinal digit, and therefore of no numerical value. But in and of itself it is a figure. And it figures. It figures in the scene as a crown without a head, or in Goneril's case, a frontlet of consternation. But more, it figures as zero, the zeroed out being, which Lear has become. The Fool's O, then, in its bare figuration, might allow us a history.

But the Fool's O is only a small porthole through which to view a much wider scene of figures, a much broader history. If Lear is an O without a figure, "unaccommodated man," as he says on the heath, his fate leaves a bleak and blank picture. "All's cheerless, dark, and deadly," says Kent to the king at the play's end (V.iii.288). If we are going to see greater possibilities than the tragic O, we need to go beyond the Fool, and beyond Lear as his figuration. It is vital to see the empty crown, the hollowed out sovereignty. But what was that sovereignty to begin with? And where does its demise lead us? We need to see the O refigured. And for that we need a different drama.

The pages to follow will allow for a dramatic figuring to take shape: the Fool's O, which is Lear's O, will lead to Shakespeare's O, and to Auden's O. This drama will then require a history, and yet this history must always be tenuous, precisely because the O, as nothing, and without a name attached to it, has no story at its origin, and therefore no history in the general sense of the term. By attaching a name, we figure it, and thus let it figure in, and out of, its pure nothing. But the name does not fully escape that nothingness we place in its possession. And neither does the history. We are caught, then, in our own circle. By taking leave of the philosopher's reasoning, and by taking the poet at his word, we name an O that will come to nothing.

FALSETTO

In the opening of his book entitled *Nietzsche and the Vicious Circle*, Pierre Klossowski describes the moment when the thought of the Eternal Return came to Nietzsche as a revelation of the *"hohe Stimmung*—the high tonality of the soul." But Klossowski then asks, "How can a tonality of a soul, a *Stimmung*, become a thought"? Only, he says, by turning back upon itself, by repeating and imitating itself, and thereby signifying itself for thought, in a move by which "an image of the Circle is formed."[2]

But already in the Introduction Klossowski had asked, "How can we speak solely of 'Nietzsche's thought'"? He is forced to put "Nietzsche's thought" in inverted commas because, in light of Nietzsche's own false voice, in light of Nietzsche's later delirium that puts into question the rationality of his legacy, in light of Nietzsche's proleptic tone, through which "he predicted that this future would be convulsive, to the point where our own convulsions are caricatures of this thought," he is forced to ask, "What then is the *act of thinking?*"[3] And here Klossowski means, What is an act of thinking if it is now always and already informed by a "thinker" who challenged what it means to think, who taught that a *"thought only rises by falling, it progresses only by regressing"?*[4] How do we identify Nietzsche the thinker and teacher, the "Professor Nietzsche" who "destroyed not only his own identity but that of the *authorities of speech"?*[5] How do we give speech and voice back to this infamous negator of the word? The response of civilized culture, of scientific culture especially, has been, according to Klossowski, to keep teaching and learning, to keep speaking the language of positivity, to keep, that is, *calculating* (the "decision that invents reality"). We calculate "so as not to have to speak, for fear of falling back into nothingness."[6] But this dilemma is also the dilemma of the O. How do we calculate with O? Calculating with O, or zero, brings us all the faster back to nothing. And when we are back to nothing, where are we? In what company? With whose voice? In whose name have we made our calculation? What names are left, and what possibilities for naming?

Klossowski struggled with writing a book about Nietzsche's thought—the thought of Eternal Return—precisely because Nietzsche himself was caught up in a vicious circle, one whereby he challenged the thought of his day, with a high pitch that has remained unsurpassed, by employing that very thought. To write about a body of *thought* as if it were stable, fixed, reliably knowable and accessible, there to be determined as a substantive entity, requires a certain position on behalf of the author (both the original author and the author writing about that author), and Klossowski shows his hesitation right at the outset. Nietzsche *was not* in that kind of position. If we are going to explore Nietzsche's notion of Eternal Return, he admits, we cannot explore it as if it were a theory that was postulated and is now to be examined for coherence and probity. Instead, we have to give ourselves over to the circular nature of the matter. Thus, he says audaciously of his book to follow: "Let us say that we have written a *false* study."[7] And by this he means that the O of the vicious circle will always displace the object under direct analysis by holding it to a certain negation. The effect of this paradox, being held to displacement, is that in reading *Nietzsche and the Vicious Circle* we hear more the voice of Klossowski than of Nietzsche. Or, we might say, the history of Nietzsche's O is always something, and someone, else.

AUDEN'S CIRCUMLOCUTION

This study, *Auden's O,* is written in a similar intonation—as a "false study." For the poet W. H. Auden too was caught up in a vicious circle, one of trying to capture in his art that which forever eludes capture: the origin and nature of the O itself. For what exactly is this O if, in its viciousness, it still allows the poet's voice to ring out, and perhaps ring out all the more, in the highest tonality of the soul? How can something, even the artifice of the song, the poem, the play, arise from the depths of an unnameable nothing? And if it does arise, in whose name does it take its form?

In his poem "One Circumlocution," Auden begins with what, on one register, sounds like Nietzsche's moment of revelation concerning Eternal Return:

> Sometimes we see astonishingly clearly
> The out-there-now we are already in;
> Now that is not what we are here-for really.
>
> All its to-do is bound to re-occur,
> Is nothing therefore that we need to say;
> How then to make its compromise refer
>
> To what could not be otherwise instead
> And has its being as its own to be,
> The once-for-all that is not seen nor said?[8]

Here Auden seems to seek a way out of the vicious reoccurrence of our bare existence, glimpsed on those rare occasions in its high tonality. For in its endless return there is nothing more to say about it. But how do we capture the otherwise, the once-for-all, which breaks the circularity, but which itself cannot be said? We are caught in a circumlocution of a particularly ironic kind: *what we can only say in a roundabout way is precisely what cannot be said.* And so we can only say it in the name of a compromise. Thus, the poem ends on a "blank I."

Auden's poetry is an investigation into the "staged importance," the "staginess," of the false voice required in naming the O. And so "Auden's O," in turn, is a trope, and throughout the pages to come it is only ever a trope. The turning in the *tropos* of this O is precisely that it must come back on itself and undo itself. Like Lear, the Fool's O, and like Nietzsche's thought on Eternal O, it must zero itself out. But as a trope, it is also a figuration, a specific circumlocution, even if one among many possibilities.

The figuration of this one as O, its staged importance, is what will transpire in what is to follow, in the name of Auden, which is to say, in the name of one who knew how, and why, to blank out his own name. *Auden's* O will thus circle around itself, in one great circumlocution, with Auden and his O at the blank center.

But to put Auden and his O at this center, to take him at his own compromising word, means also to displace him. This requires a certain indulgence: to put him elsewhere than perhaps where we might expect (the beginning, say). The talking around of Auden, yes, but more, the talking around Auden.

CHAPTER O

INTRODUCTION

But "whatever its force, the status of circular argumentation is simply that of *persuasion*" (my italics). Because of this fundamental trait [of circularity], which is linked more to persuasion than demonstration, the appearance of a paradigm in the history of any given science has many—or all—of the traits of an "artistic revolution."

—Gianni Vattimo, quoting Thomas Kuhn[1]

GIOTTO'S O

The great Renaissance painter Giotto di Bondone (1267–1337) is said to have won a Vatican contract from Pope Benedictus XII by submitting nothing more than a hand-drawn circle, supposedly perfect in its execution. The "O of Giotto," as it became famously known, has since become the stuff of artistic lore in its ability to capture, not reality (realism was not a functioning aesthetic in Giotto's time),[2] but the idea of perfection. Giotto's O is thus emblematic of the Renaissance's obsession with symmetry, with the aesthetics of geometry, with the unity of the whole, and with the spiritual features of the circle, as seen in the many Roman arches and halos that Giotto painted for churches and ecclesiastical patrons. It is also emblematic of the human ability to master an wholly integrated world, one in which the divine imprint on human nature and the created order is replicable by and within an aesthetic gesture. This gesture, perfectly rendered, is what so obviously impressed the Pope, and gave Giotto such a celebrated career. His O was a sign of the highest order.

But is there such a thing as a perfect circle in the phenomenal world? Or is the perfect circle only a theological ideal, a doctrinal construct, a philosophical dream, a utopian wish? In the medieval West, the perfect circle represented unity and oneness: a single and pure symbol of the one true divine perfection that not only was reflected in the heavens and their

1

movements, but who resided as the ultimate Sovereign in those heavens. Thus, by drawing freely his circle, Giotto proved not only his technical prowess, but his theological acumen. But with the coming of modernity, that ruling sense of one, or the One, has been plagued with division. It is not just that the perfect circle was applied to humanity, as in da Vinci's famous Vitruvian drawings. Nor that the Catholic Church lost its catholicity in the upheavals of the Reformation. It is also that the true and perfect circle was finally seen for what it was: a spiritualized *aesthetic*. Thus, the seventeenth-century Johannes Kepler, himself a spiritual man, signally wrote:

> For if it was only a question of the beauty of the circle, the spirit would decide with good reason for it, and the circle would be suitable for all bodies, principally for celestial bodies, since bodies participate in quantity, and the circle is the most beautiful form of quantity. But since it was necessary to rely not only on the spirit but also on natural and animal faculties to create motion, these faculties followed their own inclination, and they were not accomplished according to the dictates of spirit, which they did not perceive, but through material necessity. It is therefore not astonishing that these faculties, mixed together, did not fully reach perfection.[3]

Hence, the ellipse. Material necessity distorts the circle, brings it up short of perfection (the etymology of the Greek *ellipsis*). Only a spiritualized circle remains purely whole, as a kind of beatific vision. The real, phenomenal circle remains bound to "quantity." That is, it exceeds one. There is no one true and perfect circle phenomenally, says Kepler. The spirit and nature divide. In modernity, the circle departs from the One, or the One is no longer at its center. "The centre cannot hold," wrote Yeats in his now most quoted line.[4] "Something is missing that would make the circle perfect," wrote Derrida in "Ellipsis."[5] "*No centre there where the circle is impossible*," said Jabès.[6]

As circle, the round O has now come to represent many things. This book will explore these representations. What it no longer represents is pure unity and divine wholeness, the virtues that endeared Benedictus XII to Giotto. Such unity and wholeness have been broken. This book will also explore that brokenness. Division has entered our modern world as a common feature, and we have many circles, many centers, many Os. "Once the center or the origin have begun by repeating themselves, by redoubling themselves, the double did not only add itself to the simple. It divided it and supplemented it."[7] That is to say, like an ellipse, the O, which is no longer one, no longer with a single and perfect center, opens us up to something beyond ourselves as one, as "I."[8] Let us then begin our discussion by going beyond one.

THE BINARY

Let us begin with two characters, a pair that, in their most basic forms, stand within both the numerical and the alphabetic systems of Western symbology. They are, of course, the characters "1" and "O." The first signifies the Arabic numeral one, the second the cipher zero. The first also signifies the modern Roman alphabetic characters "i" and "I," the second the letter "o." No other characters in either system are common to both. This fact alone says something about their fundamental nature as symbols: they seek to encompass both measurement (cardinal, ordinal, and geometric) and description (graphic, phonic, and figural).

The first is the most rudimentary of characters, the vertical straight line. It is pure linearity, possessing a clear beginning and a clear end. It is the mark of progress, for the child begins by marking out in random direction, but the adult starts and stops with exactitude, keeping to the vertical axis at the same exact point along the horizontal axis. Precision might be obtained by an unwavering hand, in a determinate resolve to "hold the line." Perfection might be obtained by the aid of a straight edge, whether in its mechanical, logical, or even methodological (i.e. inductive, deductive) forms. The drawing goes up or down, from earth to sky, or sky to earth, and in that passage humans aspire beyond randomness, beyond themselves, while the divine might descend to the human. Figurally, and figuratively, the "I" is where we begin and where we end, the most basic determination of our being, the upright species who is self-reflexive, self-conscious, and, at its best, clear about where it came from and where it is going.

The second is also rudimentary, but more elaborately so. In theory, the circle is perfection par excellence. But in practice, Giotto's claim notwithstanding, we know there is no perfectly drawn circle. True circularity requires, necessarily, instrumental aid, and even then, ellipticity is always a threat. The circle has no discernible beginning and no end. It has a center, but its center is only notional, and not part of its delineation. Its hub is null, its core void. The circle, and its theoretical perfection, is thus based on a determination that is, geometrically and figurally, irrational: the irrational Pi that allows its calculation, and the nullity that constitutes its inner and outer limit. The O is therefore the containment of nothing, or the nothing of containment—the human ideal to circumscribe, delimit, and incarcerate the negation at the center of our being, an attempt to corral our feral psyche and the imperfectability or randomness of chaos. The O is the expletive of our fear, and of its eternal return.

Now for such rudimentary inscriptions, it may very well be said that these projections are too fanciful. Perhaps the straight line represents nothing more than our intentions for order, the circle nothing more than the idealization of order, construed out of straight lines equidistant from a given center.

Or perhaps even this is too much. Perhaps Saussure was right: the straight line signifies nothing other than the absence of curvature, the circle nothing other than the absence of straight lines, the hollowing out of all radial components.

And yet, these basic characters have opened up possibilities for us that go to the very heart of our thought in the West (if not beyond the West), and the fact that much wider meanings have reverberated through our imagination, like ever-expanding concentric waves, with implications for the very nature of our being, suggests a relationship based on something more than mutual difference. The two may hold an incommensurability, but as Hegel observed, such incommensurability is part of the essential nature of our world and its formal expression (in art and beyond), and we must always keep the two together, the curves of the organic plant with the straight lines of the inorganic crystal.[9] There is something, then, about these characters that invokes primordial qualities that seem to belong together, as if in a binary system. And such a system suggests mutual dependence as much as difference: without spokes, the wheel collapses.[10] These characters are fundamental characters because together, whether intersecting, tangential, or incontiguous, they have provided the forward movement of our symbology. As pure line and pure curve, they have allowed geometry to advance beyond itself, transporting new possibilities of meaning by taking, in their purity, the brunt of that weight metaphor ultimately places on any one signifier, allowing it to be translated from one sphere to another. Thus, "spoke": it is both the supporting radius, as well as that past verbal form by which, through inscription, what is said can be retained for the future, repeated again and again—the fundamental principle of all written language.

This book is about the reading of the "I/1" and "O" as primordial characters, but characters that have opened up well beyond what they may first appear to be. This book is about *reading characters*, characters that have stepped into our history to make tremendous marks on our self-understanding and thought. And we begin with characters that are nothing more than fundamental inscriptions, to see how they become translated into something much larger than their mere form as geometric shapes. So this book is also about translating characters, taking them from one sphere to another, with sometimes powerful and disconcerting effects. And it is also about this very process of translation, of bearing across different spheres, and how one sphere may give way to another, or become possible from another. Finally, it is about the nature of the sphere itself, and especially the sphere we capture by writing "O," which, as we shall see, is more than just a written signifier, leading to any one signified or field of meaning. It is a sphere of thinking, and thinking differently, which we are only now beginning to encounter with any kind of intention and embrace here in the late modernity of the twenty-first century. It is a sphere we may attach to a certain character, just as we may attach the "I" to ourselves, as "I" the author, but ultimately, it is a sphere that cannot be captured by anyone, or any one, or any one thing. It is a sphere of a completely different dimension, well beyond the comfortable "I" of authorship. But nevertheless it is a sphere we live with daily, even if the "I" becomes lost in it.

THE BINARY CODE

If it still seems too fanciful, here at the outset, to read so much into these simple characters "I" and "O," and to give them such "primordial" importance, we need then to consider the most revolutionary language of our late modern times: computer code. At its very basis is a binary system made up exclusively of "O" and "I," now in their numerical forms, zero (0) and one (1). Why these figures, and only these figures? In one sense, the choice is arbitrary, for all that is technically needed for computer programming is a simple binary function for two steady states of the memory unit, the labeling of which is immaterial. But in another sense, the concatenation of 0s and 1s, in a string of ever-expanding and complex variations and computations, allows for an arithmetic efficiency that, as the philosopher Leibniz first saw, would not be as possible if other signifiers were chosen—A and B, say. Leibniz was obsessed with finding a symbolic system that could represent not merely sounds but concepts. His ultimate goal was a universal alphabet of logical thought. For him, his invention of binary notation, in which any number could be written with just the digits 0 and 1, was the beginning of such a quest, and he believed these two fundamental digits could reveal to us properties of other numbers that would otherwise remain hidden from us.[11] Though this hope went unfulfilled, later mathematicians and philosophers kept his ultimate goal alive. George Boole, for example, took the symbols 0 and 1 to represent classes, since their own mathematical functions were unique: any number times 0 is 0, while any number times 1 is that number.[12] These digits might therefore be able to stand, metaphorically, and function, logically, as something greater than their mere numerical designation. The hope of arriving at a universal symbolic language of rational thought culminated in the logical positivists of the early twentieth century, whose system of logic was intended to convey, through advanced symbolic notation, a comprehensive language of all logical relations. Logical positivism may have had its day, philosophically, but it carries on in the new guise of computer programming, which has returned to the "simplicity" of Leibniz's first binary scheme, with all its technical convenience. Even if we think beyond this convenience, we know that the 0 and the 1 are also the beginning points of the numbering system, the place, we might say, of origin, of things arising from nothing into singularity. It is no sheer coincidence then that the origins of a new language, one computational at its core, should be founded upon these two primary units, coded together in a binary system.

Nor is it difficult to see how translation arises here from the rudimentary to the complex, for in computer code we see the best example of the kind of metaphorics Leibniz and Boole (et al.) were striving for: from the workings of binary code, 0s and 1s transcend their numerical function and become other base codes, which in turn translate into numbers and words of a given written language, and more complexly, into sounds and images, and then into a highly sophisticated interplay of graphics, phonics, and interactivity, none of which necessarily has any inherent significatory relationship with its coded substructure, other than the rules of the code. That this particular text—these very printed words I have written—originated from a word processing program whose origins are reducible to 0s and 1s is remarkable enough; that speaking "live" on screen to my family members across the sea in real time is also reducible, in the end, to 0s and 1s is almost inconceivable. And yet, increasingly the developed world accepts this metaphoric leap as part of our everyday realities. It even gives it a name, a name that, in its own origins, evokes the force and standing we associate with essential natures: virtuality. If the computer revolution and its attendant virtual nature translate us to a new way of thinking and being, then we are in no strong position to dismiss the metaphorics that inhere in the very forms that constitute its structure, the 0 and 1. They are, we might say, more essential than ever.

In establishing a mutual relationship between these two basic forms, a fundamental binary connection that begins at the geometric level, and extends to the numerical, computational, logical, and notional levels, we begin to see the power they accrue. But the issue of power raises the question that now accompanies our understanding of any binary system: is this power one of parity, or one of disparity? For as we know, late modernity has forced upon us a great suspicion of binaries, and expended much energy in showing us that parity never exists in those conventional binaries we have taken for granted for so long. If we are to point out yet one more binary system, and claim for it a metaphorics as prolific as any other—human/divine, male/female, white/black, etc.—is there here too an imbalance of power, a privileging of one side over the other? Is there ideology at work even in these most rudimentary of forms?

THE BINARY CODE CRACKED

If we begin at the basic geometric level of line and curve, and ask which has held supremacy, we have seen the pendulum swing back and forth. In the exemplary field of architecture, where these forms manifest themselves most directly in our cultural experience, each has had its day, depending on the prevailing thoughts and trends of the time. In the Classical period, the erect column stood tall and foundational, the curve merely embellishment. In Romanesque architecture, the circle took on new precedence in the formation of the arch. In Gothic architecture, that arch was compromised by an intersecting straight line, which, though only notional, disrupted the perfection of the (half-) circle, and returned verticality (and hierarchy) to cosmological and theological conception. Subsequent periods vacillated back and forth between the linear and the florid, reaching a pinnacle (or zenith) in the modern and postmodern periods, when the former took the grid to its farthest extreme (e.g., Le Corbusier), and the latter took curvature to new heights (e.g., Gehry).[13] Of course, tangent to all curves is the straight line, and architecturally we know that buildings must be built on flat surfaces if they are to stand the test of time. And here we might begin to see a power difference emerge: what is straight is foundational, either as base or as strut. But even given this advantage, the picture has never been one-sided in architecture, since the pure arch, with its keystone, could bear its own load, and in some respects more forcefully. Line and curve then have always worked together in putting a solid roof over our head.

In astronomy, and cosmology, the circle of course plays a more defining role. Ptolemaic astronomy spent much of its time trying to save the appearances of perfect circular rotation in the heavens, necessary as this was to its sense of centripetal harmony and order. Copernicus caused spectacular upheaval with his heliocentric revolution, and the centrifugal implications it had for our place in the cosmos, but the circle was still central to the operation of his heavens. Kepler was the first to bring acceptance of elliptical deviation as the norm, and thus introduce the straight line into the center of astronomical understanding. But it takes theology to keep pure verticality in the heavens, since no matter how many concentric spheres one places between humans and God, the path to or from the divine is still envisioned as a direct line, whether Jacob's ladder or Mary's annunciative call, Dante's rays of *Paradisio* or Milton's "golden Chain" of *Paradise Lost*.[14] When we move to modern astrophysics, line and curve break down, as the infinite universe lends itself to the calculability of neither. What is infinite does not conform to spatial parameters, or at the very least makes those parameters meaningless, so that "space" becomes a kind of cipher, a black hole into which anything, and nothing, might be poured, or pour out. This suggests a move toward a different understanding of the form of O, where space, if it is to be numerical in any geometric or spatial way, must resort to the nature of zero, in all its impossible ambiguity of working both within and against any system of accounting.

But we refrain from making this metaphorical jump to the numerical quite yet. If we stay with the figural, we can conclude that "I" and "O" as basic shapes have had a competing history, but that, correlated in a binary, no one side has maintained an uninterrupted sovereignty over the other. The wheel seems to require the spoke; the heavenly sphere is reached by the straight path. And if one does dominate, it is only for a time. Perhaps this is because as a geometric pair, the two do not yet function fully as a binary system, since in most working contexts the forms are usually seen or treated segmentally. Architecture, for all practical purposes, is a science of segments, as is, for all theoretical purposes, the calculus at the basis of modern astronomy and astrophysics. And segmentation works against strict binary systems.

But when we go beyond geometric figures, beyond linearity and curvature, beyond the straight line and the circle, beyond all their segmentation, what happens? What happens when we make that crucial metaphorical move at the heart of all signification, and impose upon the circle the notion of the nought, and upon the straight line the notion of the one? What, in this translation from figural geometry to cardinal numeration, transpires? A shift does take place. An "ideological" shift. We begin to see privileging: the notion of the one takes precedence over the notion of the nought. Not so much computationally, since in mathematics all numbers, rational and irrational, whole and fractional, maintain in theory a neutrality by virtue of their purely quantitative function (even if "zero" works against the concept of "quantity"). But we see the privilege notionally, speculatively, even metaphysically. We might even say the one, since the early Hebrews and the early Greeks, has not merely taken precedence, but has reigned above. And above not only zero (the Greeks did not even have a symbol for zero), but above all other numbers, at least in the cardinal if not the ordinal sense. The one, we shall see, takes on a supremely cardinal function, and above all marks the philosophical, theological, and cultural heritage of the West (and as some have argued, even the East).[15] The one becomes the ultimate metaphorical destination in the series of metaphoric moves from the figural to the figurative, because in the end the one is the purely abstracted One, the apotheosis of all truth and reality, the unifying figure whose manifold nature reduces down in the end to pure and all-encompassing singularity, whether from some other manifestation (e.g., The Three in One), or from its omni-nature (e.g., the Universal). The One in its capital form is, we know, God, and it is hard to count against God.

In Part I, chapter 1, we will try to confirm this claim, this cultural hegemony of the One. At this point, let us simply state that the notion of the One has held immeasurable sway over our Western understanding of reality from as early as the Ancient Israelites and the Presocratics. The One has not only defined monotheistic traditions (Judaism, Christianity, and Islam), but has helped determine all subsequent philosophical and cultural manifestations of these traditions. Philosophically, this One is seen in the obvious examples of Plato's metaphysics and Aristotle's teleology, and then in all the subsequent philosophies that work out of this Greek tradition, from Neoplatonism onward. Theologically, one sees it in the contentions of the Patristics, in the scholasticism of medieval thought, and in the reactions of Protestant hermeneutics. Historically, one sees it in Western conceptions of linear development and its concomitant historicism and progressivism. Culturally, one sees it in national and global politics, in all forms of ethics and judicial rule, in the mimetic as well as the expressionist conceptions of art, and in the working assumptions of scientific research and exploration. One ultimately see it in the use of the indefinite generic pronoun *one*, where the singularity of subjective origin is generalized to capture the universality of the all—*one* functions as everyone.

If this privileging is still in question, we might consider the following terms: *unanimous, unified, uniform, unique, united, universal.* As terms built upon oneness, they are often set as standards, and only in rare contexts do they connote something negative or disagreeable. *Universality* especially remains a potent word and concept, even this side of the postmodern critique, since, like *unity*, it invokes agreement, and civilizations are built upon agreement, even if it is the agreement to critique structures that have become too universal. Compare these terms to their counterparts, those either with the prefix "un-" (where an all-important "i" must be left off) or "non-." The privative forms are rarely, if ever, used as standards, since they presuppose a situation undesirable or in need of negating. "Unimpeachable," for example, is predicated upon an understanding of impeachment, and as a standard it assumes one ought to be evading the entrapments of bad faith or practice inherent to a given situation. "Nonproliferation" assumes a similarly negative context, and it arises as a standard only because of an inimical set of preexisting conditions. With virtually all terms utilizing a privative prefix, and thus invoking the O as zero, we seldom if ever see the makings of virtue. We privilege the affirmative. We give credence to what can be set out positively. As *the* first positive integer (and the definite article becomes highly significant here), the one becomes a standard like no other.

Chapter 2 of Part I will propose something radical by comparison. It will look at the difficult nature of the O, and claim that, beginning in the twentieth century, the hegemony of the one begins to give way, so that by the end of the century, and indeed at the beginning of this new millennium, it has all but given up its hold to another way of thinking altogether—a way represented by the figure of the O. The chapter will try to show that, in the binary of "O" and "I," the balance of power has shifted, the O standing poised, finally, to outweigh its rival. Of course, what this O actually stands for, beyond geometric circularity, will be worked out in some detail, for as we have already hinted there is no simple and straightforward metaphor at

work here. (There is nothing straightforward with the O, we will see.) The
metaphorics of this figure are complex, manifold, and ultimately open-ended,
despite what appears to be a tightly closed circle. The O will become a new
way of conceiving reality, a new way of situating ourselves within and over
against that reality, a new way that leads beyond precedence and hegemony.

How are we to figure this new O? In Part II, chapters 3, 4, and 5
will argue that it is not the geometrician, the mathematician, the scientist,
the philosopher, or even the theologian who gives us the first sustained
glimpse of this modern O, as we might expect. Rather, it is the poet, the
creative writer. We will return to Shakespeare, and to his dramatization
of the O in various guises. But we will come to focus on the poet W. H.
Auden (1907–1973), and his commentary on that dramatization. Now, it
might well be asked, or asked again with greater insistence, why such a late
focus for a name made central by the title? Is such displacement not deeply
mischievous and misleading? But the roguish nature of the O—the other
titular figure of the title—is such that it always displaces those who come
into its orbit. And it is the artist who best understands this, who in fact
works with this, who makes it work for the art. Or in Auden's case (but not
only Auden's), makes it work *as* the art. Auden's O, as the O of negative
centrality, rewrites the center as it rewrites from the center. And thus the
central figure is swallowed up in his own creation.

But in such a self-displaced position, how can the artist best serve the
coming of the O? Will not the dramatist and poet move the figure out of
the realm of the conceptual, by virtue of a craft materially embedded in a
given language and the concretions of life? How then can a poet's O, bound
to *terra firma*, compete with the magisterial metaphysics of the One, much
less displace it? These central chapters, and their artists, will elaborate a
different way of thinking about structures and systems, binary and otherwise,
as absolute modes of defining our reality. Shakespeare will begin to question
the sovereignty of absolutes, in which the One reigns supreme. Auden will
move us from a prevailing doctrine of absolutes to a "doctrine" of *poiesis,* in
which creation, or better *creating,* becomes the operative and defining term.
In doing so, he will not move us out of this world. In fact, he will *ground*
us all the more. But he will not ground us in the universals of this world.
Rather, he will place us in his creating, which remains unbounded, even if
his creating first comes to us from a particular historical period, with all its
mid-century anxieties. As we shall see, the kind of poesis that comes from
Auden's O extends beyond past, present, and future, and becomes *parahis-
torical,* not dispensing with, but working alongside history in a radically
open-ended manner. So even if Auden the historical character will become
central, that character will be translated by the workings of its own O into
something other than itself.

The poet, we know, grounds us by creating a world within the poem for our dwelling. Even the philosopher has understood this, and we think of Heidegger's famous rendering of Hölderlin's poetry, in which ground and dwelling become "essential."[16] In Auden's expansive poem "The Sea and the Mirror" we quickly encounter the unexpected, for the ground of this poem is not the ground of Hölderlin's *Grund* upon which Heidegger could set his philosophical remarks. It is quite the opposite, the *sea*, the most ungrounded of earthly places. The O then becomes a kind of ocean, an expansive sea whose depth, regardless of the solid perimeters that may surround it, we can never fathom. But the O is also an island within that ocean, a place marked out from the chaos of the watery depths. And that island we will recognize: it is Shakespeare's play *The Tempest*. (It is also *in* Shakespeare's play *The Tempest*.) Thus, we will be placed both on familiar ground and over unfamiliar waters, and this combination, or paradox, is a reflection of the very nature we have seen in the binary that is made of the figures "I" and "O." The circle is built out of the radius, which nevertheless does not figure, or is negated, in the final shape; the number one is a whole integer that comes into existence only because zero precedes it in the series (and separates it from negative numbers). This paradox is also seen in the reflecting image of the *mirror*, so that the O further becomes a speculum into which we gaze, and see ourselves, our "I." The paradox of the mirror, of course, is that the only time we can ever truly see our "I" (or eye) is in a mirror, and yet what we see in the mirror is not *truly* our "I" (or eye)—it is only its reflection. So the "I" never exists in our own eye truly. It exists only in the O as speculum, which of course is no "I." All these reflections will be born out in Auden's commentary, which is a "reflection" on Shakespeare's *The Tempest*, in order to explore the question: Where is the reflected original that is being reflected in the reflection? Where is the "I" of the "O" (the notional radius), the eye of the mirror (the notional self)? What is actually being created in this paradox, and between all these reflective surfaces?

It is clear from these preliminary questions and remarks that figuring the O is a disruptive process. What we think might be a straightforward picture is continually being broken open, as if the slit of the "I" was rent apart to produce a conspicuous hole. The circle invites its own void into view, and however much we wish to focus on the circumference, the void is always staring us in the eye. The O will never not carry a negating force. But its figuring is also a storied process, for the O provides the parameters from which the void can be both seen and filled. In this sense, the negating force negates its own self—a deepening of the paradox, in which we begin to wonder what begat what. Is it the story of O, or the O of story? Chapter 5 will examine more closely the question of origin, and of its storied, and storying, nature. This will become a dilemma of history: How do we trace the origin of nothing, when nothing has no fixed origin? How do we situate the O as a specific historical emergence when history itself is undercut by that emergence? Maurice Blanchot will help situate the space we must occupy in trying to work our way through this dilemma, as we orient the twentieth century around the O and its literary figuration. Here the center of that century will gain particular prominence, that center so often lost as an interstitial space between two conceptual markers, modernism and postmodernism. The convenience of those markers will break down upon a central lacuna inhabited by numerous writers in concord with Auden, as the power of negation is harnessed anew in an explosion of contemporaneous literary activity that tries to write its way through the cavernous darkness made ever-present by the spectacle of O's emergence from its closeted history. But then we will be forced to ask again: Did the spectacle originate this period, or did this period originate that spectacle? And we will feel the force of O's disruptive powers disrupting our history even as we construct it.

This question of history will transpose itself, as we saw in our opening gestures, into *whose* history. Who embodies the O, or how is O embodied? If the O must be storied, whose story is being told, whose body (or *corpus*) is being worked out? The embodiment of O, even at its most corporeal, will also work in two directions, toward the body and its desires, and away from the body in ecstasy. The "ex-stasis" of the figure, the "placing outside"—this we have already seen, as the circle places the circumferential perimeter outside of its own center and radii, or as the zero is placed outside of rational numbers, if not outside the notion of quantity altogether, retaining an irrationality at many levels, as it works against the concept of *ratio* at the heart of the *rational*. This irrationality resides in the concept of paradox that marks the O at the various stages of its metaphorics. It will also be made manifest in an erotics, whereby the body through desire is both embraced and abandoned. A shift to the O also becomes a shift to a certain eroticization of our experience, one that, if it is not wholly sexual, is at least predicated upon a new intensity of desire, a desire for desire, which of course holds its own negations and paradoxes. Here, Auden will further figure the O, as his own homosexual history is both made and unmade in his poetics. And from this history the question of gender will arise, as a masculine erotics is emasculated in the binary of gender and gender roles that will finally fall prey to the complications of O's negating nature. Here, the seminal work of Auden's French contemporary Simone de Beauvoir will inform our reading, as the feminist O is redrawn outside the power structures of male domination.

Will the O really be able to uphold such a shift in thinking, and at all these levels, from the conceptual to the erotic, from the existential to the gendered? For the paradigmatic upheaval that seems to be inevitable here would mean an entirely new way of conceiving all these levels, including the very nature of humanity and the very nature of the divine. Are we truly prepared for such a colossal shift?

THE PARADIGM

In the foregoing binary setup, we see a cracking of the system, whereby the O refuses to play the game, and disrupts the system from within. Of course, there are further disruptions we could mention, such as the fact that the binary never holds 0s and 1s only, since the binary itself, by name and by definition, introduces the concept of 2 into the field, as all binaries must. And from this 2, the question of plurality begins to invade, a question that will agitate over the entirety of our discussion of One and O, and especially of the latter as it ushers us, speculatively, toward the infinite.[17] The shift from One to the figure O then represents a shift away from the binary system itself, even if "1" and "O" are still bound to each other in some mutual relationship. Perhaps then we ought not to be thinking in binary terms at all, however much parity or disparity may exist among the two constituents, and consider that what we are really talking about here, if the suggestion has any credibility, is a *paradigm shift*. We had seen the world, structured the world, understood the world according to one framework, where the concept of the One reigned supreme, and now we see the world by means of another conceptual framing device, that of the O. The shift then is paradigmatic, to utilize Thomas Kuhn's now-famous idea, as we move from one system (including the binary) to another. This is a compelling way to look at the matter, and could provide us with the makings of another revolution, this time not merely scientific but philosophical, theological, even aesthetic, one that would lend itself to a new and all-encompassing paradigm.

If the O, and Auden's O, represented such a paradigm, we could gain the advantage of presenting something that gives Auden a new reputation, and something that could finally act as a clear and distinct label to the condition that for so long has been mired in the imprecision and relativity of the term *postmodern*. This might seem an attractive and welcome proposition. But unfortunately the story of the O is not quite so categorical as to impute a paradigmatic function. The disruptive complexity of the O carries through even to the notion of the paradigm. It is thus worth stepping back again to science—for the O leaves no discipline untouched—to understand why the ecstatic nature of the O places it outside even the structure of the paradigm.

THE PARADIGM SHIFT

What gave Kuhn's book *The Structure of Scientific Revolutions* such power and currency in 1962 when it first appeared was a thesis that those in the

West were primed to accept: that revolutions come about because a set of assumptions about how things operate, about how things ought to operate, and about the questions that need to be asked concerning their operation, shows up a flaw that cannot be accounted for within the set itself. Science, as a rigorous discipline whose very purpose is to fix the world of nature into predictable and stable states or mechanistic systems, finds itself in crisis when an anomaly persists. A revolution takes place when someone within the community—a rogue—steps outside the given paradigm, and challenges or un-fixes its very assumptions, proving in the end that they need to be radically modified or discarded. The idea of a paradigm shift appealed, first because it showed us that we do construct paradigms, often tacitly, through which we participate in giving meaning and stability to this world; and secondly because it showed that these constructs, though at times themselves unstable, do not simply disintegrate into nothing when challenged, leaving us to regress back to a state of permanent anomaly, but lead to new paradigms, and eventually to new stabilities. For a world still reeling from the excesses of two cataclysmic world wars, and finding increasing tension in a cold war where competing political paradigms could lead to even further global destruction, the possibility of a new emerging paradigm was welcome news. The effect of Kuhn's argument was that we still could progress, because revolutions separated by periods of normal practice or fixed paradigms are precisely what make the world (of science, and by extension of all human endeavor) advance. And this process can even occur "without benefit of a set goal, a permanent fixed scientific truth, of which each stage in the development of a scientific knowledge is a better exemplar."[18] This thinly veiled Hegelianism was embraced by a world beginning to think that the next revolution or upheaval would lead to total annihilation. To suggest a continuing advance appeases the anxieties, so that regardless of what is happening, or has happened, to disrupt the accepted state of things and affairs, a new stable condition is waiting on the horizon. This progressivist belief also reveals that Kuhn's notion of revolution, scientific or otherwise, still operated within the provenance of the One: the "turning over" of the revolution becomes flattened out in a linear movement toward the next paradigm.

A paradigm shift, then, can take place only within the meta-paradigm of the One. As a system (linguistic, scientific, etc.) of structure, taxonomy, and exempla, a paradigm assumes a unifying origin at its base: all material in the system conforms to a singular conception that governs its arrangement and interpretation. Kuhn's scientific revolutions simply overturn one such system with another. They do not actually move outside the singular conception of the defining frame. To do so would be to halt the "evolution" of science, and indeed "halt" his own thesis of a shift from one paradigmatic structure to the next. The One is needed to keep the paradigm a paradigm. But the meta-paradigm of the One Kuhn does not address.

His text does show, however, and in spite of itself, the creaky nature of this meta-paradigm, whose deterioration was already well under way in other spheres of thinking by the 1960s, as we shall see. From Kuhn's title alone we can educe the inherent tensions between One and O. A *structure*, in the sense being elicited by the title, assumes, like the paradigm, a given whole to which the constituent parts are mutually related. This structure, "*the* structure," must have a singularity or uniformity as its fundamental nature in order for it to function as a structuring entity. This oneness therefore draws in the second half of the title, the *scientific revolutions*, so that whether we take the preposition "of" subjectively or objectively, the net result remains bound to the limits of the structuring wholeness, where the whole, as an integer, is the wholeness of one. Revolutions, then, either structure or are structured by this wholeness. What Kuhn is ultimately arguing is that revolutions as events are both: they are events that structure the advance forward of science, and events that are structured by certain consistent and repeatable features within history. But here the concept of *revolution* begins to disrupt the structure. For to have it both ways assumes an even larger wholeness that itself must be immune to any revolution, or we could never speak of the "structure of revolutions." This meta-structure allows revolutions to revolutionize, or, as we could say, to restructure. The revolution as a pure revolutionary force of disruption is domesticated back into another wholeness, where disruptions are dampened or done away with altogether. The zeroing effect of the O of revolution is made whole again. And yet, the O still remains part of the picture, hidden within Kuhn's revolutions like a caged animal waiting to spring its trap.

The unease in keeping a lock on this O manifests itself at several places within Kuhn's main text. Of course, in using "revolution," Kuhn wants to refer both to the circular movements of the heavenly bodies and to the disruptive force of overthrow, borrowing especially from the Copernican heritage, whose revolution famously embraced both meanings. But the more radical nature of the turning in revolution, the O that cancels out, finds its way into the picture through repeated acknowledgment of the tautological nature in describing the paradigm shift. Let us restrict ourselves to only one salient example. Kuhn writes near the center of his argument: "When paradigms enter, as they must, into a debate about paradigm choice, their role is necessarily circular. Each group uses its own paradigm to argue in that paradigm's defense."[19] Of course what Kuhn does not admit here is his own paradigmatic position, which allows him to give meaning to paradigms in the first instance, and thus meaning to his entire thesis. But were he to admit such, his argument would be so circular as to be of little use as a scientist, or as a historian of science, since he would effectively be arguing that the *structure* of the title ultimately does not hold, and that the enterprise of science, with its structuring intentions, is founded upon a very questionable base. He does later admit in a "Postscript" of 1969 that his own text falls prey to a certain circularity: "The term 'paradigm' enters the preceding pages early, and its manner of entry is intrinsically circular. A paradigm is what the members of a community share, *and*, conversely, a scientific community consists of men who share a paradigm. Not all circularities are vicious . . . but this one is a source of real difficulties."[20] To follow through this circularity fully, Kuhn has to admit that at the center of the concept of a paradigm is a deeply hermeneutical problem, which begs the question of where one begins and ends in the definition, a problem that the Postscript raises but in the end does not resolve.[21] Here is the closest Kuhn comes to acknowledging the O at the center of his revolutions, and their structure—the disruptive O that will not be counted within the whole, the zeroing effect that leaves a black hole at the core of the logic. It is because of this hole that, in moving from the One to the O, we cannot speak of a *paradigm shift* as such.

THE PARADIGM RIFT

What we have, rather, is a rift in the concept of paradigm itself. The paradigm becomes split open by the O, as if the O were the face of a weighty hammer. Moving from the One to the O does away with the meta-paradigm altogether, leaving no provision for any one paradigm (least of all the paradigm of the One) to give itself over to another paradigm. Instead, it gives itself over to something *new*. Not something *wholly* new, since the O does not trade in wholeness any more than it does in straightforwardness. Zero is not a whole number. But something new and *other* arises nevertheless, since the loss of the whole, the zeroing out of the structure, as paradigm, necessitates a going outside (ecstatically) of that which was once self-contained. The number one, and the concept One, is a fully self-contained notion. What impressed Pythagoras so much was that as the ultimate prime number, one is divisible by no other number but itself. It thus represents pure unity, pure self-containment. But what does zero contain? Figurally, the circle's circumference would suggest pure containment, but what is actually being contained, the inside of the perimeter, is nothing. Kuhn might have struggled with paradigm's tautology, but at least he could fall back upon *something*, if only self-containment—argument from within, paradigm justified by its own parameters. But the O does not allow even this. For within its own parameters there is a void. The O therefore is the greatest disruption of all, since it can only contain itself paradoxically: "Nothing is at my center" (the great paradox the East has wrestled with so much more profoundly than the West). The rift then is wide and bottomless. *And yet,* it is precisely because of this deep and fathomless zeroing that something other gains its possibility. The new is made available out of the nothing that centers the O, the Other, beyond, or within, what has been given. Here, *pace* Levinas, we cannot even say *wholly* Other, for that would be a betrayal of itself. The best we can say is that the O is the most emergent place possible, since it starts from nothing. It is *so* new, this place, that we are at pains to describe it. We can only figure around it. But that figuring, that "staging," will become immensely important, as we hope to show.

So if we are not describing a linear movement from one (binary or paradigmatic) structure to another, what exactly are we trying to isolate? How would we account for a *shift* that would be away from and outside of binaries and paradigms, and therefore a *rift?* And how could we account for it historically, without resorting to the very linear structures of historical movement that allow one phase to follow on from the next with some kind of logical succession or coherence? The rest of these pages will try to furnish an answer, as it moves through a metaphorics of the O. For now, we might see the problem as a fundamental problem of modernity itself, and in many ways the zenith of that problem now in modernity's latest (and last?) stages.

THE MODERN

If we remember that the term *modern* is built upon the Latin *modo,* "just now," we can see that a historical component is forever implicated in the concept that follows, "modernity." To be *modern* is to be thinking from the vantage of the now, to *begin* from the vantage of the now. Cartesian thinking shows us this move at its most formative and intensive: excise *pre*-supposition from all modes of cogitation, and begin from a *tabula rasa.* The *cogito* begins when one simply thinks, before the content of thought enters the picture. To gain this position of pure abstracted cogitation, one has to zero out the past, and its history (materially and conceptually). History can be brought in later—inevitably so, according to Descartes—but the emerging existing self begins from the point of the ahistorical now, and moves forward (or backward) from there. What this move suggests is that the starting point for reality is never, either cardinally or ordinally, prior to us. We inherit our past, yes, but this inheritance comes into operation only a posteriori, once our existence has been established in the now. In such a way of thinking, even in this crude reduction of it, the new gains a force hitherto unseen. For it is the new, the *just now,* that grounds our existence. As David Leahy describes, "[F]or Descartes, who appropriated from sacred doctrine a natural reason essentially altered from previous metaphysical identity, reason is that 'universal instrument which can serve for all contingencies,' that is, for knowing not *what is*, but *what is new*."[22] It is no longer the God who led our forefathers out of Egypt, or the Eternal Absolute known through anamnesis, or the Prime Mover, or any variation on these premodern notions. It is the "I" thinking here and now. It is the state of the new that comes from zeroing out the past. And from here on we will no longer be able to "accept" the past as we had done before. Modern science is still our best example of this "paradigmatic" shift: we accept the past because it works *now*. But if, for whatever reason, it ceases to work now, we discard it, never to return to it. Modern science progresses because, when verified by experiment and experience, it takes the new as always outstripping the old. When heliocentrism supersedes geocentrism, there is no turning back to the old model. The modern structure is always forward-facing. As a result, there is no longer a cosmology as such, in which all features of existence, past and present, fit into a tightly bound hierarchical framework. There is, instead, only an outward expanding universe, which can be known through an ever-progressive unveiling of its own structures. Scientific revolutions are simply a removal of one layer of fabric to reveal a more accurate view below or beyond. Only in modernity, therefore, does the past become "history" proper as we now know it—not that which has taken place yet still inheres meaning for us now, but the appropriation of the past from the privileged position of the present.

THE MODERN CRISIS

But this aggrandizement of the new, this privileged positioning of ourselves in the *just now*, was always bound to reveal its holes. For the new, the purely *just now* of the *cogito*, must start from zero, at least at its most reduced level, and to get there, one must zero out the prevailing forms and norms. For Descartes, this zeroing came in the form of doubt, and for Cartesians afterward this doubt has always been a necessary preparatory gesture. But if we think further about the radical nature of this doubt, it is more than a preparatory gesture—it is central to the conclusion. For in the *cogito*, the "I am" is not merely predicated on thinking, but on the doubt that allows thinking to be reduced to mere thinking. For we remember that in the end one can still doubt all the doubt, but one cannot doubt the thinking that is required for doubting. Thinking and doubting bear here a structural equivalence. One therefore might rewrite the *cogito* and still be within its logic: *I doubt, therefore I am*. And if thinking and doubt can wear the same cloth, then the O enters at the very heart of existence, since to zero out requires a thinking mind.

The crisis of modernity, right from its inception, is that we have never come to terms with the O. It has always been present, but we have tended to write it away in the One. Of course, since Descartes, the O as crisis, the negating disturbance attendant to thinking, the irrationality incumbent in rationality, has taken on many forms, for better or for worse: Hume's skepticism, Kant's antinomies, Hegel's antitheses, Marx's revolutions, Nietzsche's death of God, Freud's Id, the concentration camp,[23] nuclear proliferation, deconstruction, Lacan's Real, 9/11, global terrorism, and with it, the ultimate crisis event of our times, suicide bombing, where thoroughgoing negation is used as positive (theological) assertion. In Part III, chapter 6, we will return to philosophy and religion/theology to see how certain formative thinkers, in response to these various crises, began to figure the O in such a way as to allow it occupation in the very domain where the One had gained its sovereignty and held on to it most firmly.

But the O need not remain at the level of crisis. The twentieth century will reveal a shift not only in what the conceptual fields of philosophy and theology concern themselves with, but in how they approach that concern. Here we will concentrate on the O's double powers of irruption and eruption, as philosophy rewrites negation into a potent source of both taking away and adding, both nihilation and generation, while theology considers the very negation of God as the new point of departure for theological renewal. In both fields, O's creative nature will actively surface, not as an object for abstracted interest—the philosophy of art, or religious aesthetics—but as a *mode for doing* either discipline, or both together.

We will thus see that the O also carries with it the possibilities for something creatively new and constructive. It is from its zeroing process that the new as new is allowed to emerge at all. The nature of this new is what we will explore fully in all the pages to follow. But we need to be absolutely clear from the outset: the fact it still is the *new* tells us that we have not moved out of the sphere of modernity, however we wish to label the present. Postmodernity tried to capture the sense of the newness beyond universals and absolutes, while still reliant on the language of those universals and absolutes, even if deconstructively. In this regard any shift to the O is propelled forward by the postmodern venture. But as the list of crises above tells us, postmodernism has run into its own crisis, its own O, as it stands toothless before the post-9/11 realities of our day. Auden's O had already reached a similar conclusion: poetry, Auden eventually conceded, was largely ineffectual in changing the political realities of fascist Spain in the 1930s. Postmodernism's O exposes the fact that playful deconstruction has little to offer in response to the suicide bomber, other than the obvious fact, which we do not need deconstruction to tell us, that radical adherence to one form of truth will always be destructive, that zealotry and militarism are always a short breath away from each other. Postmodernism has been unable to provide for us any kind of ethics in response to a growing radical militarism,

where terrorist and freedom fighter become wholly interchangeable, and it
is clear that an ethics is increasingly demanded. (Guantanamo Bay is the
paramount example of a befuddled ethics in the West, as it represents, even
in its geographic location, the jumble of conflicting and incommensurate
positions: justice without justness, law without legality, democracy without
freedom, enemy without status, retention without warrant, etc. As a "judi-
cious" response of a democratic military, it is the manifestation of a classic
aporia—one cannot move forward, one cannot move backward. One can
only dismantle.) An ironic position of impassibility is no longer sustainable
in the "free" world. One ends up blown apart, or blowing oneself apart
(either literally, as was experienced on various Coalition front lines, or
figuratively, in the implosion of cultural stability).

If there has been a crisis in postmodernism, then what does this shift
to the O signify, beyond that crisis? What is beyond postmodernism, and
yet still within modernity? Post-postmodernity? Advanced modernity (in
the pathological sense)? For lack of a better term, we will continue to use
the label "late modernity," less because modernity seems to be in its later
stages of existence, advancing toward a state of expiration, and more because
modernity is *late* in confronting its own inherent O. To this end, we stress
that a move toward the O is a necessary and salutary move, insofar as it
brings us to confront the *new* anew. If we still fetishize the new, as seen for
example in the manifestations of the O as an erotics, or a sexualized metaphorics, we need to rethink the new. Every orgasm is *new*, we are told; it
makes us new, and thus the negation and recreation of sexual encounter is
a kind of eroticised *cogito*, a coming into being, as it were: *climaco ergo sum*.
And this is played out purely on the individual level, where my "I," as one,
has been eroticized into a "new" singular existence. (And the autoeroticiza-
tion of virtual sex keeps the one away from any coupling beyond itself.) Of
course, what virtually all pornography strips from our view is the possible
newness that is the very source of life: procreation. *This* new, a new life,
conception, with all its labor and attendant responsibilities, is not erotic
in any way, and so we dis-imagine it. But it is this kind of new we need to
reconceive, if we are to translate the metaphorics of the O beyond merely
an erotics of personal desire. Fetishization of the new needs to give way to
a responsible new, a new we hold responsibility for, culturally and ethically,
as a new life brought into this world. To keep the new moving forward
responsibly, the O must lead beyond the negating void we experience during
and after climax, and toward a newness of life in the fully conceived sense
of a newborn. The O must always be present as the otherness to ourselves,
even if (again *pace* Levinas) within ourselves, and not merely as negation,
but as the circular negation of negation, or the conception of something
new. We resist, once again, saying *wholly new*. But that new being will have

to think of itself as one come about through the O, and whose own being never dispenses with the O.

It is in this sense that we will hazard in chapter 7 a reading of O's possible appropriation of the ethical realm, through a Brechtian drama closely associated with Auden (*The Caucasian Chalk Circle*) in which law is turned inside out, and the newborn must be kept alive through the responsibility of looking after O. Here, the O will show its disruptive power within one kind of revolution—the overthrow of sovereignty in the name of a more powerful sovereignty—and its generative power within another kind of revolution—the chalk circle of ethical potency, that gains its force by withdrawing force. Here, the question of the legitimacy of O will be raised, and the legitimacy of its own future, in light of its inherently roguish behaviour. This, of course, will not be a prescriptive reading, but rather a parabolic trial in how the O might lend its powers to an ethical demand during a time when legitimacy is thrown into question on both sides of a revolutionary confrontation.

The being of this newborn is nothing more than a metaphor, of course—and we'll see this clearly enough in the parabolic circumference of the "chalk circle." In the case of some—Auden, for example, the homosexual—conception will play itself out in different terms. What those terms are that make up this metaphorics figured by the O is precisely what we aim to explore, beyond system, beyond paradigm. But even as the form of the circle makes clear—Giotto's O will be a constant reminder to us—the borders and limits of figuration, system, or paradigm are never entirely erased from view. So we must return to the figure of the One, and understand first how its paradigmatic force has kept rule for so long.

PART ONE

FROM RELIGION AND PHILOSOPHY
TO ARTIFICE

ONE

THE SOVEREIGNTY OF ONE

Multiple sovereignty is not good. Let there be one sovereign!

—Aristotle, *Metaphysics*

If one, or One, can be operating in something as unlikely as a drawn O, at least in Giotto's case, then the prevalence of One as a ruling paradigm is surely more extensive than what first meets the eye. How do we uncover this prevalence, especially within the vast history that constitutes the West and its thinking? Let us begin in a less lofty, even more unlikely place, to show the full extent of its reach. Let us begin in the mundane and often crass realm of humor, and with the variations on a joke.

ONE'S PUNCH LINE

Among the most paradigmatic of joke structures is the light bulb joke, built around the disparagement of a particular class of people (ethnic, special interests, etc.). The base joke runs: How many [fill in the blank with chosen group] does it take to screw in a light bulb? Answer: Ten—one to hold the light bulb, nine to turn the ladder. The joke is so stale now it no longer provokes a laugh. But the variations are infinite: "How many Scots does it take? Sixteen—one to hold the light bulb, fifteen to get drunk and make the room spin"; "How many Pentecostals? Three—one to turn it, and two to catch it when it falls"; "How many Surrealists? To get to the other side." And so on. (The latter example cleverly combines two of the most common joke paradigms.) Why does the light bulb joke keep turning out new variations? Why its longevity? (We have recently had: "How many Coalition fighter pilots in Afghanistan does it take to change a light bulb? No! You mean it was one of ours?") We could here invoke Nietzsche, who said that laughter simply means "to gloat, but with a good conscience" (the German word used here is literally *schadenfroh,* or taking malicious joy at the expense of others).[1] And certainly the light bulb joke would support this definition. But we could say that the joke owes its long life also to a structure predicated upon the concept of one. And this at several levels.

First, we know what the answer should be: it only takes *one* person to screw in a light bulb under any normal circumstances. If somehow more than one is needed, this shows incompetence, deficiency, ignorance, or stupidity, or it shows up a general or specific foible. And precisely the message being sent by the joke is that one or more of these qualities is present in the group being mocked. The obvious right way requires one person, and only folly, or ridiculous circumstances, would require more than one. When we laugh at any variant of the joke, we do so from a firm grounding in the standard that is one (not just the original version of the joke, but the implied singular answer).

But this standard operates at another level. The joke structure presupposes an agreed sense of normality, and that those who do not conform to the norm, for whatever reason, are worthy of ridicule. We know that racism, upon which this joke first gained its popularity, assumes a superiority, where one's own race stands above others, so that the norm is defined by a specific group of people and their custom. But even in milder versions, where the particular habits or foibles of a people are being pilloried, a unifying sense of normality exists, beyond which lies excessive behavior: Scots are excessive in their drinking habits, Pentecostals in their worship practice, Surrealists in their view of the world, Coalition fighters in their lack of discriminatory power, etc. To belittle, in any degree, is to discredit one's attainment of the accepted standard.

But jokes as a whole operate beyond the normal: what makes a joke a joke is that which goes beyond what we expect. Even contemporary comedians, who trade in humor based on common human traits, make us laugh only when those traits are presented to us outside their normal context. And to "stand up" in front of a crowd may be all that is required to take us outside of normality, since relational or sexual habits (to use standard material) are for the most part not funny *in situ,* but become funny when presented to us at some remove, where our normalities suddenly become strangely, and ridiculously, eccentric. The light bulb joke reduces this remove to its most basic. (Whereas the original chicken crossing the road joke gains its humor precisely by frustrating our expectations of being removed from the norm: "to get to the other side" is the very thing that mundane normality expects, and therefore we laugh, because we were not expecting the expected.)

But the joke structure is a testimony to the one at even a more complex level, at the level of hermeneutics. For the joke assumes a single shared meaning. We know that when meaning is not grasped it can be terribly unforgiving, as everyone has experienced the embarrassment of being left alone in puzzlement after a punch line. We have to "get" a joke, and if we fail, we are left to chagrin. Language's obvious fact is that it is predicated upon shared meaning, and meaning is predicated on a shared acceptance of what the semiologists call the referent, what any sign is referring to in its signification. The overall referent for a joke, the punch line, *must* be sin-gular, or the joke simply fails to engender laughter. Multiple meanings may work for irony, but irony seldom makes us laugh out loud. Joke tellers and professional comedians base their entire careers on whether or not people laugh out loud, which is to say they trade on a singular meaning, one that everyone interprets the same (or at least broadly the same). Hermeneutically, they assume—they require—*one* "punch" to the punch line. Only the most sophisticated of jokes can make people laugh through multiple interpreta-tions, and in such cases the laughter is usually more muted, as the mind thinks through the various possibilities of meaning. (I suspect the Surrealist variant of the light bulb joke would, on average, cause the least amount of overt laughter, since its punch line begins to introduce several ways of interpretation—not least because the crossing chicken joke is in many ways an anti-joke, with a punch line that uses the expected unexpectedly.) The punchiest jokes are those we all agree on immediately, from a gut reac-tion, which is why body (and bawdy) jokes remain so endless—"How many eunuchs does it take to screw in a light bulb? Answer: Eunuchs, screw?" Cerebral jokes, jokes that make us think at some deeper level, are generally not funny: "How many light bulbs does it take to change a human? Answer: It doesn't matter—humans remain forever in the dark."

Why begin with a joke? The light bulb joke shows us how permeating the concept of the one can be, at any level of culture or society. The *one* person required to screw it in becomes a metonym for the one meaning, the one interpretation, the one structure that we all share, even though it remains unacknowledged. It takes at least two for a joke to work (jokes told to oneself are not jokes as such—they are preparations for a future encounter), but the one in the joke remains the binding factor, the thing that *unites* two or more people in a common venture. And though it remains unacknowledged, the one nevertheless remains present throughout, under-girding the entire structure and encounter, a tacit hegemony. Of course to mention it ruins the joke, which is why the above analysis saps the humor out of the original contexts (if humor there ever was). But the one is nev-ertheless *understood*, and it is that unspoken activity of understanding that lies at the heart of Western conceptions of ourselves and reality.

A joke is a *conceit* par excellence. It is first an idea played out in the mind, and then a trick played out on, and with, others. At the root of the

word *conceit* is conception, and we should begin any analysis of the one by
understanding that it, the one, especially as One, is a *concept*. As understood
in philosophy (at least from the dominant Kantian tradition), a concept we
know as a notion that unites a manifold together under a singular entity.[2] It
is a process that originates in the mind, as opposed to a percept, an object
of perception received through our sensate faculties. A concept is understanding, at least insofar as a manifold is comprehended as sharing certain
features that can be reduced to a single description, category, or idea. When
Kant talked about concepts, he understood this as the capacity of the mind
to *synthesize* disparate entities together into a single notion, a synthesis that
of course requires the rational ability to discern the one out from the many.
The concept of the one is therefore standing under our entire notion of
rationality, *as concept* (even as its own paradox: the One's own manifold
is a series of other singular ones). Which is why it can be understood, but
need not necessarily be articulated as such. It may take a philosopher like
Kant to analyze the concept in detail, but operationally we have assumed
its existence since long before Kant.

The light bulb joke evidences this concept to us in a conceit. We
conceive of something that allows us to agree on the one without actually
acknowledging it, and when we understand, when we "get" the joke, we can
keep the reality of its existence unspoken, though we "acknowledge" it by
laughing. Laughter acts as the outward gesture of understanding, which itself
is kept silent in the conceptual chambers of the mind (one can pretend to
get a joke just by laughing). The one is therefore *understood*, implied but
not expressed. The one has largely been *understood* throughout the West
in this way. It is a concept that sits at the heart of all our understanding,
tacitly. And when we bring it to light, so to speak, we see how pervasive it
is. Just as light pervades when it is present, so too the one, as One, becomes
a conceptual radiance that allows us to see beyond the mess of multiplicity and nothingness. Thus, the philosophical and theological history of the
connection between divine unity and light. Not only does it take the One
to set the light in place ("Let there be light"), but the One *is* Light ("I am
the light of the world"). This connection becomes the joke (as parody) of
Thomas Pynchon's "Byron the Bulb" story in *Gravity's Rainbow*, in which
Byron, a light bulb, becomes not only sentient but *immortal*, never burning
out, desiring to exceed his role as "conveyor of light energy alone," but
"condemned to go on forever, knowing the truth and powerless to change
anything."[3]

But what allows us to make such metaphorical leaps? How can we
move from a bad joke to profound notions of understanding and conceptualization with such apparent ease? Let us then look now at how this *concept*
of one may have come about, as something more than a mere joke.

FROM THE MANY, ONE: THE HEBREWS

There is no one starting place from which to trace out the history of the One. It would be convenient, and corroborating, to say there was one origin, one beginning point. But the truth is, we have to construct a story from out of many, a history of ideas that functions as a conceptual thread through the many possibilities that undoubtedly exist. If we approach the matter chronologically, we might well begin with the Hebrews, whose monotheism has been so formative for us here in the West.

The Ancient Israelites of course were not strictly monotheistic from the start. Their God was one among many gods. His role, as the first version of the creation story in Genesis makes clear, was one of primordial separation. His first act was separating light from darkness, according to Genesis 1.3: in the beginning was a formless void (the void that resides in our O), and God split its pervasive darkness into two entities, darkness and light. The rest of the days are spent likewise, separating out the various features of the cosmos, so that by the end of the sixth day, the heavens and the earth are finished as a "multitude" (Gen. 2.1), and the story ends with "generations" (2.4a). Even God himself, as Elohim, is plural, as he speaks to a creating "us" upon whose image he will base humankind (1.26–27), whom in turn he will instruct to be fruitful and multiply (1.28). The second version of creation (2.4b–25) is less cosmological, more earthbound, and focuses on the budding forth of creation as some kind of grand exfoliation. The culmination of this story is also the creation of humankind, but it goes in the opposite direction. Where in the first version humankind began as a singular creation—"male and female he created them" simultaneously (1.27)—ending up among the multitude, in the second version they begin as separate entities—"for out of Man this one was taken" successively (2.23)—and end up as "one flesh" (2.24).[4] Here in this redaction, we already see the direction the ancient Hebrew scholars wanted us to move: from the many to the one. Through separation, we are then united. From the manifold, we become one.

Becoming one for the Hebrews was part of their very self-identity. Yahweh had brought Abraham out of Ur, the land of the Chaldeans and their gods, to possess his own land, Canaan. His offspring would be manifold, and Yahweh would be their God, Abraham the great patriarch. This pattern is then repeated with Moses in the exodus out of Egypt. There, Yahweh leads His people from slavery back to their own land, the land of their forefathers, and makes his claim upon His people even more exclusively. Despite apparent confusion ("If I come to the Israelites and say to them, 'The God of your ancestors has sent me to you,' and they ask me, 'What is his name?,' what shall I say to them?" [Ex. 3.13–14]), He and only He is their God. This movement toward monotheism, though not yet strict ("Who is like you, O Lord, among the gods?" [Ex. 15.9]), reaches the level of commandment on Mount Sinai, where Yahweh's first injunction is that his people should have no other gods before them (Ex. 20.3). By the time of the Deuteronomic Yahweh, God has become more exclusive and singular—jealous, even—and, as he now makes repeatedly clear, there is no other god besides Him. Thus, in the great *Shema* of Deuteronomy 6.4, the Lord is *one* God. And His chosen people are selected "out of all the peoples on earth to be his people, his treasured possession" (Deut. 7.6). One God, one people.

The Hebrew Pentateuch, therefore, gives us the full trajectory of this movement from the many to the one. It does not operate simply within the heavens, but, perhaps more importantly, within the peoples of the earth. And though the one is always seen against the backdrop of the many (the one chosen nation is defined by the promise of its multitudinous progeny; the Israelites' neighbors are never not a threat), it remains prominently in the foreground as the defining feature, upon which the cultic laws and practices are formed, administered, and adjudicated. Holiness and purity here are concepts deriving from the one, as the first separates out, and the second maintains singular distinction. *Religiously*, then, we have inherited the one as that which underlies the marks of piety, of faithfulness, and of righteousness. The God who is One, or who is our God alone, demands from us unalloyed allegiance and obedience. In return, we will be blessed as one people, the chosen people of God.

The curious story of the tower of Babel in Genesis 11 can be read in this light. To select one from among the many, not only does the One have to be drawn out as separate, but the many must be maintained in order for the One to be selected and held distinct. The end of chapter 11 begins the story of Abram, the future patriarch who will become Abraham, the one called out to be the forefather of a great nation. The beginning of chapter 11 sets us up for the power of the One. Following the flood narrative of Noah and his descendants, we learn in its opening verse that the whole earth had become one in language and speech. This linguistic unity leads to enterprise and ambition, as the people gather and say, "Come let us build ourselves a city, and a tower with its top in the heavens, and let us make a name for ourselves; otherwise we will be scattered abroad the face of the whole earth" (v. 4). We have already seen what such a tower can represent: the straight line as human aspiration beyond itself, that figure which becomes one in all its pure verticality and numerical consolidation. And a "name for ourselves" is merely an extension of this consolidation, as the manifold is consolidated in the name, which then bears identity and reputation. But Yahweh takes umbrage at this ambition. It is more than just hubris; it is threat. In a response reminiscent of Gen. 3, when Adam and

Eve have eaten from the tree of the knowledge of good and evil, He says (again to His plural "us"): "Look, they are one people, and they have all one language; and this is only the beginning of what they will do; nothing that they propose to do will now be impossible for them" (v.6). The power of the one is too great even for the divine sovereign here. Thus, He and His plural divine come down and confuse the one, scattering the people over the face of the earth in multilingual exile. Yahweh will have no threat to His power, and therefore no conditions of homogeneity which consolidate power. Not unless He initiates those conditions himself. And that is precisely what chapter 12 entails: God taking the One into His own hands. Out of the heterogeneous, the homogeneous may come, and when God sets the conditions, and governs the consolidation, the one can truly become the force He meant it to be, as it moves toward its promised land, a beacon for all nations.[5]

This familiar story of becoming one, of course, is not only a religious story. It is at the same time political (theocracy and monarchical kingdom), social (tribal Israel), judicial (the Levitical law), genealogical (the descendants of Abraham), ethnic (the Jewish people after the Diaspora), historical (the history of the Jews), textual (the Book), and national (the nation-state of Israel). Of these, we may pause for a moment with history. One of the great legacies this story has passed on is the outworking of God *in history*, as the Israelites are continually reminded to recall their history in the prescribed rituals and rites. The very centerpiece of Hebrew ritual, the Passover, is a celebration of Yahweh's historical delivery, which set in motion that progression of events which later German theologians would call *Heilsgeschichte*, the history of God's workings (taken both ways together: God's workings *in* history, and God's workings *as* history). This historical trajectory is likewise predicated on the one, the one historical timeline, divinely set out, that unfolds from beginning to end in linear fashion. It is what will allow later Jewish theologians their messianism and later Christian theologians their eschatology, as world affairs align themselves to a singular narrative, prescribed and preordained. Seeing history as one, as one coherent narrative, grounded not in mythic retelling and circular reinvention but in a procession of factual events, with chronological succession and internally cohesive development, is what lies behind our general historical understanding to this day, however we interpret the manifold events that make up any one history. We continue to see History as one meta-event. Even the premise behind Kuhn's paradigm shift owes its historical rationale to this meta-event, as does the suggestion in this book that we have been moving from the One to the O. We cannot escape this linear view of history, it seems, and whether or not we impute progression into its movement, we still conceive of its unfolding as we do any narrative—predicated on a singular story line, plot, argument, or thesis. This book is no exception, we repeat.

We begin with the Hebrews because their story of the One is a story embedded in history, unfolding in the vicissitudes of life's messy details, in order that a single sacred narrative might emerge. But, the *Shema* notwithstanding, the story does not yet *conceptualize* the One. In Hebrew wisdom, the One is not present in any defining way. Proverbial wisdom takes its aphoristic truth from the manifold of life experience (and in the compilation of many sayings), the Psalmist gives voice to devotional concerns (in the compilation of many hymns), the Preacher in Ecclesiastes tells us there is a season for everything, and Job's narrator is concerned with justice, which clearly does not have one interpretation, despite what Job's friends contend. It is to the Greeks we must turn to see the conceptualization of One in its most emergent form.

THE NATURE OF ONE: THE PRESOCRATICS

The earliest Greeks might at first seem the most remote from singularity, if we take their mythology and their pantheon as indicative of their thinking. But with the coming of Greek philosophy, in what we know today as the Presocratics, we start to see a new approach to the question of reality. Instead of narrativized accounts for what we find in our world—how the gods and humans came to be, how and why great battles were fought, how great heroes rose above the rest, how humans and the gods react under certain epic circumstances—the philosophers began observing the world and contemplating conceptual ideas that might unify reality under one explanation. What accounted for this radical shift in thinking has been the cause of much and varied speculation. But without this shift, we would not have conceptual thinking as we know it today, and would certainly not have what later philosophers have called *henology*, the rationalizing concept, or conceptual rationalizing, of the One.[6]

The earliest of the Presocratic philosophers, the Milesians, asked questions of the cosmos in ways not dissimilar to modern scientists: What is the world made of, and can it be reduced to a single substance? Each of these material monists put forward his own theory: for Thales it was water, for Anaximander it was the *apeiron,* an "indefinite" substance that had no boundaries but remained in motion, and for Anaximenes it was air, at least in the form of a dense atmospheric mist. These elemental reductions accounted for not merely nature in stasis, but the entire cosmic reality in motion and change. The question of change, or the mutability of all things, was of crucial concern for these early thinkers, and the attempt to deduce the cause of change from a single substance provides the concept of One its chance to sediment out from the flowing currents of mythic narrative. It is one thing to unify the many under one. We might say the Homeric epic functioned in this purpose. It is quite another thing to account for the flow of change, of the many begetting more, by claiming that the change itself is a result of a single substance, which has been transformed into the multiplicity and flux we see and experience in nature. This paradox of the one from the many the Milesians never fully resolved, except to concede that however material the single explanatory substance may be, it still can be viewed in divine terms.

Heraclitus of Ephesus had much better success with the unity of opposites by claiming fire as the elemental or archetypal material, not to which all things can be reduced (sea and earth were also primordial), but by which all things can be explained. Fire is in constant motion, forever changing its aspect, and yet it always remains the same essential substance. By maintaining this internal contradiction, fire allowed Heraclitus to account for the coexistence of opposites. "Change reposes," he famously said.[7] Or more famously, he turned it around, and said we never step into the same river twice. The one constant, "river," is by definition forever changing. What of course allows this *coincidentia oppositorum* is the concept, which we capture by the inverted commas. The label or signifier "river" is the name we give to the synthesis of all features we associate with naturally flowing fresh water bordered by two opposing banks. We reduced it to the one name as concept, "river," which universalizes the shared traits under a single entity. Likewise, if all things can be explained as a material we call "fire," our multitudinous world, normally in flux, can be fixed in place, at least as long as we capture it in the unifying concept that is one (fire), much as a camera captures the frozen moment of moving reality, to be preserved in the one that is the photograph.

This conceptual move, fire as an archetypal element, is closely associated with another of Heraclitus's essential terms, the *Logos*. As understood by Heraclitus, the Logos is an underlying coherence of reality, by which all things find their proper ratio or measure or balance with each other and with the totality that is the cosmos. The Logos is the great uniting concept behind all relations, and all opposites. It provides commensurability to that which may at first seem incommensurable. It gives common measure, harmony, proportion, or ration. "Listening not to me but to the Logos it is wise to agree that all things are one," Heraclitus says.[8] The Logos, as unified measurement, allows us to properly account for things. It is therefore related to rational thought (discerning measure) and eventually to language, and the words that make up language. It is by rationality that we conceptualize, unify, bring things together under one structure of commensurability, and it is through language that we fix this commensurability in place (the word *river* providing the constant signifier for the notion or concept of flowing fresh water bounded by opposing banks).[9] The Logos functions as the ultimate conceptual unifier, and thus, even in Heraclitus, it is linked to the divine.[10] It is no wonder then that Yahweh felt threatened by the singular language of Babel. The Logos we do not *see*; it is hidden, operating in the background like a barometric pressure. But its hidden nature is its power. "Essential nature is accustomed to hide itself," says Heraclitus.[11] The mistake of Babel was in bringing this hidden power to view in the form of a tower. Had the Babelites spent more of their efforts in constructing concepts, rather than tokens, they may have been spared their fate. Or so Hegel might have said, that grand absolutizer of rational thought.[12]

With Heraclitus's introduction of the Logos, we move into a whole new phase of the One. No longer does it manifest itself through the historical particularity of a people singled out. Rather, it sits behind all reality as something *understood*, as our rational thought brings it to an understanding common to all. "Therefore it is necessary to follow the common; but although the Logos is common, the many live as though they had a private understanding."[13]

Perhaps the most particular understanding of the One as One comes with Heraclitus's contemporary, Pythagoras. This famous mathematician was also in his way a religious leader, and his followers, the Pythagoreans, were split into two camps, those who followed his religious teachings, and those who followed his more philosophical and conceptual teachings. But it is important not to separate these camps too widely, since the conceptual and the religious are deeply entwined for Pythagoras, as they are for most numerical mystics (e.g., the Kabbalarians). Central to both sides is that number is the reality of all things. By this Pythagoras meant that the cosmos was constructed out of harmony (*harmonia*, or "attunement"), which itself was constructed from numerical and mathematical principles. Most important of these principles was the *tetractys*, or the first four cardinal numbers (1, 2, 3, and 4), which through their various relations governed all of reality, including the very music of the spheres.[14] The heavenly harmony was foundational to the earthly harmony, and by understanding and interpreting numbers, one developed a key to the cosmos and to the underlying principles of all we experience. Hence, number *as* reality. Rather than an elemental substance like water or fire, all things can be reduced to number as principle. And not just ontologically, but epistemologically: we cannot know anything unless it is, in effect, countable.

Of the first four numbers, the first, number one—the Greeks, we recall, did not admit the concept or symbol of zero—held natural priority. What fascinated the Pythagoreans was the consistency of this most prime of numbers. When multiplied with another number, it consistently yields that other number, but when multiplied by itself, it was the only number to yield itself as the other number. Moreover, as Aristotle tells us, the essence of numbers for the Pythagoreans is their property as either even or odd, the first being unlimited, the second limited. What makes the number one unique is its unity as *both*: the number one is even *and* odd simultaneously. It is, therefore the generator of all other numbers.[15] It coheres all extensions of itself together in unity, and remains both limited and unlimited. Like Heraclitus's fire it thus holds together opposites within itself, and makes them commensurate.

By extension, the number one is also the generator of reason. Reasoning entails measuring, and measuring requires some scale, and some unit of measurement. The One is the unifying principle of all measurement, since it allows both the limited and the unlimited their existence under the concept of the "unit" as such, a word etymologically built upon the one. The One is Unit, and as Unit it is therefore the unifying element behind reason, which is a faculty of measuring with conceptual units (the unit itself, as the undivided whole, being the primal concept). Even Reason itself is a Unit, if we take it as the whole of that ability to measure in ratio. The One then is, as the Pythagoreans thought, foundational even to our thinking about numbers, so that by Euclid's time several centuries later, One, as Badiou reminds us, was not even considered a number, but "supra-numeric."[16] If numbers are about measuring and ordering, then thinking about numbers is itself numerical, even supra-numerical. Reason is accounting (for): reckoning by enumeration.

THE METAPHYSICS OF ONE: PLATO, ARISTOTLE

Plato

It is not surprising that Plato and his metaphysics owe a tremendous debt to Pythagoras, as is universally acknowledged. While other Presocratics argued around the points of the one and the many, some siding with the latter (the Pluralists Anaxagoras and Empedocles), more siding with the former (Xenophanes, Parmenides, Zeno, Melissus, and, arguably, the Atomists Leucippus and Democritus), it was clear which side would eventually prevail: Plato's rendering of Socrates's ideas sealed the matter. Many observable things there may be, even many unities, but only one thing can unify them all, and that is the One, when "the *one* is not taken from the things that come to be or perish," says Socrates.[17] So how can we determine whether there are things, or *a* thing, that does not come to be or perish? That is the very question driving virtually all of Plato's dialogues, and which yields up Platonic metaphysics.

Yet we most often associate Plato and his metaphysics not with a monism but a *dualism*. Metaphysics assumes two realms, the perishable physical world of instability and change (*phusis*), and the absolute eternal world of immutable truth *beyond* the material (*metaphusis*). And we think of those great dualistic distinctions such as body and soul, or matter and mind, as immediate products of metaphysical thinking. How then can we say that Plato leads us to a One that surpasses even his supposed dualism? How does the One come together in Plato, either from the many, or from the dual nature inherent in a metaphysical structure of reality?

The consolidation of One in the metaphysics of Plato would require extensive analysis to do full justice to the complexities that it involves throughout the corpus of philosophy's most august Greek, far more extensive than we have space for here. Let us limit ourselves to the dialogue with the most pervasive and concentrated discussion of the One—that is, *Parmenides*, that fanciful invention of Plato's that brings together the Presocratics, the young Socrates, Plato's half-brother, and a figure named Aristotle. Here, the venerable Greek philosophical tradition seems to coalesce into one, as the question of the One figures centrally in the discussion, leading to that famous conclusion, which remains the most quoted line from the dialogue: "if one is not, nothing is."[18] In briefly exploring this work, we can see how the One might emerge as the ruling paradigmatic or conceptual force.[19]

The dialogue itself is a complex piece of argumentation, an intricately constructed text in two basic parts, and we cannot take their every detail into account without overextending ourselves greatly for our present purposes. Let us then limit ourselves to how the One comes to the fore of the dialogue within the context of the one and the many. We first need to set up the scenario. Present in the discussion is the title's namesake, Parmenides, the Eleatic Presocratic whom we deliberately have not treated in any detail above, and Zeno, a younger Eleatic philosopher, noted for his paradoxes, and here a devoted disciple of Parmenides. Parmenides's thought, we can now say, was handed down to us largely in the form of a didactic poem, or proem, which discusses the nature of being and of not-being, and leads toward a monism in which all of reality possesses the same aspect or character, seen as a whole one that does not admit opposites.

> There still remains just one account [or story, *mythos*] of a way, that it is. On this way there are very many signs that being uncreated and imperishable it is, whole and of a single kind and unshaken and perfect.[20]

From this quote, we can see what attracted Plato, and why he placed Parmenides as a main character, so suited is Parmenides's account to the development of Platonic Forms. Zeno, the disciple, had argued that Parmenides's claim about reality dictates against plurality necessarily, since plural things would be both like and unlike, and such contradiction or paradox could not obtain. The one must therefore supersede all appearance of contradiction or paradox. At the beginning of *Parmenides*, Zeno is just concluding the reading of his book that details this argument against the many, when the young Socrates challenges Zeno for clarification. To Socrates, the apparent contradiction seems unproblematic if we restrict ourselves to sensible objects, where we encounter the coexistence of the one and the many continuously, even in the same thing (one body has several members, etc.). But were these opposites to exist at the level of intelligible forms, this is another matter. And it is to the question of the Forms that the first half of the dialogue is devoted.

The first sections examine the young Socrates's theory of the Forms.[21] What is the precise nature of these Forms ontologically, if they are, as Zeno claims, to surpass the binary distinction of likeness and unlikeness, and maintain oneness or unity? This Socrates wonders, and draws the elder Parmenides into the conversation. Parmenides proceeds to challenge some of Socrates's basic assumptions, culminating in his metaphysical belief that they exist in a realm distinct from the mutable world of sensible things. If this is so, Parmenides concludes, how could the Forms have any intelligible connection or relation to the sensible world? On what would that connection be based, and how, ultimately, could we *know* the Forms? Parmenides shows that contradiction is the only basis, and that, if Socrates wishes to maintain an absolute distinction between this world and the metaphysical world of the Forms, the latter will ultimately be unknowable to us. Thus, the dualism of this world/other world, of *phusis/metaphusis*, of body/soul, which marks the doctrine of the Forms as it is more familiarly found in the later *Republic*, for example, is here drawn into question. And we can see why Plato uses Parmenides to elicit the doubt—he who held a thoroughgoing monistic belief that all things cohere in a one that does not admit opposites. If the Forms appear to lead to a defining dualism, Parmenides is the one to test the case, and push the matter to its farthest limit.

Socrates's dilemma is in many respects the Kantian distinction of phenomena and noumena anticipated much in advance. To overcome the dilemma, Parmenides tells the callow Socrates that he must train himself further in the ways of philosophical discourse, particularly in the method of dialectical thinking. And in the second part of the dialogue, Parmenides is convinced by his interlocutors to demonstrate the rigors of such a dialectic, as a model, a *paradigm*, for how the promising young philosopher might sharpen his skill, and "achieve a full view of the truth."[22]

The method of the dialectic, as Parmenides sees it, involves not only testing a positive hypothesis ("if each thing is"), but also its inverse ("if that same thing is not"). One must go through all the possible permutations in both cases, and do so dialectically by engaging one's interlocutor in question and answer, so that (at least) two minds are working through the matter by the dictates of rational discourse and the measurements of reason (Logos). Only then can one arrive at a trustworthy conclusion, one grounded on tested and sure knowledge. Parmenides, after much reluctance, agrees to demonstrate, using the young Aristotle as his interlocutor. But he now must find a suitable topic on which to employ the method. "Shall I hypothesise about the one itself and consider what the consequences must be, if it is one or if it is not one?" asks Parmenides. "By all means," responds Zeno,[23] and the paradigmatic demonstration begins, ending many hypotheses and cogitations later with the famous litotes, "If one is not, nothing is."

We could spend many pages, as others have done, analyzing every last turn in the demonstration, and all the various hypotheses concerning the one (eight in total) that are weighed and counterweighed.[24] But this would steer us too far off course. Suffice it to say here that the one, in being put through its paces, and tested against limit and limitlessness, likeness and unlikeness, part and whole, equality and inequality, coming-to-be and ceasing-to-be, being and nonbeing, can finally be summed up in the negative phrase "If one is not, nothing is." Or so Parmenides would have us believe, in a conclusion that would seem to suggest that all depends on the one. But this famous apophatic conclusion is not the last word. For Parmenides goes on to say, as the very final words of the dialogue:

> Let us say then this [the previous summation in the negative]—*and also* that, as it seems, whether one is or is not, it and the others both are and are not, and both appear and do not appear all things in all ways, both in relation to themselves and in relation to each other.[25]

Thus ends the dialogue. So what really has been concluded? Is there one, or is there not one? The final lines, with all their ambiguity, or contradiction, have caused many to conclude that *Parmenides* is aporetic, and belongs with the other aporetic dialogues in which no conclusive position is reached by the end, and the discussion simply ceases as if the exercise itself was more important than what was actually reached or agreed upon in the exercise. So seems to be the case here. How then could we draw out the one as supreme?

We might hold on to the penultimate conclusion—"If one is not, nothing is"—as the *real* conclusion, and lay the matter defiantly to rest, despite its negative rendering. And this would certainly serve our purposes. But we could also take the entire dialectical exercise as a parody, directed by Plato either against Zeno or the Eleatic philosophers in general. Or we might defend Parmenides, and say that dualism is done away with here by a more mystical (even Neoplatonic) understanding of the relation between the metaphysical realm and the changeable physical realm, in which neither side can be thoroughly dismissed ("both appear and do not appear all things in all ways"), and truth emerges in a seeing that goes beyond any dualism, where the One is grasped in a Being beyond all being (and nonbeing).[26] Or, we might look at a more structural or literary way in which the one comes to gain the upper hand.

We must remember that the question of the one that occupies the second part is really only set up as an example of how to employ the dialectic in a more effectively rigorous manner. Granted, it directly pertains to the example that Zeno had raised in his book at the outset, and it is at the heart of Parmenides's own thought. But it is still only an example, to show a more important point that Parmenides wants the young Socrates to understand: that the doctrine of the Forms needs to go through a greater and more reliable fine-tuning. But if the last point about the Forms in the first part—that they act as a kind of paradigm—was put into doubt, because their paradigmatic structure still could not account for how they might bridge the gap between the physical and the metaphysical, does this not put all paradigmatic structures into doubt, including the very one structuring the dialogue, the second part as paradigmatic of how the questions in the first part ought to be pursued and answered? If Parmenides's example cannot convey the truth it needs to, that one truth will arise out of a multiple of (contradictory) hypotheses, how will the Forms? The possible aporetic conclusion of the second part concerning the one—that it appears to be one and not one at the same time—would seem to deny validity to the dialectic itself, as the one paradigmatic method by which to arrive at truth.

But if the one and the many seem to coexist in the dialogue at the level of basic structure, perhaps Plato is trying to point toward the One that allows this coexistence itself to exist—the Paradigm that keeps all things, including opposites, contained within our capacity to talk about them. And to see this One more clearly we need to move away from the minutiae of dialectic or disputation, especially in the second part, and consider the narrative structure instead. We know that it is divided into two basic parts: the first in which Socrates's view of the Forms is critiqued by Parmenides, and the second in which the dialectic is actively demonstrated by using the one as an example. How are these two conversations relayed to us? The overall narrator is a certain Cephalus, who reports to us the content of the dialogue. At the beginning, Cephalus tells us that he met a friend in the marketplace, who knew another friend, Antiphon, who met with a figure named Pythodorus, who recounted to him the famed meeting of Socrates, Zeno, and Parmenides in the Great Panathenaea. Cephalus and his friend go to Antiphon's house in order to hear him recite from memory this great encounter. Cephalus then writes that Antiphon said that Pythodorus said

what exactly transpired at this meeting, the entire dialogue that is to follow. Narratively, then, the dialogue comes to us at four times removed: the
actual event, as related by Pythodorus, as related by Antiphon, as related
by Cephalus. Hermeneutically, we have an account that requires five levels
of signification: Plato, writing as Cephalus, writing for Antiphon, reporting for Pythodorus, reporting on the interlocutors of the supposed original
event, Socrates, Parmenides, and the rest of the philosophers in company
that day. How are we to trust the transmission of truth through these five
levels? Even if we take the whole thing as an elaborate narrative ruse, why
such elaboration? Why could not Plato simply relay the words of the original participants as he does in many other dialogues, or assume the voice of
Socrates himself, as he does in the *Republic*? Why this excessive distancing
from the original?

We can assume this deliberate narrative approach has a purpose, and
we might say that Plato is trying to show us a unity, a One, amid what
seems like apparent multiplicity, even structural multiplicity. Is this not what
the dialectic is supposed to bring about ultimately, a unified truth through
multiple interlocutors in dialogue? But rather than showing the Logos of
dialectic bringing this about unequivocally, Plato opts to show us another
possible route—a certain unifying structuring across the multiple planes of
reportage, as seen even in the choice of names of the three reporting characters involved here: Cephalus (which means "head") writes of Antiphon
(which means "sounding in return") who recites the words of Pythodorus
(whose name evokes the locality of Delphi—"*Python*"—with its oracular pronouncements from the divine through the "*Pythia*," the priestess). We should
always be wary of investing too much into the use of names, especially with
Plato, yet one cannot help but see an intention here, as if the oracle of
the original divine event, given by a priestly mouthpiece, is repeated as an
antiphon to be captured by our thinking minds. It is as if Plato wants to
show that despite the multiple layers, the original event still comes to be
possessed by our thinking selves as a single event,[27] one whose transmission
is unified by the narrative structure, despite the undecidability of the argument's conclusion, or the dialectic's aporetic nature. The narrative remains
universally applicable. The One is one Truth, which emerges from the many
as a single account that we engage in narratively. That "account" may be
Logos (rational argument) or Mythos (story), as it was for Parmenides (and
we should keep in mind that Parmenides's Truth came in the form of a
poem, and not in the form of discursive reasoning). Or it may be both, as
it seems to be in *Parmenides*, where Logos and Mythos must be unified in
order for the account to be accounted for. As Heidegger reminds us, "For
the Greeks, the opposite to 'barbarism' is not 'culture'; it is dwelling within
μῦθος [*mythos*] and λόγος [*logos*], for 'μῦθος [*mythos*], ἔπος [*epos*] and λόγος

[*logos*]' belong together essentially."[28] If the Forms are to have credibility, if the dialectic is to work, they both must let themselves be narrativized in a single form that allows knowledge to be transferred from one realm to the next—precisely the dilemma that initiates the central discussion of the dialogue: How would we *know* the Forms if they had independent being apart from our world? How would we know the One if it had independent being apart from the manifold that we live in? We could not, unless that One somehow inheres in the many that constitutes both the realms of Logos and Mythos. The metaphysics of the One for Plato here, in a dialogue most devoted to the One, is thus more sophisticated than merely a bifold distinction that keeps two worlds in their place, the one sovereign over the other: mutable/immutable, body/soul, *phusis/metaphusis*, etc. We should remember that the very "meta-" prefix carries the sense both of something changed, substituted, or set beyond, *and* of something common or shared. These opposing lines of semantic force are precisely the kind of thing that fascinated much of Presocratic thought, and certainly preoccupied the Eleatic philosophers, and so here in Plato they come together in one synthetic narrative, in which the One is One by virtue of being narrativized in the one dialogue. This is to say, that despite the apparent manifold, and aporia, the discussion is One as narrative. And through that narrative, we participate in the One that grounds all narrative.

We will see in a moment how the Neoplatonists took this One even further, and made sure any dualism would not creep back in. But let us briefly point out that this One has, even recently, been seen as primarily *logocentric*, or requiring the Logos to ground all being and reality, whether in human existence or in human language and reason. But *Parmenides*, if our reading has any merit, shows us that a Platonic One is not simply Logos alone, that Logos and Mythos can and should themselves be unified (and we could enlist other dialogues in the Platonic canon to support this further—*Phaedo, Symposium, Phaedrus*, etc.). The narrative or form must never be fully separated from the content—which is to repeat the old saw that Plato is as much an artist as he is a rational philosopher. And this view will help us later as we move into the O. For now, let us return to our brief rendering of the One as it moves through ancient thought, and, before the Neoplatonists, briefly look at Plato's successor, Aristotle.

Aristotle

Aristotle had much to say about unity and the One, especially in his *Metaphysics*, where he begins with discussion about the Presocratics and their theories of explanation. In fact, much of what we know about the earliest Greek philosophers arises from this book. Numbers come from unity, he said, speaking of the Pythagoreans (986a).[29] Or quoting Xenophanes: "Unity is God" (986b). But unlike the material monists, Aristotle himself does not think we can reduce all things to one substance, or unlike the Pythagoreans, to numbers. What interests him more is of course "primary being," that which is "never attributed as a predicate of something else," but of which other things are predicates, or that which is intrinsically defining of such a being, its "shape or form" (1017b). Primary beings are "first in all ways, first in discourse [logos], in knowledge and in time" (1028a). They are the essential nature of any thing, its "what-it-is." This being, as primary, already shows a predilection toward the unity of One that defines reality. But there are many primary beings, not just one. Is there a larger unity that grounds all other primaries?

After devoting the entirety of Book Iota to the complexities of the one and the many, Aristotle turns his attention to the nature of divine being in Book Lambda. He begins by distinguishing three kinds of primary beings: sensible primary beings that either can perish (such as plants and animals) or cannot perish (such as the heavenly bodies), and an immovable being, which is neither perishable nor changeable. Aristotle is concerned ultimately with the question of motion, and that which motivates or moves something is a primal force with primary ontological status. He thus equates whatever produces movement or rest with primary being, saying that "without primary beings there would be neither active nor passive change" (1071a). But where does the process of change itself come from? For Aristotle, change does not come into being, but has always been (1071b). So how do we account for it? The problem with Plato's Forms, for Aristotle, is that they tend to be seen as static. They may have the capacity to enact change, but this capacity does not necessarily mean they will act on their potential. They therefore cannot account for change themselves. There needs to be some primary being that exists not with potentiality, but solely with actuality, remaining forever "in act," in order for the process of change itself to remain accounted for, and to keep changing. This necessitates a primary being that is eternally in act, a being that moves all other beings, and provides the possibility for movement itself. But of course this primary being cannot itself be moved—it must be eternally in active movement, or we could ask, regressively, and ad infinitum, what moves it, and what moves that which moves it, etc. Thus, Aristotle's famous "Prime Mover," the first mover that sets all movement into motion, but which itself is not moved, or is forever moving. This eternal, imperishable Mover is of course divine, God, the One who is always, and always One. It is not a Form that remains discontinuous with this physical world (Aristotle's complaint against Platonic Forms in general), but, by virtue of its eternal motivation, is driving everything, within *phusis* and *metaphusis* alike, along its designated path and toward its designated goal as a unified whole. Thus, Aristotle ends this Book on the Prime Divine with the following significant passage:

> And no one has thrown light on what it is to which numbers, or soul and body, or, in general, form and thing owe their unity. Nor is it possible to explain this unless one says as we do that this is due to the mover. And those who say that mathematical number is first and hence there must always be one thing after another and different principles for each, present the being of the universe as a series of episodes, in which none, by being or not being, contributes anything to another. Thus, their first principles are many, but actually things do not wish to be misgoverned. "Multiple sovereignty is not good. Let there be one sovereign!" (1075b–1076a)

The discussion ends with a political analogy, and a message that is clear: unity is found in the One that is the Prime Mover, unifying all numbers, and all levels of experience and reality, *body and soul* together. The sovereign is the head (*cephalus*) that keeps all things moving and functioning together. Working himself against a dualism, Aristotle solicits motive force not merely as the agent but as the very actuality by which all things cohere in unity and oneness. And thus, the form of the One becomes the teleological goal to which all things are driven. This One is not numerical as such: it is what allows numericality in the first instance, as he says later against the Pythagoreans in the concluding Book Nu (1088a). It is therefore generative, a being in eternal act—a pure Principle or Being that drives all other principles and beings. It is primary in the most comprehensive sense.

The metaphysics of the One in Plato and Aristotle, then, continually works toward *unity*, despite the duality inherent in the structure of metaphysical thinking itself. Aristotle tries to overcome this duality even more than his predecessor, and his *Metaphysics*, as a series of philosophical disquisitions about the nature of first principles as explanation, attempts to unify the concept itself of explanation under the category of the One, since thinking itself is a category of movement, generated by the most prime of all primary beings. The Prime Mover explains all rational explanation, then, just as in Plato the narrative generates the unity that allows us to speak of unity. These are essential developments, where ultimately, in both thinkers, the One leads to the divine, so that as in the quoted Xenophanes, God becomes unity itself. We see the apotheosis of this movement as we now turn to the Neoplatonists, who gave One its most supreme position, unifying philosophy and divinity together in a way that would have profound influence on all Western thought to come.

THE WHOLLY, PLENARY ONE: PLOTINUS

Where Plato and Aristotle remain implicit in their sense of unity, struggling against an invasive duality between this world and an ideal reality behind or beyond this world, the Neoplatonists are explicit about the One and unity. They do not speak about unifying two worlds, where the notion of unity carries the necessary act of bringing a manifold together under one entity (as in the concept). Their unity, their One, is primal in its most primordial sense. In the beginning there was only One, which defined all—as one. There was no manifold, no multiplicity, nothing to unify, only pure oneness.[30] This renders the concept of One commensurate with nothing, since if everything is One, there is nothing but One, and all is One as much as nothing is One.[31] In Neoplatonism, there is always a thin transparent line between nothing and One, that is, between 0 and 1, since by making singularity consummate and all-encompassing, the concept of singularity itself runs the risk of dissipating altogether, at least in any quantitative sense.[32] Neoplatonism tries to avoid this nothingness by keeping the One as purely qualitative—that is, as a kind of infinite and unlimited plenitude. The One is a plenary power—a fullness not only beyond all actuality, but beyond even Being itself. A fullness purely transcendent, beyond anything Aristotle could countenance, and beyond what Plato had envisioned. It is a fullness that reaches mystical levels, and begins to take itself out of the realm of philosophy. That is, it is Oneness beyond, ultimately, comprehension.

The great Neoplatonic figure, to whom we restrict ourselves here for the sake of space, is Plotinus (204–270 CE). His writings, *The Enneads*, as compiled by his disciple Porphyry, detail a system of thought that, though deeply indebted to Plato and his understanding of the metaphysical realm, goes beyond the question of Forms and the eternal absolute. It even takes the question of the Prime Mover farther. Where the Forms assumed that the world of *phusis* was illusory, at least insofar as its changeability and perishability did not make it *real* in any eternal and absolute sense, Plotinus's One did not discount the natural world as something to be discarded or dismissed. Where the Prime Mover took us back sequentially to a primordial generative force of Being, a pure actuality from which followed all other potentialities and actualities of being, a first source or cause, as it were, to which all being traces its roots, Plotinus's One stands prior to being, or Being.[33] It is pre-ontological in the sense that it does not rely on some first principle of being to account for itself, but brings all being, including Primary Being, into existence itself: "[I]n order that Being may be brought about, the source must be no Being but Being's generator, in what is to be thought of as the primal act of generation."[34] It is therefore before even Principle. It is also before all actuality and potentiality, completely self-enclosed or self-sufficing, both wholly internal and wholly external to itself, acting neither upon nor toward anything outside of it:

> That his being is constituted by this self-originating and self-tendance—at once Act and repose—becomes clear if we imagine the contrary; inclining towards something outside of Himself, He would destroy the identity of his being [which is not-being, or pre-being]. This self-directed Act is therefore his peculiar being, one with himself. Thus He created Himself because his Act was inseparable from Himself. If then this Act never came to be but is eternal—a wakening without a wakener, an eternal wakening and a supra-Intellection—He is as He waked Himself to be. This awakening is before being, before Intellectual-Principle, before rational life, though he is these; He is thus an Act before Intellectual-Principle, and thought and life; these come from Him and no other; his being, then is a self-presence, issuing from Himself.[35]

This hyper-transcendence takes us beyond the usual dualities we create with Act/repose, actuality/potentiality, or activity/passivity. It even takes us beyond metaphysics itself, as Plotinus's One collapses all dualities or multiplicities that might issue from it.[36] Neither does it remain a purely abstracted concept with concrete manifestations, but is the perfected unity of all abstraction and concretion at once. This is the One that remains plenary, supreme, divine, alone in the most comprehensive sense possible,[37] since it is neither all things nor no things, and it is *both* all things and no things simultaneously. It therefore exceeds even description: "The One is in truth beyond all statement: any affirmation is of a thing; but 'all-transcending, resting above even the most august divine Mind'—this is the only true description," says Plotinus.[38] Or again:

> We are in agony for a true expression; we are talking of the untellable; we name only to indicate for our own use as best we may. And this name, The One, contains really no more than the negation of plurality: under the same pressure the Pythagoreans found their indication in the symbol "Apollo" (a = not; pollôn = of many) with its repudiation of the multiple. If we are led to think positively of The One, name and thing, there would be more truth in silence: the designation, a mere aid to inquiry, was never intended for more than a preliminary affirmation of absolute simplicity [The Simplex] to be followed by the rejection of even that statement; it was the best that offered, but remains inadequate to express the nature indicated. For this is a principle not to be conveyed by any sound;

it cannot be known on any hearing but, if at all, by vision; and to hope in that vision to see a form is to fail even that.[39]

This apophatic vision transports the One to purely mystical realms, beyond rational thought, beyond the powers of language and description, beyond even vision itself. It is a mysticism in concert with the great mystics of all religions, East and West, whether Bonaventure, Eckhart, Teresa of Avila, Lao Tzu, Al-Ghazali, Nāgārjuna, or Śamkara, to name but a few.[40] It is in concert with Wittgenstein's famous conclusion about the necessity of silence beyond a certain point in the philosophical game. And it is in concert with the great poets, from Rumi to, as we shall see, Auden. It is a purely contemplative mysticism, not bound to any text or sacred scripture, the One being beyond both the narrativity of Plato and the explanatory principles of Aristotle. It is the "Wholly Other" of Otto et al., except that it is beyond even the distinction of Self and Other, being Wholly One. It is wholly impersonal then, unlike most other religious mysticisms. How then can we even contemplate it or know it?

The One, for Plotinus, of course is not all that is. In its state of being wholly and comprehensively One, its plenitude or superabundance "spills out" and overflows into what Plotinus calls *hypostases* (the division of which, significantly, he derives from Plato's *Parmenides*). The first hypostasis to follow upon the One is called the Intellectual-Principle. This represents both intellection itself and Being itself—Divine Mind and Divine Ideas. This is the Principle that most accords with Socrates's and Plato's understanding of the Divine as Absolute Reason, to which our minds aspire, or ought to aspire, in their original purity.[41] This hypostasis is the Contemplator of the One, allowing us to contemplate the One ourselves. But as such it is no longer pure Unity in the comprehensive, plenary sense. It is the "One-Many" distinction brought to existence, unity within duality, as Plotinus describes it (V.6.1), or "a secondary god manifesting before there is any vision of that other, the Supreme which rests overall."[42]

The second hypostasis, to follow upon the latter, is the Soul. This is the experiential side of the equation, the living out of the Intellect in Oneness, the essence of existence both individually and collectively. As the "Act of the Intellect" (VI.2.6), it comes closest to what Aristotle was intending for the Prime Mover as pure Act. Like the Intellectual-Principle, it brings a certain division, but now not merely "One-Many" but "One-and-Many":

> Soul, then, is one and many—as many as are manifested in that oneness—one in its nature, many in those other things. A single Existent, it makes itself many by what we may call its motion: it

is one entire, but by its striving, so to speak, to contemplate itself, it is a plurality . . .[43]

This plurality is still ensconced in the Primal One, along with the Intellectual-Principle. The three thus make a kind of triad, or Trinity, whose components are nevertheless interconnected and inextricable, though distinct through hypostases, by which the Many becomes primarily an extension of the One.

It is important to note that the hypostatic extensions are not a lessening or a degradation of that original One, but its pure manifestation as either the principle of Intellect or the activity of Intellect. The activity, as Soul, further extends to sense and nature, which Plotinus calls the Soul's living "image" (V.2.1), and thus to Body, the physical reality of our existence in the cosmos. But here again we ought not to assume, as did Plato, and Gnosticism, that in moving to the realm of *phusis*, we move to a lesser, degraded realm. The body is not a source of illusion or inherent fallibility, but part of the overall unified plenitude that the Soul actualizes in its contemplation. As the embodiment of consciousness, the Soul allows immanence into the unified transcendence, an immanence that is not an alloyed expression of transcendence at some remove, but is coextensive with transcendence: "Side by side exist the Authentic All and its counterpart, the visible universe."[44] And thus the material is not fallen, but part of the Soul's act of contemplation, of which it passively gives form, the Soul "having brought the corporeal-principle, in itself unlovely, to partake of good and beauty to the utmost of its receptivity—and to a pitch which stirs souls, being of the divine order."[45] Any hint of a dualism is kept well from sight: "The secret is: that this All is one universally comprehensive living being, encircling all the living beings within it, and having a soul, one soul."[46] Granted, like any religion, there needs to be an intentional return from the body back to the Oneness that encompasses that body. But the important thing for Neoplatonism is that the body itself, or physical nature as a whole, does not constitute evil, depravity, or inferiority. As Reiner Schürmann tells us, "The one will not be the supreme *noumenon*; its way of being will have to be sought among phenomena, but not in light of them."[47] Though we must contemplate the One that is prior to the body, prior to even the Soul and the Intellect, we do this not because that body *constitutionally* is keeping us from eternal delights or rewards. It is because that body is only one aspect of the overall picture, the All that is One. It is the difference between leaving a location because it is enemy territory and leaving a location because it is only a small part of a larger, more bountiful and enriching area that awaits our experience.

The One encompasses all—comprehensively. And in that encompassing, the circularity, with its dividing perimeter, gives way to pure Unity, into which all and nothing, inner and outer, transcendence and immanence, spiritual and material, are subsumed. And here we begin to leave the territory of familiar and accountable bearings completely, and enter into the sphere of an absolute undifferentiating monism. This is the plenary sphere of the One, which, in its movement, is beyond movement itself: the *coincidentia oppositorum* of pure act and repose, a motivation of rest into a transcendence that no longer transcends.

With Plotinus and Neoplatonism, we have an understanding of the One that surpasses any paradigmatic function. It is neither formal in the Platonic sense, nor causally explanatory in the Aristotelian sense. It is not a model or structure in any conceptual understanding of the terms, and therefore cannot be represented as such. This is the highest reach of the One we have looked at so far, an apex that, in its mystical heights, leaves behind comprehension and enters the heightened spiritual experience of ineffability. Few can dwell in this rarefied air. And thus it is not surprising that Neoplatonism did not develop into a religion of its own. But in its adaptation of Platonic ideals, in its refutation of other systems of thought and religion (Peripatetic Philosophy, Stoicism, Epicureanism, Gnosticism, and Zoroastrianism), and in its distinct overlapping with the emerging Christianity of its day, it is clear that it would have an immense influence on thought to come, as it gave utmost supremacy to the One. After Neoplatonism, the One would never go beyond such mystical heights again, for there is really nowhere else it could go beyond. But the power of the One would continue to emanate as a principle force, or a force of Principle, in various manifestations, as the subsequent millennia have patently shown.

THE CHRISTIAN ONE: PAUL

We have focused much on the philosophical heritage of the One, because it is there that the One gains its most stable footing, and perhaps its most far-reaching effect. We began with the Hebrew religion, however, and we might return again now to religion, this time in the form of Christianity, following after a Neoplatonism that seems to correlate so well with what came to be orthodox Christian theology. Curiously, however, the founder of Christianity is the least monistic of all we have examined so far. This should not surprise us if we consider that the account of Jesus is not one but *four*—four Gospel narratives, each with its own emphases and variations. We might try to harmonize these accounts, or consolidate them into one, as the early Tatian did with his famous *Diatessaron* (ca. 175 CE), and as have countless theologians thereafter, but the fact that we have multiple accounts of Jesus and his words already dictates against a Oneness in the forms that we have so far encountered. Jesus, like Socrates, wrote nothing down. But unlike Socrates, Jesus did not have one amanuensis, or one disciple gifted with and devoted to the skill of writing. Plato may have written at several levels removed, as he did (or feigned) in *Parmenides*, but his own metanarrative keeps the one amid the many. The Christian Gospels may have their own structure of one amid the many—and no doubt the arrangement of shared pericopae shows a similar attempt to distil one narrative out from the many—but that there are four versions of such attempts tells us that the One of Jesus, if there be such a thing, is viewed from even a greater remove.

More to the point, in these several accounts, Jesus has very little to say about the One. In the Synoptic Gospels, he certainly points toward the Judaic monotheism of his upbringing: "And call no one your father on earth for you have one Father—the one in heaven" (Mt. 23.9). And this single God alone is good (Mt. 19.17; Mk. 10.18; Lk. 18.19). But these pronouncements would be meager support for the *concept* of the One we have seen elsewhere. John's Gospel is different, with its evident influence from Hellenistic and Gnostic philosophy. So in the opening of John's Prologue we have the use of the *Logos*, which begins to think in terms of principle, and the idea of a hidden God made manifest by the Son, which accords with later Neoplatonic conceptions: "No one has ever seen God. It is God the only Son, who is close to the Father's heart, who has made him known" (Jn.1.18). Of course the great, and deeply provocative, admission in 10.30 that "I and the Father are one" certainly presses the issue, supported later in Jesus's deeply personal prayer of chapter 17, when four times he unifies himself with his Father (vs. 11, 21, 22, and 23). The last instance culminates them all: "I in them and you in me, that they may become completely one" (vs.23). But even here this Oneness is hardly comprehensive: it is still set off from those who do not believe, even though it should act as an inducement to believe ("so that the world may know that you have sent me and have loved them even as you have loved me" [vs.23]). But this is about the extent of Jesus's (or John's) sense of the One. It still remains largely Jewish, notwithstanding Jesus's blasphemous equation with the Father, insofar as the unity being called upon here is not an abstract principle or concept, but is for the people, and always directed toward the people ("that they may be one," repeated each of the four times). And though John's Jesus himself may be the way, the truth, and the life for these people (Jn.14.6), the Synoptic Jesus is far less a unifier, and in many ways sets out to disunify, whether among family members (Lk.14.26) or among any complacent relations one may have fallen into with another (Mt. 10.34–39). The Jesus of the Gospels is not interested in universal unity, we might say. He is more interested in one's positioning of faith, and the inclination of the heart, and these do not lend themselves to the harmony of the One, and may even, he warns us, go contrary to it.

It is to Paul we must turn to find the universal Unity that comes by way of Jesus as *Christ*. We might best gain entry into Paul's universal under-standing if we look at his encounter—the only one recorded—with Greek philosophy, as we find it upon Paul's visit to Athens in Acts 17. The passage begins with Paul's distress in seeing the city full of idols. His subsequent perorations against idolatry draw certain philosophers his way, among them Epicureans and Stoics. Ironically, they accuse him of further adding to the superabundant Greek pantheon by preaching "foreign divinities." For this they call him "*spermologos*," a wonderfully descriptive Greek word combining "seed" (*sperma*) and "word" (*logos*) to mean someone who randomly picks up seeds, like a bird, and in the RSV translated as "babbler" (vs.18). We are taken back to Gen. 11, and the Tower of Babel, as if Paul were here one of the multilingual diaspora, scattered abroad to keep from consolidating into a powerful One (through language, as *logos*). Paul, for his part, takes the multi-plicity of the Athenian religious context, and turns it back toward the One, as if marshaling the people back to its monolithic tower. The chosen route is through the "Unknown God," that inscription set up to cover all bases in the Greek world, lest a god should be unwittingly neglected and religious obeisance ignored, simply because it was not known. This great insignia of polytheism and multiplicity is precisely the base on which Paul erects his monotheistic claim. The "Unknown God" is actually the God of the Jews, the one who made the physical world[48] and, "from one" (v.26), made all other people and nations. This God, not reducible to material form in any way, has sent a man to earth to judge it in righteousness, and in validation of this man's authority and power has raised him from the dead. Here we have the essence of Pauline theology: the One true God sends his Son as the arbiter of righteousness, and in his resurrection from the dead, this Son gains the stature reserved only for the Divine One, becoming unified with that One by conquering death. The tower is reconstructed, but again, as from Genesis 12 forward, reconstructed on God's terms, here theologized by Paul. The Unknown is now Known—we must choose, believe, and become one in Christ, the eternal One. This is Paul's reinterpretation of the Jewish story of the chosen One (as people and as Messiah).

Paul's theology of unity in Christ finds common language in the mem-bership of the many in one body. As he says in the context of worshipping idols, "Because there is one bread, we who are many are one body, for we all partake of the one bread" (1Cor. 10.17). And again, two chapters later, "For just as the body is one and has many members, and all the members of the body, though many, are one body, so it is in Christ. For in the one Spirit we were all baptized into one body—Jews or Greeks, slaves or free—and we were all made to drink of one Spirit" (1Cor. 12.12–13).[49] And of course this unitarian political theology finds its paramount assertion in Galatians 3.28: "There is neither Jew nor Greek, there is neither slave nor free, there is neither male nor female; for you are all one in Christ Jesus." For Paul, Jesus *as Christ*, that is, as the One resurrected, is the great unifier, and all become one in Him and through Him.

Much has been made of Paul's universalism. Even now outside of theology, especially with Alain Badiou's *Saint Paul: The Foundation of Universalism* (orig. 1997), Paul's role as the one who consolidated a unified and unifying understanding of Jesus and his role has regained much ground and been reintroduced into contemporary philosophical and political debate. For Badiou, Paul is an antiphilosopher, one who is not interested in the *concept* of Unity or the One: "Paul is not a philosopher precisely because he assigns his thought to a singular event, rather than a set of conceptual generalities."[50] This singular event, of course, is the resurrection, that stumbling block even to the Athenian philosophers of his day (Acts 17.32). What makes Paul's universalism unique for Badiou is that it is a universal claim always and only "for all," superseding the particularity of law and the conceptualization of the Logos:

> His genuinely revolutionary conviction is that *the sign of the One is the "for all," or the "without exception."* That there is but a single God must be understood not as a philosophical speculation concerning substance or supreme being, but on the basis of a structure of address. The One is that which inscribes no difference in the subjects to which it addresses itself. The One is only insofar as it is for all: such is the maxim of universality when it has its root in the event. Monotheism can be understood only by taking into consideration the whole of humanity. Unless addressed to all, the One crumbles and disappears.[51]

Whether this conviction can be revolutionary in the nontheological way Badiou suggests (the revolutionary subject being one "who maintains the universal" as "immanent exception," and not as "conformity")[52] is up for debate. But Badiou's characterization of Paul's sense of the One is helpful here. For it shows us that for the One to be One it must reach out and apply to all as the unifying event of One, that event being something completely other to what conceptualization (and law) will allow. Such reaching out is what we call *love*, the love that is expressed in Christ's death on the cross, which we share in as a reconciled humanity (Eph. 2.15–16), in Christ, in God, through faith and hope. This love, the uniting of all (faith, hope, and those who possess them), must carry with it a boundless personal force, the force captured by *agape* or *caritas*; the One must be and remain comprehensively personal as the giver of love. This expressly personal factor is what separates Paul's One from all the Greek philosophical conceptions of One we have thus far seen (a factor missing even from Badiou's account of the event for Paul).[53] The "for all" is really only such as a gesture of pure, unsolicited love and self-giving. Thus, Paul entreats us toward the One always in the context of love:

> I therefore, a prisoner for the Lord, beg you to lead a life worthy of the calling to which you have been called, with all lowliness and meekness, with patience, forbearing one another in love, eager to maintain the unity of the Spirit in the bond of peace. There is one body and one Spirit, just as you were called to the one hope that belongs to your call, one Lord, one faith, one baptism, one God and Father of us all, who is above all and through all and in all. (Eph.4.1–6)[54]

THE PARADIGMS OF ONE

In our very brief sketches of the treatment of the One above—and we must stress they are all too brief, and incur all the perils of such brevity—we might then, in both challenging its supreme unity and confirming its singular influence, construe six different models or paradigms of the One, paradigms that, following after Neoplatonism and early Pauline thinking, will be adopted in some form or other, or in some combination or other, by all subsequent thinking till the twentieth century. These paradigms can be categorized as such: *the One as genealogical* (Hebrews), *the One as substantive* (Presocratics), *the One as metanarrative* (Plato), *the One as meta-explanatory* (Aristotle), *the One as mystical* (Neoplatonism), and *the One as self-giving* (Paul).

Summarily, the One as genealogical pertains to the One as it first comes from the many, separated out (the fundamental nature of the holy, and of God's people of holiness), and then traced back to the one source, as event (Passover), as forefather (Abraham), or as beginning (Elohim/Yahweh as creator). Genealogical unity engenders the One as always embedded in the chosen lineage, passing from one generation to the next, and hence always embedded in history. The One, we might say, *is* history, though not in any absolute Hegelian way: history of a people, history as God's people, history as God's working out of that people, chosen specifically for this purpose. This paradigm assumes the divine as One, but it also understands history's trajectory as one, set in place by the Creator God who separates out and then unites.

The One as substantive pertains to the One as defining substance, the bedrock of all things, whether material, cosmological, in stasis or in motion. Like the early material monists, it reduces reality to a single entity, though like Parmenides and others the entity need not be material or elemental but ontological (being or Being) or idealist (as in Leibniz's monadology). This understanding is the clearest monism, as it explains all multiplicity, and therefore all that exists, in terms of a homogeneity or singularity. It seeks out a single foundation, upon which all else can be based and accounted for.

The One as metanarrative pertains to the One as part of a metastructure of both "with" and "beyond": unifying together ("with") by standing over ("beyond"). The Platonic One is the ultimate paradigmatic Form that stands over or behind all we know as reality, the absolute Good, allowing all things to cohere. In that coherence is any one narrative, grounded in the Absolute, the metanarrative, which allows the recounting or reforming of all that lies beneath it, whether in the form of *logos* or *mythos*. Here, both rational argument (or dialectic) and storytelling (or myth) come together to form a bonded whole. In this understanding the One unites not by reducing all things to one thing, but by providing the absolute narrative possibility in which all things can find their place and articulation.

The One as meta-explanatory pertains to the One as an etiological structure. In many respects it combines the latter two, substantive and metanarrative, by allowing a single explanation to emerge through the act of explaining. But where the former explains all things by reducing them to a single *entity*, and the latter explains things by narrating "together beyond," the meta-explanatory unites explanation itself, as the force of Reason allows us to arrive at and account for the Cause of cause. This understanding sees the One therefore as *teleological*, not in a historical sense, but as principle, a principle of (prime) being governing the etiology of movement and the movement of etiology. It therefore works both backward and forward, giving both cause and effect their singular and united purpose.

The One as mystical pertains to the One as so absolutely One that it loses its distinction altogether, and dissolves into an ineffability that can only be experienced through mystical union. This One is even beyond the metastructure, since the "with" always overwhelms the "beyond," and encompasses all in a unitary plenitude of indistinction. This understanding is ultimately beyond understanding; it requires some form of spiritual contemplation, which carries one beyond intellect as principle. This One is the most plenary One, the most fully pure in its Oneness, and therefore will always come close to, and perhaps even interchange with, a pure nothingness.

The One as self-giving pertains to the One as wholly personal and which gives (of) itself as a universal gift, especially as unifying love. It pertains not to principle or concept, but to a universal embracing through the act of giving as gift. That giving may be purely Pauline, and focus on the death and resurrection of Christ. Here, it unifies through faith and hope in an event, an event open to all, and for all, as pure love (even if this, as Paul, has its roots in Hebrew thinking). Or it may be institutional, focusing on the Church that embraces all. Or it may be less defined, focusing on subjective experience, the giving of oneself to oneself or another. Either way, it unifies not through genealogy, but through universal relevance and application, where all selves are necessarily implied.

Now, the fact that we have just enumerated six paradigms (and we might have enumerated more),[55] tells us that the One, for all its predominance since the Hebrews, has not been uniformly One. In theory, and with irony, we can think of the One many ways, as already shown by the backslash in "O/one" that separates the divine One from the numerical one. But paradigmatically, the One, as paradigm, allows us at least to model our thoughts on the One, however conceived, and this modelling, as a metastructure, is what is most significant as we try to understand the legacy of the One in our Western thinking.

We therefore suggest that, given these six paradigmatic formulations of the One, we can account for what is to follow in the Common Era, moving approximately from the third to the nineteenth centuries, as dependent on the One in one paradigmatic form or another. For what we see after Neoplatonism is an adoption or adaption of one or more of these paradigms as a way to make sense of the reality that any one period or any one people has encountered or has created. This may seem an overreaching claim, given the breadth and complexity of social and intellectual circumstances experienced under the vast time span in question. But we risk such abbreviation, in order to exemplify, and amplify, the nature of the One at work in our basic understanding of ourselves as a developed civilization. Our history of ideas, as it pertains to the One, has thus become utterly paradigmatic, as we dare to use paradigms paradigmatically, and hazard the generalizations that will inevitably—if corroboratively—arise.

The Catholic One

The term *catholic* we know means "universal" (literally, "concerning the whole"). And as we move into the Catholic era of Christendom, we find the whole of Europe caught up in one universal, as put forward by the Church. Of course, this is a rich and variegated history. But let us put our paradigmatic theory to test, and account for this history using the possible six paradigms we have developed above.

The era of the Patristics, those early Church Fathers coming to terms with a Christianity that, by the fourth century, would be made the official religion of the Roman Empire, is an era marked by a pressing need for unity. It is not only that one faith was to rule as a result of Constantine's military victory over his rivals and his conversion to the "Supreme God," but that the one faith had to be unified itself, made homogeneous amid many competing influences, systems, ideas, and doctrines. Early Christianity was many things, but among its most salient features is the effort of consolidation through orthodoxy, creed, and canon. The Roman Empire's greatest accomplishment—both its greatest strength and its greatest weakness—was its ability to maintain a plurality of cultures, voices, peoples, and beliefs under one system of government. This is, of course, the great challenge of any empire. With Constantine's victory, the move away from the plurality of paganism and toward one official religion introduced a unity that would be set in place for well over a thousand years.

If we consider the concepts of orthodoxy, creed, and canon, we see in each case the paradigm of the One as metanarrative under employment. The first, orthodoxy, is about correct belief, or correct doctrine. It is predicated upon a singular understanding of Truth. To be orthodox means to be aligned perfectly with the Truth that aligns all beliefs and practices. The early Church Fathers understood that there were many ways to articulate belief, and when it came to belief in the One true God as revealed by the narratives of the Gospel, their intent was to forge a metanarrative in which all other articulations could be measured and assessed. Orthodoxy is precisely this metanarrative: the standard by which all narratives could be deemed either truth or heresy. Even Constantine himself was interested in the master doctrine, for to rule comprehensively, one needs a unified and shared agreement about what will define the terms of rule: "one God, one Lord, one faith, one church, one empire, one emperor."

It is not surprising that the central issue to emerge during this formative period of orthodox religion was the triune nature of God. For how does one reconcile the Supreme God of monotheism with a second divine figure, the Son, and a third divine figure, the Holy Spirit? What keeps this trio unified, and how do we speak of this unification? The doctrine of the Trinity, a question of the Many from the One, is an age-old problem, we know, going back to the Presocratics at least. The immense amount of energy and controversy that went into this problem in the first three hundred years or so after Christ's death shows how crucial the question of the One became for Christian belief. How precisely *do* we understand an incarnated God, if that God is to remain supremely One? This conundrum opened up not only the question of divine nature, but the relationship of that nature with the material world—*metaphusis* and *phusis* all over again. A doctrine of creation is thus made inevitable, as well as a doctrine of God, of Christ, and of the Spirit, respectively. The fact that the Triune God still maintains absolute unity and Oneness is one of the great feats of Christian thinking, and owes its possibility to a metanarrative that keeps One both "with" and "beyond." For the concept of the Trinity itself reveals a metastructure fundamentally at work: there are three personages—three "hypostases," to use Neoplatonic language—but those three cannot in any way have meaning apart from the unified structure from which they come. That structure, the One, functions *beyond* the three, to remain the supreme true God of all, but is also wholly *with* that three *as* that three, fully integrated and completely inextricable as three-in-One. The early Trinitarian debates were about this very structure, making sure that it would be the ruling paradigm from which all other mani-festations of Many-from-the-One, whether political, social, or ecclesiastical, would find their ground. And this included even the concept of orthodox belief itself: all articulations would find their ground in the one orthodoxy that governs and unifies the manifold.

Closely connected with orthodoxy is creed. If orthodoxy is about the correct way of thinking, creed is about unification through shared and fixed expression. Creed is still about belief (*credo*: "I believe"), but it is the out-ward expression of that belief in a manner that brings the many together under one system. Only through creed could the people be called a church, and only through creed could that church be called "catholic." Creed then unifies through its emphasis on unity, which underwrites its entire structure. A highlighted look at the Nicene Creed (first devised and ratified in 325 CE at Constantine's behest, and expanded upon in 381) reveals the One in all its centrality:

> We believe in **one God**,
> the Father, the Almighty,
> maker of heaven and earth,
> of all that is, seen and unseen.
>
> We believe in **one Lord**, Jesus Christ,
> the only Son of God,
> eternally begotten of the Father,
> God from God, Light from Light,
> true God from true God,
> begotten, not made,
> of one Being with the Father.
> Through him all things were made . . .
> We believe in **one holy catholic and apostolic Church**.

We acknowledge one baptism for the forgiveness of sins.
We look for the resurrection of the dead,
and the life of the world to come. Amen.

By instituting and reciting this creed, one is grounded in the metanarrative that is One, just as the creed unifies all other narratives, and makes them one in purpose and truth.

The creed, as a rule of faith, as well as a regulatory mechanism for keeping heresy at bay, functions at the doctrinal level in the way that the canon functions at the textual level. With so many possible texts circulating about in the early centuries of Christianity, some form of standardization and consolidation was needed to keep out texts that did not conform to orthodox belief. The concept of the canon is metanarrative in its paramount form. Canonization is not simply the process of selecting out texts that adhere to prescribed criteria; it is also, and for that very reason, the formation of a narrative of narratives, in which text collated with text reveals a broader story, whose whole is effectively greater than the sum of its constituent parts. The biblical canon is about the unity of texts within orthodoxy, creating a One that is made sacred by its consolidation into one, while at the same time creating a sacredness that is made One by virtue of its exclusive character. The Bible is sacred precisely because it has gone through the process of selection and deselection, in order that a whole might emerge to reflect the One true Sacred. Without the canon, textual authority would be inherently undermined, and this the later Reformers fully comprehended, and exploited as far as they could, though with consequences that became one of history's greatest ironies: without catholic orthodoxy, the very One that canon meant to preserve became fractured and multiple, leading to the modernity of Self, in which concepts of the One have greatly eroded. But this was not the Reformers' intention, as their adoption of the credal formulas makes clear. For the canon is a paradigmatic metastructure, and meant to consolidate authority. That the Reformers wagered upon this consolidation with such exclusivity—*sola scriptura*—shows they were still committed to the One in all its glory. That the Patristics held the canon as part of a more integrated One—including eventually apostolic succession (which brings in the One as genealogical) and Church hierarchy (which brings in the One as meta-explanatory)—only shows a difference in how One can be understood and interpreted. Canonical authority, as metanarrative, nevertheless holds out the promise of an *already interpreted One*. And such arch-hermeneutics is its greatest achievement, even if, as we shall see, it could never fulfil the promise.

If we give any credence to orthodoxy, creed, and canon as metanarratives in their own right, all operating within an even higher metanarrative of the One, we can apply this to how individual figures in this period adapted this scheme for themselves. We cannot go through a roll call of names, or we would never leave this chapter, but foremost among the Church Fathers in this regard is Augustine. In his seminal *Confessions,* we see the One as metanarrative united with the One as self-giving. The *Confessions* unfolds a narrative through which one personal story is given as one long confession— a confessing into truth, to modify Aeschylus's famous phrase "to suffer into truth." This truth, on one level, is the truth of the personal narrative as an honest autobiographical account. But by giving this account of the self, the Truth of God's personal story also comes to light, so that Augustine is not only admitting his own personal weaknesses, but also disclosing God's personal salvation in the midst of that weakness. The unity of Augustine's life with God's love, made evident by the end of Book 10, then gives way to the unity of God as Father, Son, and Holy Spirit (the final three books, 11–13). The trajectory of Augustine's own unity—his self-giving to us as readers and to his God, his ultimate reader—transposes itself to the self-giving of God in his creation through the Trinity in the final three books. The *Confessions* in its entirety, then, provides a unity between the narrative that is Augustine's life and the narrative that is God's being. This metanarrative, the *Confessions* as a text, is similar to what we saw operating in Plato's *Parmenides,* where only through the confessing itself, that is, through the narrative structure, is the unity grasped as unity. The concept of the One may be informing the content, but the form of that One is not instantiated fully and concretely until the confession is actually made and made available through the written text. What makes the *Confessions* so groundbreaking is that for the first time individual being and individual identity are defined in terms of a comprehensive unity—a unity, that is, comprehended *through the text as self-giving.*

The self-giving of the text will become an important feature of later modern hermeneutics, as we shall see, and for this reason Augustine remains a proto-modern figure. For now, we can see Augustine's appropriation of the paradigmatic One as the perfect fusion of metanarrative and self-giving. He will, of course, go on, in such works as *The City of God Against the Pagans,* to espouse a One that owes much to Plotinus's *Enneads* and Porphyry, whereby God is the point of unity for all that follows after Him. And this he will put to work against not only the dualism inherent in Platonism as it came to be understood, but also the dualism rampant in such heresies as Manichaeism and Gnosticism, which Augustine castigated tirelessly. Yet his more philosophical One will always be compromised by his dim view of physicality and bodily appetite, so that his most enduring legacy, at least in terms of the One, remains with the gift that is his confessional text, his unified *self* as given.

The rise of the Church within Christendom moves away from Augustine's individualism, as the *Ecclesia* incorporates metanarrative at all levels of orthodoxy, creed, and canon to become itself a metanarrative—a metanarrative of corporate institutionalization. We have already indicated that papal authority and hierarchy bring genealogical and self-explanatory aspects to this institutional One, the first by way of apostolic succession, the second by way of empowering this authority to administer between various levels of corporate being, so that the effect at one level is justified by the cause at another, and so on. But the Church is also seen as self-giving: as a bride gives to a bridegroom, and the two become one, so the Church as Bride is wedded to Christ as Bridegroom, and the two are perfectly united in Christ. In giving oneself to the Church, one is giving over and given up to union with God. The ecclesiastical structure thus acts as a paradigm itself—to become part of the Church, one unites with divine and cosmological structures, all of which are integrated in one system of creation. The Church can thus dictate a master narrative because it is fully representative of that narrative through its self-giving union with Christ. It is no wonder, then, that the Catholic Church became such a powerful institution. It was able to subsume all paradigms, and become a master paradigm itself—in ecclesiastical language, a master sacrament, or in Thomistic language, a master analogy of the Triune God, the "highest exemplar" of unity.

The monumental figures of medieval Christendom are a richly complex manifold. Frederick Copleston, who has well covered the philosophically religious thought concerning the One in his *Religion and the One*, claims that "the metaphysics of the One and the Many, in some form or other, runs from John Scotus Erigena in the ninth century to a Nicholas of Cusa in the first half of the fifteenth century."[56] We can add that, paradigmatically, Scholasticism as a whole was largely guided by a concept of the One as meta-explanatory, as the rediscovery of Aristotle in the twelfth century drove much of the Scholastic approach and agenda, culminating of course in Aquinas's work, the *Summa Theologica* in particular. There are exceptions, as always, especially in the approach to the One as mystical—Bonaventure and Eckhart, as but two examples—but medieval theology was largely a time of explaining theology as the explanation of explanation. As Aquinas says, in trying to explain the unity that comes out of diversity,

> knowledge is higher to the degree that it is more unified and extends to more things. Hence God's intellect, which is highest, has distinct knowledge of all things *through something one*, which is God himself. So too . . . this science [theology] is highest and derives its efficacy from the light of divine inspiration itself and, while remaining one and undivided, considers diverse things.[57]

The Modern One

We have been dealing almost exclusively with the question of the One on the same level at which it has been forged, the level of philosophical and religious ideas, knowing that these ideas shaped manifold cultural expressions, from politics and science to art and technology. We have earlier alluded to, for example, the geocentric model of astronomy, and how its framework of the One was shattered by Copernicus's heliocentric hypothesis. In this light of transition, we could also mention the printing press, and how its practical application brought a new sense of "original" and "copy," which made both the original all the more singular and the copy all the more plural. As we move into the modern era, with its sense of newness, the old C/catholic assumptions quickly fall away on all levels, and even the varying paradigms of the One become more varied. If we can say that the medieval One was predominantly modeled on the meta-explanatory, there is no predominance in the modern era. We see all of our six paradigms in operation in one form or other, but now increasingly under threat. The "modern," we said in the Introduction, was marked by an "O" at its very inception. Early modernity tried to hide that O, the Enlightenment tried to rationalize it away, while modernism acknowledged that it was finally irrepressible. Each assumed a paradigmatic One in its stance, but that stance was never as stable as any had hoped. As we remain at the level of philosophical and religious ideas, we will see briefly why instability would necessarily encroach.

The Renaissance period, with its return to classical ideals, certainly offered varied approaches, but the humanism at its center adopted a meta-narrative understanding of human nature: we all share in one common humanity, a humanity worth glorifying. It is this humanity as a master narrative that lends itself to the many possible narratives we might explore in the arts, the sciences, education, etc., and that unifies them all. With its emphasis on human freedom and rationality, this humanism would create the appropriate conditions for the Reformation, and the further instability of the One as C/catholic. But it still maintained a one that was defining of humanity, even if that humanity, by virtue of its freedom, was no longer fully unified with nature.

Luther's One is the God of the Bible, which involves the self-giving of Paul, and by extension of Augustine. But self-giving for Luther takes Augustine's individualism to an extreme: it is not self-giving *as the text*, as it was in the *Confessions*, whereby the metanarrative emerges as one's self-text is unified with the self-text of God; it is self-giving *to the text*, which must be read in freedom and faith as the self-text of God. The metanarrative of One emerges in the authority of *sola scriptura* as the already interpreted One. And in Reformed theology, the believer has to read this One for him- or herself, and become unified with it. As Luther says in "The Freedom of a Christian": "Just as the heated iron glows like fire because of the union of fire with it, so the Word imparts its qualities to the soul."[58] For Augustine, the One came about in writing the confessing text, through which the confessor is unified with God the One. For Luther, and those who came after him, the text is already written, and already interpreted, and one must simply embrace it in the act of faithful reading, wearing the "spectacles of belief." The difference between the two positions is more than a difference between writing and reading. Augustine's metanarrative is textual in the comprehensive sense: all things are a unified text, so that an act of personal testimonial brings one into the unified whole that is God's cosmos. Luther's metanarrative is possible only through personal faith, and the act of personal reading, even in faith, does not necessarily bring one into a unified cosmos. Luther mistrusts wholesale unity, because it necessarily includes the Church and its hierarchy. By confessing to God, Luther is confessing an individual position, not a comprehensive whole. The whole, as Church, is precisely what distanced Luther from his God. Personal faith in the authority of God's textual revelation is what brings him back. It is metanarrative, as self-giving, but now the metanarrative is much more dependent upon the individual as such—that is, upon someone who gains their ontological, psychological, and spiritual bearings not from the predeterminations of the ordered and unified world but from the inner self. And with such dependence, such reconceived self-giving, the entire status of the "meta" comes under threat.

We might think of this important transition from C/catholic to individual thinking this way. However much Augustine personalizes his experience in the Confessions, he does not subjectivize his faith. Faith, for him, is part of a unified comprehensive whole. This is why he can say that the Platonists and Neoplatonists come close to this faith, and indeed remain a worthy path to it. But for Luther, coming to God means subjectivizing faith, removing it from any external structure (the Church or the law of "works") and confining it to one's internal disposition toward God and His text. Pagan philosophy cannot lead one into this disposition. Nor can any institution or figurehead. Each person must find this disposition of faith on their own, as their own priest and their own interpreter. In the language of Scholasticism, then, Catholic faith operates within an unum per se (intrinsic unity, where the believer and the structure of reality are one), Reformed faith within an unum per accidens (unity by aggregation, where the believer is unified only to fellow believers as individuals). For this reason, the One itself becomes subjectivized, and once this move is made, the C/catholic One begins to slide from its position of sovereignty.

Descartes, a Catholic, was a poignant witness to this decline in the seventeenth century, when competing sovereignties were clashing in the brutal Thirty Years' War of religions across Continental Europe. Having served near the front lines, Descartes retreated into his private hovel to contemplate the nature of certainty, and why, in his times of turmoil, it seemed to have disappeared. The resulting Cartesian dualism between mind and body—certainty is found only in the thinking mind, not in the bodily senses—would irretrievably alter the map of medieval and scholastic cosmic *unum per se*, and give way to a permanent subject/object divide. Where Luther subjectivized faith, the Cartesian *cogito* subjectivized reality. Or, we could say, it made reality a feature of subjective thinking and knowing, not by reducing it to pure solipsism, but by making the certainty of the objective world contingent upon the subjective mind. One could always doubt phenomenal appearances, but one could not doubt the thinking mind that allowed one to doubt in the first place. We must begin, therefore, with a stability of the self, and work outward from there to the objective world. We might still bring in God to ratify objective reality, but God is now on the other side of the equation, as it were: He no longer underpins or defines the initial step of explanation. Cartesianism may therefore still hold on to a vestige of the One as meta-explanatory, as the *cogito* itself becomes meta-explanation, but now the One, as it was with Luther, rests on subjectivity, and thus loses its capacity to circumscribe all of reality, both that within and that without. The One is reduced to the subject (as *unum per se*) in disengagement from the world (as *unum per accidens*). It is not *we think, therefore we are*, but the first person singular. The One as capitalized and the one as genericized becomes the one, the "I," as individualized.

Subsequent philosophers of the Enlightenment period attempt to adapt the various paradigms of the One in spite of this Cartesian disturbance. Spinoza's metaphysics very much adopted the One as substantive, where all reality is reduced to one substance, a Necessary God, in a pure monism by which God becomes the ultimate paradigm for all things within reality (a monism but not a monotheism—Spinoza's God is not personal). And Leibniz's "monads," we have seen, also draw upon this substantive model, in an attempt to eradicate the Cartesian dualism between body and soul, matter and mind, through a "preestablished harmony" or unity between all substances (which ultimately is God, the supreme substance, in a return to the *unum per se*). And along with this substantive thinking can be placed the rise of science (to which Descartes, Spinoza, and Leibniz all contributed significantly in their way), and the rise of empiricism, which shifted the question of certainty back onto the phenomenal world and our senses. So whether mind or matter, substantive explanation takes us back to the Presocratic idea that basic singular substances or entities can explain all reality. It also brings us full circle to the scientific paradigms of Kuhn, which we saw in the Introduction, though now we can see even more explicitly how, by this period in history, the One had already lost its firm hold, and was slowly giving itself up as a ruling paradigm.

The critiques of Kant may be said to conceptualize the concept itself—that which brings the manifold under one entity—and therefore present the One in a meta-explanatory model of explaining explanation. Here, following the individual shifts above, unity is found in the unity of (self-)consciousness, whereby one's experiences, including the experience of oneself experiencing, is brought together under one conscious whole by virtue of the transcendental self-reasoning mind of an individual. Of course, bracketed out of this unity is the "thing itself," or *noumena* (in opposition to *phenomena*). But critique in the Kantian sense is about limit, and within the limits of the phenomenal world the self-conscious mind, now fully conscious of its own consciousness as never before, engages in a participatory unification—the Kantian term is *synthesis*—of all known reality, keeping the One in place as meta-critique.

Hegel's system of absolute dialectics brings, for many, this unity of self-consciousness to its greatest modern pinnacle, as the movements of history and culture culminate in an Absolute One of pure idealism, in which there is a perfect amalgamation of the material and the spirit, where spirit can be understood in a phenomenological sense—*The Phenomenology of Spirit*. Standard readings of Hegelian idealism would suggest here too a paradigm of meta-explanation, as the rational forces of reason themselves are manifested in this all-unifying *Geist*. But such a reading of Hegel would have to ignore the negating component of the dialectic as absolutely fundamental, as it did for more than a century and a half. Only recently has this negative component, not merely as "anti-thesis" but as a constitutive core of the structural logic of the system as a whole, been appreciated.[59] With negation placed centrally, the Hegelian system brings an "O" to the heart of its operation, a zeroing out. As Hegel himself says: "[T]he simplicity [i.e., the singular nature] which constitutes the very nature of the universal is such that, through absolute negativity, it contains *within itself* difference and determinateness in the highest degree."[60] With this emphasis, Hegel's thought would suggest a Neoplatonic paradigm that moves toward the One as wholly absolute, and therefore mystical, where the "with" overwhelms the "beyond" to a point where the "with" itself loses all distinction, and becomes one with negativity. We can see then that by the time of Hegel's radical philosophy, the One paradigmatically is no longer on sure ground, and, if Hegel is to be believed, begins to break apart from within. We will return to Hegel in the sixth chapter, to see his side more from the O.

Romanticism drew upon Kantian unity of self-consciousness to further emphasize the interiorization of the paradigmatic One. Much of German Romanticism struggled to reconcile the dualism in Kant's own system between a determined natural world run by necessary laws and a free subject able to choose at will, or between things in themselves and appearances of things, the troubling phenomena/noumena division. The philosophy of Schelling is exemplary in this case, as is Hegel's system that reacts to it, but the same concern runs through those more associated with German Romanticism directly, such as Herder, F. Schlegel, and Hölderlin: how to repair the subject/object or human/nature divide. "To be one with all that lives, to return in blessed self-forgetfulness to All of Nature," yearned Hölderlin.[61] Or as Schleiermacher offered:

> The Universe is ceaselessly active and at every moment is revealing itself to us. Every form it has produced, everything to which, from the fullness of its life, it has given a separate existence, every occurrence scattered from its fertile bosom is an operation of the Universe upon us. Now religion is to take up into our lives and to submit to be swayed by them, each of these influences and their consequent emotions, not by themselves but as a part of the Whole, not as limited and in opposition to other things, but as an exhibition of the Infinite in our life.[62]

For Schleiermacher, this divine Infinite was One: "The sum total of religion is to feel that, in its highest unity, all that moves us in feeling is one . . ."[63] This pursuit for (re-)unity led to a new kind of self-giving, a submission "to be swayed" by and become part of a unified harmony of the Universe, drawing on human passion, inclination, intuition, and imagination in their most sublime forms. We can think here of Coleridge's primary imagination, which repeats the eternal act of creation of the infinite I AM within the finite mind, unifying nature and spirit. But here, as with all the Romantics, this unity can only be found by going inward, so that the One becomes *self*-giving, or self-giving becomes the One only as it is sourced from within the individual. Charles Taylor calls this self-giving "expressive individuation": "If our access to nature is through an inner voice or impulse [imagination], then we can only fully know nature through articulating what we find within us . . . its realisation within us is also its form of expression."[64] In giving or expressing ourselves, we are brought into the One, but a One that is paradoxically individuated. Romantic unity thus goes in two opposing directions: toward harmony with Nature on the one hand, and toward individual self-realization on the other. This fundamental fracture, which modernism will bear out, and postmodernism will celebrate, is captured succinctly by Hölderlin's "The Root of all Evil":

> Being united is godly and good; but why this obsession
> Driving all humans, that only One and One only must be?[65]

ONE'S RETREAT

Where and how do we draw this history of an idea, the history of One, grand and sweeping as it is, to an appropriate close, as it clearly and increasingly ebbs in the nineteenth century from its place of supremacy? Of course the concept of the One will not disappear, and remains even in our present day, operating at manifold levels of our society, as the joke showed us at the outset of the chapter. But where does it lose its sovereignty, its preeminent position of power? With Nietzsche's madman, and the death of the unified God of Christianity and religion?[66] With Existentialism, that reinscription of the one from noun to verb, the one as purely individual *being* no longer in harmony with Nature, except through some self-committed resignation? With modernism and its experiments—in T. S. Eliot's famous "heaps of broken images" or Yeats's famous center that cannot hold, in Joyce's polyphony or Beckett's absurdity? Or does it take a more political event: the rise and defeat of European totalitarianism, after which the idealization of the One can no longer be countenanced, either in religion, in philosophy, or as Adorno implied, in art?

We have focused on religion and philosophy almost exclusively in this chapter, because it is here that the One is forged conceptually and paradigmatically. As we reach the twentieth century, we find few religious or philosophical paradigms left that have not either relied on traditional renderings or have given way under the unsustainable weight of modernist thinking. Granted, positivism, and its offspring in analytical philosophy, assumed a unity of logical, at times even mathematical, proportion, in which the laws of contradiction continued to play a central role in defining the nature of truth, or "truth value." But logical positivism or logical empiricism, in its move away from metaphysics, was beholden to the scientific model, which showed tremendous limitations in dealing with the full spectrum of human concerns, ethics especially, and which in the end was reduced to a philosophy that, in Bertrand Russell's words, simply "diminishes the risk of error."[67] And analytical philosophy, for its part, ceased to talk about unity or the one in any real sense, especially after its move away from linguistics proper (where at least it could talk about a unity of rules of the linguistic game), and speaks now only of shared "truth-conditions" (Davidson) or "solidarity" (the earlier Rorty). That we do not have a ruling paradigmatic One philosophically in the twentieth century shows us how far the One has moved from center stage. And when religion loses its position as a central social force, no longer governing political and cultural activity and decisions, religion likewise retreats from the One, and finds itself unable to maintain not only an ecumenism, but worse, denominational unity, as the ongoing divisions within long-established churches make evident today.

The full end of the paradigmatic One cannot be told without discussing the rise of the figure "O" as its rival, and to this we will turn in the next chapter. What we have seen here in this chapter, in a highly selective and overly abbreviated history of ideas (and how differently it could have been written), is a positioning of the paradigmatic One, immovable till the modern era, that controlled how we think about reality and the relationship with our world around us. We could embark on many different analyses of how this One determined everyday living in the West, but we will have to leave this kind of employment of the paradigms to others in more specialized fields (anthropology, sociology, psychology, etc.). Important here and now is to understand the sovereignty—how it arose, how it sat upon a throne supported equally by religion and philosophy, and how that throne became brittle and unstable.

We then return back to the world of Genesis 11, where the consolidation of a people's striving is manifested in a unified language and a single edifice, reaching to the heavens in audacious hubris. But we seem this time to have been scattered by our own doing, and not by a jealous and worried God. And therefore we do not move toward a new consolidation as a chosen and holy people, since God, as One, is no longer present. We are post-Babel, but without a divine sovereign to draw us together out of the many. And this is a position that, for all intents and purposes, we have not occupied before.

In Milan Kundera's novel *The Joke*, one of the main characters struggles to hold on to his Christian faith in the midst of a crumbling world in which previous certainties—given this cause, this effect will follow—no longer obtain. Each action has led to an unpredictable outcome, and even the certainty of his faith, which may once have rested upon meta-explanatory ground, now teeters on loose and slipping soil. And so at the end of his long chapter as a soliloquy, this character, Kostka, asks, "But how to recognize God's voice among so many other voices?"[68] The irony of *our* post-Babel situation is that even God's voice is lost among the cacophony of multiplicity and polyvocality. Or the joke, it might be construed, is now on God: by scattering the people's voices, if that is what He has done, even God's own voice cannot be heard. "O God, is it truly so?" Kostka laments, "Am I so wretchedly laughable? Tell me it is not so! Reassure me! Make yourself heard, God, louder, louder! In this chaos of confused voices I cannot seem to hear You."[69]

The joke is no longer laughable, having lost its One. But does this mean we stop laughing altogether, and lament? Rather than forging forward or upward in a straight line, we return to the beginning, in a circle. But does that mean we have lost the story, the plot, the punch line, and have become a joke of our own history and ideas? Or can the "O" be a prelude to another kind of laughter, as the artist might suggest?

TWO

THE REVOLUTIONS OF O

The language we thought was reporting on the reality of negation turns out to take part in the activity itself, to have its own negating function and, indeed, to be subject to negation itself.

—Judith Butler, *Subjects of Desire*

"*O how that name befits my composition!*"[1] —
THE ROMEO EFFECT

"O Romeo, Romeo! Wherefore art thou Romeo?" So goes one of the most famous lines in literature. But in all the recitations, the repetitions, the parodies, the lampoons, does any of us take note of the opening "O"? Why should we? As an interjection, it intensifies the cry for Romeo. Juliet pines for her man with intense longing, and the O deepens her emotion. But that intensity is already present in the redoubling of Romeo's name, and so it merely mirrors, or amplifies, the longed-for yet absent Romeo. As an expletive, an expression that might fill in that absence, it is semantically empty. Its point is to fill up the space left by Romeo, and to do so by emptying itself in order that what surrounds it might be brought into greater relief. As an apostrophe, it addresses the absent with an emphatic turn.[2] Grammatically it is without connection, semiotically it is without function. As a word, as a thought, as an expression, it is as nugatory a "signifier" as we have.

Poetically, and prosodically, the expletive is used to fill the line, here allowing the iambic pentameter its proper scansion, the full five feet of the metrical beat (though this line has always been difficult to scan). It compensates for an absence, and, ironically, for a lack of quantity or number. Given its syllabic structure, it can only compensate for the quantity of one. The O stands in for one, then, a cardinal vowel standing in for a cardinal number.

67

But in and of itself, outside of its metrical context, it is grammatically and semantically nothing. At best it points to absence, the hole within whole.

As Juliet stands at her balcony, looking into the night, she questions both the presence and absence of her new love. Romeo, wherefore art thou? ("Wherefore" in Shakespeare means "on what account," "for what purpose," "why.") But as far as she is concerned, the nature of his existence is in his absence. The whole opening phrase then might be seen to have an expletive function, as it tries to compensate for the absence of presence of Romeo. The opening "O" thus spills through to the end of the line, in the hope that it might fill in for the absent one. But there is yet more hope of compensation, for where Juliet wishes something present that is absent, in the next line she wishes something absent that is present: Romeo's family name, Montague. "Deny thy father, and refuse thy name," she says. And if this will not work, Juliet will reverse the hope, and wish absent her own name: "Or, if thou wilt not, be but sworn my love, / And I'll no longer be a Capulet."[3] So Juliet's entire four-line passage is colored by an expletive role signaled by the opening "O": her intensifying words of desire try to compensate for the absent Romeo, while her love tries to compensate for the lack of family accord.

But Romeo is *not* absent in the scene. He is present, even if not yet visible to Juliet. He stands in the orchard, listening to her words. His response—"Shall I hear more, or shall I speak at this?"—betrays a dilemma. Should he remain absent to her, and hear more of her compensatory words, her "O," or should he reveal himself? He is thus caught between absence and presence, which is always what the stage direction "[aside]" indicates, a place that, dramatically, is there and not there. This place "[aside]" is further expression of the "O" itself, as expletive, which is both there and not there, both present as compensatory and absent as nothing, as zero. Romeo, here in his response, fully manifests the O: caught between listening and speaking, he resides in the space between passivity and activity, or in the space that is both at once. This reveals the peculiar and paradoxical nature of the O, simultaneously passive and active, receiving and giving, not being something while acting as that something. Wherefore art thou indeed?

As Juliet tries to absent the Montague name in her continuing speech, with Romeo secretly listening on, she returns again to the expletive. "O, be some other name," she cries. But can this O be a mere trifling here? Be some other name, something else, she seems to ask of the O, as if addressing it vocatively. And as a cipher, as homonym, this is precisely what the O does best. It becomes some other name—"Romeo," she hopes, and only "Romeo," not "Montague." The O both adds and cancels out. Become Romeo, and cancel Montague, she requests, as if this were possible. She then poses a further thought, "What's in a name?" and gives us that now famous example of the rose. What *is* in a name, we might ask, the name of the "O"? Nothing, we have repeatedly said. And this is exactly what she is hoping for, Romeo as a kind of cipher, a pure container or containment of nothing, into which she can pour herself and her love. In the next line she takes these hopes farther, and dispenses even with the given name "Romeo": "So Romeo would, were he not Romeo call'd / Retain that dear perfection which he owes / Without that title." Here the young girl betrays her naive sense of love, as if her lover could be so neutralized or hollowed out of all that has made him, of all that has given him his name(s). "Romeo, doff thy name / And for that name which is no part of thee / Take all myself." So Juliet has turned her love completely into the expletive with which she began, the O that means nothing except the intensification of herself.

Now precisely at this point Romeo makes himself present before Juliet. And as if to present the very O that Juliet has desired, he says:

> I take thee at thy word
> Call me but love, and I'll be new baptized;
> Henceforth, I will never be Romeo.

Here, Romeo washes himself of himself, in a baptism of cipher purification. He remains the O, taking Juliet "at her word" (the word of "O," which is Juliet's love). He is both present and absent—present now before Juliet in full body, absent as the old Romeo. This is the paradoxical place of either/nor, a place without a name, except the name of O. Thus, Romeo can only say, "By a name / I know not how to tell thee who I am." Wherefore is this O? Wherefore is Romeo? And yet, there he remains, wherever, and why ever, this *there* is.

So the intricacies of the O are born out here in this famous episode between Shakespeare's two young lovers. What seems invisible, innocuous, immaterial, becomes the very core of the matter, the heart of disturbance or disruption, and what was is no longer considered as it was. This is the typical nature of the O, with which we begin our analysis. When it seems absent, it is present, and when we want to make it present, it is also absent. How do we place such a figure then? Or how does such a figure come to be placed? How do we talk about it, analyze it? How do we give it meaning, when it inherently seems to divest meaning as the archexpletive?

"O thou senseless form"[4] —ZERO AND ITS HISTORY

The paradox of the expletive—it is empty, but in its emptiness it acts to fill up—extends to the figure of the O in its most basic form. Two-dimensionally, the O is pure containment, with no opening or gap, and yet what it contains is nothing.[5] This paradox also extends to the cipher. Arithmetically, the cipher has no inherent value, but it takes on value by its positioning around whole numbers—increasing or decreasing by tenfold, depending on its place-ment before or after a number and its decimal point. This paradox likewise extends to zero. Zero does not hold numerical value, but as the dividing line, or the threshold, between positive and negative numbers, it becomes extremely valuable, and modern mathematics is impossible without it. If we were to try to trace a history of the form of O, we would find the paradox continuing to work. For unlike the One, with which we could mark out a clear and paradigmatic history, the O does not lend itself to model forms of development, conceptual or otherwise. There are periods where the O as zero did not even exist. And yet, without it history becomes muddled. We would not know where to begin. But how do we historicize zero, when zero ruptures history as a linear progression, by rupturing the unity between cardinality and ordinality (numerical value versus the ordering of that value taxonomically in a sequence)? When 0 is present (but always without cardinality itself), the cardinality of subsequent numbers is never synonymous with their ordinality, but always one out: 1 in a series beginning 0, 1, 2, 3 . . . is always the sec-ond, 2 the third, 3 the fourth, etc. Hence we have the "twenty-first century" whose written dates (2011, 2012, etc.) refer only to twenty hundreds, and not twenty-one. This lack of synchronization comes to complicate any attempt to date across "the year of our Lord," which the ancient monks had calculated without zero. That they did not possess a firm concept of zero already belies the eclipsing nature of the One in Western history (eclipsing even the void of Genesis 1, from which life began). That they started with AD 1 makes calculating the number of years between, say, 4 BC and AD 4 problematic. We think it should be 8 $(4 - (-4))$, but in fact it is 7, since for the monks 1 BC moves directly to AD 1 with no zero in between.[6] The zero then, despite its cardinal nothingness, is nonetheless crucial for historical accounting, and yet itself has a broken history, at least in the West.

The Greeks, we have said, did not have a symbol for zero. This is because they could not entertain the *concept* of nothing. Parmenides, that great champion of the changeless One, averred the impossibility for *what is not* to be, or even for *what is not* to be thought of. We therefore must not try to think on it. And this is what the Greeks did: they largely shunned thinking about the nothing altogether. We can see why. If Greek thinking since the Presocratics is about *ratio*, about ordering things in relation to one another, reality must remain accountable, or countable. The Pythagoreans, we saw, took this countability to its extreme, where reality becomes number. But with O, or "0," a void is introduced, and a void, by definition, cannot be counted. It lacks all quantification. If the universe is structured on an idea such as the *logos*, and its attendant rationality or proportionality, which allows us to speak of it, or (ac)count for it, it must remain positive. Negativity cannot enter into the equation. Thus, the Greeks never developed a symbol for this nothing in their numerology.[7]

Neither did the older Egyptians, whose system of accounting was notated in pictures. With pictographic language, a positive referent is needed in the world. But how do you picture nothing? What does it look like? You need to turn nothing into a concept, beyond pictures. But famed for mathematics as ancient Egyptian civilization may have been—the pyramids proved their excellence at geometry—they never developed a need for zero in their computations. Even death was not about returning to a place of nothing, as evidenced in the Book of the Dead, where the ferryman who transports the dead soul across the river to the netherworld would deny passage to anyone "who does not know the number of his fingers."[8] As with the Greeks, accounting systems were crucial, as they must be for all civilizations that base their governance on some form of taxation. And so the avoidance of nothing, which troubles accounting in every regard—financial accounting as much as philosophical and religious accounting. It is not surprising that the Egyptians developed such a sophisticated system of bodily preservation upon death. Mummification is a gesture against the void, or an attempt to contain and preserve that which lies within. The pyramids, we remember, functioned similarly as tombs. Thus, the O, as zero, figures neither in the pyramidical shape nor in the afterlife—zero would be a perilous ticket for the ferryman.

Where does the symbol of zero enter our Western world? A look at the etymology of the word may best describe its history.[9] The origins stem from the East, and India in particular. In Sanskrit, the word for "empty" or "blank" is *sunya*.[10] The East, and both Hinduism and Buddhism especially, were much more accepting of the idea of nothingness, or void. In both religions, all reality not only stems from the void but returns to the void. Coming to terms with this void is, one might argue, the very essence of these systems of religious thought and practice. The Atman, the supreme principle of the universe in Hindu belief, for example, is very much like the mystical One, where its total and all-encompassing infinity is synonymous with a pure nothing—everywhere and nowhere at the same time. This is a paradox the Western mind still, to this day, cannot fathom. E. M. Forster dramatizes well this inability in his *Passage to India*. The center of the novel is also the center of a cave, in which the old affrighted Mrs. Moore hears the echoing "boum," that circular motion of sound "entirely devoid of distinction."[11] She flees the midst of the cave, the center, deeply disturbed by this void, and by the comprehensive nothingness it represents, "because it robbed infinity and eternity of their vastness" and reduced her Christianity, with "all its divine words from 'Let there be light' to 'It is finished,'" to an empty echo, a "boum" of nothing. So the Marabar caves themselves stand on a reputation of nothing—"nothing attaches to them," Forster tells us, literally and figuratively; and if excavated, "nothing, nothing would be added to the sum of good and evil."[12] This zeroing effect the poor Mrs. Moore cannot comprehend, like the West she represents. Nor is it by accident that Forster's entire plot is predicated on an event in the center of the caves that he never actually describes, and which, we suspect by the end of the novel, never actually happened. It is the great if enigmatic Brahmin professor Godbole who knows best this *sunya*, this zero: when asked earlier to describe the caves and what makes them so famous, he agrees, and then says absolutely nothing. But in saying nothing he reveals, in his Brahminic mind, everything. This is the revelation of the zero, which far from being feared has been revered in the great Hindu traditions of old. It is not surprising then that Sanskrit numerology is the first to provide a symbol for zero, the "0" as we know it today.[13]

Sunya is transliterated *çifr* in Arabic. Thus, it was the Islamic world who picked up the zero form of O from India when they conquered it in the eighth century, passing it on to the West. (This Forster seems to know implicitly: Aziz, charged with indecency in the caves, is a Muslim who understands India, but less the Marabar caves, and still less the English.) In accepting the concept, Islam was also rejecting the Greek heritage, and here, we might argue, is the real dividing line between the Western and Arabic worlds: the Arabs, through their contact with India, chose to accept the void of Genesis over the *Logos* of the Greeks, or over the ruling Aristotelian cosmological view that had rejected any possibility of the void.[14] By allowing for the void, they invited the zero into what became the Arabic system of numerical notation, which the West still uses today, even if in defiance of the void and its "infidel symbol."[15] From *çifr* we get the Latin *cifra* or *ciphra*, and hence our "cipher." And from cipher we get *zefiro* or *zephiro*, which through cognate Latinate languages (French, Italian) becomes *zero*. (Connected to *cifra* is also the French word *chiffre*, which means "digit.")[16] So the zero is not indigenous to the Hellenized West, and the passage back to India is one fraught with tension, unease, and incomprehension.

In his aptly named *Zero: The Biography of a Dangerous Idea*, Charles Seife writes: "Zero and infinity were at the very center of the Renaissance. As Europe slowly awakened from the Dark Ages, the void and the infinite—nothing and everything—would destroy the Aristotelian foundation of the church and open the way to scientific revolution."[17] Seife stresses the inherent relationship between zero and infinity, both mathematically and philosophically. And it is the likes of Descartes and Pascal who wrestle most profoundly with this relationship, as they try to reconcile its implications for their cherished Christian (Jesuit) faith in the seventeenth century. In Descartes's case, infinity was used as a new proof of God's existence (since we are finite beings ourselves, the concept of infinity must come from somewhere outside of us, i.e., God, who is perfect Infinity). And yet what we now call the Cartesian coordinates also introduced the zero as the center of the x/y axes (rather than 1, as the earlier monks might have done), even though Descartes repudiated any concept of an ultimate void.[18] Pascal, inventor of one of the earliest calculators, also embodied this tension. "Les silences éternels de ces espaces m'effraie [The silences of the infinite spaces terrify me]," he said.[19] And yet, he was willing to admit an infinity into the universe, and even proved the void in his experiments with vacuum. As for his faith, this was left now to a wager. It was no longer a matter of natural science or philosophy underscoring belief; it was a matter of hedging our bets on a calculation that now admitted a zero. As Pascal writes:

> After all, what is man in creation? Is he not a mere cipher compared with the Infinite, a whole compared to the nothing, a mean between zero and all, infinitely remote from understanding either extreme? Who can follow these astonishing processes? The Author of these wonders understands them; but no one else can.[20]

Descartes and Pascal were working in those early years of modern science when the consequences of infinity—the result of the Copernican revolution, in effect—would necessitate a full embrace of the zero. And yet that nought, as with the infinity, was terrifying. "Zero and infinity are two sides of the same coin—equal and opposite, yin and yang, equally powerful adversaries at either end of the realm of numbers."[21] The problem with zero is its infinite nature. Anything times zero is zero. Anything divided by zero is infinite. And vice versa. As modern mathematics and calculus developed, a reconciliation with and between the two would arise, as both became workable numbers in and of themselves. Yet even in the most arcane and abstruse of mathematical formulae, this relationship, and the zero especially, remains troublesome. "We must know also that zero and the infinite are precisely *that which does not succeed*," writes Alain Badiou.[22] In the most esoteric theories of physics—Einstein's' theory of relativity, for example—zero leads to anxious conclusions such as the black hole. The greatest problem with nought is describing what it is once we have arrived at it. On any level, atomic or cosmic, it remains a thoroughly black hole, like the void of a deep and endless cave. Where are we when we are in its darkness? Where is nowhere, or what is nothing? Zero is ultimately senseless, but yet without it, other things lack sense. How do we live with this vexing reality?

"O barbarous and bloody spectacle!"[23] — GROUND ZERO

The advance of modern science and mathematics has led to some of the most sophisticated utilizations of the zero, especially in technological development. Of course the most significant and far-reaching developments are also the most dangerous. Introducing zero, or the void, or any sense of a vacuum, destroyed the fundament of Greek cosmological thinking, so that heavenly spheres, which eventually stopped at an outer sphere, the divine realm, beyond which was only God (the nutshell theory of the cosmos), gave way to the concept of infinity, and eventually an ever-expanding universe. The development of calculus, which arose from the need to account for areas within curvature, allowed for the harnessing of natural forces and energies, leading to such notions as the *absolute zero* or *zero point*. But zero-point energy—the lowest point of energy in a quantum mechanical system—emerges from Heisenberg's uncertainty principle, where interference from the observer alters the "true" state of a particle, so that the truth of that state can never be fully known. That is, the zero point derives from an inherent uncertainty about the true state of things. Heisenberg's uncertainty principle has always been a dangerous idea, and not just to scientists. Its implications are vast: If we cannot know the true nature of things because our own interference alters the reality, how are we to know when we are engaging with true reality? (How are we to know, for that matter, when we are altering?) We are left with a kind of philosophical zero point, which returns us to a Kantian phenomena/noumena distinction, although in the case of modern science, such a zero point is now at the level of phenomena. Zeroing in this regard explodes our empirical sure ground.

And yet modern science has not been held back, and continues to find ways of working with, or around, the dangers of this rogue we call zero. The tension between useful and dangerous technological advance is no better seen, and this throughout all of history, than in the military context. The military has found good use of the concept of zero. It speaks of "zero day" and "zero time," the moment, general or precise, when a military operation is to begin. Unlike the ancient monks, modern militaries require indisputable precision in the timing of things, a precision unavailable if starting with 1. They also demand precision in targeting, and hence they have given us the term "ground zero," that location in the ground under an exploding bomb, and carved out by the explosion. With the greater utilization of zero in calculation, modern military technology can pinpoint this location with greater and greater accuracy when directing missiles at a specified target. But only so far. The zero in ground zero or point zero still disrupts exactitude and certainty, and we have witnessed this repeatedly even in the most up-to-date war arsenals.

Exactly what, or where, is ground zero, we can ask? The term gained its currency during the atomic age of the twentieth century. When the American military brought World War II to an end by dropping atomic bombs on Nagasaki and Hiroshima, it was necessary to establish where the initial point of contact was made by the bomb within the cities, since the devastation caused by the atomic explosion was so vast. "Ground zero" at least gave a reference point, even if, for all intents and purposes, that point was completely lost in the immensity and severity of destruction wrought by the blast. During the cold war, the concept of ground zero took on greater significance the greater the destructive capacity of the nuclear bombs being designed, and the greater the stockpiling of the arsenal. But by the height of the arms race, the idea of a ground zero became ludicrous—it would not matter where the initial bombs had hit, since the destruction wreaked would be so widespread as to make any zero point of reference negligible. With perverse irony, the zero truly zeroed out the precision.

In contemporary warfare, the precision may seem to have returned with missile guidance systems, the kind we see in operation, for example, during military briefings, where video clips of descending missiles are shown from the underbelly of the attacking jet fighter. The missile hits its target, "ground zero," and the ensuing explosion zeroes out the target. But of course, even here, we now know, the missile often goes astray, or the intended target turns out to be something different than what was thought—a civilian object, in the worst of the cases. Hence, the popular term *collateral damage*, damage brought to objects situated collaterally to ground zero. The "zeroing" then always exceeds the precise point of contact—the whole point of bomb warfare. And it is this excess that makes the zero so dangerous. And paradoxically so, since the zero itself does not carry quantification. Ground zero, like the zero point of energy, has inextricable links with uncertainty.

Of course, the term *ground zero* has taken on new signification since September 11, 2011. "Ground Zero" in the United States now has a very precise location, the perimeter of which can be marked by street blocks in downtown Manhattan. But this is a metonymic use of the term. Technically, the ground directly beneath the point of impact of the enemy "bomb" in the case of 9/11 is not ground at all, but a floor or two very high up on a pair of skyscrapers. What is called "Ground Zero" was the result not of the initial explosion, but of the collapsing of the initial ground zero itself, the zeroing out of ground zero high above it. "Ground Zero," then, really has no ground on which to call itself ground zero, and really no ground, for the crater that was left on prime real estate in Manhattan that everyone calls Ground Zero is not the original site of the explosion. It would be, in any other context, collateral damage. But because the impact of the initial explosion, and the subsequent collapsing of the Twin Towers, had a significance so well beyond the phenomenal reality of a missile hitting its target—this was the first foreign terrorist attack on American "soil" since Pearl Harbor (which too was not "soil" as such), and on the financial center of American capitalism—the zeroing effect of the phenomenal was almost instant. The attack was immediately construed as symbolic by the West; the collapse of the Twin Towers was immediately construed as symbolic by the Islamic world; and thus the term *Ground Zero* immediately took on a symbolic force. The "Zero" was symbolic for something other than "nothing." It adopted its ciphering role, and became symbolic first for the zeroing out of zero (the making of a ground zero when a ground zero did not exist, or had itself collapsed, a double negationary act which brings to mind the philosopher Heidegger's famous phrase *das Nichts nichtet*—lit. "the nothing nothings"), and then for the ground on which something new was to be built, a memorial. (But a memorial to what—ground zero? the lack of ground zero? the zeroing out of a distinct urban skyline, of twin symbols of America capitalism, of the lives that supported it, of American innocence, of American insulation from global terrorism, of American dominance in warfare strategy? But are all these good grounds for a memorial?)

It is not surprising that the rebuilding that is (on) Ground Zero has been beset by so many problems and controversies in the last decade. Ground Zero itself is a problematic symbolization of a problematic concept (ground zero) and a problematic reality (a terrorist attack of tremendous magnitude that, technically, is mostly all collateral damage). How do you build on zero? *What* do you build on zero? *Why* do you build on zero? Why add to something that was never there in the first place? Of course, the need to memorialize lost lives is not only understandable but necessary. Yet Ground Zero symbolizes much more than lost lives. If it did not, then the memorial site would have become only that other "ground of zero" we have as our cultural expression against the nought—the graveyard, or the memorial grounds. This was, in fact, one of the first suggestions for Ground Zero, which received little support. Why? Because Ground Zero always meant more than lost lives. But what exactly that *more* was remained open to multiple interpretations, and hence the inability for the rebuilding of the site to maintain a harmony of consensus.

A telling editorial headline appeared in the *New York Times* on March 29, 2007. It read, "The Vanishing Arts at Ground Zero." The editorial bemoaned, amid cost overruns and impractical schedules, the cancellation of three of four planned art institutions at Ground Zero. The article wanted to show how government support for the arts is desperately on the decline. But unwittingly, it showed something else: the inherent challenges in creating anew from zero. The lack of agreement on what and when to build is symbolic enough of the problematic nature of ground zero in general; the fact that the arts—whose location at Ground Zero was "to make sure that the redevelopment site wouldn't be monopolized by grief or commerce"[24]— could not gain a secure footing drives the symbolic point home. It is hard to create ex nihilo; it is even harder to create when the *nothing* has so many different and competing interpretations. Why does the form of O invite so many interpretations?[25]

> *"O flattering glass"*[26]—MIRROR/SPECULUM/EYE—
> *"O, let me view his visage, being dead"*[27]

The nature of the cipher, we have said, is such that it does not bear any meaning in and of itself, but furnishes meaning by virtue of its positioning relative to other (numerical) figures. Who positions, then, is as important as where the position is. This is why the cipher's emptiness is often seen as something to be filled, a blank space to be occupied. What or who occupies will determine the cipher's role. Thus, in cryptography, the cipher is a secretly interpreted or reinterpreted character or set of characters, the meaning of which resides with the cryptographer. It carries no inherent meaning of its own. So the O, as the quintessential cipher, depends on an interpreting other to have a function. Its fundamentally vacant and neces- sarily neutral character (neither one nor the other) is also the source of its immense risk: the O can be appropriated by forces as sinister as benign, and remains in its nothingness open to all. It was more than just the threat of the void that kept the zero out of the Greek and Hellenic world. It was also its arch-democratic nature: there is no greater leveler than an empty O, available for anyone and everyone to interpret or fill in as they may. (0 plus a number is always that number.) Even the seminal democracy of ancient Greece did not extend its system to this length. No one or no group can govern at the pure point of zero.[28]

The O, then, has several levels to the nature of its nothing. There is the O as *constitutionally* nothing, a pure nullity, a zero quantitatively and qualitatively empty. There is the O as *actively* nothing, a force that negates, a zeroing out or emptying of some other existent thing. And then there is the O as *proactively* nothing, a cipher that gives or fills by its relative position set in advance.

On the surface, it is the proactive nature of the O that leads to the image of the speculum, or mirror. Both terms, "speculum" and "mirror," are derived from verbs "to look" (the Latin *speculare* and *mirare* respectively), and hence both lend themselves to the image of the round eye. The O as eye encompasses the pupil, which in the mechanism of sight allows light to reflect an image onto the retina. In this sense the eye is passive. But the O as eye also directs the vision, the gaze, while the pupil expands or retracts to let in the right amount of light. In this sense it is proactive, having first to position itself relative to the light in order for an image to appear within. Yet the eye never achieves pure active seeing, that is, never brings that which is seen into existence by its own internal powers. The eye sees only what is brought to it (by light), and not what it produces from within. Light does not come from within the eye, as the Presocratic Empedocles once taught, and Plato[29] and medieval optical theory adopted. The eye is an instrument or agent for outside forces. This limitation is best portrayed in the eye's inability to portray itself, to see itself as eye. True seeing sees itself as seer (just as full consciousness, modernity has told us, arises only in self-consciousness). Thus, we talk of *insight,* a sight that sees not only within, but *from* within. The physical eye never sees itself directly; it is never *within itself* in this sense, seeing from within, with insight. The eye is an empty receptacle (or receptor). But its positioning is crucial.

The eye only sees itself when positioned in front of a reflecting surface such as a mirror. There, it finally sees itself for what it is. But what, phenomenally, does it see? It does not see itself, of course, but only its reflection. If the eye, with its retinal screen, functions itself like a mirror, mirroring back an image to the brain, then we could say that when it sees its mirrored reflection, it is seeing its true self (as mirror). But "true" here has only a functional capacity, not an essential capacity. For the nature of the mirror is not to show the real thing in its essence, but only its reflection. If the eye is only a mirror-like instrument—and whether the numerous theories of perception argue for or against this metaphor, they most always admit that the eye merely transmits something to the brain, where real perception lies, somehow, some way—then the eye is very much like the O as cipher, whose positioning (left/right, up/down, open/closed) alone determines what is to be captured elsewhere (in the brain, as percept, as sense, as meaning, etc.). The mirror mirrors the eye, then, or the eye mirrors the mirror, but neither is anything other than a cipher that proactively allows for image to take place. Nothing is *in* the eye of the beholder, other than the mechanism of the optical apparatus; and yet, by virtue of that apparatus, everything is *with* the eye of the beholder, as she or he directs that apparatus to its desired location. So too the mirror: nothing is *in* the mirror, per se, other than light reflecting off the back of its tain; and yet, everything is *with* the mirror by virtue of its position before it. (Add a 0 to anything, and it retains the anything.)

It is commonly thought that we double ourselves when we step in front of a mirror. But this is only true for someone who steps in front of the mirror with us. For ourselves, we only double that part of us we normally see when not in front of the mirror. Excluded in our normal sight is, naturally, our face, and most extremely, our eyes. We can never double our eyes. This is why we stop in front of mirrors when we pass them to look at ourselves, or why we look for and at ourselves first and foremost in a photograph (a frozen reflection of ourselves). We never fully see ourselves otherwise. We never fully see our seeing. The mirror and the photograph allow us to see into our eyes, to view our own seeing. We have pathologized narcissism as an over-fixation with the self at the expense of all other things, but perhaps the common experience of seeking out ourselves in a mirror, or in a photograph, shows us that, rather than an unhealthy fixation, what we are fascinated with is ourselves finally as a whole, the fullness that comes with seeing our own seeing. We finally get to "be" what our eyes tell us everyone else is, but cannot tell us or confirm to us of our own self. We get to be a whole self. The mirror completes us, empty as it is in itself. 1 is never fully 1 until it is 0 + 1.

But of course, this whole is only an illusion of the whole, a reflection. Reflection has a circular effect, with the gaze returning to its original point of departure. But in our attempt to make equivalency with the reflected and the reflection, we must introduce a break into the circularity. O becomes ⊃ which becomes = which becomes ≠.[30] Our fixation on the apparent whole is therefore as much a fixation on the lack of whole that this mirroring brings, whether consciously or unconsciously. This Lacan has taught us. For Lacan, the psyche is never whole, since the unconscious always makes divisive inroads into the conscious. The psyche is driven by narcissistic drives, hidden desires, and repressed verbal myths, all of which make wholeness illusory. This "split ego" comes to know itself only through the discovery of Other, or what is not itself even in itself. Lacan's famous pre-mirror and mirror stages of infancy and childhood attempt to explain this coming to self-realization of self-fracture. During the pre-mirror stage (first six months of human life), an infant has no sense of worldly or bodily coherence. Everything it perceives is fragmented, with no sense or premonition of individual selfness. During the mirror stage, at which the child looks in a mirror and begins to recognize itself, self-identity starts to take shape in the realization of itself as a bodily whole. The mirror objectifies the child so that it can perceive a totality in its own being, and later a totality of the larger world in which that being shares a *Gestalt*-like relation. But because the mirror objectifies, it also splits. As Ragland-Sullivan has described, "[T]his early identification also constitutes the first alienation for an infant, a split between outer form (big and symmetrical) and an inner sense of incoherence and dissymmetry."[31] As the mirror image reduplicates, and creates an Other, a second self that is not-self, the child comes to self-knowledge through an internal fracture. This is very similar to the Hegelian notion of self-consciousness, whereby knowledge of oneself is obtained through something other to oneself, the negation of oneself from within—Hegel's difference between "in-itself" and "for-itself," where the latter has split from within to know itself as self. But whereas for Hegel a unifying synthesis is available in the name of self-consciousness ("in-and-for-itself"), for Lacan fracture and difference inexorably remain. The mirror continually shows cracks, we might say, disturbing the drive toward unity or synthesis. In Lacan's narcissism, the self comes to knowledge not through reflection but re-cognition of itself in something alien. This is a "false or aborted Cogito. . . . There is no whole 'self' in Lacan's epistemology."[32]

Yet it is precisely from this mirroring that we can talk about a whole self in the first place. The eye sees itself seeing, the mirror reflects to us our wholeness, the depths of our eyes, only to drive home the point that this wholeness is predicated on a splitting. The mirror simultaneously acts as the place of wholeness and fracture. And it is within this paradox of the O as mirror, containing fullness and emptiness at the same time, creation and destruction, presence and absence—the whole Romeo effect—where we become aware that our selves are always dependent upon a certain nothing in order to become who we are. (Romeo can only become who he is now, after falling in love with Juliet, by ridding himself of himself, by zeroing [out] himself, figuratively and, by the end, literally.) This awareness relies on the proactive nature of the nothing: it is only by positioning ourselves before the empty O that we can make ourselves into something coherently possible. It is perhaps in this sense that the post-Freudian/Lacanian Deleuze and Guattari can say: "The unconscious ceases to be what it is—a factory, a workshop—to become a theatre, a scene, and its staging."[33] Narcissism makes a necessary show of ourselves.

We have said that the positioning of the mirror (or the eye) is everything, not because *everything* is captured in the mirror at once, but precisely because *not* everything is captured by the mirror at once. A mirror can only reflect what stands before it, but not everything can stand before it at any one time. Every mirror has a limit or border, every O its perimeter. It is because of this perimeter, or *frame*, that the O becomes such a creative device—the empty figure providing the creative space. And the space must be delimited, or it is no space to speak of. Art, but even philosophy, and to a similar extent religion, are languages that rely upon the frame, which means that they are caught in the double act (in the case of religion, the double bind) of delimiting and adding, of setting up boundaries to mark out the scope of one's reflection, just as one adds a frame to a mirror and, in doing so, creates something *other* to what is supposedly reflected—the *other* of the framed mirror and its reflection. This paradox has, paradoxically, both plagued and invigorated art, philosophy, religion, and in fact all other manner of disciplinary reflections. For the placing of boundaries invites a *coincidentia oppositorum*—limit and addition, what is within the perimeter and what is without—and thus a collapse of the stability or uniformity the boundary or frame was meant to provide. But unlike philosophy and religion, art has always made its framing an integral part of its work, if for no other reason than it knows that the frame, the concretion of delimitation, cannot in any way be avoided. The philosopher remains uneasy with the frame (as Derrida has shown us in *The Truth in Painting*, for example);[34] the artist, on the other hand, is all too aware of their ironies, and many an artist has made much capital of them. Shakespeare is one such.

Consider Hamlet's speech to the players practicing their play. "Suit the action to the word," he admonishes, "the word to the action, with this special observance, that you o'erstep not the modesty of nature. For anything so o'erdone is from the purpose of playing whose end, both at the first and now, was and is to hold as 'twere the mirror up to Nature to show Virtue her feature, Scorn her own image, and the very age and body of the time his form and pressure" (*Hamlet* III, ii, 16–24).[35] At first glance, Hamlet's description appears to reflect a traditional mimetic theory of aesthetics. "Hold a mirror up to nature," and in so doing the play, out of a supposed equivalency with reality, will "catch the conscience of the king." But can this really be Shakespeare's own understanding of art or his own theory of drama? The problem is that the theory is imbedded within the drama, spoken by one of the characters and directed at a play within a play. What then is going on in this dramatized poetics? First, Hamlet tells us that there ought to be a correspondence between word and action, the one always appropriate to the other. This appears to be nothing exceptional, for most actions can be described, and many descriptions can be acted, and it has always been the playwright's task to breed one from the other, to bring forth descriptions from actions, and in turn actions from descriptions. That plays are never acted the same way twice is proof that the correspondence between the one and the other is never strict. So Hamlet instructs that, given this dramatic leeway, a certain "modesty" must be maintained, at least in correspondence with nature. Here, we see the first sign of mimesis in the imitative sense. But it is weak mimesis, for Hamlet does not say that dramatic actions must correspond *exactly* to nature (how could they ever be judged to fit *exactly* to nature when actions are so wide and fluid they resist the measurement and determination the word *exact* intends?) Hamlet says, rather, that dramatic actions must "o'erstep not the modesty of nature," must, in other words, not be so extravagant that nature itself could never conceive of them. The enactment of any action must remain *possible*, and here Hamlet is closer to an Aristotelian view of art, which tends to be misrepresented in its prevalent characterization as strict mimesis. As Aristotle says in the *Poetics*, "the poet's function is to describe, not the thing that has happened, but a kind of thing that might happen, i.e. what is possible as being probable or necessary." Or more succinctly: "A likely impossibility is always preferable to an unconvincing possibility."[36]

Hamlet's poetics here begins to raise questions, for knowing his words are spoken within a play, what "modest nature" then can we take him to mean: our own as readers or listeners of the play called *Hamlet*, or the nature according to the action found between Act I and Act V of this play? If the latter, can Hamlet's world of actions rightfully be called "modest"? Or if these are really Shakespeare's views, can the world of actions in, say, *Midsummer Night's Dream*, or *King Lear*, or *Winter's Tale*, or, ultimately, *The Tempest*, be called "modest" in any sense of the word? We suspect more than a little irony here. If we take the world of drama as our guide, "modesty" would hardly be the first trait we should ascribe to nature, however we define nature. We wonder at Hamlet's sense of mimesis. He goes on to say that the whole purpose of the play is, and always has been, "to hold, as 'twere, the mirror up to nature." This often-quoted phrase seldom retains the little subjunctive qualification, "as 'twere," when quoted. Why does Shakespeare throw it in? Is it just another expletive? It is a signal that what follows is simply a figure of speech, a trope, an unreal condition. Art is only *like* a mirror held up to nature. Art in and of itself is not that mirror (unless one's art is to make mirrors, which clearly is not what Hamlet means). Art reflects in a similar manner to a mirror. Hamlet is conscious of making a metaphor do the work of his poetics, whereby the function of one thing is transferred to another, the function of the mirror transferred to the function of the play. What exactly is this function? To reflect "feature," "image," "form," and "pressure" (impression) back upon the viewer, he tells us. It is not to reflect a given "reality," but made things, as each of his words suggests. This is all a mirror ever can do. The function of Hamlet's poetics, then, depends upon a metaphoric transference, for his poetics *is* metaphor itself, inasmuch as the play carries over one framed thing (the action, the art) to another framed thing (the description, the mirror). And this poetics is supremely manifested shortly thereafter in the play within the play, a mirroring of the mirror, a framing of the frame, in which the king is caught and framed.

"O, he hath drawn my picture in his letter!"[37] —
THE ARTIFICER'S CIRCLE

The frame, as perimeter, sets the limits of art, and in fact allows art to be art, distinct from quotidian life. We would not know something was art unless a frame existed in some form, whether the edge of a canvas, the platform of a stage, the covers of a book, etc. This distinction is also at the center of the artificer's circle in the magic ritual. The artificer, wizard, or conjuror drew a circle around himself or herself in order to distinguish normal or natural reality from paranormal or preternatural reality, and to ensure protection from outside and everyday influence. It became the *locus in quo,* the place of divination and/or creation, the zone of the spell. This goes back to ancient religious practice, where confrontation with divinity required holy ground—a temple, a grove, a standing circle of stones. The artificer remained under "divine" inspiration only when in the perimeter of the protected circle. The old, blinded Oedipus has protection in the sacred grove outside Colonus, for example, from which he leaves his mortal coil to join the gods. Or in pagan places such as Stonehenge, the divine circular motions of the sun and moon, as they form the moments of solstice in the seasons, when they themselves are perfect orbs, become a place of intense worship within the bounds of concentric circles.

Perhaps the most self-conscious artifice of the circle is seen in Coleridge's famous "Kubla Khan." The poem, we recall, is often subtitled "Or a Vision in a Dream. A Fragment." The fragmentary nature of this title becomes evident from the outset, particularly in the poem's later 1816 published form, when Coleridge begins not with the poem but with a prose description of how the poem came about.[38] It is an autobiographical account, telling us how, after taking an anodyne (of narcotic strength), he fell asleep upon reading a passage about the historical Kublai Khan: "'And here the Khan Kubla commanded a palace to be built, and a stately garden thereunto. And thus ten miles of fertile ground were inclosed with a wall.'" The image of protective circles is first drawn here with the palace's wall, within which lies fertility and creativity. The author then relates how he falls into a deep "sleep," and has a vivid dream, vision, or narcotic "trip," in which he composes a poem of some considerable length based on Kublai Khan's palace. Upon awakening, he begins to write these lines down, but is interrupted for an hour by some necessary business with the now famous "person from Porlock." When he returns to the poetic task, the vividness is gone, and all that remains on paper are a few lines, which he then later expands into the fifty-four lines that make up the fragment we now know as "Kubla Khan."

We are told in the very first lines of the explanatory notes that the fragment is published on the request of another celebrated poet (Lord Byron), and published more as a "psychological curiosity, than on the ground of any supposed *poetic* merits." The psychological features are well on the surface—the vision takes place within the protective confines of "sleep," as if the opium had erected a psychological, if not psychedelic, enclosure. Here, on the fertile grounds of the psyche, the poetic palace is built. The circular perimeter is the threshold of consciousness, set in place by the drug. Without lies the historical account of Kubla Khan,[39] sitting on his lap as an open book like a cat to be stroked; within lies the poetic vision, playing out the *poesis* of pure and heightened imagination. As long as he is within the circle of the drug's O, the composition remains unimpeded. As soon as

the drug wears off, the purity of the vision is lost, and only hazy recollec-
tion is possible. To see the purity of the vision again, he must look into a
mirroring surface, and capture the reflection of the original. But of course
that reflection is not whole; it is fragmentary, with only "eight or ten lines
and images" remaining, the rest having passed away "like the images on the
surface of a stream into which a stone has been cast."

Coleridge then quotes—he is still "explaining" the poem—from his
own earlier poem *The Picture, or The Lover's Resolution*:

> Then all the charm
> Is broken—all that phantom world so fair
> Vanishes, and a thousand circlets spread,
> And each misshape the other. Stay awhile,
> Poor youth! Who scarcely dar'st lift up thine eyes—
> The stream will soon renew its smoothness, soon
> The visions will return! And lo, he stays,
> And soon the garments dim of lovely forms
> Come trembling back, unite, and now once more
> The pool becomes a mirror.[40]

The quoted fragment here of the earlier poem begins by evoking the
artificer's circle, whose charm is broken, and ends by evoking the image of
the mirror, which recaptures the charm. Even this fragment is a kind of
circle, then, beginning with the artificer's spell and returning back to that
spell in its restored form, though now only its mirror image. The circles
within circles of the fragment (the "thousand circlets spread") mirror the
circles that Coleridge is trying to draw around his poem "Kubla Khan,"
here in the form of explanatory notes. And the final mirror image itself
mirrors the experience of the later poem. The "pool becomes a mirror"
becomes the reflection of "Kubla Khan" the poem, which arises from the
broken images of the lost vision, broken by the wearing off of the drug
and the supposed interruption of a business call (scholars differ on whether
the person from Porlock was actual or fictional), and restored again by the
recollecting imagination. So before the poem proper has even begun, we are
made conscious of having been encircled about, as if by a wall of mirrors.
The poet has erected the ultimate artificer's circle, the ultimate fortress of
protection from outside intrusion—a wall of reflecting surfaces—for a poem
whose very genesis is marked by outside intrusion, fictional or not (but all
the more significant if fictional).[41] Thus, the "explanatory notes" drop their
explanatory function, and become instead the circle around which the poem
will emerge. They become the O of the poem's creation.

In Xanadu did Kubla Khan
A stately pleasure-dome decree:
Where Alph, the sacred river, ran
Through caverns measureless to man
Down to a sunless sea.
So twice five miles of fertile ground
With walls and towers were girdled round:
And here were gardens bright with sinuous rills,
Where blossomed many an incense-bearing tree;
And here were forests ancient as the hills,
Enfolding sunny spots of greenery.

But oh! that deep romantic chasm which slanted
Down the green hill athwart a cedarn cover!
A savage place! as holy and enchanted
As e'er beneath a waning moon was haunted
By woman wailing for her demon-lover!
And from this chasm, with ceaseless turmoil seething,
As if this earth in fast thick pants were breathing,
A mighty fountain momently was forced:
Amid whose swift half-intermitted burst
Huge fragments vaulted like rebounding hail,
Or chaffy grain beneath the thresher's flail:
And 'mid these dancing rocks at once and ever
It flung up momently the sacred river.
Five miles meandering with a mazy motion
Through wood and dale the sacred river ran,
Then reached the caverns measureless to man,
And sank in tumult to a lifeless ocean:
And 'mid this tumult Kubla heard from far
Ancestral voices prophesying war!
The shadow of the dome of pleasure
Floated midway on the waves;
Where was heard the mingled measure
From the fountain and the caves.
It was a miracle of rare device,
A sunny pleasure-dome with caves of ice!

A damsel with a dulcimer
In a vision once I saw:

It was an Abyssinian maid,
And on her dulcimer she played,
Singing of Mount Abora.
Could I revive within me.
Her symphony and song,
To such a deep delight 'twould win me,
That with music loud and long,
I would build that dome in air,
That sunny dome! those caves of ice!
And all who heard should see them there,
And all should cry, Beware! Beware!
His flashing eyes, his floating hair!
Weave a circle round him thrice,
And close your eyes with holy dread,
For he on honey-dew hath fed,
And drunk the milk of Paradise.

"Kubla Khan" itself is encircled by O within. The poem begins by mirroring the image of the last lines read before falling asleep, the image of the O encircling the palace of the emperor Kublai Kahn. "So twice five miles of fertile ground / With walls and towers were girdled round." Within these walls is lush and verdant growth, the fertility, we might say, of creative imagination. But in its very midst is also a sacred river running deep into a fathomless chasm. A "savage place" we are told, from which erupts the chaotic energy of creation itself, "holy and enchanted." There, the dome of pleasure mingles with the bottomless void, the nothing of the O's inner core. And at this very moment of commingling, another vision is recalled ("A damsel with a dulcimer . . ."), and another mirroring takes place: the mirroring of the poetic creation itself, now the stuff of the very poem, as the poet longs to revive within him the song of the vision, just as in the "explanatory notes" he longed to revive the vision of Kubla Khan (and "Kubla Khan"). The poem then ends with explicit reference to the artificer's circle:

Weave a circle round him thrice
And close your eyes with holy dread,
For he on honeydew hath fed
And drunk the milk of Paradise.

The poem comes full circle at several levels. The first is an internal level, where the O around the palace (the sacred space of creation) and the O of the dome (the pleasure of creation) become the O of the artificer's circle, in which the holy dread of the chasm's nothing spills forth into Paradise. The second is an external level, where the generative circle of the poem, with its central void, mirrors the generative "explanation" of the opening notes, which itself can only explain by fragments. Thus, the poem comes to be only in the O of creation; but it remains in that O of creation by being a poem precisely about that O (*about* it in every sense). "Kubla Khan" remains the great poem it is because it remains true to the poetic origin of its own existence, even if that origin is only ever recollected. It is a poem about the pure *poesis* of poetry, drawing upon itself for its own power. Such is the nature of the O. It brings to life purely from within, and lets its own nothing become something. As in Forster's Marabar caves, caverns measureless provide the point from which, and around which, a vision—happy or sad, pleasing or problematic—emerges.

The intense Romantic vision of Coleridge's *poesis* shows a subjectivity that has since marked our understanding of creation. We create from a private experience within, and that private experience itself becomes an integral part of the art. Hence, Coleridge writes his *Biographia Literaria*, Wordsworth his *Prelude*, as direct literary expressions of the self being formed by the poetic moment, just as much as the poetic moment being formed by the self. Yet when that poetry is put into the public domain, the self loses its hold on the moment, and the moment is now open to becoming something other than what it was at its original inception. This is the source of a new and prevalent artistic angst since Romanticism: the subjective self, by virtue of being part of the framing that is art (both the frame and that which frames), is released to something over which it will no longer have any control. It is one thing to give your craftsmanship over to another for appropriation or misappropriation; it is quite another to give the chasms of your very being over to another. It is no surprise that the poetic genius of the modern period is stereotyped by an angst-ridden and brooding hero, in whom the creative life burns brightly but with "tragic" brevity (Coleridge's contemporary Byron, for example, the very one who asked Coleridge for explanatory notes to "Kubla Khan," as if by premonition). We can see Coleridge's own attempt to protect himself from such self-exposure by ringing himself with the artificer's O. Even the poetic fragment we know of as "Kubla Khan" betrays its own protective mechanism. "Beware! Beware!" it cries to itself. "Beware lest you should recollect too well, and expose the chasm that lies at the core of your being. Weave a circle round your self, and bury the original vision in the darkness of the internal void from which it sprung."

Can we rightly give "Kubla Khan" its own voice in this manner? Can we rightly interpret the poem in such a figural and circular way, with its O spreading out to include, necessarily, its explanatory notes? Is this really what Coleridge meant to convey? Do I not run the risk, as interpreter, of manipulating this poem to conform to my particular notions of the O? Do I not neglect the poem's own warning, or the warning of another of Coleridge's contemporaries, Shelley, that we humans are "a many-sided mirror / Which could distort to many a shape of error / This true fair world of things"?[42] We have seen how the O opens up a blank space for reinscription. But how do we determine what should rightly be reinscribed there? It is the dilemma Coleridge himself faced—how, after the interruption in which all vividness was gone, does he remain true to the vision and reinscribe from what is lost? Paradoxically, he draws a circle that both protects him and his readers from the original vision and at the same time allows that vision to be redrawn. The O both erases and creates: it voids the original vision, by drawing a circle around what is no longer there, and it re-creates the poem anew from the remaining spectre of its original lineaments. Where does the *origin* lie, then? The origin is the void, which, being void, is no longer available; but that very origin, as void, is made present as the measureless caverns, mingled with the dome of pleasure.[43] If we try to get to the origin then, we are caught in a *circulus vitiosus*, the same as that presented to us in the phrase "nothing is." This problem is more than one of contradictory logic. It is of a viciousness that keeps us going around in circles. If the void is truly present, it is present as void, and therefore it is not there. But not being there means being there in its purest form, as void. Likewise, if the origin is a place we cannot access, because it is lost to a void (of memory, of self, of the holy dread of ex nihilo), how do we talk about it not being accessible, or having been lost? How do we originate, that is, the lost origin? Or how do we originate *in* the lost origin. This is the central question of "Kubla Khan."

"*O, some authority how to proceed*"[44] —
THE HERMENEUTICAL CIRCLE

The O presents to us the problem of the origin of meaning. And this is a question of hermeneutics. As the art, or science, of interpretation, hermeneutics attempts to bridge the gap between text and reader, whatever form the "text" may take, and whatever form the "reader" may take. (These terms themselves are open to hermeneutical questioning.) There is already a circle formed between these two poles of "origin": on the one hand, the text brings to us fixed sets of inscriptions, while on the other hand the reader brings a history of assumption and experience concerning how to read those inscriptions. At which pole does meaning originate, or reside? Does it begin with the pregiven text, with its author's intention, its specific linguistic arrangement, and its predetermined semantic fields? Or does it begin with the reader, who must give that arrangement and those fields a specific and directed meaning and significance? The hermeneutical circle arises when we realize that both poles are not only necessary, but *are logically dependent upon each other*. That is to say, the "origin" lies simultaneously at both, or as some hermeneutical theorists would say, en route from one pole to the other (and back again). The text may be said to furnish meaning, but not until someone actually reads it; so *how* it furnishes its meaning will necessary depend on *how* it is read. Meaning therefore cannot be said to lie solely in the text, if reading itself plays an active role in letting the text speak. Meaning then moves around in a circle from text to reader, and from reader to text. The text brings something to the reader, while the reader brings something to the text, and both are altered in a looping dance of semantic interchange. This circularity is made superabundant in Coleridge's experience with the genesis of "Kubla Khan," when he becomes the reader of his own "text" upon wakening. In order to "give meaning" to the original poem of his drug-induced state, he must first take and retain what little his memory will furnish (eight or ten lines, he claims). Then, finding this incomplete, he must furnish the rest "on his own," that is, from a state of normality or sobriety outside of narcotic amplification. Where most of the "origin" of the final poem actually lies—before or after the opium (and in some cases long after, with multiple revisions over the course of almost two decades)—we will never fully know. At best, we can say the origin lies in *both* places.

This circle circumscribing text and reader, even if the reader is the very author of the text, plays itself out on two more specific levels of hermeneutical enquiry. The first is the relationship between part and whole within the text. The whole of a text cannot be understood until each of its constituent parts, which make up that whole, is understood. Each constituent part, on the other hand, can only find meaning in relation to the whole. If part is defined by whole, and yet whole is defined by part, we have a circular definition, and thus immense difficulties in trying to situate meaning. Do we start from the whole or the parts? But how do we do this without invoking the other? Again, "Kubla Khan" supplies us with a paramount example. The poem itself is entitled "A Fragment," which tells us that it is only a fragment or part of a larger piece that is lost irretrievably. But this "fragment" now stands as the whole of the poem. Whole and part are, in effect, one and the same here, and we could argue that the "meaning" of the poem rests on the fact that the fragment is the whole, and vice versa, or that the "meaning" is precisely that the fragment should be understood as a whole in its own right. But further, we could say that the "fragment," as a poem, cannot be fully understood without knowing how the poem came about to be a fragment, described to us in the opening explanatory notes. We know of its fragmentary nature only because of these notes, so that the fragment (the poem) only makes sense as a fragment in relation to the whole of both the notes (which themselves are fragmentary) and the poem *together*. But this *together*, as whole, makes sense only when we understand the constituent fragments that constitute it. Now the poem can stand on its own, as it often does, and still invite or grant meaning. And we suppose that the explanatory notes too could stand on their own, to say simply, "I had a vision, while in a dream, but upon wakening I lost it," and leave it at that. ("Tomorrow is yet to come" are the last words of the notes in many versions). But the fragmentary nature of the vision, and the visionary nature of the fragment, gain their greatest potency when they are set within the whole. When, that is, fragment and whole fully merge, and become wholly fragmentary. Coleridge, whether he knew it or not, was giving vision to the hermeneutical circle.

The second specific level of the hermeneutical circle is related to the first, but now played out as less a feature of the text, and more a feature of the reader. Similarly, it involves the nature of understanding, but instead of working within a spatial field (part and whole), it works within a temporal field (before and after). To understand anything, one has to have some pre-understanding of what is to be understood. If no pre-understanding exists, there is no *context* for the text to make sense. It is as the philosophers say: in order to pose a question, one has to have some understanding of what answers could possibly be available. "Understanding requires presuppositions in order to get underway," as John Caputo puts it.[45] But where do these presuppositions come from? They come from understanding itself, already given in advance. But if already given in advance, how could we arrive at them later? Martin Heidegger was the first to show us the full circular nature of this kind of existential or ontological hermeneutical circle. For him, interpretation was an essential feature of our existential selves, not a technique or a methodology we come to acquire later, as we would, say, the skill of violin playing. Interpretation of our world requires a pre-understanding of that world, in order for things to exist as situated beings to be grasped. But since understanding, at any point, requires interpretation, we are caught once again in a vicious circle. How do we proceed without becoming impossibly vertiginous? For Heidegger, it was not a matter of trying to escape the circularity. Rather than seeing the circle as vicious, we need to accept it as part of our very nature and being. As Heidegger now famously said, "What is decisive is not to get out of the circle but to come to it in the right way."[46] The right way, for Heidegger, means not trying to resolve the illogic of the circle, but trying to work out an understanding, an interpretation, a knowing, *from within*. This *within* (within oneself and within the circle, which is one and the same thing, like fragment and whole above) would mean not discarding presuppositions altogether (as if we ever could) but letting them be further shaped by what becomes known in the encounter with world and what will be known as a result of that encounter. The "pre-," that is, is never fully before, and never fully complete. It only marks out the shape of a movement, which transmits itself across past, present, and future. In the case again of Coleridge and his "Kubla Khan," he builds his poem on a pre-poem, without which the poem could never take shape, but which itself cannot be understood until the poem, as its fragment, is shaped. This, it might be said, is the true "psychological curiosity" of the vision—a poetic fore-knowing that is grounded existentially on the present being that is to know.

Hermeneutically, the O asks us to enter into interpretation with an understanding that comes only after that interpretation. It therefore demands that we move in circles around ourselves, first between what we are and what we are not, and then between what we possess and what we do not possess. These circular paradoxes attend first and foremost to our own identity, our own "Romeo," and frustrate us with an inability to locate our identity's origin or ground. Our very Cartesian legacy, by which we obtained absolute certainty with both sides of the *cogito's* equation, first the "I think" and then the "I am," is drawn here into its own doubt. And this is what makes the O so bewildering. If we cannot give indubitable meaning even to *ourselves*, because the hermeneutical circle operates from the outset upon or within our capacity to be in the world as interpretive beings, as Heidegger has suggested, then how are we expected to exist at all in any kind of grounded manner? Once again, the O pulls the ground out from under our feet. Yet we must remind ourselves that, as we have seen repeatedly, the nature of the O does not lend itself to fixed origins and grounds. When we move within its circle, when we encompass ourselves by the holy dread of its perimeter, we relinquish not only the surety of origin and ground, but also their horizon. This is not to say that origin and ground are not called forth by the O. As Heidegger says, it is a question of moving toward possibility, as opposed to surety. And in possibility, as in the chasms of Coleridge's sacred space, the origin might burst forth anew, this time as pure origin (as opposed to retrieved origin), or, to reappropriate a term that has long since been made banal, as *originality*, the pure state of the coming-to-be before it is encased in a peremptory history.

Modern hermeneutics, as a general discipline about the nature of interpretation, continues to struggle for legitimacy among the academic establishment precisely because of this tendency to founder the sure bases upon which we presume our knowledge to rest and move forward. No one wants to delegitimize his or her own grounds for existence, and yet since the beginning of the last century, we seem to be moving increasingly toward such self-foundering. It is no coincidence that the development of modern hermeneutics, well beyond the reading practices within such specialty fields as biblical scholarship, literary criticism, or law, corresponds to the move away from the paradigmatic One and toward the O. The more the One loses its sovereign power and the O gains in stature, the more the complex nature or demands of interpretation become evident. And the more we explore the complex nature or demands of interpretation, with all their paradoxes, the more we must yield to the O as a space from which to interpret. This is a daunting place in which to reside. It echoes with "Beware! Beware!" Yet here, with growing prevalence, we find ourselves.

We can think of the many labels of identity that have now become problematized in our late modern world. There are those that, as a result of globalized forces, are no longer semantically stable categories: West, East, Occident, Orient, colonial, white, black, foreign, domestic, etc. We have developed a lexicon of terms to account for the ambiguities that exist among and within such labels, many now beginning with the prefix "post-." But like "pre-" above, the prefix does not merely signify a simple temporal designation. It means something that is neither before nor after, and something that is *both* before and after. The "post-" attempts to go beyond, in a critical manner, the term that it attaches itself to—post-Enlightenment, post-industrial, post-modern, post-colonial, post-metaphysical, post-human, post-feminist, etc.—and yet also signals a complete reliance upon that term. It marks a position that is both beholden to and a further development of what came before. It thus operates in a circular manner, evoking the hermeneutical circle. What comes after is an understanding that is possible only by virtue of a pre-understanding that comes before. But that pre-understanding already carries with it the post-condition. In the case of "postcolonial," for example, a country having gained its independence from a colonial power has understood, and most likely gained, that independence completely from within the colonial framework, "independence" becoming a sensible term only once the colonial power has colonized it (with nationalism being an "invention" of the Western colonial powers in the first place). Its new independent existence is itself not an erasing of its colonial past as it is a modulation of it. Thus, its colonized existence already showed the shift in "paradigm" that would allow for its post-condition. The same circularity can be applied to each of the "post-" terms now in regular use.

More troubling is that this problem of identity operates on a much more personal and existential level. When I want to mark out my own identity, the hermeneutical circle encroaches in upon me. When I go to give myself meaning, I find myself in the double-double bind of the part/whole and pre-understanding/interpretation circles of hermeneutics. In order for the individual experiences of my life to have meaning, I must understand them against the backdrop of my entire life-world, or they would not make much sense; but that very life-world has meaning only by virtue of the component parts that make it up, each of my individual experiences, with which I do not yet have meaning. Or, if I am to understand who I am, I must interpret the various features of my life to construct a valid identity; but in order to interpret, I must have pre-understanding about what it is I am to interpret. I go forward then with a task that requires its completion in order to go forward. How do I begin? Or, to put the problem even more existentially, when I want to ground my origin, or place it in the surety of a known and stable location, how do I proceed if the very grounding of my origin is itself an origin, which bursts forth upon any previous origins I might think to be retrieving, and alters the situation? This was Coleridge's dilemma, played out poetically. And of course it is the dilemma of Heisenberg's Principle, playing out now on the self as much as on any scientific phenomenon we may hope to observe.

"O, put me in thy books!"[47] — I THE AUTHOR'S O

Amid this acknowledged aporia of the self, the question of my own situation as an author must now arise and be addressed. Until now, I have largely and deliberately remained a "one," or a "we," precisely because the paradigms in question operate themselves with the requirement and assumption of a neutral but knowing author, who lets the text speak for itself in a language of universality, through the tropes of "one" and "we." But when one reaches the heart of the O, or when we reach the heart of the O, one, or we, can no longer hide amid the "one" or the "we." For the O is about the exposure of origins, outside of paradigms. I therefore can no longer remain the one author every reader can simply assume. The O outs me, as it were.

It has become part of a recent critical expectation that I should "situate" myself as the author in order to keep full transparency within my argument's "position," or to bring my complicity within my critique out into the open. So theoretical discourses more and more proceed along the lines of constant self-disclosure. The O has brought us to a point where we the readers can no longer "assume" an author's position, especially when that author's own positioning may contribute to the very structures his or her discourse may be intending to question or analyze. Yet, there is a general problematic attending this critical demand, one that involves the hermeneutical circle.

In order to situate myself within my text, I must have some pre-understanding of myself outside the text. But from where do I draw this understanding, particularly as it remains relevant to the text I am about to write? (For not all aspects of my understanding would remain relevant to a text like this one—my thoughts on ornithology, for example, or mundane thoughts such as how and when I brush my teeth.) The problem is, having not written the text yet, I cannot say for certain where relevance might lie. I do not know what "relevance" would mean until I have a text to relate or be relevant to. There might be two responses to this dilemma. I could wait till after the text is complete, and then insert myself retrospectively as an openly situated author. But then, I would not be situated "in" the text properly; I would merely be imposed onto a text that was written without my open situation informing the writing. This would be paramount to adding a biographical preface or appendix, the purpose of which would be very different than a critical situating of myself amid the very origination of the argument. I could therefore situate myself during the writing according to *what I think* will be relevant, as I try to anticipate the whole of the argument before it has taken shape. (And no author knows the final shape of the whole argument before they have written it.) But then, my situation would only be provisional each stage along the way, and, at any given point, would not be representative of the whole. It may even differ or conflict from beginning to end. This would be paramount to a constant authorial intrusion where, even if honesty might persist, incoherency, inconsistency, and a certain kind of literary narcissism would become an overriding threat to the critical nature of the task. There is a part/whole circularity therefore frustrating my situation, as well as that of a pre-understanding dependent on what is to come afterward. We might say it is Heisenberg's Principle at work in my authorship: the moment I try to situate myself in my text, I alter the text, and therefore I alter what I thought I was being situated to. I cannot have both my situation and a whole that is relevant to that situation at one and the same time. So how, and where, do I place myself as author, when there is no text *proper* (that is, etymologically, no text of my own)?

Those who insist on authorship that is fully and openly situated within the text do so most often from a critical position that believes authenticity will reveal complicity, and complicity will temper authority. Admirable as such a position may be, the O as hermeneutical circle shows us that we can never be truly "authentic" (in the sense of a simple and guileless transparency) with(in) our own texts. The O unveils to us our own void, or our lack of origin as author. This, of course, is not to say we are *not* the authors of our own text, or that our situation prior to the text does not inform the text at all levels. But it is to say that the notion of author here within the O is different from that assumed, or desired, even by those with complicity as their critical concern. Authorship will always be a creative position, and its situation will always be within an O that allows things to come into being, but where origin is forever shifting, restarting, or emerging anew. I can be self-reflexive about this lack of fixed origin, about the ongoing loss of my origin, and this might now constitute my authorship, but this kind of authorial position cannot reveal a stably situated self whose complicity or noncomplicity is patently clear for every reader to see. It can only reveal a self, an "I," being constructed—Augustine-like—out of the void of its own self. And this self will have an authenticity, if we continue to insist on the term, very different from that of an already situated author capable of being whole, and wholly transparent.

What, then, can I say about myself? I began this text knowing full well that the very twofold distinction between One and nought, which structures the entire book, was a certain contrivance in order to get an argument under way. I understood that this contrivance would eventually threaten the argument internally, because the very claim of a twofold distinction, in which the first gives way to the second, cannot survive without resorting to the language of One, both in terms of historical trajectory—a history of ideas is *a* history, which inevitably excludes other possible histories—and of posited thesis—I argue for one prevailing thesis, around which all other material is meant to cohere. Why then did I proceed, if my initial motivation was self-conscious enough to know the contradictory nature of the venture?

We might approach this personal question by resorting for a moment back to the general "we." Why do we academics in the Arts or Humanities write books? Or why do we academics write the particular books that we do at any particular moment? There are manifold reasons. At our best, we say we write for a high and noble reason: we are impassioned by ideas, and feel they can actually change the way we live. But if we are honest, few of us can claim that this is an exclusive reason, or even a dominant reason. We also write because we are pressured by the system: in order to get tenure or promotion, to win research funding, or to justify research leave, we have to produce worthy scholarship. But we also write because of our egos: there is a certain self-importance that comes from making grand claims, a self-importance that is always under threat from rival academics, who either write more, or better, or in a manner critical of our own work, and against whom we are always measuring ourselves, in an attempt to maintain our pride. I say "we," but I must admit I am personally involved in each of these reasons, to one extent or another. (As a matter of record, one reason does not factor in, for any of us: money. There is nothing less economically viable, in terms of the time/remuneration ratio, than writing academic books.) But my own story would have to go much deeper—be less generic—than this. To attempt pure transparency, I would have to divulge why I chose a book with a working title "Auden's O," especially when I promised, on my application for research leave, a book on Hegel. How and why did Auden, who, curiously, has yet to figure properly in these pages, usurp Hegel?

My interest in Hegel began when, in reading again the *Phenomenology of Spirit*, I could see there was a way to read Hegel that put much more emphasis on one part of the famous (if suspect) Hegelian dialectical triad (thesis, antithesis, synthesis) than the others. This part was the antithesis, or better, *negation*. And in fact many contemporary theorists I had been reading seemed to confirm that such a reading was not only possible but preferable. The subsequent reading of Hegel's *Science of Logic* made this patently clear to me, and I wanted to explore this in relation to how the role of imagination in Hegel differed from his predecessor Kant: imagination, as a faculty, did not put things together, but instead pulled things apart. Thus, I would look at Hegel's *Aesthetics,* and explore how a heightened understanding of negation might force us to rethink our view not only of Hegel's conception of art but our own view of origin, *poesis*, and creativity. But how best to approach this? From a purely philosophical point of view, or from an aesthetic point of view?

I felt I had to prepare some "groundwork." My early interest in Auden returned now with a new possibility: Auden, whether he knew it or not, seemed to be preparing a kind of "ground" for a shift in thinking about how and why we create as human beings, a shift involving the figurations of the One and the O. And since Auden was not a philosopher, but a practicing artist, perhaps I should begin with the very material(ity) of art, as Hegel would want me to, and see how that might fit into the workings of this apparent nonmaterial shift. And thus, with a certain thesis in mind, I embarked on a preliminary text of a poet/essayist/thinker who came well *after* Hegel.

But now, how best does one—how best do *I*—write about an author? To write about Hegel or Auden with some kind of claim on authority, as a sovereign author who *knows*, after rigorous research and scholarship, what we should be thinking about Hegel or Auden, seemed to undermine the very "premise" upon which, ironically, I was undertaking my task, the premise that negation is somehow intimately involved in our creative processes, in however disguised a form. If negation was central, could I rightly write as if the identity of "Hegel" or "Auden," or their respective work, was some-thing to be positively put forward in unequivocal terms, in a thesis that was straightforward, and supported by all the demands of scholarly erudition and reference? How could I postulate such identity, when I myself felt my own identity as author, and my own position in the O, were in question? The hermeneutical circle raised its ominous self again.

It seems appropriate, as a summation of this general problem, to quote Blanchot quoting Hegel:

> "An individual," says Hegel, "cannot know what he [really] is until he has made himself a reality through action. However, this seems to imply that he cannot determine the *end* of his action until he has carried it out; but at the same time, since he is a *conscious*

individual, he must have the action in front of him beforehand as *entirely his* own; i.e. as an End."

In illuminating this passage, Blanchot illuminates the authorial circle with perspicuity:

> Now, the same is true for each new work, because everything begins again from nothing. And the same is also true when he creates a work part by part: if he does not see his work before him as a project already completely formed, how can he make it the conscious end of his conscious acts? But if the work is already present in its entirety in his mind and if this presence is the essence of the work (taking the words, for the time being, to be inessential), why would he realise it any further? Either as an interior project it is everything it ever will be, and from that moment the writer knows everything about it that he can learn, and so will leave it to lie there in its twilight, without translating into words, without writing it—but then he won't ever write; and he won't be a writer. Or, realizing that the work cannot be planned, but only carried out, that it has value, truth and reality only through the words which unfold it in time and inscribe it in space, he will begin to write, but starting from nothing and with nothing in mind—like a nothingness working in nothingness, to borrow an expression of Hegel's.[48]

How, then, to write? How, then, to write of someone? Is it right that a titular figure of a book should not properly appear within the first four chapters? Is it right that an author should confess that the book he has entitled with the name of one figure might really be a book about another? Is it right that by confessing he does not know precisely how to locate himself in his text, an author should go ahead and locate himself in his text, even if the "location" is that point where he confesses there is no easy location? Is it right, then, that the O should be invoked at all, if it plays this much havoc with the actions of writing?

"O, call back yesterday, bid time return"[49] —
ETERNAL RECURRENCE

The revolutionary nature of O is that it keeps returning back upon itself in self-disruption. In the preamble of this book, I invoked Pierre Klossowski, and his notoriously difficult book *Nietzsche and the Vicious Circle*. Nietzsche's notion of the Eternal Return of the Same is itself notoriously difficult, and few, if any, can claim success in describing this notion in definitive and comprehensive terms. The notion does not lend itself either to definitiveness or to comprehensiveness. And thus the struggle Klossowski admits at the outset of his text in describing the man Nietzsche as if he were a teacher of a theory or a doctrine. Nietzsche the author "destroyed not only his own identity but that of the *authorities of speech*," we have already highlighted.[50] How then does Klossowski write about him? Certainly in no straightforward manner. But perhaps his text has had such influence, standing above most others on the question of Eternal Recurrence, precisely because it does not fully give in to the positivities of philosophical, explanatory, or biographical discourse. And perhaps this only because Klossowski, like Nietzsche himself, was an artist as much as a discursive writer, and defied disciplinary boundaries in his varied works as novelist, philosopher, essayist, translator, actor, and painter. Perhaps it was his artistry that most allowed him access to the Eternal Recurrence in a way that philosophy could not. That is to say, perhaps it was his own "I" he was willing to give over to the eternally recurring O in Nietzsche's thought and writing, an "I" willing to lose its own origin in order to re-originate out of the circular viciousness that remained after the One had, for all intents and purposes, been erased from the horizon.

Nietzsche's death of God cry of the late nineteenth century certainly heralds a crucial and decisive point in the overall trajectory of One's descendancy and O's ascendancy. We might say it explodes the idea of trajectory altogether, of movement forward, of movement up and down, abruptly forcing a change of metaphor by which we can describe the shift from One to O. If the previous chapter worked out a linear history of One's reign, this chapter, in light of this Nietzschean turning point, was forced to work itself in a totally different manner. If we had difficulty in articulating the declination of One's historical trajectory leading up to the twentieth century, it is because the One had become uncertain about how to proceed, while the O did not impose itself in a clear and defiant usurpation. The O, rather, insinuated itself into the equation of developing modernity, like an algebraic variable that suddenly, by virtue of its revealed value (a valuation we owe in large part to Nietzsche), alters completely the way one goes about its computation. It is no longer a movement from beginning to end, but a circular movement, whose end is also its beginning, or an implosive movement, whereby all lines of trajectory collapse in upon themselves. What were even the most critical of philosophers and theologians after Kant supposed to do with such an impossible movement?

The idea of Eternal Recurrence that Nietzsche taught in such a broken and unsystematic fashion, as if through whispers, is on first encounter a pointed critique of metaphysics' reliance upon linearity, and of the universality this linearity inheres. Whether from cause to effect, from the material to the absolute, from this world to the afterlife, the universal nature of *teleological* truth was a constant target for Nietzsche's pen. So too was the concept of individual unity through stable and transcendent (and transparent) self-consciousness. The One that is "I" is always foundering on its own fracturing impulses, never able to sustain its internally rational coherence. But what could Nietzsche offer in the place of this One? The idea of the circle, in contradistinction to the linear path, still carried the vestiges of a premodern ideal, structured around wholeness and perfection. The idea of Fate still carried the Greek vestiges of divine control or manipulation. Nietzsche was not adverse to circularity or divinity per se. Indeed, he first sourced the idea of Eternal Recurrence in those early Greeks, whose god Dionysus would play such a central role in his own thought. The challenge was to find a way to understand identity, beginning with his own identity as "I," that did not rely on Presocratic theologies of Oneness or the later teleological theologies of Plato, Aristotle, and their Western progeny. The idea of a return *back to the same* that was not unified, of a circle that is *vicious* insofar as it returns us to a completely unindividuated condition, beyond all sense of stability, coherence, and unity, this is what Nietzsche hoped might revolutionize our thinking and our being.

How does Klossowski try to convey this revolutionary notion of Nietzsche? How does he describe Nietzsche's identity as author outside of the "I"? The first step, we have already said, involves treating Nietzsche other than as a theoretician in any pure sense. The paradox is to present a study of a thinker whose very thought undermines thinking as we have traditionally understood it. Thus, he will appeal not to Nietzsche's "theoretical texts," the books for which he is best known, but only to his letters, to his posthumous fragmentary writings, and to *Ecce Homo*, Nietzsche's own "false study" of himself. But despite all these biographical sources, the second step also involves treating Nietzsche other than as an autobiographer in any technical sense. What Klossowski offers is a commentary on Nietzsche's personal writings, confessions, and views, but a commentary that must not reconstruct an "I" of Nietzsche, a person or personality we can then say we grasp and understand, even justify.[51] What arises is not any identity of Nietzsche as such, but a commentary, a text, caught up repeatedly within the *circulus vitiosus* of the O that Nietzsche was striving to figure through Eternal Recurrence. Klossowski's own book is difficult to read because it functions outside any dispensation of the One, and embraces the O as its own mode.

The language of identity outside of the One, as Klossowski presents it to us, must trade outside of the traditional certainties of universality and unity. Instead, then, of the soul, mind, spirit, consciousness, and ego, he speaks of intensities, impulses, and tonalities (*Stimmung*). The latter phenomena, as biological states, do not cohere, either among themselves, or with any fixed interpretations one might give them. We do give them meaning, but only after the fact, as phantasms or simulations. There is no One around which or by which they can form a firm "once and for all" identity. They are random, chaotic forces, at best fortuitous, but largely arbitrary. Their identities are always plural, and pluralizing. The idea of the Eternal Recurrence was put forward by Nietzsche as a means to allow this pluralizing nature to maintain infinite plurality, and in doing so, to be lost to a sameness that such infinity eventually brings. As Klossowski describes it (resorting, contradictorily, to the old language):

> The emphasis must be placed on the loss of a given identity. The "death of God" (the God who guarantees the identity of the responsible self) opens up the soul to all its possible identities, already apprehended in the various *Stimmungen* of the Nietzschean soul. The revelation of the Eternal Return brings about, as necessity, the successive realizations of all possible identities: "at bottom every name of history is I"—in the end, "Dionysus and the Crucified." In Nietzsche, the "death of God" corresponds to a *Stimmung* in the same way as does the ecstatic moment of the Eternal Return.[52]

In linking here the death of God (as One) with the Eternal Recurrence (as O), Klossowski figures for us, through Nietzsche, a new way of historicizing identity: "[A]t bottom every name of history is I," which is to say, the "I" can conceive (of) itself, can "will itself," in so many different ways that its endless self-interpretation comes back upon itself, to where it first began, in a circularity that is eventual:

> But *to re-will myself one more time* indicates that nothing ever succeeds in getting constituted in *a single meaning, once and for all.* The circle opens me to inanity, and encloses me in the following alternative: *either* everything returns because nothing has ever had any meaning whatsoever, *or else* nothing has ever had a meaning except through the return of all things, without beginning or end.[53]

These complex views, however else they might be theoretically extrapolated, clearly reveal a hermeneutics of self-identity, of the self as author of itself, a hermeneutics of "I" (One) operating within and being subsumed by a vicious circle (O). For "given this plurality of perspectives," Klossowski writes later, "it not only follows that everything is an interpretation, but that the subject that interprets is itself an interpretation."[54] Here, we might say, is the hub of the entire commentary, a hermeneutical circle that of course implicates Klossowski himself as author.

The entire text of *Nietzsche and the Vicious Circle* might then be summed up—singularly interpreted—in a passage that questions the very nature of interpretation at its core, beginning with Nietzsche's own words:

> "*To be able to read a text without any interpretation*"—this desideratum of Nietzsche expresses his revolt against the servitude implied in all signification. What then is it that will free us from a given signification and restore us to *uninterpretable existence?* . . .
>
> This is the question that underlies Nietzsche's "autobiographical" writings. He opened himself up to an act of understanding, he explicated himself by *implicating himself* in a preconceived *interpretation* of the "text."[55]

Here we find a new manifestation of the hermeneutical circle. It is not simply that Nietzsche, in writing about himself, implicated himself problematically in an already given interpretation of his "I," as we saw above with my own attempt to "situate" myself in this text. It is that the "text" we are talking about here is the *same* that we are brought back to in the Eternal Recurrence, that ahistorical, or "supra-historical" (as Kaufmann calls it),[56] condition in which all temporal existence and all possible identity collapse into an all-encompassing, infinite "moment." This "moment" is what Nietzsche understands as the "text without any interpretation," or an "uninterpretable existence," in Klossowski's words. The O, at its most advanced (that is, its most circular), leads us to this uninterpretable moment, a moment from which we then retreat back wilfully into signification, into meaning, into interpretation, in order to remake ourselves anew. This is what Klossowski does—he remakes Nietzsche anew, and by extension, he remakes himself anew, by showing us how "Nietzsche's interrogation describes what we are now living through,"[57] in this moment, the moment of the O, which, as Eternal Recurrence, is always upon us.

The circumlocutions of O designate a continual return or recreation of itself as a figure. O's own identity is under constant renewal, out of the false appearances of its cipher logic as manifold nothingness. But its false appearances, like ancient Greek theatrical masks, are precisely what keep its self-renewal possible, even in the worst of circumstances. In *Romeo and Juliet,* that tragic play where the titular characters first meet amid masks, appearances, despite all first impressions, become "false" under the hermeneutical problematic of being "misread." And death is the grandest of these appearances. Romeo takes his own life thinking Juliet is dead—the most tragic of actions. Earlier, after Romeo has fought and slain Juliet's cousin Tybalt, Juliet's nurse comes before Juliet with the news: "he's dead, he's dead, he's

dead!" (III.ii, 39). She even repeats Juliet's famous line in her announce-
ment: "O, Romeo, Romeo!" Juliet does not know how to take this. About
whom is the nurse really talking here? Juliet solicits the "I" in her response,
but an "I" that has now become something other than the I of One that
she hoped had united her with Romeo (III.ii, 45–51):

> Hath Romeo slain himself? Say though but "I"
> And that bare vowel "I" shall poison more
> Than the death-darting eye of cockatrice.
> I am not I, if there be such an "I"
> Or those eyes' shot [or shut] that makes the answer "I."
> If he be slain, say "I," or if not, "no."
> Brief sounds determine of my weal or woe.

Juliet's identity as "I" is negated if this "I" she solicits from the Nurse
is something other than what it appears (i.e., if it is "ay" or "eye"), since
this would mean Romeo's "I" is no more, and she in turn will be no more.
The shift from One to O is inaugurated for these characters here by the now
negative impact of "I" and the positive impact of its opposite, "no." If one
says "ay" to death, if one's eye beholds death, even imparts death, a hom-
onymic force has invaded the I with heteronomic effect—yes has become
no and no become yes. The Nurse seems to confirm this translation into
circular paradox, when she is sent by Juliet to the Friar's cell on the charge
of delivering a ring to the hiding Romeo. She finds him laid out upon the
ground, a position she equates with Juliet, and in calling him forth, like a
Lazarus figure—"rise and stand!"—she adds: "Why should you fall into so
deep an O?" (III.iii, 90). But that deep O is precisely what has caught up
both lovers, and all their "I"s. Its negating force will now be unavoidable.
"Death's the end of all," the Nurse admits in her following line. But Romeo
here too is confused: does she mean Juliet or not? The circle has embraced
both figures in a confounding hermeneutical perimeter, presaging the one
act that is I's ultimate negation: self-negation, suicide.

Nietzsche never took this course. Nor did Klossowski. (Though one
did who was immensely influenced by Klossowski, and offered his own idiosyncratic interpretation of Nietzsche—Deleuze.) Madness was Nietzsche's
fate. Does the O in all its modern permutations then lead inexorably either
to self-negation or madness, the self-negations of Romeo and Juliet, the
madness of Nietzsche, and his forbear Lear? How do we get out of this so
apparently vicious circle? Or, how are we possibly to conceive of coming
into it the right way?

PART TWO

POESIS' FIGURE — THE MAKING OF O

THREE

SHAKESPEARE'S EYE OF THE STORM

"Sovereignty is NOTHING."

—Maurice Blanchot, quoting Georges Bataille

LEAR'S TRAGIC O

One of the attendant symbols of Lear's emasculated sovereignty in the first half of *King Lear* is his retinue, that band of slack men whose raucous antics reflect the waning control of the king to whom they have remained in service. When the Fool calls Lear an "O without a figure," a "nothing" (I.iv), he anticipates the source and consequence of Goneril's vexation: the unruly band of a hundred she is about to halve. Goneril safeguards her ill-gotten power by exercising it against Lear, the very source of that power, reducing his men accordingly. Enraged, Lear leaves for Regan, as if this shift will prove his sovereignty properly acknowledged and maintained. But of course he reaches Regan's domain only to find his loyal servant Kent in the stocks. In appeal to Regan, he tells her, "Thy sister's naught" (II.iv, 323). But Goneril's wickedness will be matched by Regan's wickedness, and both will lead to Lear's utter nought. Later in the same scene, the two sisters come together, and in joint attack they cut down the remainder of their father's rule. With an audacity and calculation that mortifies Lear, his fifty remaining loyals begin to disappear. "What, fifty followers? / Is it not well? What should you need of more?" asks Regan. "I entreat you / To bring but five-and-twenty. To no more / Will I give place or notice." Lear's response is heartbreaking: "I gave you all" (II.ii, 436–38). He then tries to cut his losses, and return to Goneril: "Thy fifty yet doth double five-and-twenty, / And though art twice her love" (448–49). But still operating on the false economy of power for love, his currency now plummets in value. "Hear me, my lord," says Goneril. "What need you five-and-twenty? ten? or five?" And then Regan's final blow: "What need one?" (449–52).

"What need one?" With this *coup de grâce*, which is the ultimate *coup d'état*, Shakespeare gives us the paramount expression, the defining apothegm, for the modernity to come. It is a question of sovereignty, a question for sovereignty, as embodied in Lear. The one, in dividing itself, is reduced to O.[1] When the usurpation of the one is complete, shut out from its own sovereign domain, the O must relocate to another place, to the raw elements of nature:

> . . . In such a night
> To shut me out! Pour on; I will endure.
> In such a night as this! O Regan, Goneril,
> Your old kind father, whose frank heart gave all—
> O, that way madness lies . . . (III.iv, 17–21)

The madness that is O, the loss of one's reason, is what exposure to the elements out on the heath becomes. "What need one?" Regan had asked, and Lear responded immediately, "O reason not the need!" (II.ii, 453). This is not a question of need, but a question of one's very nature. Yet what Lear cannot fathom, what he cannot bear to behold, is that very nature as something divested of sovereignty. To him, his own nature is sovereign. To see it otherwise, to see nature, and human nature, reduced to the barest of beasts and elements, where the sovereignty of one has lost all footing, that way madness lies. And so, in Lear's speech in II.iv, as he rails against the "unnatural hags" that are his daughters, and asserts his "noble anger," we get the first appearance of the storm and tempest. Nobility and sovereignty are no longer natural traits, no longer blood inheritance, and the rule of one gives way to "terrors of the earth." All reason gone. "O fool, I shall go mad!" (II.ii, 475).

To be true to Shakespeare's prophetic vision here—"What need one?"—the *mise-en-scène* of those moments on the heath in Act III would be best served by having the barest of stages possible. If there is a hovel, it ought to be small and inconspicuous. Emptiness ought to dominate. In fact, the hovel itself might be simply a drawn circle on the stage—the eye of the storm. Lear is never fully alone on the heath, and less so in the hovel. But this is the place where he becomes completely disrobed of his sovereign oneness, and must come to terms with the madness that is O (as presaged by the Fool, as mourned by Kent, as courted by Gloucester, as feigned by Edgar, as lived by Lear). Outside the hovel, as the storm rages, Lear strips himself of all former vestiges (III.iv). Inside the hovel, his wits give way— "who alone suffers suffers most i' th' mind / Leaving free things and happy shows behind" (III.vi, 100–101). The storm enacts the transformation, the purgation of the one who thought himself reasonable, by nature. And now nature exacts its revenge, with a tempest that ravages the inner landscape of the soul, like a nightmare, and renders the king a fool's madman, an "angler in the lake of darkness" (II.vi, 7–8), like the ruined sovereigns before him.

Here, Lear must face the question "What needs one?" for himself. But we too are asked to face this question. There are of course many ways to read this play, but perhaps the most trenchant for us now is to see Lear as that moment in the history of modernity when One's hegemony as a natural right, as an in-built feature of reality, as a divine inheritance, gives way to the privatizations of inner self and the opening up of the Os that attend (to) them. Lear still has a band of men, but now they are either forced into disguise (Kent, Edgar), blinded (Gloucester), or already given to O's folly (the Fool). The final sustaining power of his old role, the one whose "nothing," ironically, invoked the very processes by which this role would unravel, Cordelia, he loses outright. What can come of nothing? For Lear, the only possibility is the awareness, if not the acceptance, of this inexorable shift from One to nought. Tragically, for him, nothing else avails. For us, Lear as the Fool's O, attended by the last remnants of his train, allows us to behold this passing of the old guard. We might even say that what we see dramatized before us is the paradigm shift away from the old political sovereign, or, as expressed in the final lines of the play by the solemn Kent and Edgar, the mourning of its departure. A new era is awaiting. Kent's final lines are thus: "I have a journey, sir, shortly to go. My master calls me; I must not say no" (V.iii, 320–21). But the features of this new master we are not given.[2]

The storm in King Lear is, we might say, nature giving up the necessity of a preordained world. In the first third, before the tempest on the heath, nature is perceived as still hanging together in a cosmological whole. Aberrant heavenly movements, eclipses, foul weather still augur a change in fortunes, a discord and disaster in the offing. Edmund, the bastard son of Gloucester, whose villainy sends Edgar into the guise of Bedlam and Cordelia to her death, dismisses this old cosmology. Nature, to him, is reduced to its physical "base." Natural forces do not inhere within or ally themselves to social conventions. If he is born of a mother, there is no "legitimacy" or "illegitimacy." If there are any inherent correlations, the quality of the physical act of conception would dominate over any social constructs one might impose thereafter (I.ii, 1–22). People do not act from astrological influence, but from their own lusty drives (I.ii, 118–33). So he will defy convention and contract himself maritally to both Goneril and Regan. Edmund's world is a pre-Nietzschean will to power, a naturalized, individualized self operating outside conventional systems, except without the irony to see the self's own hand in its amputation from these systems. It ordains itself, and moves forward not out of necessity but desire. In this sense, Edmund represents the coming reality beyond the old paradigm. His fate is circular in its way. If he comes to life by "lusty stealth," he dies by the same force. The "dark and vicious place" of his conception becomes the dark and vicious place of his demise.[3] Even Edmund, upon capture, admits this to Edgar: "The wheel is come full circle; I am here"—here, that is, where he began (V.iii, 172). Yet this is a different kind of circle than Lear's O. In the storm on the heath (the middle third of the play), Lear is not returning to his very nature, now stripped of all social convention. He might think this, as he compares himself to Tom O'Bedlam, the "poor, bare, forked animal" (III. iv, 105–106). But in fact he doesn't *return* anywhere. He comes to a new place altogether, losing all sense of what is understood as natural or what can be natural. The storm for him is not a natural expression of a portended inevitability. He is moving into the very nothing beyond nature itself. Thus, the emptiness of the heath.

The last third of *Lear* has little mention of cosmological forces. Albany, early in Act IV, signals the shift from heavenly influence to human self-direction (and self-destruction) when he berates Goneril:

> If that the heavens do not their visible spirits
> Send quickly down to tame these vile offenses,
> It will come,
> Humanity must perforce prey on itself,
> Like monsters of the deep. (IV.ii, 47–51)

Otherworldly experiences are quickly transposed into human realities: Gloucester's "fall" from the cliffs of Dover, Cordelia's "spirit" before Lear upon their reunion. The ruling metaphor here is the ripening and rotting of fruit: humans, like still life in painting (*nature morte* in French), are reduced to their base organic selves, poised in life between birth and decomposition. So Lear's last words over his dead Cordelia are not of some divinely created spirit now returning heavenward, but of basic animal materialism:

> . . . no, no, no life?
> Why should a dog, a horse, a rat, have life,
> And thou no breath at all?
> Thou'lt come no more,
> Never, never, never, never, never. (V.iii, 312–15)

Lear's O ends without renewal. If, in staring into the pale face of Cordelia, he sees himself, a voice that now, as then, speaks nothing, says nothing, issues nothing, it is a mirror upon whose surface no breath will ever cloud. In his final gesture, preceded by "O o o o" in the Quarto text, which the First Folio edition then excised, he points to her lips—"Look, her lips / Look there, look there"—but nothing comes, and he himself expires, in a clear mirror image of his daughter. Nothing has come of nothing.

SHAKESPEARE'S SPECULAR O

The Tempest represents another kind of storm, one wholly disconnected from cosmologies, natural forces, or tragic failing. For the storm in this late, and reputedly last, play in the Shakespearean corpus is a human conjuration, a ruse played out through the artful manipulation of nature. It therefore represents a different kind of mirroring surface, one designed to trick, to give the illusion of something that is not, or to recreate something in the absence of some other thing no longer available. It thus presents an O very different from Lear's, an O that, as self-conscious artifice, does offer some sense of renewal. If *Lear* enacts the decline of the One, the decline of unitary sovereignty, *The Tempest* opens the Ô in all its modern possibilities. Ripeness gives way to recultivation, madness to captivation, and usurpation to brave new worlds.

Prospero, *The Tempest's* main figure, is still largely seen as Shakespeare the playwright looking into his own mirror. This, his swan song, represents his self-analysis, in the form of a grand farewell to his company, his audience, and his art. This may be so, but the image of the mirror, and indeed the mirror image, plays a much more extensive role than the speculative nature of an autobiographical gesture.

The entire surface of the play's action appears broadly reflective, as if it is played out within the frame of a mirror. We can find mirroring suggested or manifested throughout. There are images that come and go, illusions conjured by Prospero and effected by Ariel, bringing a world of immaterial creatures and sounds and sights like the play of light across a polished surface. One moment they appear, the next they are gone. There are also images that materialize and vanish within each character's head, dreams and visions that, in sleep or out, idealize (Gonzalo), amaze (Miranda), infatuate (Ferdinand), perturb (Alonso), take revenge (Caliban), conspire (Antonio and Sebastian), indulge (Stephano), covet (Trinculo), free (Ariel), and retire (Prospero). Like a mirror, "the quality of one's dreaming is an index of character," suggests Northrop Frye.[4] There is only one explicit reference to mirrors, when Miranda says to her suitor Ferdinand that she remembers no other woman's face "Save, from my glass, mine own" (III.i, 50),[5] but this image gives way to a host of other reflections on different levels. Miranda and her father Prospero have been stranded on an island since Miranda was a young child. The only faces she remembers are those of her father, of Caliban, of herself, and now of Ferdinand. The island, framed by water, has been a mirror allowing her to see only that which resides within its frame. On this particular level, we can see the unnamed island as a speculum into which characters peer. Miranda so far has only seen a handful of images, and the discovery of this new one in the form of Ferdinand is a thrill by which she is captured. Of course, there is a "brave new world" that will later enter the frame, but this only after she has given her affections over to the one who has returned them. The rest of the shipwrecked party too will peer into this frame, but they in large part will see only themselves, as the island shows up their strengths or, more often, their deficiencies in character. In bringing this group within his frame, Prospero himself sees his past, his present, and his future shaped within the island's activity. For him, the island is not only a mirror with which to play tricks, but a mirror in which the entire compass of his life unfolds. Any who peer into the frame, then, receive a vision of self-realization: whether through love, through flaw, or through manipulation. In the language of the One, pre-Lear, such self-realization becomes redemptive, and society is righted, with the proper sovereign back in power. In the language of the O, such self-realization becomes disturbing, as the self is realized on the basis of a cracked and discomfiting image.

Looking at the island in this metaphorical light, we can see the trope of Hamlet's "mirror held up to nature" used in several ways. The island, as a speculum, reflects back to the characters their various dramatic aspects. On one level, the speculum works microcosmically, equating or relating the island with the selfhood of each character, and the shores of the island with the boundaries of that selfhood, much as if each individual held up a round mirror to their face. On another level, the speculum works macrocosmically, reflecting back to the characters the entire dramatic world in which they are collectively bound. Everything that takes place on the island becomes the dramatic terra firma from which all else is defined. The island offers up the possibilities of a society, with rulers and subordinates, with economy and labor, with factions and alliances, with establishment and disestablishment, with the privileged and the impoverished, the sober and the dissipated, the greedy and the content, the seditious and the honorable. So Gonzalo in his utopian speech can envision a commonwealth world, free from sweat and sovereignty, where people live in prelapsarian harmony. So Caliban can envision a primitive world, peopled by the fruits of rape, and run on savagery. So Miranda can envision a "brave new world," her naïveté making all things good. The island becomes a world ready to be made, or remade, by the characters who inhabit it.

The island, then, is the woven circle of the play, Shakespeare's O. On either side of its perimeter, in the first scene and in the Epilogue, there is action presented beyond the limits of the shore. The opening scene is where the play receives its title. But why *The Tempest* and not *The Enchanted Island,* as some later versions were renamed?[6] Why did Shakespeare title the work on something that happens beyond the frame of the main action? As the island is a mirror image of the characters' self and their world, so the sea and the storm are traditionally seen in like manner: the tempestuous waters mirror the internal states of those who have fallen their victim (everyone short of the sprites and fairies), much like Lear's experience on the heath. But here, what lies outside of the world to be made is what, potentially, is both the greatest source of threat and the greatest source of rehabilitation. The storm brings ashore the possibility of both subversion and restoration (of society), of both iniquity and repentance (of the self). The duality of inner and outer, inside and outside, thus becomes confused, as the boundary of the circle itself begins to dissolve. The external gales that blow outside the main arena of action—though a result of Prospero's arts, we must always remember—become the internal gales that define action within it. Even at the end, those gales will not abate. This is something Auden will highlight. Everyone, Ariel sings, "doth suffer a sea-change" (I.ii, 403), but this change includes the island's O itself, and its sense of solid ground on which to rebuild in the face of the storm. Shakespeare's O is more than just a happy image of restoration.

On the far side lies the Epilogue. Like the opening storm scene, the Epilogue points to action beyond the ground of the island, action situated upon the insubstantial surface of the waters ("Gentle breath of yours my sails / Must fill . . ." [Epilogue, 11–12]). But unlike the opening action, the Epilogue does not claim to stand within the continuity of the plot. It does not claim to be action at all. (Again, something Auden will highlight.) Rather, it steps outside of the plot and the action to address the audience members who have just been witness to the plot and the action. Prospero is still Prospero, the administrator of the preceding events, but his plea is to be released from these events by the audience. He pleads to leave the island. Were his words part of the main action, he would have directed them to one of the characters, Alonso or the Boatswain. But he directs them to those sitting on the other side of the stage's plane of activity, to those who have viewed the island from without. This move is more complicated than it may first appear. By addressing the audience, and breaking through the "fourth wall" of the drama, Prospero has consciously demarcated another boundary in his artifice, this time a boundary defining his artifice as a whole. The Epilogue holds up another mirror, though one that claims to reflect not merely features within the play, but the play itself as it can be viewed from outside. Like *Hamlet*'s play within the play, a distinct mirroring of the mirror, Prospero invites the audience to view a similar picture in *The Tempest,* wherein the main character of the play, Prospero himself, shows the play as *play*, shows the mirror by turning the mirror back upon itself, and giving his own role as spellbinder over to the viewing public. "You have been watching a mirror image," he says in effect, "and now let me pass the mirror over to you, dear people, to mirror the mirror image, and show you clearly the frame of this performance. We have come to the end of the frame. Set us free now by creating another frame into which we may escape." The indulgence of the audience is to accept kindly the performance as artifice, the goal of which has been "to please," and then to release Prospero into the artifice of their own minds. With this request, Shakespeare simply shifts the frame. The audience becomes part of the mirror, or, we could say, is framed, in the same way the king is framed in *Hamlet*. But here we must acknowledge that being part of the frame does not make the performance correspond any more to an external "reality." The performance itself is the "reality," along with our participation in it. The mirror, whether held by us or by the play itself, is only ever held up to the *play's* nature.[7]

The Epilogue invites us to rethink our notion of mimesis. As much as we may wish to find the concepts of "original" and "imitation" in Prospero's parting words, we search in vain. Nothing he says can point us to an "original" beyond or preceding the five acts; any "original" must come from our inference within the five acts, or following the five acts, none of which can be "original" in any *prior* sense. The effect of the action, Prospero says, has been to enchant. It has not been to evoke some phenomenal reality outside of itself, to show things outside of the frame that are the sources of the mirror's reflection. Prospero, from within his O, has cast a spell, a spell operating equally upon the play and the audience. The play charms us while we in turn charm the play, granting it the run of its own nature. Such a granting is our act of framing, while the running of its nature is the play's. The Epilogue does no more than state this mutual dependence, this mutual framing. It holds up a mirror before us only insofar as it shows us holding a mirror back. The only thing "original" is the made thing, original not in temporal priority but in unique self-generation and self-subsistence. Here Shakespeare appears deeply modern: art is always "original" in the latter sense, never an "imitation."

Is art, then, even for the great Bard, no more than a house of mirrors, unable to picture anything beyond its self-enclosed world, unable to show the traditionally understood "human nature" with which we are all universally endowed, and in whose limitations we must live, outside the realm of art? Is the movement from infirmity to wholeness or from iniquity to repentance simply an artifice, with no correlation to the way we conduct our lives in reality? The better question is this: If there seems to be a correlation between the sea and the mirror, is this because there is something in the play that exceeds artifice, or because there is something in our real lives that is bound to artifice, as reflected by the play? Shakespeare's O does not deny either possibility.

The mirror, we have said, confines by its frame. In its own way, it acts as a prison-house. The image of the prison is one readily found in *The Tempest*. Prospero on several occasions calls his place on the island a "cell" (I.ii, 20, 39; V.i, 291, 301); and in the Epilogue, his plea to the audience is wrought with the imagery of imprisonment—"I must be here confin'd by you," "But release me from my bands," "Let your indulgence set me free" (4, 9, 20). As a place of exile the island has had precedence, for Sycorax, Caliban, and Ariel all experienced their own detention, whether imposed by the shores of the beach or, in Ariel's case, by the trunk of a "cloven pine" (I.ii, 277). When Prospero and Miranda begin their twelve-year ordeal, they take Caliban as a creature to be civilized. But when his actions prove intractable and his motives perverse, he is confined to yet a further jail, a cave-like rock from which he must yield to hard labor. His toil is briefly inherited by Ferdinand, whose fondness for Miranda gives him the endurance to withstand his captivity: "All corners else o' th' earth / Let liberty make use of; space enough / Have I in such a prison" (I.ii, 494–96). As a jailer, Prospero is none too kind, either to Ferdinand or to Caliban, even if his tyrannical edge is shown to have some salubrious motive by the play's end. The two shipwrecked parties, those of the court and those on the bottle (Stephano and Trinculo), are no less free than the others, and their captivity comes to a visible summation when in the final Act the court party *"all enter the circle which Prospero had made, and there stand charm'd"* (sd. V.i), held in bondage until their captor releases them, while the hapless pair are held with Caliban by hounding spirits until released by Ariel. Even those characters nonessential to the plot, the Boatswain and his crew, are holed up in their ships under a spell of slumber until they are needed again at the play's conclusion. Everyone, without exception, is in some sort of imprisonment by virtue of being on or associated with the island. So it is not inappropriate when Prospero's final lines in the Epilogue stress the image of confinement. The whole of the play's actions, from the opening scene onward, is wracked with captivity.

The O of *The Tempest* becomes a prison-house from which its captives cannot escape. The artistic creation, or delimitation, of anything, whether an unnamed island or a named character to dwell on it, erects its own boundaries of identity, and each is caught inexorably within that space as long as the desire to be identified as art remains. No art is completely self-determining; some kind of frame must be set up in advance.[8] Art by definition, we have said, imposes limits, or we simply do not call it art (a limitless or unbounded "art" would go unnoticed). *The Tempest* turns and calls attention to its own limits by making the action itself a delimiting process. Prospero is a spellbinder, closing off certain areas of existence and awareness in order to bring other areas of existence and awareness into being. Drawing the court party into a closed circle where they are bound by a spell is a symbolic crystalization of the artistic moment. This moment, in turn, is a homology of the play as whole: the island is the circle where all characters and spells are cast, and by which the five Acts become a spell-bound circle for the audience. We can see this sense of imprisonment earlier in Shakespeare, as in the famous Prologue to *The Life of King Henry the Fifth*:

> Can this cockpit hold
> The vasty fields of France? Or may we cram
> Within this wooden O the very casques
> That did afright the air at Agincourt?
> O, pardon! since a crooked figure may
> Attest in little place a million;
> And let us, ciphers to this great accompt,
> On your imaginary forces work.
> Suppose within the girdle of these walls
> Are now confined two mighty monarchies . . . [etc.] (lns. 11–20)

Art is a poetic incarceration, an incarceration of *poesis*, a making of walls to confine. Prospero in the end calls for his release, but in vain, for as he has made walls for others, so too he is penned. The audience can only move him to another pen: another written or staged performance, or an ongoing performance within their minds or memories. Either way, his sentence is fixed, his release ungrantable. And the audience has become implicated, for they too are bound as long as they sit before the stage. The performance has drawn its boundaries around the spectator, a drawing of limits to be noticed. These limits then cannot be wholly erased by the viewer. Is this not the lesson of Dorian Gray, whose self-portrait incarcerates the artist irrevocably, in a manner that suggests life imitates art, not art life? "It is the spectator, and not life, that art really mirrors," Wilde had said.[9] By gazing into the mirror the spectator is trapped, trapped by the made thing, trapped by artifice.

The nature of this entrapment calls for a kind of grace or mercy. With framing comes judgment (the King in *Hamlet*, Macbeth, Dorian Gray, even, as we will see later, Brecht's notorious Judge). Yet as Prospero shows us in the Epilogue, judgment in art calls for *indulgence*, and not only indulgence in the sense of gratifying one's wishes, but more significantly in the theological sense of remitting punishment for a sin. Prospero's "faults" for which he asks relief lie, as he states it, in a failure "to please" (Epilogue, 13, 18); but they also lie, we might say, in his godlike assumption of the divine Creator's role, which recreates both a heaven and hell within the "earth" of the island, and requires mercy and pardon from without. As Blake later paraphrased Prospero in "Jerusalem": "*dear* Reader, *forgive* what you do not approve, & *love* me for this energetic exertion of my talent," by which "Heaven, Earth and Hell henceforth shall live in harmony."[10] But as Prospero seeks mercy for the godlike exertion of his talent, so he implicates the audience in asking that they, in godlike capacity, grant such mercy. The moment of grace equals here the moment of condemnation, as both sides of the plane of the mirror, both the work of art/artist and the spectator, stand in need of a mutual release from the judgment of the frame, which can only be granted by the other—the spectator grants pardon to the work, while the work grants pardon to the spectator for granting pardon to its work (since the spectator is implicated only in terms of the work's frame of reference). For, "by your words you will be justified, and by your words you will be condemned" (Matthew 12.37), and as all words are imprisoned within the frame of the creative work, the work becomes both a limit and a freedom, both a judgment and an acquittal, both a binding and a release, just as the work of the cross becomes for the Word both death and salvation. Or in the case of Dorian Gray, his refusal to confess and seek out mercy condemns him, as both an artist and spectator forever caught within his own framing, and to his own self-destruction: "Was he really to confess? Never. There was only one bit of evidence left against him. The picture itself—that was evidence. He would destroy it."[11] In the case of Prospero, the boundary between judgment and mercy is further confused by the figure of Caliban, his own Dorian Gray.

CALIBAN'S NEGATING O

Of all the main *personae* on the island, Caliban is the only one whose situation remains unresolved. The shipwrecked parties, having their iniquities exposed and the consciences chastened, having received both judgment and pardon, prepare themselves for their journey home. Prospero and Miranda, one with a restored dukedom, the other with a pending marriage, are set to join them. Ariel, after two dozen years in fetters and service, has finally gained his liberation. But Caliban leaves the stage sulking in self-reproach and spite, and we are given no indication as to his plight. Prospero appears to offer him pardon—"as you look / To have my pardon, trim it handsomely" (V.i, 292–93)—but only after he has sent him back to his cell. How he then gets on, whom he then sides with—these are all left unanswered. His own last words suggest that he too has come to some new awareness: "I'll be wise hereafter / And seek for grace" (V.i, 294–95). But his apparent contrition is no more than a show of regret for having inflicted pain and misery upon himself. "What a thrice-double ass / Was I to take this drunkard for a god / And worship this dull fool!" (V.i, 295–97). He does not say he will worship Prospero now instead; his seeking of grace is simply to avoid punishment ("pinch'd to death" [V.i, 276]). His idea of freedom is not autonomy, but a new master: [*singing*] "'Ban, 'Ban, Cacaliban / Has a new master: —get a new man / Freedom, high-day! high-day freedom! freedom, high-day, freedom!" (II.ii, 184–86). Never does he suggest that he can be out from under someone's rule, only that he wishes to be out from under Prospero's torment, which would be freedom enough. Never demanding complete self-rule or release, never demanding complete condemnation or justification, Caliban is never granted them. We don't know what he is granted. He remains inconclusive, a deep fissure upon the play's mirror.

He also remains inextricable from Prospero. Adopted once, enslaved later, Caliban acts as an irreparable split on the surface of all of Prospero's dealings, and indeed on the surface of Prospero's thoughts. The attempts to civilize Caliban prove fruitless. The attempts to tame him prove impossible. The attempts to corral him prove temporary. Prospero may appear to be omniscient to everything Caliban does, but this is because he cannot be rid of him. Of the parodic trio, Prospero says to Alonso: "Two of these fellows you / Must know and own; this thing of darkness I / Acknowledge mine" (V.i, 274–76). Such an admission of possession, of a kind of paternal duty, of an almost psychological union, makes Caliban a contumacious force in Prospero's own psyche, a crack on Prospero's own mirror, a deep crevice around which Prospero must continually negotiate. At certain points his negotiation falters. Fittingly, the most vivid of these moments comes during *The Tempest's* own play within the play. As Ferdinand and Miranda sit watching a wedding masque in the fourth Act, the entire scene is abruptly dispelled by a startled Prospero, who thinks,

> I had forgot that foul conspiracy
> Of the beast Caliban and his confederates
> Against my life: the minute of their plot
> Is almost come. (IV.i, 139–42)

In a mirror-like manner to *Hamlet*, Prospero's conscience is awakened by or during the watched performance. Perhaps because of guilt, most certainly because of self-preservation, here too the performance has to be stopped. What has reminded Prospero of the foul deeds awaiting him? What is Caliban's link with the sprightly dances of the masque? Why does the moment of darkness coincide with the middle of the performance? As if looking into a mirror, Prospero has not been able to avoid the cracks in the images he himself has made. Caliban, his most extensive, always intrudes upon the view. The framed scene is wrought with its own imperfections. Framing always suggests a break, a split, a fall.

This framing, as we have already suggested, begins with the capacity for language (Matthew 12.37). Upon adoption, Prospero and Miranda try to sophisticate Caliban by teaching him their own tongue. Miranda says,

> I pitied thee,
> Took pains to make thee speak, taught thee each hour
> One thing or other: when thou didst not, savage,
> Know thine own meaning, but wouldst gabble like
> A thing most brutish, I endow'd thy purposes
> With words that made them known. But thy vile race,
> Though thou didst learn, had that in't which good natures
> Could not abide to be with; therefore wast thou
> Deservedly confined into this rock, who hadst
> Deserved more than a prison. (I.ii, 355–62)

When Caliban did not know his own meaning, he was given words to make his purposes known. But the very expression of his meaning and purposes led to his imprisonment. Language, the supposed revealing of inner intent, was wisdom of another kind for Caliban. It became fruit from the tree of the knowledge of good and evil. It became the cognizance of a difference from others, and a move to be like them. Hence, it became a fall, a malediction:

> You taught me language, and my profit on 't
> Is, I know how to curse. The red plague rid you
> For learning me your language! (I.ii, 365–67)

Language becomes a prison-house that defines, because it confines, the curse.[12] The fostering of Caliban invites the dark side of creation, and the teaching of language invites fault lines to break through creation's surface. Prospero is plagued with these fractures, because they plague his very work; Caliban's own curse begins to take effect throughout the play, as it rids Prospero of the wedding masque in action, as it drives a plot to vanquish Prospero altogether, as it forces Prospero in the end to call for deliverance from the play's entire structure—the structure of language as it has been formed around action. Prospero too is caught in his own prison-house of words, and his Epilogue is a kind of reverse cry to Caliban's curse. May your own designs and devices plague you to death, cries Caliban to Prospero; may I be released from my own designs and devices by your good hands, pleads Prospero to the audience. But as Caliban remains Prospero's "thing of darkness," Prospero is in an eternal bind. For to be released from the bounds of the play realizes fully Caliban's curse: Prospero is rid of existence. But to remain within its bounds is to remain forever on the island, forever facing Caliban, the voiding O of his artifice. At the end of it all, Caliban has the upper hand. Having endowed Caliban with the means to express himself in words, Prospero is bound to those words, and will live or die by them in judgment or acquittal.

Shakespeare shuffles Caliban into the wings at the end of The Tempest. But both for Prospero and for any subsequent reader or viewer, Caliban remains the central and inexorable disturbance of the action, the deformation which, far from aesthetically marring the dramatic structure, intensifies it, providing space with which to maneuver inward, a deep black cave to explore, like the cave to which Caliban himself was impounded, or the Marabar Caves of Forster. It is inevitable, then, that of all the play's characters, Caliban would gain the longest afterlife. Shakespeare keeps him unresolved within the play, and as a result he continues to rear his head outside the play, usurping the very plea of his master. He does not leave the bounded world of art altogether, of course, but is reframed, in a variety of settings from literature to painting.[13] Artists continue to remain fascinated by Caliban, far more than they do by Prospero, because it is with Caliban that the very question of the origin of creation lies, and not with Prospero. Prospero may be the grand artificer of the play, and thus may be closer to Shakespeare than any other Shakespearean role, but his arts are delimited enough and his character prescribed enough that one can ask of him questions about *what* is created, but less questions about *why*. Caliban's character raises more profoundly the question of *why*, why any art. Prospero tells us that his project was to "enchant" and "please." But Caliban, with his "vile race," threatens artifice with a breaking down of itself, and poses questions not simply of closed systems, but of how closed systems come into existence, and how they share in, or retain, the abysses of open systems, of nonexistence and negation. Why create or bring into existence at all, if creation necessarily brings with it its own demise? This question is a question resting upon Caliban, and links him much more closely to the spirit and concern of tragedy than anything offered by Prospero. We are reminded here again of Hamlet, and the main character's monologues, or of Lear, and the nothing that comes of nothing. Yet the late play of The Tempest probes the question of the *will come* of nothing by merging tragedy with the act itself of creating. As Hölderlin had said in his brief but immensely important "The Significance of Tragedy" (1802):

The significance of tragedy is most easily understood [*begriffen*] through paradox. Because all capability is divided justly and equally, everything that is original appears not in its original strength, not truly, but genuinely only in its weakness, so that in reality the light of life and appearance belong to the weakness of each whole. Now in the tragic, the sign is in itself meaningless, without power, but that which is original is straight out. For really the original can only appear in its weakness, but insofar as the sign in itself is posited as meaningless = 0, the original too, the hidden ground of everything in nature can represent itself. If nature genuinely represents itself in its weakest gift [Gabe], then, when [nature] presents itself in its strongest gift, the sign = 0.[14]

Or as Derrida later paraphrased: "In the beginning, at the origin, there was ruin."[15] Caliban remains Prospero's because Prospero cannot create without him—it was, after all, Caliban who showed him "all the qualities o' th' isle" (I.ii, 339). Caliban is not only a negative counterpart to Miranda, Ariel, and Ferdinand; he is the necessary inverse to Prospero's creative abilities—an "inverse" in the sense of a turning inward, a turning creation back upon itself, or within itself, to probe the darkness that resides there, the inner vortices, the crevasses that show up the tain of the mirror, the blank space within the perimeter of the O.

The language of Shakespeare provides the space for such inverse exploration. And the territory, as with the language, becomes theological. What began as a speculum has become something quite other, internal reflections leading to dark spots with no label or "value," only ineffability, emptiness. Larry Bouchard has suggested the term *kenotic integrity* in relation to Shakespearean creation, play(ing), and suffering. In play we empty out ourselves, or are emptied, and "in this emptiness, there can be a meeting place for those who suffer."[16] Prospero and Caliban meet as co-sufferers, not to transform their suffering into good, but as in a Blakean marriage of heaven and hell, in which neither is ultimately sovereign over the other, where joys might impregnate, but where "sorrows bring forth." Their own created frames have not been overcome, and Caliban has escaped no less than Prospero. It is that Caliban takes us to the center of the O, and there to a new kind of integrity, or a new kind of "ground."

This "ground" of course has no being of its own. Like the tain of a mirror, it is a place that allows something to take place, but which itself has no ground of reference. It is a place beyond all speech and metaphor, but which, to speak of, requires metaphor, only to deny it. It is this contradictory "ground" that Auden will try to extend even farther, using the metaphors of "the sea" and "the mirror," both of which collapse into one another, as they do upon their own selves.

FOUR

REFLECTIONS OF AUDEN

We shall be judged, not by the kind of mirror found on us, but by the use we have made of it, by our *riposte* to our reflection.

—W. H. Auden, "Hic et Ille"

W. H. AUDEN

W. H. Auden (1907–1973) is sometimes considered the last of the "great English poets," before poetry left the center of civic activity altogether and devolved into a cottage industry of private practitioners and specialist academics. By "great" here is meant a poet who approached poetry still as a comprehensive art, one informed by the classics, one conversant in multiple genres, one maintaining a learned sensibility of what is or what has traditionally been "high" versus "low" culture, and one that sees itself in terms of a vital and indispensable vocation. Of course, we no longer subscribe to this understanding of "greatness," its categories having been ground down by the apparatus of critical theories. And though Auden himself may have still held these categories in esteem, his own work, if not his own life, was already suggesting otherwise. We could say that, after Auden, there no longer could be a "great" poet in the same regard. Or, that Auden helped to undo (his own) "greatness," even before postmodern theory would overtake the literary world and dissolve such "greatness" categorically. Or we could say that Auden, informed by Kierkegaardian and Kafkan despair, and thus keenly aware of his own obliteration as self and artist, was all too aware of dwelling in the O.

The self-negation of the O, however, is not about annihilating one's own existence, even if many Western artists of the twentieth century, in Europe and America, took this course. It is, rather, about reinventing oneself, or reoriginating the "self," by moving or removing the borders and

121

frames that were once set up to constitute the self, and placing them anew elsewhere. Auden was fascinated with borders. He crossed geographical borders regularly throughout his life, at times momentously; and he crossed literary borders with habit. His career included poems in every form, plays for both radio and stage, essays, libretti, film and documentary text, tracts— virtually all literary genres publishable, and even a few not publishable. It is thus not without significance that his early published career included travel journals—*Letters from Iceland* and *Journey to a War*.[1] Within each genre Auden crossed boundaries of form as a rule, and was proud to claim in his later years that he had written a poem in every poetic form known to the English language. He would even blur the boundaries of poetry and prose, so that his poetry could sound very prosaic, while his prose take on a very poetic role. Here was a poet who not only celebrated form, but seemed happy to reside at form's threshold, as it gave way to new form. (*On the Frontier* is the title he gave to one of his plays.) This threshold is the place of O, the womb of new beginning. But how, we keep asking, do we place this O?

In the history of aesthetic ideas (and ideals) from the Renaissance to the present, Auden stands in a pivotal position. The lead into modernism saw the sovereignty of the One collapse fully and decisively with Nietzsche's clarion call that "God is dead." In between the height of modernism and the present late modernism stand the two great wars. Auden was too young to participate in the first world war, and too old to join the ranks of sol- diery in the second. He nevertheless felt compelled to address politics and play his part, and as a rising and leading star of a young Oxford circle of poets and writers ("The Auden Group," including Stephen Spender, Cecil Day-Lewis, Christopher Isherwood, Edward Upward, and Rex Warner), he sought to improve society by charging his poetry with a Marxist socialism. (Is not twentieth-century Marxism, as Žižek frequently implies, a similar grasp for ideological unity and oneness in the West, before Marxist ideals became but a specter?)[2] But as his fame grew throughout the 1930s, and his political and social influence did not—wars were raging in China and Spain, and a severe one was brewing in and about Germany, and Auden felt helpless in the face of them all[3]—he came to realize his errant aim as a poet. Sovereign oneness, whether in the guise of fascism or socialism, was unsustainable without further bloodshed. He thus effected a major change in his thinking and being when, in 1939, on the eve of World War II, and to the outcry of his fellow countrymen, he crossed borders (and seas), moved to America, and shifted his concerns from politics to religion. With these moves, his poetry took a decided turn. Gone was the unified and shared humanity of "Lay your sleeping head my love." Gone too was the desire for social, political, or moral change in "Spain." Instead, Auden increasingly came to stress the limits of poetry and art, that is, their inability to manifest

any moral value outside of themselves. In this he anticipated Blanchot: a
work of art only "is"; beyond that it is nothing. In his own words, laced
with hyperbole, Auden said: "If not a poem had been written, not a picture
painted, not a bar of music composed, the history of man would remain
materially unchanged."[4] This is to say, Auden had been contemplating the
shift of art from the One, to which it might lend some moral gravity, to
the O, which in itself is bereft of "value."

There is reality, and there is artifice. But if all Auden discovered by
his transatlantic move and his disaffection with political systems was that art
had only to do with artifice, and nothing to do with reality, then we would
have little justification in using the term *great poet* by any definition. The
prevailing scholarly view of Auden focuses on his later understanding of art
as "frivolous."[5] But even Auden understood that frivolity had an important
place in what, and how, we conceive of reality. It is not that artifice, as
frivolous, merely stands outside of reality as we know it; nor is it that reality as we know it never penetrates artifice. Auden's insight concerns the
"as we know it." The reality that we know *is not necessarily the only reality*;
it may not even be *the* reality we think persists in our existence. And it is
art that must bring us to this realization. For only art can disturb, disrupt,
and negate the reality that we know, and lead us to an understanding of a
reality that we might originate. Art itself, then, is an O, a bordered void
of negation as much as a woven circle in which newness arises. It thus sits
between the earnest and the frivolous, between reality and artifice, allowing
each to merge with, and to emerge from, the other.

Not long after his move to America, Auden wrote his longest and most
important work, *The Sea and the Mirror* (1942–44). The title metaphorizes
these common binaries: reality/earnestness (the sea) and artifice/frivolity
(the mirror). Coupled with an "and" not an "or," the two do not stand in
opposition. They sit side by side, and during the course of the complex poem
bleed into each other. The sea can act like a mirroring surface, whereas the
mirror can provide its own fathomless depth. If there is frivolity here, it
cannot be the kind we normally associate with triviality and insignificance.
It will be of the nature of Kundera's *The Joke*. It will be the frivolity of the
cipher O, whose joke is that its valueless feature is its greatest and most
profound value. Along the surface and within the depths of *The Sea and
the Mirror* we find circumscribed this O, Auden's O.

This O will circle around many other dualities in the course of the
poem. Auden, as Arthur Kirsch reminds us, was obsessed with dualities in
the early goings of his career,[6] and the poem's form, though tripartite in
structure, is built around a series of binaries, as we shall see below. Yet Auden
was all too aware of the provisional nature of these structuring binaries. "All
the striving of life is a striving to transcend duality."[7] Here is where the O

operates, in a transcending that is as much an imploding, a zeroing out of the binary strife, which leaves a nothing that is nevertheless an echo (a Hegelian echo) of the two forms it has erased.

The O then circles around the title and the binary of sea and mirror. But it also circles around the subtitle, which presents its own binary: "A Commentary on Shakespeare's *The Tempest*." Here, the internal duality between "original" and "commentary" will also be redrawn, as the "original" is commented upon in such a way that its "origin" becomes lost, and the commentary becomes more original than what it ostensibly points back to. The O thus circumnavigates Shakespeare's *The Tempest* in order to remap the play, if not Shakespeare himself. But of course this too will be a "false study," and reveal more of Auden than of Shakespeare. Or, we should say, it will reveal more of the originating than what was first originated.

THE SEA AND THE MIRROR

We have just read Shakespeare and his *The Tempest* from a particularly late modern vantage, in which the O, as speculum, as artificer's circle, as prison-house, as Caliban, as kenotic negation or integrity, continually overwhelms the unity, wholeness, and restoration previous generations would have granted to the play's general sense and meaning. We could not have read in this manner without first being informed by Auden, and his mid-century commentary, as it moves us from the idea of "origin" as One to "origin" as *poesis*. Let us now peer closely, then, and at last, into this vast poem of words, rhymes, meters, voices, styles, images, and references—a flaunting of sheer craftsmanship—to see how Auden's commentary is, in effect, a commentary on late modernity's emergent O.[8]

The Sea and the Mirror is a flowing verbosity, which, like an ocean itself, shifts, swells, breaks, collides, rests, and storms over areas both shallow and deep. But while it seems all over the map, its cartographical features are in fact highly contained. Like all commentaries, it analyzes a given work, *The Tempest*, by addressing each component, each character, as it fits into the larger grid of the whole. As a genre, commentaries are not poetic pieces; they are discursive prose. But the only prose we find in the poem is Caliban's final speech, whose prose is so heightened and mannered its very contrivance assumes a poetic role. Why then combine or confuse two genres, one traditionally belonging to exposition, the other to imagination? What is Auden attempting, or implying, by merging the critical approach with the creative and imaginative? Is his commentary an explanation of a Shakespearean play, or the furtherance of it, the sequel to it? Where does the original lie in this commentary/commentaried binary?

Title Page

The traditional origin of creative endeavor is, of course, divine. The artist drew upon the Muses, those ancient goddesses who furnished the power to imagine, and who guaranteed art a heavenly nature. Auden knew these Muses well, but for him their roles had long been lost in the modern world. In his later "Homage to Clio," for example, Clio, the Muse of History, is a "Madonna of silences" who neither speaks nor inspires words. "I dare not ask you if you bless the poets," says the poet in the final lines, "For you do not look as if you ever read them, / Nor can I see a reason why you should."[9] A decade or so earlier, Auden opened the *Sea and the Mirror* with an epigraph also about divine inspiration. The lines are the final stanza from Emily Brontë's poem "Plead For Me":

> *And am I wrong to worship where*
> *Faith cannot doubt nor Hope despair*
> *Since my own soul can grant my prayer?*
> *Speak, God of Visions, plead for me*
> *And tell why I have chosen thee.*[10]

In this invocation, the Muse here, the "God of Visions," is also not playing her traditional role. Though she is asked to speak on behalf of the author, it is not as a direct and authoritative inspiration, issuing words from on high, but in order to justify the Muse's own existence. The poet interrogates her new role, if not capacity, with some doubt. Is it now the gods or God who grant the poetic vision, or one's "own soul"? This thoroughly modern question reveals a more fundamentally modern concern: Is art about that which is already expressed (positive discourse, mimesis, reflection, divine revelation) or that waiting to be newly expressed? Does origination mean returning to an already placed and singular original, a One as we have been describing it, or creating an immediate original in the now of the present, *extempore*? The modern commentary deals with the former, the modern poem with the latter. But there is doubt invoked at the outset, for we do not know where or how we are to situate Auden's work that follows this epigraph. In Brontë, the poet tries to justify her exchange of Reason's wealth, power, glory, and pleasure ("These once indeed seemed Beings divine") for an "ever present, phantom thing"—the world of imagination. For her, the "God of Visions" and "her own soul" have become one and the same. Since the poet has control over her creative thought (her new "God"), since she can, thus, answer her own prayers, she wonders if this new religion—a religion of Art—deserves her devotion. Is it right to

worship where faith is always constant and hope always secure, because
the faith and hope are within a self-contained world, and never transgress
the imaginative realm? The poet, despite her early assurance, seems now
to demur, as if doubt and despair, not faith and hope, are the very things
that gnaw at her conscience. She pleads with this new "God of Visions"
to plead in turn for her, and tell her why she has renounced the earlier
pursuits for a veneration of Imagination. "Bring me a vision to justify the
Vision," the poet in effect asks, uncertain still of her chosen sympathies. But
can the imagination exceed its own boundaries? Is the imagination divine
in this sense—that it can authenticate its own self? The poet, informed by
this Romantic ideal—Auden was right to source the dilemma in Romanticism—has already shifted the boundaries of origin. But there remains a
lingering uncertainty, as if the shift is too much for the imagination to
bear. Auden's "commentary" (imagination's opposite—the supposed Reason
Brontë left behind) will test this.

The Frame

The context of the poem to follow is the Shakespearean stage, but *after*
the performance has taken place. Here, the cast of *The Tempest* takes stock
within the O that is, geometrically and figuratively, The Globe theatre—and
an *emptied out* theatre, with only the cast remaining.

The main body of the poem is structured into three chapters. On
either side sits a Preface and a Postscript, as if to mirror *The Tempest,* with
its Scene One and Epilogue. The first chapter, "Prospero to Ariel," consists of
a long monologue, itself divided into three blank verse sections that are followed by shorter refrains, the first two rhymed. In the monologue, Prospero
addresses both Ariel and himself, as he takes stock of the play's actions now
behind him. In the second chapter, "The Supporting Cast, *Sotto Voce*," every
other character inhabiting *The Tempest's* island, short of Ariel and Caliban,
receives a voice in the form of a poem, each one differing in structure, style,
content, and length, so as to reflect the respective *personae*. Even peripheral
characters such as Adrian and Francisco, the Master and Boatswain, get
their say. Following each poem is a standardized refrain spoken by Antonio,
whose poem leads off the section, and whom Auden in many ways presents as the most self-aware of the secondary characters. The chapter ends
with a poem from Miranda, whom Auden presents as the least aware. The
third section, also divided into three parts, is a lengthy prose monologue,
"Caliban to the Audience," in which Caliban, in the grandiloquent prose of
Henry James, addresses various types of supposed theatre-goers. The Preface,
subtitled *"The Stage Manager to the Critics,"* prepares us for the journey to

be taken "on stage." The Postscript, subtitled *"Ariel to Caliban. Echo by the Prompter,"* prepares us for the journey off stage. The former marks out the two boundaries outside the actual play on stage: the stage manager behind the scenes, who controls the running of the play, and the critics in front of the curtain, who subsequently judge it. The latter is made up of three stanzas, each followed by a rhymed echo, ". . . I," the voice of the prompter from the wings, cueing Ariel as he responds diminutively to Caliban's preceding oratorical *tour de force*. The entire framework is thus constructed outside the action of the original play. Though its five parts mirror the five acts upon which it "comments," these new "acts" are of their own device, beyond the original, beyond action. They reflect.

Preface

The Preface takes us behind the stage to the Stage Manager as he addresses the critics upon the end of the performance. But he makes it clear we are not outside "performance": though none of the action, nor the *dramatis personae,* of *The Tempest* are mentioned, the poem begins nevertheless *in medias res,* as if in the throes of a circus performance. The image of the circus ring is important here, for it is the continuing O of the artificer's circle, where the conjured performance takes place:

> The aged catch their breath,
> For the nonchalant couple go
> Waltzing across the tightrope
> As if there were no death
> Or hope of falling down;
> The wounded cry as the clown
> Doubles his meaning, and O
> How the dear little children laugh
> When the drums roll and the lovely
> Lady is sawn in half.

It is the "aged" who are first described, as they sit on the edge of their seat in suspense or anticipation of the daring feat's accomplishment. Children are later laughing, finding nothing but pleasure in these acts of illusion, but it is the adults who understand the balancing act of the circus performance, the balance between life and death. It is they who catch the double meaning of the clown, whose role it is to fuse comedy with the tragic, to disguise the melancholy in joy. The adults see through both the visual and the verbal artifice, and, having lost the innocence and naiveté of childhood, become "the wounded" who cry. This wounding loss is prefigured in the "O" of line 7 before the mention of the children, that weighty expletive that anticipates Antonio's refrain at the end of the second chapter. Like the tightrope walkers dancing before death, the "O" in line 7 stands on the edge; it is a sigh, a nullity, but also a completed circle, which death signifies for life, cutting us off like the end of a series, as in the final number of a countdown. The children laugh as the "lovely / Lady" is sliced in half—the macabre dressed up to please—but their "O" will one day come when the illusion of the trick is known. The performers, for their part, side neither with the crying adults nor the laughing children; they are "nonchalant," waltzing with a sense of ease and diversion, as if death did not factor in, not even a "hope of falling down." The performers are caught in the artifice of their performance, and as long as they are performing, as long as they are in the "as if," death does not figure, and no "hope" of escape is open to them. The audience, however, are outside the "as if," and must see both life and death in each performance: the tightrope walk (a death-defying feat of skill and bravery), the clown (duplicitous, punning comedy revealing the tragic), magic (the illusion, through smoke and mirrors, of conquering mortality). The Stage Manager's message is already clear: creation's O will always carry a death at its center. The circus performs a dance of death.

This "O" begins the second stanza: "O what authority gives / Existence its surprise?" The Reason of Brontë's "Plead For Me" poem, as manifested in science, likes to think it can account for these unexpected moments, the ghosts that haunt us, the desire, passion, and bravado of human affairs. But it fails: "Our wonder, our terror remains." Art too would like to claim authority over these moments, but in the third stanza, it is no more successful in satisfying our state of predicament in between the interrogative and the future indicative, between question and resolve. Art's "fishiest eye" (Caliban, etc.) leads only to the maw of the O that "no metaphors can fill." Art forces us into the dark or fiery places where speech is inadequate but heroism required. We hear again Brontë's echo: "*tell why I have chosen thee.*"

But there is no telling in the end. Not only are the Muses quiet, but the divine is itself a place of silence. The final stanza attempts to answer Brontë's question with another question.

> Well, who in his own backyard
> Has not opened his heart to the smiling
> Secret he cannot quote?

But the secret it not always smiling. Or, as in the circus ring, smiles are mixed with sorrow, fear, and trembling. Auden, who immersed himself in Kierkegaard during this period, certainly had *Fear and Trembling* in mind throughout the Preface:

> Thanks! And thanks again, to whoever holds out to one who has been assaulted and left naked by life's sorrows, holds out to him the leaf of the word with which to hide his misery. Thanks to you, great Shakespeare!, you who can say everything, everything, everything exactly as it is—and yet why was this torment [the *horror religiosus* of Abraham] one you never gave voice to? Was it perhaps that you kept it to yourself, like the beloved whose name one still cannot bear the world to mention? For a poet buys this power to utter all the grim secrets of others at the cost of a little secret he himself cannot utter, and a poet is not an apostle, he casts devils out only by the power of the devil.[11]

The O is voiceless, as much for the genius scientist as for the greatest wordsmith. Both "this world of fact" and "the unsubstantial stuff" must give way to an O that utters nothing. "All the rest is silence," as Hamlet had said (V.ii, 342).[12] We meet that silence in the ripeness of our maturity, ready and prepared, as Edgar states in *King Lear* (V.ii, 9–11): "Men must endure / Their going hence, even as their coming hither; / Ripeness is all." Our silence in nonexistence stands ever present before us, as Heidegger taught us; our maturity is our ripeness within the silence, ready to fall to the unknown, the *circulus vitiosus*. Thus, neither Reason nor Imagination wins out in the end, and Brontë was right to doubt. The O wins out: that place where both Reason and Imagination, both the world of fact and the unsubstantial stuff of art, both the divine and the demonic,[13] give themselves over to the negation that is silence.

All this is said to the critics. What, then, are they to make of the performance? As the Stage Manager has been critical of science's and art's capabilities in the face of surprising existence, so he admonishes the critics to beware of their judgments, for those judgments too will ultimately succumb to the O. Following Kierkegaard, Auden's understanding is that only the religious sphere can bring us to this place of disquieting silence on the other side of the wall, not the ethical or the aesthetic. But Auden's O goes farther, for the other side of the wall is in fact *nowhere but within the circle itself.* Auden is, after all, writing a poem/commentary, in whose very boundaries this silence issues forth in resonance. It is the old Derridean problem of how to pass on a secret without betraying it. The secret of silence is meaningless outside of the circle. It is more than just a matter of pointing to it. (How does one point out silence anyway?) It is a matter of creating it, by creating the O.

Prospero to Ariel

The silence of the O is drawn into the first chapter, where Prospero (the artist) bids farewell to Ariel (his art). The three-part poetic speech (and song) is much informed by an existentialism in which the journey beyond the island and upon the sea becomes a journey of the Self into the stark realities of its own nakedness, beyond the drapery of art's performance. Prospero's voice is more polished and mannerly, his songs more witty, than Camus's Dr. Rieux or Sartre's Roquentin. But there is a similar plaintive note sounding across the whole section, as if the impending journey is a weight one would like to unload, a kind of malaise, to which one is nevertheless resigned. Some critics have pointed to autobiographical links, in which Ariel becomes Chester Kallman, Auden's American partner whose infidelity and eventual departure shook Auden profoundly just before *The Sea and the Mirror*'s composition.[14] Others have suggested that, despite Auden's own dislike of Shakespeare's Prospero—"He has the coldness of someone who has come to the conclusion that human nature is not worth much, that human relations are, at their best, pretty sorry affairs"[15]—Auden nevertheless identified deeply with Prospero, and Kirsch quotes Auden's 1947 lecture on *The Tempest*: "That art cannot thus transform men grieves Prospero greatly."[16] Thus, bidding goodbye to Ariel means a harsh separation on several levels. These interpretations certainly have their validity, but there is yet a deeper reason for the plaintive tone. We might recall Blanchot's words that it is the artist who most "obeys the fatality of the circle,"[17] and here in Prospero's speech to Ariel we find this resigned obedience at its most salient. The existential question is one of death and nonexistence, separation of or from oneself, and Prospero, who admittedly may not be the most likable of characters, comes face to face with his own O. The surface of this O is Ariel; its depth Caliban. Prospero now peers beyond the surface, where "death is inconceivable"—art will always aestheticize death, make it something for the living—as he anticipates the recesses below. But as artist, he cannot yet dwell there. He must, in Blanchot's terms, keep that instance of his death in abeyance.[18]

    The relinquishing of art to the void of the O is seen at the beginning of the second stanza:

> But now all these heavy books are no use to me any more, for
>   Where I go, words carry no weight: it is best,
>   Then, I surrender their fascinating counsel
>   To the silent dissolution of the sea
>   Which misuses nothing because it values nothing . . .

The sea now becomes something more than real *life*. It even becomes more than its traditional literary symbol, mortality. It becomes, rather, the primordial negating force that is nevertheless still a *force*, still an effective power. In giving up his books, his arts, Prospero abandons one particular power, "the power to enchant." But this power comes from disillusion, he admits. Art illusions, but by that very fact it also disillusions, in showing us all the more plainly the demarcations between what is our self and what is our not-self. "I am that I am" is Prospero's self-appellation, a usurpation of that divine name which mirrors pure existence back upon itself. But this pure reflection is soon itself negated; what art can do is teach us to us "ask for nothing," and thus to show us that, in staring into its mirror, "All that we are not stares back at what we are." "I am that I am not" is the real refrain, the "ripe" refrain. "*Hold up your mirror, boy,*" Prospero says in his first song, "*One peep, though, will be quite enough.*" We can so easily misperceive our own nakedness as something other than negation.

In the pure economy of this silence and negation, operating in both sea and mirror, nothing would be misused because nothing is valued. This is to say, one can always value nothing two ways: there may be *nought* value; or nothing, qua nothing, may be highly *valued*. The cipher can always work either way. As Prospero speaks his farewell to Ariel, he is trying to come to terms with the second value, as he senses it emerge in the O. But he never truly embraces it. He has a premonition that it lies most emphatically with the "*loud beast*" that is Caliban, Ariel's negative inverse, but he stills sees Caliban as an "impervious disgrace," for whom both he and Ariel hold responsibility. He admits incompetence in knowing what more to do. Prospero here is, in many ways, the quintessential twentieth-century pre-postmodern. And if Auden identified with his Prospero with any degree of intimacy, however reluctantly, he too might also assume this position. For there is a reflective knowing, a glimpse of the negative void that looms within the constructed walls of our temples (be they art, ethics, or religion), but there is misgiving in making that void a private possession. "The journey really exists," but the feet are wary to start. He tells Ariel, "*But should you catch a living eye, / Just wink as you depart,*" but he himself can no longer take this frivolous approach. His own sense of knowing is fraught with Kierkegaardian anxiety and uncertainty:

> . . . shall I ever be able
> To stop myself from telling them what I am doing,—
> Sailing alone, out over seventy thousand fathoms—?
> Yet if I speak, I shall sink without a sound
> Into unmeaning abysses . . .

Before the O, seen now for what it is, one demurs. One abides at the "deferred imminence" of the instant of the O, to alter Blanchot, and Derrida, not too far.[19] The demurring and deferring is by way of speech, by Prospero's own continuing poetic reflections and injunctions (since old habits die hard). "Can I learn to suffer / Without saying something ironic or funny / On suffering?" he wonders. "I never suspected the way of truth / Was a way of silence. . . ." (Ariel gave no forewarning, though Caliban did.) This is a man not completely prepared to launch himself into that silence. This is a man clutching his words tightly, staring at the O, knowing full well it is of his own doing, but hesitating, like the child on the higher diving platform, who having decided to climb, finds he cannot bring himself either to jump or to climb back down. Derrida best captures this dilemma, as he sees it in the later Blanchot: "One thus finds oneself in a fatal and double impossibility: the impossibility of deciding, but the impossibility of remaining [demeurer] in the undecidable."[20] This is Auden's Prospero, perhaps even Auden himself (though whether this poem is fiction or testimony we cannot say), the mid-twentieth-century paragon of liminal demurring before the O. His last request, before he makes his onward way, is of Ariel to sing "Of separation, of bodies and death"—the Ariel for whom death had been inconceivable. It is all too conceivable now: the separation from the one that is ("I") to the one that is not ("O"), a separation we will see again in Ariel's Postscript. Prospero, the artist beyond art, yet beyond only by virtue of being ineluctably within (the "double impossibility"), makes way for this "silent passage" he can never enjoy.

Supporting Cast

In Hegelian terms—and we can never dismiss a Hegelianism filtered through Kierkegaard in this period of Auden—if Prospero is a thesis of artistic accomplishment, even if one on the threshold of abandoning the means to that accomplishment, Antonio, his brother, is his anti-thesis. As usurper of the throne, he comes by this role naturally, and here, well after The Tempest has ended, he continues his subversive ways. It is common to read Antonio as the unrepented or unreformed antagonist, and thus as the evil and disorder that continues to plague this fallen world, and that art in many respects is trying to rehabilitate. Hence, Antonio will place himself outside the circle of art, and claim art is wholly dependent upon his kind. Yet Antonio solicits the O more directly and defiantly than Prospero himself. As anti-thesis, even aesthetic anti-thesis, Antonio understands fully the negating power. Yet he, and he alone, calls the O for what it truly is—"Creation's O." Rather than a mere foil, then, we need to see Antonio, for all his faults, as one who also stands on the threshold of the O. He is the negative inverse of Prospero as the One ("One" is the beginning word in each of his refrains), whose function does not concern artistic accomplishment, but artistic disruption. And this disruption, Antonio says, will be as necessary as the order art traditionally trades upon. In terms of the O, we ought to see Antonio as the orchestrator of its consciousness. Which is why he dominates the second chapter.

This middle section of the commentary involves all "The Supporting Cast," those who have stood inside Prospero's circle of magic. Because they have been enchanted, and in some sense still are enchanted, they speak "Sotto Voce," in a hushed or whispered voice. Their reflections are muted, as if speaking from within a sealed but transparent cage. And thus their world is highly, exaggeratedly artificial. Of the ten poems that make up this display, each differs in length, style, form, meter, rhyme, diction, and tone, relative to the characteristics of each speaker. The second chapter is thus cornucopian, with differing poetic forms spilling forth, waxed and polished in precise arrangement, as if to show the fruit's plastic yet perfectly shaped moulds.

Their order is also significant. Antonio ends his opening poem with a formulaic refrain that will act as a coda to each subsequent poem. These poems alternate between a *courtly* figure and a "low" figure: *Ferdinand,* Stephano, *Gonzalo,* Adrian and Francisco, *Alonso,* Master and Boatswain, *Sebastian,* Trinculo, and *Miranda.* Antonio claims to stand outside this group, for reasons that will soon be evident, and so the group from Ferdinand to Miranda makes up a certain circular arrangement, with Alonso at the bottom half of the circle, and Ferdinand and Miranda at the top half, though not yet joined (the circle is kept apart by Antonio). Lucy McDiarmid sees this circle as a suggestion of "the emotional community and aesthetic harmony of a wedding feast," where the wedding party and guests are joined in a ring of dance, much like the wedding masque in *The Tempest* itself.[21] But as much as Antonio's refrains act to link each character, they also subvert each character, and keep them apart from one another (much as the thought of Caliban disrupts the wedding masque in *The Tempest*). Here, "Auden has his wedding cake and eats it: he includes a wedding feast, and he includes characters who undermine it."[22] So the image of the circle goes beyond that of harmony. What is being joined is also being separated: the O is intercalated by Antonio, the foil of *The Tempest* who, in this existence now beyond the stage, functions dually as both link and severance. He claims to stand outside the circle, but in reality he also stands irrevocably and necessarily within the circle. He enacts the paradox described by the Stage Manager in the Preface: "The lion's mouth whose hunger / No metaphor can fill" is described by the metaphor of the lion's mouth. For all the heightened self-awareness Antonio boasts, his words are still *sotto voce,* caught within artifice. He may intend to subvert, but in doing so he orders as well. And not just through linking up the supporting cast—in his acknowledgment of the void within/without art, Antonio also links chapter 1 (Prospero, who reflects on the threshold of his art), with chapter 3 (Caliban, who reflects outside of Prospero's art). His position is thus integral.

> As all the pigs have turned back into men
> And all the sky is auspicious and the sea
> Calm as a clock, we can all go home again.

Antonio's terza rima sets the scene for the entire middle chapter: the cast are on the boat home to Italy, the weather is the very opposite of a tempest, calm and serene, and the travelers are all about the deck of the craft, meditative and at ease. There is no action to accompany their inner dialogues, only contemplative musing. The magic spells have worn off, the "pigs" have resumed their normal human form, and thoughts turn back toward the island as much as they turn forward toward the sea journey. The picture is a fairy-tale ending, as the two lovers sit kissing, "silhouetted against the sails" like a Hollywood finale, as the comical fool (Trinculo) has gained some worth, as the stock butler (Stephano) has tidied himself, and as the courtly passengers (Alonso, Sebastian) have come off their high horse and learned to be genuine, more genuine than even the rustics. All the characters have found awareness of their own proper place through guilt, humility, thwarted schemes, and folly. The microcosmic world of the Island, now the microcosmic world of the ship, is a neatly arranged vignette, perfect in its felicity and fortune.

In the forefront of this scene Auden places the cynicism and sedition of Antonio. As he usurped the king in Milan, so now Antonio turns upon his brother's artistic rule, and sneers at the seductive power with which the entire scene has come together. Prospero's clear manipulation of the outcome has made his "peace" and "greatness" things to be scoffed at. He deserves no applause because he is stuck in his magic. His wand will always repair itself: incomplete objects will always come together in an appearance of wholeness, and order will always emerge from the chaotic sea, because the desire and power to create order are for Prospero irrepressible. But this desire is only possible because order is lacking in the first place:

> . . . as long as I choose
> To wear my fashion, whatever you wear
> Is a magic robe; while I stand outside
> Your circle, the will to charm is still there.

Antonio still sees Prospero's circle in terms of the O of Giotto. Where Prospero stands on the threshold of a modern O and looks forward, Antonio stands on that same threshold and looks backward. Imperfection, disorder, rebellion, sedition, and subversion will always accompany the vestments of charm, even though charm gives the illusion of winning out in the end. The circle, though looking perfect and complete, remains distorted or broken, as Antonio's refrains attempt to manifest by their disruptive placement among the rest. More, he professes to negate the circle maker himself, as the antithesis by which all charms gain their charm: "As I exist, so you shall be denied." Prospero loses more than his freedom here. Having become the mature artist, "adult in his pride," the parent (and originator) of society, Prospero is caught in the negating space between fabricated order and inexorable disorder, between suspended time and real time. Auden employs the image of a clock in Antonio's poem, in both the first and final stanzas, as if to draw a full circle. Prospero can never rest at "the center / Time turns on when completely reconciled." That place is the suspended time of art, when the encircling hands are nonexistent, and all that remains is the timeless center point, the sea when "Calm as a clock," as in the phrase of the opening stanza. Prospero, adult Prospero, knows too well the sea as a raging tempest, knows too much ever to enter the "green occluded pasture," the framed world of idyllic or idealized art, the "Cockaigne" of his own poem—knows too much to enter it innocently or charmed. His brother is always there to remind him of the space outside the clock's circle, or of the one figure that is not present on the clock's face, but which that face, as circle, represents—zero.

Like the twelve stanzas of his poem, Antonio's refrains all address Prospero. Their framework is consistent: five lines, each ending in the same word or phrase—"Prospero," "my own," "know," "Antonio," and "alone," and all ending, intentionally, on the rhymed vowel "O." Taken together, the words make up the essence of what each refrain is saying: "Prospero, [only does] my own [self] know Antonio alone." Neither you, nor your Giotto's O, can know it or convey it. Here, we might see again Auden's shifted understanding of art, that art is constitutionally limited, and can never show what truly lies in reality. But even Antonio, who claims to be this reality, is no more than a highly artificial acknowledgment of artistic limitation. Thus, we can read Antonio from yet another angle: the reality we think we know or experience may be no more than Antonio, the aesthetic disorder that allows art its aesthetic arrangement, gives it its raison d'être. Antonio is still art, though in his egoism an art that is highly self-conscious of its own internal fractures. This is the art of Blake's devil, the diabolical necessary for salvation. Or it is the art that purposely negates itself. Antonio claims Prospero has no choice but to be art as it strives toward the O of Giotto. "Your all is partial," therefore, since it will always fall short of its goal. Antonio, on the other hand, claims a choice. He can be not-art; he can embrace imperfection. And yet he can only do this in an aesthetic way. (And here Antonio may be represented by much of the anti-art movement of the first half of the twentieth century—Dada, for example.) "I am I, Antonio," he says, in a tidy refutation of Prospero's "I am that I am." Prospero's version is the sovereign creator's claim. Antonio's version simply mirrors the pronoun: "I" am "I." The verb is unrepeated; it is mere copula, joining the subject, the ego, outside of any action. This is what Antonio does in the poem, joining "I"s outside of action. He is no sovereign creator in this regard. The "I"s, and his own "I" especially, are hollow. But he is still deeply aesthetic.[23] Antonio has a great regard for himself—and Auden allows us to treat Antonio as the self-involved, hypocritical antagonist, should we insist—but by the end we see what his "I" is made of—the O of his last refrain. And this O is more than mere aesthetic antagonism.

The journey to this last refrain travels through the poetic contrivances of the remaining characters. Ferdinand's Petrarchan sonnet, with its confused syntax and ambiguous meaning, conveys the young adolescent in love, with his focus on flesh, the opening word. The poem's apparent inaccessibility, the abstraction of physical love to a metaphysical level, was addressed by Auden later in his poem "Dichtung and Wahrheit" (1959), which explored the inability of poetry to return to or translate the original experience and motivating passion of love. The later poem, in fact, was subtitled "An Unwritten Poem," was written in prose paragraphs, and ended: "This poem I wished to write was to have expressed exactly what I mean when I think the words I love you, but I cannot know exactly what I mean; it was to have been self-evidently true, but words cannot verify themselves."[24] Fifteen or so years earlier, in Ferdinand's sonnet, Auden tried to suggest what might happen if such words as I love you were to be true to their original passions: they would necessarily obscure, falter in coherence, or be reduced to a barely scrutable amalgam of epithets and private images. The poem is still written, even within a highly contrived framework, and the words do carry some sense appropriate to its speaker, but the language proceeds as if in a cloud. Antonio, in his refrain, sees through the haze. Ferdinand, driven by lust, however idealized, cannot know the infernal flames of the void. "My person is my own": the "O Light" of artistic love turns to darkness, Antonio says, and the "Dear Other" becomes one's own O.

Stephano's ballade is a "low" counterpart to Ferdinand's heightened passion, in which the gluttonous butler tries to make his own sense of the relationship between mind and matter. His "Dear Other" is his own belly ("dear daughter"), and swollen with drink he asks it, philosophically, "who / is self or sovereign, I or You?" Neither I nor You can answer. Stephano can only repeat: "A lost thing looks for a lost name." Antonio, forever sober, points to the lost name: "One and One alone." What is this One, if neither the mind nor the body, nor any divine Sovereign, nor even Antonio himself as existential reality beyond art? Only the final refrain will tell us what the One really is, as it gives itself over to the O.

Gonzalo, the next to speak, presents a thoughtful meditation in syllabic verse on the experiences of life that hearken death. The calm seas encourage one last backward glance. The linking of "Sea and silence" links Gonzalo to Prospero: "Gonzalo is a variation on the Prospero-Antonio reaction of age to the preparation of death."[25] But where Prospero's sea demands poetic silence, looking ahead, Gonzalo's sea is a place of poetic extension, looking behind. Death for Gonzalo is still an aesthetic matter. What is silenced are his own ideals of innocence and optimism. For "There was nothing to explain," he now realizes. He should have "trusted the Absurd," the unreasonable, inexplicable, insensible force behind all the apparent misfortune, should have abandoned himself to the raw realities, and not padded his songs with false notes. But his false notes remain: there is "nothing to forgive," he feels, because everyone has had their own private storms and self-reformations. Gonzalo, the "ruined tower by the sea," looks back with consolation, having come through his own storm, altered but alive. Death, "The Already There," can now be a comfort, as it comes to the lonely and says "'Here I am,'" and "To the anxious—'All is well.'" We hear the artificer's cry: all's well that ends well. Antonio ridicules Gonzalo's eloquence and utopian poetry: "*One tongue is silent, Prospero, / My language is my own.*" Antonio's has long been in dialogue with his shadowed, dystopian self.

The sideline characters Adrian and Francisco offer a short nursery rhyme–like couplet:

> Good little sunbeams must learn to fly,
> But it's madly ungay when the goldfish die.

Their basic thought is quaint but naive: don't disrupt the wonderful little play, either on stage or off. Antonio can see that these two minor figures have no possible life beyond art. Their theatre is a small circle with no depth. Antonio's drama, by contrast, is forever "censored" by the death that is O.

Alonso's ninety-six-line poem is the longest of the section. It functions as a central pivot for the four poems on either side (excluding Antonio's), "a hinge of the symmetrical pairs" or concentric circles (Ferdinand/Miranda, Stephano/Trinculo, Gonzalo/Sebastian, Adrian and Francisco/Master and Boatswain), "whose speech is about the 'tightrope' or middle way between the sea and the desert, the 'temperate city' precariously balanced between opposite extremes."[26] The eight stanzas model a Horatian epistle in syllabic verse, and are addressed to Ferdinand ("Dear Son"),[27] in a letter to be opened after Alonso's death. The passing king begins by comparing the surface image of kingly rule with the disruptive realities that lie underneath it, described by the picture of a scepter penetrating the surface of the sea to reveal itself to uninterested or oblivious fish below. "Sit regal and erect," he also tells his heir,

> But imagine the sands where a crown
> Has the status of a broken-down
> Sofa or a mutilated statue . . .

Remember that there is a sea (a "cold deep") and a desert (a "sunburnt superficial kingdom") adjacent to every supposedly stable ground. Among the many dualities within this poem, Auden critics have pointed to the central contrast between the sea and the desert here as one between, in Auden own words, "primitive potential" and "actualized triviality," or as Nelson describes it, between "the sea of too little consciousness" and "the desert of too much consciousness," both ideas coming from Auden's later essay about the Romantic use of the symbol of the sea, *The Enchafèd Flood*.[28] The contrast between the king's public image and the reality he must rule continues in the second stanza with things controlled and made safe (a sense of "Progress," zoos, "synchronized" time) and things uncontrolled and dangerous (scorpions, sharks, octopuses, the "ocean flats," and the "desert plain"). In light of such contrasts, "Only the darkness can tell you what / A prince's ornate mirror dare not": the sea brings the tyrannical ruler to ruin, while the desert brings the emperor to naked poverty. The primitive power goes amok and drowns, while the triviality is stripped to show the horrors beneath—both are to be feared, but both, discovered in the darkness of one's dreams, can teach "what you lack." This lesson in psychology (which evokes the O) is in opposition to Ferdinand's own understanding that, like Romeo, in Miranda is where his "omissions" lie; the father tells his son that "as your fears are," and not as your loves are, "so you must hope."

Alonso then returns to the image introduced by the Stage Manager to describe the nature of a sovereign's rule: "The Way of Justice is a tight-rope," negotiated between this hope and fear—just as Alonso's poem is a tightrope negotiated between poems motivated out of hope (Ferdinand, Gonzalo, Sebastian, and Miranda—court life) and fear (Stephano, Adrian and Francisco, Master and Boatswain, and Trinculo—low life). "The Way of Justice" also stands between the sea and the desert, between the left side of one's conscience where "the siren sings" temptingly of peaceful dark waters, and the right side where an evil demon ("efreet") dangles "a brilliant void" in which the mind feels clear and free from all constraint and limitation—just as at the middle point of the poem (lines 47–48 of 96) the young prince must negotiate this narrow traverse, or failing, "soon disappear / To join all the unjust kings" in the abyss below. This center point, which is the center of the chapter and indeed the center of the entire *The Sea and The Mirror*, opens up the "brilliant void" as an O. This O had already been anticipated in Prospero's opening line of his final stanza: "O brilliantly, lightly / Of separation, / Of bodies and death / . . . ," where once again it is far more than an empty and meaningless expletive. It will also be implied as that which subsumes the final "evaporating sigh" of Ariel's final words, which bring the commentary to its close. But here, it is explicitly drawn as a central vortex, seen by the good king as he goes to his death.

In the second half of the letter, Alonso continues to counsel balance between extremes, and warns to trust not the seeming permanencies of a kingdom, but, rather, painful self-reflection (the "darkness" versus the "ornate mirror" of the first half). The sovereign is always precariously perched: the space between the sea and the desert, the "watery vagueness and / The triviality of the sand," is so very slight:

> Remember that the fire and the ice
> Are never more than one step away
> From the temperate city; it is
> But a moment to either.[29]

If the sovereign should falter, he should believe in the reality of his own pain, should be thankful for desert heat and ocean storms. Alonso here speaks of a salvation in facing one's inward conflicts, a purgatorial rinsing where the flesh and the mind are restored and revitalized to a position of trust, as if they had come upon a "spring in the desert" or a "fruitful / Island in the sea." Alonso's belief remains within the Island's O of salubrious charm, where conviction leads to purgation, and purgation to improvement.[30] This is his only real hope.

The passing of sovereignty is at issue here. If the O is to come, it must come as a tonic, as a positive force, as a restorative outcome, as a middle way between perilous extremes. Alonso cannot see beyond *The Tempest* as traditionally read: a romance that, despite dark undertones, ends profitably if uncomfortably well. Should Ferdinand inherit anything, it ought to be self-awareness that leads to hard-earned love, beyond the physical love of Miranda, and to hard-earned peace, beyond the "well-fed pigeons" of the green parks. Death may be present—imminent perhaps, in the case of Alonso—but it will be overcome: the "mutilated statue" will come back to life, and like Leontes before Hermione at the end of *The Winter's Tale*, the illusion will be forgiven in the resurrection. The play's end reveals its true colors. Become like Prospero in his Epilogue, Alonso entreats (and not like Gonzalo, who sees no further need for forgiveness). Indeed, become like Shakespeare himself in all of the last plays, and learn to forgive the performance. The true sovereign knows the O he wears is a crown of thorns that leads to new love and new peace.

"*One crown is lacking*," says Antonio in his refrain. The passing of Alonso's sovereignty leads to lack, not gain. So too does the reinstatement of Prospero's sovereignty. Prospero's arts can no longer furnish forgivable illusions. The new diadem, the one Antonio wears, does not rest on some Aristotelian purgatorial reform or middle mean, nor on some dramatic redemption that reunites the broken and the separated. It binds one even further ("diadem" means literally to bind round) to the dark hour that has no face, the death that is unforgivably final.

The Master and the Boatswain's short poem in lilting tetrameter is a vulgar semblance of domestic stability parodied by whores and their patrons in a sailor's tavern. A yearning for genuine love attempts to rise above lascivious carousal, but is lost in refusal. The Master and the Boatswain undermine any happy ending where lovers embrace in marital bliss. Marriage is mere entrapment. Fast love fills no voids.

> Tears are round, the sea is deep:
> Roll them overboard and sleep.

The cheap erotic O yields a maudlin and barren self. Its tears fall to nothing. Only sleep can drown the emptiness. Antonio's O goes well beyond this kind of cheap pathos and stupor. His compass encircles a different sea, his eye a different void.

Sebastian's poem is an elaborate sestina, with repeated words ending each line—"dream," "sword," "day," "alive," "proof," and "crown"—in variant order per stanza. In direct contrast to the poem it follows, Sebastian's thoughts *come* to consciousness (not depart from it), as if he has woken from a sleep, and from an unrealizable dream.[31] Now "it is day," and the visions of overthrowing his brother's throne have crumbled, like Coleridge's vision of Kubla Khan. But for Sebastian, "Nothing has happened" and everyone is still alive. There is nothing then to rescue or re-envision. Not even his depraved nature. His awakened self-consciousness is not a result of his rehabilitation, nor is it toward rehabilitation: "I am Sebastian, wicked still, my proof / Of Mercy that I wake without a crown." Sovereignty is for Sebastian desire of a dream fulfilled; but unlike Prospero, who wakes to "unanswered wishes" as if waking from a dream of some "tremendous journey" only to find the "journey really exists" (*Prospero to Ariel*), Sebastian's journey is simply to accept his error in believing that such sovereignty was ever possible. He does not repent, and certainly does not forgive.

The unattainability of sovereignty for Sebastian leads to a notionally negative nothing. "Nothing"—he capitalizes it—is a lie, a false promise to shadows, desire, and weakness. "O blessed by bleak Exposure": his O is about bringing the lie to light, and principally his own lie and failure. There is nothing redeeming in the exposure (unlike for Alonso), and if there is any hope, it lies only in being shamed. His failure is proof that the happy scene around the boat is "no lover's dream," that the O conjures no illusion, only disillusion. Sebastian sums up his thought in the poem's envoi (as all the six repeated words come together): "dream," where "all sins are easy," is contrasted with "day," where "defeat gives proof we are alive"; it is only through the suffering "sword" of self-inflicted wounds and naked exposure that we can see our lack as preferable. But Sebastian's lack is not the pure nothing of the O. He cannot peer beyond his own cracked surface. He is merely happy to see himself alive amid all the cracks.

Antonio calls his partner in arms "*Pallid Sebastian,*" a pale imitation of the real O. Antonio's "*face cries nothing,*" the pure nothing, the cracks in all their depth and void, yielding no face of empty compunction and fruitless dreams, but the blank face of no thing. If Antonio harbors any dreams of fanciful making, they are ones in which he "*Fights the white bull alone.*" He is his own adversary.

As Sebastian is the courtly inverse of Gonzalo, his symmetrical other from the chapter's first half, so Trinculo the jester is the low inverse of Stephano, the drunken butler. But Trinculo's low station as clown brings us closer to the O than any of the courtly figures. As with all of Shakespeare's court jesters—Lear's Fool is our best example—the penetration of comic insight dissolves the hierarchy of "high" and "low," and sovereignty is corrected, humbled, admonished, advised without a public fall from grace. Trinculo regains his stature here from the drunken knave he plays in *The Tempest.* He is an artist of sorts, "Whose head is in the clouds," and his jokes and witticism warm the crowds (at all societal levels, "Mechanic, merchant, king"). But he is also the tragic clown of the Preface, who stands in the circus ring as the paradox of sadness and smiles. The children laugh, but the adults cry. His six four-line trimetrical stanzas may have a jocular rhythm, but Trinculo speaks out of fear, the comic who cannot enjoy his own comedy, "the cold clown," all too aware of the "Nobody" he references in the original play (III, ii, 125).

The joke distances, we have said. This is why we can laugh at ourselves in a comic's routine—humor sets us apart from our own being. The jokester lives with this separation internally and perpetually. Trinculo remains in solitude, ungrounded, insubstantial—like Ariel, though thoroughly and irremediably human. "My history, my love, / Is but a choice of speech." Like the rest of the low figures, Trinculo claims no "I am. . . ." His existence is

predicated upon a pun, a witticism, a clever turn of phrase, an ironic gesture. He lives for the single punch line, but the joke comes from a negating
place that disrupts all unity. In his height he is shaken by terror, and humor
flies out of his branches, winged not by pleasure but by fright. The final
stanza is the joker's invocation to his Muse. His call is not to the divine,
but to "Wild images." Their place is not a heaven but a "freezing sky." His
entreaty is not for inspiration but merely to "get my joke and die." The
audience may die laughing, but the jester longs to die as way of release from
the terror. Prospero, the "high" artist, wonders if he "Can learn to suffer /
without saying something ironic or funny / On suffering" (*Prospero to Ariel*).
Trinculo, the "low artist" knows that saying something funny is sourced in
suffering. The "one" that is supposed to constitute the joke's structure is
in fact haunted by an O at its center. Trinculo is the clown of the *Preface*
who, himself wounded more than any in the crowd, desires to leap through
the "O" and into the lion's mouth no witty words can fill. Then, and only
then, will he get his own joke.

Antonio hears the "*jarring*" note of Trinculo's strain, as it stands out
of tune with the rest. Trinculo is "*Tense*," like the paradoxes and ironies he
employs. Antonio, not in the sky, but "in woods," laughs at his own jokes
amid the shaking trees of his own dark paradox. Of course, he himself is a
jarring note in his own refrains. He, with Trinculo, remains out of tune with
the rest. And yet, paradoxically, Antonio is hardly alone. He surrounds the
entire supporting cast, as if a circular forest, shading each character with
the "one" that is, ultimately, not one.

This one, as One, emerges into clear light in the chapter's final poem
by Miranda, with its opening and repeating line: "My Dear One is mine
as mirrors are lonely." The poem, a villanelle, is contrived in extreme: five
tercets and one quatrain in syllabic verse (eleven syllables per line), with
two entire lines (a^1 and a^2) repeated in a prescribed pattern (a^1ba^2, aba^1,
aba^2, aba^1, aba^2, aba^1a^2), and a rhyme scheme where the first and third lines
always rhyme with "sea" and the middle second line always with "king." The
poem is a culmination of all the contrived forms that have gone before it.
And yet, as exaggerated artifice, it also still leads us to the O.

"My Dear One is mine as mirrors are lonely." While Ferdinand, with
his "Dear Other," objectifies his love, Miranda, with her "Dear One," sub-
jectifies and unifies hers. This One may be seen to contrast Antonio's "one"
that opens each of his refrains, that egotistical one that can never see beyond
its own mirror image. As McDiarmid argues, both Ferdinand's and Miranda's
poems "begin at the point where the ego ends, in a compassionate love."[32]
But this compassionate love is still bound by the frame of artifice. Mirrors are
lonely without someone looking into them; and when someone is looking,
narcissism prevails. But mirrors are also lonely because, like our eye, they can

never see themselves or their own reflection. Miranda thinks that by using this image of the lonely mirror, she can contrast her own experience, and manifest true love for her Dear One, into whose eye she looks directly. But of course, she must use the mirror image, and use it negatively, to describe this true love. As Auden states later in the *Dichtung and Wahrheit*, true love, when reflected upon, is inescapably aesthetic. It inevitably holds up another mirror. Miranda's reflection, then, can only be of herself reflecting. Her "One," "mine," and "lonely" are, in effect, an image of herself. And this, ironically, she cannot see.

What Miranda also cannot see is the O of the mirror she employs. Her One becomes present to her only insofar as the mirror absents the Other. The apophaticism of her image undercuts the sovereignty of the singular possession. Auden is setting us up for the O to follow in Antonio's final refrain. Miranda can no longer possess the One, because she never could. It was always undone by the "O" with which the One begins.

The lines that join this repeated refrain reveal Miranda's young mind, and its inability to grasp the O. "And the high green hill sits always by the sea" is the second repeated refrain, and this too juxtaposes contrasting elements, the verdant solid ground with the changeable watery sea, permanence with mutability, order with chaos. Trinculo has just told us what terrors shake the heights. She is no safer above than below. Yet for her any such terrors are tame realities, goodly things in the end. Caliban, "the Black Man," has no foul or salacious intent, only a playful regard, with a somersault and a wave. Caliban's mother, Sycorax the witch, though venomous, dissipates into air as if only a specter. Her father, "the Ancient," has been a model of virtue, while her Prince Charming kissed her awake without any malcontent from those looking on. "The sun shone on sails, eyes, pebbles, anything." The entire island, their place of paradise, where great changes took place (though none lapsarian)—the young bride-to-be sees them all joined as if in a hymeneal ring, "linked as children in a circle dancing," singing the immutable (and circular) refrains she herself has been singing throughout her poem:

> My Dear One is mine as mirrors are lonely,
> And the high green hill sits always by the sea.

She is unaware that this circle is the artificer's circle, where her charmed little innocence has its fragile run. It is the place out of time, the faceless clock. It is the round speculum framing the crack, the "O" whose center is a void, a nullity, an abyss. All of which she is blind to.

And she is most blind to Antonio, and to the circle's incompletion that is a result of his insertions: "*One link is missing, Prospero, | My magic is my own.*" Without Antonio's poem at the outset, Miranda could join hands with her lover as the circle came round. But the chief antagonist stands in the way. He does not let "*Happy Miranda*" have her happy way. The circle remains broken and imperfect. He dances his own "*figure*" within the happy "O" of the hymeneal ring. This is the zeroed figure, the disruptive figure, inside yet out of step. And so, in this final refrain, even his own pattern is disrupted, as an additional sixth line is added to his usual five, a line that qualifies all other lines, and brings his role to a culmination, just as it brings Miranda's "Dear One" to face its own lonely reflection: "*The only One, Creation's O.*"

The only One is an O. But it is not just any O. It is *Creation's O*. At the heart of all Antonio's antithesis, his self-absorbing negation, his dance of death, is a *creation*. Antonio has never claimed to stand outside art; he has only claimed to stand outside *Prospero's* art, the art of Giotto's O. But clearly Antonio is as bound to artifice as any other. He is, we might even say, the very *binding* of that artifice, the linkage, though linkage that brings together and separates in one and the same action. In his framing he himself is framed. And his own frame betrays an empty core, negated as it is negating. But by that very negating, it opens us up to a purely new creative space, one that Prospero himself has not even seen. This space, *Creation's O*, Antonio himself, is the very space Caliban will fill. But like an eye that cannot see its own seeing, or a mirror that cannot see its own reflection, Antonio cannot image Caliban. Antonio remains part of the *sotto voce*, the whispering form, or frame. Caliban must burst forth outside of Antonio's vision. But of course, that outside is totally inside, the "brilliant void" at the center of Alonso's poem, and thus of Antonio's concentric ring structure, and thus of the commentary as a whole.

Caliban to the Audience

Caliban, as the "brilliant void," as the negating power of the O that opens us up to creation, is the pinnacle of the commentary's elaborate edifice. Yet he does not speak to his fellow characters, but to us, the audience (even *as* or *for* us the audience). Prospero addresses Ariel, Antonio addresses Prospero, but Caliban must stand outside this dimension of the artifice. He is not, in Auden's hands, a person of the artifice, nor is he the artifice personified. He is the blank space that makes the artifice possible. Thus, like the Preface, he turns to face this side of the curtain. The Stage Manager had spoken to the critics, those who must, because of their position as judges, be unwilling to suspend disbelief. Caliban speaks to the general public, those who not only are willing but who have paid money to suspend disbelief. Caliban moves the discussion back off the stage, but the discussion is always and only about the stage, about "staginess."

The separation or boundary between stage and audience, the grand proscenium arch, first appears to be the dividing line within Caliban's speech, by which actors and onlookers, "artifice" and "reality," "mirror" and "sea," all find their appropriate and inexchangeable places. This binary structure we have seen Auden employ repeatedly, and here in Caliban's speech it resurfaces as if now the defining framework for the entire commentary. But the proscenium, as threshold, soon crumbles under its own weight. Like Antonio, *Creation's O,* who both combines and separates, Caliban becomes his own grand artificer who divides and merges, who builds up and tears down. Prospero, we might have thought, could he fulfil his request and get outside the bounds of his own creation, is the one to play this dual role, he who staged the drama and knows best where all the smoke and mirrors lie. But Prospero is gone from the scene. Caliban brings the commentary to its grandest height. Why does Caliban succeed where Prospero does not? Why does Caliban receive the most elevated, most self-conscious, most self-reflective voice? Would not even Ariel be a better choice for such an extended reflection on the nature of staginess itself? Why, if void's negation, does Caliban become the supreme manifestation of stagecraft looking into its own eyes?

Caliban's speech mirrors the "commentary" as a whole: it contains a preface, three main sections, and a qualifying postscript, and each section correlates with the issues put forward in *The Sea and the Mirror's* three parts. In the preface (the first paragraph), Caliban announces himself as Prospero's best and only spokesman, and sets out the main concern to be faced, just as the Stage Manager sets out in the Preface the main questions to be "commented" upon. In the first section, Caliban assumes the voice of the audience, as they in turn address the playwright, Shakespeare. Like Prospero in his speech, the audience make a clear distinction between their own "blancmange" world and the "Cockaigne" world of art, as they try to hold the two worlds forever apart. In the second section, Caliban speaks to an apprenticing artist in the audience who has come to the performance to learn. Like Antonio in "The Supporting Cast," the young artist soon finds that art has a disturbing dark hole. In the third section, Caliban speaks to the general audience, mirroring his own entire speech in radical self-reflection. In the postscript (the final paragraph beginning with "Yet"), Caliban speaks on behalf of all—players, audience, and himself alike—as together everyone seeks to reach that which ultimately the performance cannot reach, the "Wholly Other Life," just as Ariel seeks, vainly, in the Postscript. The ostensible point of the commentary, insofar as there is a

point, is set forth in this final paragraph, before Ariel has one final sigh.
But Caliban's point is less a thesis as it is a position. As the negating
power within which art finds its genesis, Caliban's "Wholly Other" is not
some inaccessible reality, a noumena of a completely incommensurate and
foreign nature outside the frame of our mirrored existence. The "Other"
is part of the mirror's mirroring (of itself), and thus gains a meaning that,
paradoxically, can only be spoken of or spoken about inside the frame—its
own reconstructed O.

Caliban's speech, then, is about the dissolution of the boundary
between our concept of One (as one's own) and Other. It is, therefore,
about a shift from One to O, whereby the O is not a newly arrived-at
reality or entity that displaces and replaces the concept of One (as one's
own or as the unity of coherence that allows us to be our own, our *amour
propre*), but a position or (re-)positioning of our values so that the One's
sovereignty is lost to a space whose very negation allows for (re-)creation
to take place. Thus, Caliban's voice, as expression of the O (in distinction
to Antonio, consciousness of the O), is artifice in its extreme, an artificially
ornate and grandiloquent prose, which comments on the nature of *poesis*
with such deliberate self-reflexivity that it reveals the paradox of expressing
the nothing of the voiding O (the lion's mouth no metaphor can fill). Let
us see, finally, how this expression emerges.

Caliban begins, with the final curtain lowered and the "hired imper-
sonators" (all but the Stage Manager) dismissed, by addressing the audience,
who have called for Shakespeare to come forward. He relays the impossibility
of the playwright ever to appear, and presents himself as the only voice to
answer their pressing question, their "bewildering cry," which concerns, as
it must, the very presence of Caliban in the first place. He then offers himself as the audience's echo, becoming the embodiment of this "bewildering
cry." As Ariel becomes the echo of Caliban in the Postscript to follow, the
echo generated from behind The Tempest's curtain, Caliban is the echo of
the people *this* side of the curtain, the disturbing echo from another kind
of stage, the stage we have long insisted is our "reality" but which, Caliban
must impress, is always caught up within its own artifice. As "echo," Caliban
manifests the artificiality, the already secondary nature, of the audience's
primary "real" world.

The audience, caught in the rhetorical flair of Caliban's prose ("The
whole point about the verbal style," Auden explained, "is that, since Caliban
is inarticulate, he has to borrow, from Ariel, the most artificial style possible, i.e. that of Henry James"[33]), demand a reckoning from the Bard. His
own personification of creativity, Prospero, has asked us for an indulgence,
but how, the audience ask, could Shakespeare have the gall to request such
a thing after he has imprisoned us "in the doubtful mood" by introducing

Caliban into the pages of his supposed farewell? Theatre, they say, works by solidifying the rough waters of reality into the smoothness of an ice pond, by skating "full tilt toward the forbidden incoherence" beyond the ice, but at the last minute, "on the shuddering edge of the bohemian standardless abyss," making a "breathtaking triumphant turn." Theatre cannot and should not cross the line, lest it ruin that "miraculous suspension" of reality by which the audience, novice and expert alike, become enraptured. It is appalling to see Caliban present, for he represents the clear crossing of the boundary, the manifestation of negation ("*not* sympathizing, *not* associating, *not* amusing"), the singular offspring of "unrectored chaos."

The audience invoke their own Muse to press their case. (The audience refuse to give up the notion of a Muse, and betray their fundamental aesthetic nature by calling upon "our native Muse" to support their cause.) But her role has already changed: no longer the inspiration of poetic making, she plays the arbiter of good standard in art's "mixed perfected brew." Working for the public weal, she has made every effort to shut out the Calibans of our existence, for she knows the immense disruption of their intrusion: destroying the vision of love and justice, disturbing the carefully ordered arrangements, and threatening the very purity of inspiration itself. The entire house of cards would come crashing down. How then could Shakespeare knowingly let such a creature loose within his art?

The audience insists on maintaining a strict divide between daily existence and theatrical presentation.

> Into that world of freedom without anxiety, sincerity without loss of vigour, feeling that loosens rather than ties the tongue, we are not, we reiterate, so blinded by presumption to our proper status and interest as to expect or even wish at any time to enter, far less to dwell there.

The whole point is that the play should not speak directly to us, that it remain another world, where universals apply universally, time is elastic and uninhibiting, moral law is fixed, inner life is easily translatable, disorder is tidied, problems are solved with exactness, and everyone in the end arrives back from the journey "safe and sound in the best of health and spirits and without so much as a scratch or bruise." The theatrical stage is not, nor cannot be, our real domain; it is merely a domain for the moment, a divertimento we enter and leave freely and without anxiety. Like Prospero, we call Ariel the "unanxious one." The bastard son of chaos, of fear and trembling, does not belong at Ariel's side.

Our *real* domain necessarily stands outside the artist's circle. It thus requires a third-person voice, a generic one, who contrasts with art's always

personified One. We only ever live in a segment of a circle, whose boundaries are defined either naturally (the "river" of what we inherently feel
is honest and sensible) or culturally/politically (the "railroad" of what we
feel is necessary to maintain our standards). These become our defining yet
"prohibitive frontiers." Of course, we must live around some sense of a public
whole—our boundaries constructed around the coordinates of instinct (the
vertical "river") and logic (the horizontal "railroad") demand this—but our
private realms are where we make sense of this "Whole" in the first place,
that is, in our limited personal visions and "local idioms." Thus, our circle
can never be complete and perfect: the O of Giotto is never our experience. Whatever partial circles we inhabit, they are not in art's reserve. Even
Shakespeare must admit that, had the fortunes of Time been less kind, a
greater talent might have survived, and created a more perfect circle into
which we now prefer to enter. The Tempest survives not because it is closer
to reality, but because reality, in all its vicissitudes, and because of its vicissitudes, has found room for it. The "O" of the Globe offers a reprieve from
the jagged lines and asymmetry amid which we are forced to live.

So the echoing Caliban points to the one image that Shakespeare
himself used to describe the relationship between the artist's circle and the
audience's seat, the "mirror held up to nature" (Hamlet, III, ii). Still speaking
for the audience, he throws the metaphor back at Shakespeare:

> You yourself, we seem to remember, have spoken of the conjured
> spectacle as "a mirror held up to nature," a phrase misleading in its
> aphoristic sweep but indicative at least of one aspect of the relation
> between the real and the imagined, their mutual reversal of value,
> for isn't the essential artistic strangeness to which your citation of
> the sinisterly biased image would point just this: that on the far
> side of the mirror the general will to compose, to form at all costs
> a felicitous pattern becomes the necessary cause of any particular
> effort to live or act or love or triumph or vary, instead of being as,
> in so far as it emerges at all, it is on this side, their accidental effect?

Though the image of the mirror biases the "real" (nature) over the
"imagined" (artifice), it at least shows that each is the reverse in value of
the other. This binary reversal is not only one of "real" versus "artificial,"
"substance" versus "specter," or "reflected" versus "reflection." It also involves
how one accounts for poesis, the creative impetus. The "general will to
compose" points to the origin of poesis in its originary form. How does one
locate this origin? For the audience, it is through the mirror image. On the
far side of the mirror (that is, in the mirror itself) the general will to compose
is the necessary cause of living: only in art can art's originary powers be the

basis on which the rest of our lives are lived and understood. But on this side of the mirror (that is, *before the mirror*), the general will to compose, inasmuch as it appears at all, is merely an accidental *effect* of living out our daily and mundane existence. The audience acknowledges this much: which of the two takes precedence, the creating or the living (and by extension the creation or the nature we must live in), is less a matter of *truth* than it is of *values*. There are two planes to the mirror, and Shakespeare at least shows us that we may value the two differently. What is unconscionable is to conflate the two planes. The "spirit of reflection," Ariel on the far side, must not invade our realm by calling attention to himself and giving away the magician's secrets, for then all sense of public propriety (which depends on concealments) would dissolve. Caliban on this side must not, for his part, invade the far side of the mirror, for otherwise the performance could never maintain "universal reconciliation and peace," the picture-perfect finish. Allowing one to roam in the other's territory, allowing the boundary between Caliban and Ariel to disappear, simultaneously violates both worlds. Shakespeare's audacity to allow such a thing ruins the entire spell of his magic. Worse, Shakespeare not only lets Caliban into the imaginary world, but lets Ariel go free into the real world. Caliban is unaccounted for at the play's end; but the intrusion of the "real" on the "imaginary" is nothing compared to that of the "imaginary" on the "real." Yes, the audience wonders where Caliban got to. But more seriously, what has Shakespeare done with Ariel? For if we dislike the severity of the "real" in our moments of performance, we surely cannot suffer the extravagance of the "imaginary" in our everyday existence: "breaking down our picket fences in the name of fraternity, seducing our wives in the name of romance, and robbing us of our sacred pecuniary deposits in the name of justice."

The audience demands a separation be maintained at all costs. But in and by their very demand, Caliban, their voice and embodiment, negates that demand, and indeed that separation. For in fact, no separation has ever existed. Though there is a boundary, a proscenium arch, between art's colorful, careless existence and our drab, weary existence, both realms, the mirror and the sea, are necessarily framed, are staged areas, and the only real difference between the two "framings" is not in their proximity to "truth" but in the way we place value on them. The audience values art as an escape from the constrictions of Time and anxiety. It values its everyday mortal life as the place of defining particularities, of "prohibitive frontiers" without which "we should never know who we were or what we wanted." As Prospero resigns himself to the sufferings of Milan, the audience too knows it must always resign itself to the world beyond the lights of the theatre. As Prospero leaves Ariel behind to take alone his homeward journey, so too must the audience. But to come to the theatre and find that Caliban

and Ariel walk hand in hand as one entity—our real world mucking about
in our artifice, and our artifice dallying about in our real world—this is
an atrocity for which we are not prepared. This kind of O, a thoroughly
self-negating O, a Globe emptied of the One thing we felt defined us, we
cannot countenance, much less indwell.

In the second section of his speech, Caliban returns to his "officially
natural role" as himself—but what is that role, if not self's dis-accredita-
tion?—and addresses now the neophyte artist. The reoccurring image here
is that of the magician, a conjuror creating illusions with an "artistic con-
traption." The young artist has responded to Ariel's cry for help, and by
releasing him from imprisonment, a "liberators face" now congratulates him
from the "shaving mirror every morning." Ariel, the "spirit of reflection,"
has brought not only self-reflection, but consciousness of the mirror, the
tool by which the artist must now make magic. The partnership with Ariel
soon steams over, and yet despite any and all entreaty, Ariel will not leave.
Why? Because Ariel no longer resides strictly within the mirror's frame. This
is a cutting realization:

> Striding up to Him in fury, you glare into His unblinking eyes and
> stop dead, transfixed with horror at seeing reflected there, not what
> you had always expected to see, a conqueror smiling at a conqueror,
> both promising mountains and marvels, but a gibbering fist-clenched
> creature with which you are all too unfamiliar, for this is the first
> time indeed that you have met the only subject that you have,
> who is not a dream amenable to magic but the all too solid flesh
> you must acknowledge as your own; at last you have come face to
> face with me . . .

Ariel has become Caliban. The artist stares in the mirror and no longer
finds his own conquering face staring back, but his own negation, the gross
brutishness and unruliness of the rogue Caliban. As Antonio's refrains had
echoed the inescapability of mortality, the "Dance of Death," after each of
the highly stylized poems of The Sea and the Mirror's middle section, so the
artist comes to see the Caliban beast in the eyes of Ariel here in this middle
section of Caliban's speech. Reflection has turned on the artist: what was
thought to be "a mirror held up to nature" is really a mirroring of Caliban,
but of Caliban mirroring real life mirroring art (or mirroring art mirroring
real life). Caliban and Ariel frame each other, the one dependent on the
other, like Antonio and Prospero ("as long as I choose / To wear my fashion,
whatever you wear / Is a magic robe"). The one, in fact, being the other.

And now we reach the place of the O in all its culminating form.
Art is in reality as much as reality is in art: each invades the other with

a consummate mutuality. And yet in this invasion and mutuality both are negated. This negation does not mean that both are somehow, in their original forms, wrong or weak or inadequate. On the contrary, they are both, as original form, wholly right, wholly adequate. It is just that they cannot sustain themselves in this original form, cannot sustain their origin as origin. The origin is always being zeroed out. Xanadu is always fading away, always in need of rebirth. The O is always and forever present, negating both the positive and the negative with an indifference that leaves neither side the same as before.

Caliban, in admonishing the artist's own intentions, now summons the essential mathematical nature of his own existence. The artist—Shakespeare better than most—can erect the finest of brackets around the space in which life and death cohabit, and before which either a plus or minus sign might stand. We can value life or death either way, with positive or negative interpretation, according to its presentation (aesthetic and otherwise), but true art (Ariel) knows how best to work these signs, knows how and when it is best to make the switch. And yet—"*the one exception, the sum no magic of His can ever transmute, is the indifferent zero.*" Here we italicize Caliban's words, because here is Caliban at his barest, his most naked, his most transparent, his most emphatic. The O between the brackets, completely indifferent either to plus or to minus, is itself intransmutable. The O sits between the brackets as neither one nor the other, as neither One nor the Other. The O, the 0, is the threshold between either spheres—or, the cipher that lets either sphere emerge. The O is thus outside of our binary spheres of experience, but it is outside only by being wholly and completely inside, as the pure possibility of space, of division, of figuration, and of value. It is negation, then, of a purely proactive kind, a negation not associated with the minus signs we construe as the nugatory or malign negation before the bracket. The artist, in confusion—the portrait of Caliban's young artist—might try either to destroy this O or to let it destroy itself, but either response mistakes an inexorable and necessary force for one that the worthy aspirant must keep at a wary distance. With Ariel having given way, "you are left alone with me," says Caliban, "the dark thing you could never abide to be with." The only hope of getting on is to forgive and forget that this confusion of beings ever existed, "and to keep our respective hopes for the future within moderate, very moderate, limits." These limits are, of course, Auden's new understanding of what art can and cannot do, what art should and should not strive for. But these limits are also *limit* itself, that boundary that represents the coming together of separation and propinquity, the coterminality of division and fusion, of ending and beginning, of negative and positive, of Caliban and Ariel. It is a moderate limit, because ultimately it is a completely indifferent limit, an indifference that takes moderation to a new level of compromise for all sides in the equation, whether "reality" and "art," or any of the manifold dualities we might construct.

So then, if the first section of Caliban's speech established that frames exist around both the "sea" and the "mirror," the second section establishes that Ariel's framing gives way to Caliban's O, the indifferent zero that makes creation possible. When Caliban turns back to the viewing public in the third and final part of the speech, now not on behalf of the public themselves, but on behalf of Ariel and himself as a single entity, he resorts back to the binary language of the first section. The middle has opened up the hole for the artist to see, the gaping O in all its naked emptiness, but now, back with the audience, Caliban must speak the language the audience in their habitual ways can only understand. The binary is now complicated by passage through the middle section, but the audience still only relates to the dual nature of the journey. So they "detect the irreconcilable difference between my reiterated affirmation of what your furnished circumstances categorically are, and His [Ariel's] successive propositions as to everything else which they conditionally might be." This is an advance: to recognize a more entangled, less delusive relationship between life and art. But their grasp of the situation remains bound to a binary formulation in which their attempts out of the "Grandly Average Place" can be guided still by the two poles of desire, Caliban, that which we "categorically are," and Ariel, that which we "conditionally might be." But in choosing either, they choose a destination beyond the duality from which they began—beyond all division and category, all tense and mood. This is Caliban's real message to those who have no experience with the creative O. The lion's mouth awaits them either way.

Public transportation—a train journey—becomes the guiding metaphor. At the station, trains come and go. Yet our most significant experiences are not had while actually riding one of these trains to an imaginary "Somewhere." They are had while waiting for it in the waiting room of habitual "Nowhere," occupied by the most mundane and forgettable tasks and thoughts. In the "Nowhere" we have a right to stagestruck hope, but the moment we leave, we enter a foreign and uncomfortable place where both Ariel and Caliban will be compelled to grant everything we ask and command. This to our detriment. Caliban therefore suggests we remain exactly where we are, in the cold, dark, lonely terminus. For our Nowhere, the O tells us, is always, and has always been, inhabited by a Somewhere.

But humans being humans, we will seek our escape. "Release us from our minor roles," we insist. Should we approach Caliban for deliverance, his route of escape, as measured within the dual framework we try to hold him to here, will only lead to a "purely arithmetical disorder," a place isolating in its "windless rarefied atmosphere" and "secular stagnation," our questions falling to utter silence and our tears to empty consolation. Here, we see "Liberty" for what it truly is: thorough disinterestedness. "Facts" and "values," the stuff of our previous meaning, fall to oblivion. Caliban, in complying with our request to be delivered from "every anxious possibility," has no choice but to deliver us precisely to "every anxious possibility." We find ourselves in a place *not* what we categorically are, a place in which our existence is "free at last to choose its own meaning . . . through silence fathomless and dry."

Should we approach Ariel as our guide, as do the more successful in life, who feel Ariel's way is more noble and "spiritual," we are in for no less a surprise. Here, success has proven a futile end, and we seek deliverance from the messy particularities of life that keep ruining our cause. The conditional way of life—as if, could be—is the condition beyond the affront of the untidiable fact, and in seeking this route we are really seeking to return back to the glories of the all-abiding One. Translate us, we ask, into the "Heaven of the Really General Case," unhampered by time, space, motion, dependency, individuality, or mortality. Here, Caliban, the undifferentiated O, again putting words into our mouth, translates for us our desire as that for the old conceptual unity, where

[l]ife turns into Light, absorbed for good into the permanently stationary, completely self-sufficient, absolutely reasonable One.

Ariel, the "what we might be," will guide us to this Neoplatonic ideal. What we in fact reach, however, as Ariel obliges our request, is anything but this spiritual repose of the universal. We are led instead into a nightmare where "All voluntary movements are possible," all modes of transportation available, where, that is, action is supreme, but where any sense of direction, origin or destination is completely lacking. Religion and culture might tell us something is missing, but there is no way to isolate or universalize what that something is. Other selves may exist, but there is no way of knowing who or what is genuine or ingenuine. Love might be performed, but true motives are forever uncertain. The mind might express itself, but either in anxious restraint or delirious babble. The only possible relief is to ride "toward a grey horizon of the bleaker vision," a dark hard place of personal undoing, a Kierkegaardian agony where existence can find an unequivocal meaning only by losing itself in fear and despair. Ariel's conditional mood is a negative "Not Yet" that leads directly back to Caliban.

By unveiling these alternative routes, Caliban reveals nothing other than their common end. But this terminus is not yet the brilliant void of the middle section, the indifferent zero of Creation's O. The audience have simply come to a place of existential dread, a precipice at the edge of this O. Here at least we may see and acknowledge the artist's great dilemma, if nothing else: in trying to show us our "condition of estrangement from the truth," the artist (Shakespeare, "the dedicated dramatist") necessarily fails, for the more truthful he is in its depiction, the less clear is the truth from which we are estranged; the brighter he shows truth in its order, justice, and joy, the fainter his picture of our actual drab condition; the more true he is to his artistic gift (to show the gap between what we are and what we might become), the more, that is, he defines the estrangement itself, the more he must delude us "that an awareness of the gap is in itself a bridge," that looking at our "defects in his mirror" is an unshakable affirmation of ourselves.

Caliban, in trying to describe the age-old gap between the human and the divine—for is this not the ultimate binary all others reduce down to?—can only admit that it is one that words in the end cannot express. The best an artist can hope for is "an unpredictable misting over of his glass or an absurd misprint in his text." While attempting to recreate life, the artist must all the while hope that something will show up his or her recreation as false. This something is Caliban himself, which is exactly why he holds forth here at the end, and becomes himself the artist "Beating about for some large loose image to define the original drama" while hoping "some unforeseen mishap will intervene to ruin his effect." He is his own ruin. As such, he reflects back to us the substance of his speech as a whole: the mishap of *The Tempest,* related in baroque language that attempts to capture the original drama, but only by means of negating it, by reflecting it anew, by commenting upon it. To this end, he unveils that *both* sides of the mirror are a shared space, that as much as our "original drama" was "original," it was still nevertheless "drama," that we are *all* actors on a "worldly stage," that there is no stage/audience distinction, and that our performance, the performance of "reality," where pains are felt and wounds leave scars, is "of the greatest grandest opera rendered by a very provincial touring company indeed." Our production and delivery has been appallingly bad, and as the curtain falls we all stand "down stage with red faces and no applause." And to conclude the show, Caliban returns us to the very beginning, where the Stage Manager stood before the critics. Our production, with ourselves as our own silent audience, stands as an utter disaster, for which not a kind a word is deserved from any critic. All is incompetence. And so the question in Brontë's epigraph of the title page is raised again: "Am I wrong to worship where / Faith cannot doubt nor Hope despair / Since my own soul can grant my prayer?" The answer is now a resounding "Yes." The Imagination of Ariel leads directly to the O of Caliban. If there is a divine aspect to this O, it is not one that grants the pious their prayers.

A final word, a kind of postscript, remains in Caliban's speech (as it does in the commentary). Speaking now to all and on behalf of all—actors, players, artists, critics, managers, the entire range of theatregoers, Ariel, and himself—Caliban, the artificer within whose drawn circle is the very magic he intends to conjure, does a significant turn in his final paragraph. He tries to articulate the O. He has led us to the edge of the abyss, "swaying out on the ultimate wind-whipped cornice that overhangs the unabiding void," and has told us only silence here reigns: "There is nothing to say. There never has been . . ." It is a place we are bound—"There is no way out. There never was . . ." And just when we admit this silent aporia, this predicament of total despair, this inescapable impossibility, he says we hear "the real Word which is our only *raison d'être*." What is Caliban doing? What is this "real Word," this "*raison d'être*"? Our dire and drab conditions remain the same, and our all our desires bear no resolve. But, he says,

> it is not in spite of them but with them that we are blessed by that Wholly Other Life from which we are separated by an essential emphatic gulf of which our contrived fissures of mirror and pro-scenium arch—we understand them at last—are feebly figurative signs, so that all our meanings are reversed and it is precisely in its negative image of Judgement that we can positively envisage Mercy; it is just here, among the ruins and the bones, that we may rejoice in the perfected Work which is not ours.

Caught on a stage we cannot leave, caught in a feeble language we cannot ignore, we find positive vision in the negative image. Only "among the ruins and bones" of Creation's O can we envisage a "Work," a creation, that is perfected, Giotto's O. This is our possibility, and the only possibility of reconciling (with) our "incorrigible staginess." Caliban's language here is, like Giotto, unmistakably Christian, ending with the hope of reconciliation. But its theology is outside the soteriological and eschatological frames of traditional doctrine. Caliban binds theology in the poetic frame, as he must. What remains incorrigible is our staginess. We are not the depraved souls of Christian orthodoxy. That orthodoxy is itself a stage, those souls themselves a mirror. We are nothing other than ham actors and amateur playwrights draping tattered curtains over cracked pillars in our basement. Caliban's speech here merely outlines the cracks in the metaphor—any metaphor. As such, it becomes itself the contrived fissure on the commentary as a whole, and the contrived fissure on the proscenium arch of The Tempest it comments upon.

But what is Caliban *really* doing? This "restored relation" seems all too happy an ending for the nature of the "brilliant void" we have been describing. Is this just more staginess from the one, the indifferent zero, who gives staginess its possibility in the first place? Is there here, as Fuller rightly wonders, a *deus ex machina?*[34] We know that Auden had said *The Sea and the Mirror* was "really about a Christian conception of Art."[35] Does this "conception," with its high sounded note, nullify the foregoing analysis in its rectifying negation of negation, in which the One returns disguised in a cloak of "nothing to say" only to erect again the "great coherences" of unity? Do we grant Auden such a taming of the beast he has so spectacularly displayed, so dramatically brought to life? Does Auden do precisely what he describes the audience believes theatre *ought* to do, skate "full tilt toward the forbidden incoherence," but at the last minute, before the abyss, perform a "breathtaking triumphant turn"? Or does his "brilliant void," despite appearances, outdo even Auden and his own intentions?

We must remember that the O is both complete nullity and complete possibility. Caliban, as metaphor—and we must remember too that Caliban is no more than this, a meticulously wrought metaphor of an O no metaphor can fill—stands for pure paradox. He is both silence and loquacity. He is both Trinculo's Nobody and the larger-than-life incarnation of a Jamesean persona. He is both emptiness and saturation. He is both the absence of all things positive and the positivity of all things absent. He both takes away comprehensively and gives comprehensively. Thus, if he should seem to lead us to a familiar theology not in full accord with his nature as paradox beyond all plus and minus, it is because in that paradox he appropriates all plus and all minus, all relation and all contrariety, all incipience and all consummation, all birth and all death. And in a way perhaps even beyond Auden's own conception.

But, of course, Caliban's is not the last word in this long and elaborate construction. Before we should pass judgment, on Auden or any of his characters, before we give the "Wholly Other" the final word, we need to give Ariel his say.

Postscript

Ariel is Caliban's ephemeral, insubstantial, "spiritual" Other. Thus, Ariel's words are themselves ephemeral, borrowed from the natural realm with no substantiality of their own. He has, in fact, no self, and so cannot even voice the one word that announces selfhood—"I." The "I," the echo that follows each of three ten-line stanzas, must be said by the "Prompter," he who stands in the wings and cues the speechless actors. As Echo, the forsaken lover of Narcissus, can only repeat the last lines she had just heard, so the Prompter repeats the last lines of Ariel as he stares into the reflecting pool and falls in love with what he sees—Caliban. The Prompter, like the Stage Manager at the outset, is not part of the play. His "I" is simply the

framing end of the commentary's script, thrown from the margins. Ariel's
"I" is not his own.

Ariel's words are spoken directly to Caliban, and each begins with a
command, as if Ariel now possessed the power to give out orders. But all
of the commands are negative—"Weep no more . . . ," "Wish for nothing . . . ," "Never hope . . ."—as if in salute to the negative counterpart
Caliban has played. Ariel speaks here not to the Caliban of *The Sea and the
Mirror*, the "brilliant void" who has just spoken, but to the original Caliban of *The Tempest*. As the "Fleet persistent shadow cast" by this Caliban's
lameness, Ariel, in a strange reversal of *The Tempest*, becomes the darkness
amid light, "cast" out from Caliban's effulgence, but also "cast" in a role
of a play from which he, unlike Caliban, cannot escape. He is "caught" by
artifice, but also now caught "helplessly in love" with Caliban, "Fascinated
by / Drab mortality." He asks Caliban to be true to this mortality, to his
"faults," to his "official natural role," and in that trueness voice the very
word Ariel cannot—"*I.*" "I can sing as you reply . . . *I,*" "I will sing if you
will cry . . . *I.*" The mirroring is still evident: the "*I*"s are reflected through
the song, the first within artifice, the second without.

In the poem's center, the middle of the second stanza, the mirror is
at its most detailed: "only /As I am can I /Love you as you are." Ariel's "I
am" is contingent on Caliban's substantiality and flesh, and art seems to
return us now to the human realm of passion and intimacy. But Ariel is
still caught in the duality of the perfections of art and the messiness of life.
"Wish for nothing lest you mar/ The perfection." Caliban, *The Tempest's*
Caliban, seems to possess all the human qualities Ariel lacks, so that only
after Caliban's cry can Ariel be heard.[36]

This absolute reliance reaches its height in the third and final stanza
(as if to echo the third section of Caliban's speech). Both Ariel and Caliban boundary upon the region beyond art, beyond "Heaven's kindness" and
"earth's frankly brutal drum." And when their falsehoods (Ariel's illusions,
Caliban's disillusions) are divided, they shall both become nothing. But
what does it mean here to divide a falsehood? Or to divide *two* falsehoods
(which are already divided)? Is this litotes, part of art's incorrigible rhetoric,
or something deeper, an acknowledgment of the paradox of which Caliban,
and by implication now Ariel, is the ultimate embodiment?

Either way, the end result in the final three lines is an "evaporating
sigh," the last gasp of life's breath, extinguished into nothing, thoroughly
dematerialized. The final "*I*" dissipates into a nullity, the self, the "I," without, finally, the "am" of existence. If this is Ariel's sigh, he has got his
wish for liberation from art, and the result is not an "I" at all, but pure
extinguishment in a surd, the O. If this is Caliban's sigh, it is Caliban as

the "brilliant void," as the Prompter off the stage, where he has always resided, in the margins, outside the frame of the proper drama, the original story, but by virtue of that negated original, at the center of the O, where all "I"'s disappear. Only at the end, in this last breath, does Ariel embrace the Caliban not of *The Tempest* but of *The Sea and the Mirror.*

So too only in the final exhaled breath does the mirror image cloud over, as the breath strikes the surface, and the binary of mirror and sea disappears. In the first two prompts, Caliban says "I" in mirror image to Ariel's "I," sung through the surface of the mirror. But in this final prompt—"One evaporating sigh . . . *I*"—the "I" is mirrored by "One," and the mirror is a negating force. We see here the last gasp of One as substance. And now even the "I" of Caliban will fade out on the faint strains of that "I," that "one," which had so marked Antonio's refrain *sotto voce.* Creation's O will not be seen, but it will echo quietly. Caliban's O will not be heard, but it will loom invisibly. And the fading italicized *I,* bent down by its own dissolution, will lead us back, reluctantly, but inexorably, to the beginning of the full circle.

"The aged catch their breath." Thus began the commentary. The catch of the breath, in its temporary suspension of the flow of life's air, is the exact antithesis to the long, expiring sigh. The exhalation of the final "I" obscures the mirror, and the reflection is no more; but the breath on the mirror fades as we return to the first words of the Preface, and the reflection begins to return. The entire poem/commentary is like life's breath held in abeyance, in order that reflection might have its play ("what delights us about her world is just that it neither is nor possibly could become one in which we could breathe"), until the gasp of the final "I," which clouds again the mirror.

But the end and the beginning are also the same gesture. Both capture that moment when life as we know it, as we had known it, as we thought we only could know it, is cut off from its source. And in that loss, in that separation, we realize—nonexistence, undeniably, but also, in the face of such nonexistence—the possibility of something new. The entire poem/ commentary is also one long release of creation's breath, giving artistic life to the characters and their words. And this breath, as Prospero had told us in *The Tempest's* Epilogue, is something *we* must exhale into the work if, as readers and viewers, we are in any way to participate in its circular world. We suspend and release breath at the same time: suspending one to give life to the other. The One, the I, gives way to the O, the 0, the artificer's circle. We are drawn round to the beginning, where the high-wire circus act defies the death of its linear path, and the laughter of the circular ring below is a children's delight. The lion's mouth remains both empty and filled in the pure simultaneity of the paradox. And from there we start again, as we pass over the center, the brilliant void, now with a wider awareness of its creative, originating power.

FIVE

THE EMPTY MIDDLE

Whenever thought is caught in a circle, this is because it has touched upon something original, its point of departure beyond which it cannot move except to return.

—Maurice Blanchot

ORIGINATING O (BLANCHOT)

In the beginning, there may have been origin, but in trying to re-present that origin, in the beginning, we lose it. This is why, in coming back to the beginning in the circle that is O, we do not return to a strictly historical origin, an origin that was prior, and therefore primary. Instead, we retrace that origin, now negated as origin in the retracing; but we originate a new O by virtue of that same retracing. The O is about making, even original making. But how exactly do we make the O when there are so many possibilities to be made? How can we originate O with so many seemingly competing construals and interpretations? If, as we said at the beginning, we feel compelled to give O a history, *whose* history do we give it?

This book began with an artist's O, the O of Giotto, the apparent perfectly drawn circle. Artists continue to draw circles, of course, but for very different reasons, and now with very different appearances. (We can think, for example, of the distortions in Munch's scream.) The modern artist cannot avoid the empty center of the O. And it is the artist of the last century who has seen this most brutally and most irrepressibly, amid the upheavals and tumult that century brought us. Auden's O becomes representative because, amid a specific historical period of uncertainty and strife, Auden intentionally shifts his art from any attempt at a self-asserting activism, with all its possibilities of historical intervention (political, social, material, etc.), to a self-retreating and ultimately self-effacing performance, with a now indelible consciousness of the nothing that it (as self-performance) circumscribes.

What remains historical in Auden's O is not an "I" that, embedded within a certain locality of history, can effect change by imposing an originating authorial power into or upon that history. It is, rather, an "I" who, like Prospero, must relinquish all its authorial powers, in order to originate a history of nothing itself. It is an "I" who must defeat itself as its primary artistic task. The historical Auden might never have admitted to this task in such words—Auden's prose, as in, say, *The Prolific and the Devourer*, that set of reflections about this very turn in (his own) art, reads like a series of injunctions issued with a still dogged grip on self-certainty, a kind of authorial grandstanding, or worse, pontification, which Auden was never able to fully resist his entire life. But his poetry making, as manifested in his *Sea and the Mirror* above all, gives the lie to any surety of the "I." For Auden, the "I" of the artist is given over to the O of art, or, we could say, the O of the artist emerges within the "I" as, and only as, art. And this poetic "I," as *The Sea and the Mirror* shows us, has always an eye toward its death.

We have already invoked the French thinker Blanchot, who said it is the artist who most "obeys the fatality of the circle."[1] And perhaps it is Blanchot, not, as often argued, Kierkegaard, who is Auden's truest spokesman in theorizing what *The Sea and the Mirror* enacts, and who is best placed now to help us situate any historicizing of O. They were more than contemporaries: Blanchot was born the same year as Auden (though he survived him by thirty years). They inhabited completely different intellectual and cultural universes, undoubtedly, and yet as a literary theorist who also wrote fiction, it is perhaps Blanchot who acts as the prime complement to Auden's *The Sea and the Mirror*, by imagining, theorizing, and philosophizing on the "I"'s own O in a way Auden could never do except as grand artificer. In his first novel *Thomas l'obscur*, published in 1941, which might be read as the tain to Auden's *The Sea and the Mirror*, Blanchot's character tries to come to terms with the reality of his self's own absence: "It is the property of my thought, not to assure me of existence (as all things do, as a stone does), but to assure me of being in nothingness itself, and to invite me not to be, in order to make me feel my marvelous absence."[2] Even those around him reflect this absence: "I had disappeared and I felt her gathering herself up to throw herself into my absence as if into her mirror."[3] About a decade after Auden wrote his long defining poem, Blanchot published his most read, and in some ways still most celebrated, work *L'Espace littéraire* (*The Space of Literature* [1955]). Despite its focus on Hölderlin, Mallarmé, Rilke, and Kafka,[4] we could nevertheless say this work of criticism, informed by Blanchot's other writing, might indeed become a commentary on *The Sea and the Mirror* in the way Auden's poem was a commentary on *The Tempest*.

It would take another entire book to parse fully the intricacies of Blanchot's reflections, and relate them all to the O we have been tracing out,

with its culmination in Auden. We have seen earlier the philosopher and
the theologian circumnavigate the perimeter of the circle's space. But with
only a few exceptions—Hegel, Nietzsche, and Heidegger make up Blanchot's
trireme[5]—the philosopher and theologian do so *from without*. This is because
philosophy and theology are still largely positive discourses, seeking to assert
or refine a reality that has already been in some manner expressed. But the
artist seeks to create a reality, one that has had no previous expression.
In Kafka's terms, "What is laid upon us is to accomplish the negative; the
positive is already given."[6] The artist therefore works *from within* the circle.
The O, as cipher, cannot be about the "already expressed"; the O expresses
nothing by definition. As Prospero had said, "Where I go, words carry no
weight." As Blanchot writes, "The writer belongs to a language which no
one speaks, which is addressed to on one, which has no center, and which
reveals nothing."[7] This nothing, for Blanchot, is the beginning point, the
interminable beginning point, of all literary endeavor.

   Thus, in trying to mark out the space of literature in the middle of
the twentieth century, Blanchot's work provides two important connections
to the way we have been figuring the O. The first is his understanding of
the "I"'s dissolution; the second is his attempt to rethink the question of
origin, especially of and in the work of art.

   First, if Blanchot (following Kafka) is right in saying that the artist writes "in order to be able to die,"[8] then we have some understanding
not only of why the artist must work from within the O, but also why
the artist must relinquish the concept of "I." The artist must be willing
to accept self-obliteration, must in some sense even be motivated by it,
though often with the illusion that the work of art will also spare the artist
from death, bring immortality, allow the origin, as originator, to carry on
in a living presence of the work. "The problem of every man and writer
is at all times essentially the same, namely first to learn to be himself and
then to learn to be not himself," wrote Auden in 1949.[9] This dichotomy—
self-obliteration and self-aggrandizement, the real and the illusory, nothing
and artifice—stands in tension within all great art. Blanchot is perhaps
the first to articulate theoretically that this tension is essential but never
dialectical: it is never resolved into something "higher," which holds some
basis of authority or sovereignty, whether of the artist or the work itself.
Rather, the tension remains constituted in the irremediable and unending
origination of the death, or dying, of "I." This is the author's, and indeed
the work's, solitude he speaks about so prevalently: the space where nothing else enjoins, because there is no longer an "I" to enjoin or be enjoined
with. This is Prospero's plight, his loneliness, his separation, and ultimately
his "I am that I am not." The work of art, for Blanchot as for *The Sea and
the Mirror*, stands as testimony to this originating death.

Early on in *The Space of Literature*, Blanchot speaks of the necessary abrogation of the self as "I" in relation to the one who writes. "When to write is to discover the interminable," he says, "the writer who enters this region does not leave himself behind in order to approach the universal." Nor does the writer "discover the admirable language which speaks honorably for all." Rather, and against all unifying gestures:

> What speaks in him is the fact that, in one way or another, he is no longer himself; he isn't anyone any more. The third person substituting for the "I": such is the solitude that comes to the writer on account of the work. . . . The third person is myself become no one, my interlocutor turned alien; it is my no longer being able, where I am, to address myself and the inability of whoever addresses me to say "I"; it is his not being himself.[10]

The loss of the writer's self here is more than simply the adoption of a narrative voice, a "third person" persona, assumed as a matter of narrative form. It is, in fact, the hollowing out of oneself in order for a negative (negative because blank or "neutral") space to open up where affirmation might originate.

> The work requires of the writer that he lose everything he might construe as his own "nature," that he lose all character and that, ceasing to be linked to others and to himself by the decision which makes him an "I," he becomes the empty place where the impersonal affirmation emerges.[11]

The "I" here is involved in both separation and dissolution, echoing Prospero's final refrain to Ariel ("Of separation / Of bodies and death. . . . Trembling he takes / The silent passage / Into discomfort"), and the Postscript's final refrain ("One evaporating sigh . . . I"). Kevin Hart's very fine *The Dark Gaze* explores the intricacies of this separation with philosophical astuteness. In examination of Blanchot's rethinking Descartes's *cogito*, Hart refers to Blanchot's reinscription "I think therefore I am not," and suggests himself a further adaptation: "*Scribo ergo non sum*"—I write, therefore I am not. We might describe this *Scribo* as follows: what happens in the work is that the O asserts a mock sovereignty—"Sovereignty is nothing"—and renders the "I" emptied of all its formerly constituted self. It does this because, as Hart contends, "consciousness does not necessarily imply the presence of existence . . . since the very ability to represent oneself as an 'I' means that one has hollowed out the existence of that selfhood and now has only the absence of that self. To say 'I,' even to oneself, is to have lost the presence one claims to have secured."[12] The act of writing then inscribes this self-hollowing—writing in its earliest of forms was an exca-vation of a surface, we must remember, a chiseling out, a taking away—so that the very space of literature is itself a hollowed out nothing, a cipher, which has no intrinsic meaning or value or relation. This is why Blanchot begins his book by saying that the work of art, rather than being singular or infinite, "is neither finished nor unfinished: it is. What it says is exclusively this: that it is. Beyond that it is nothing. Whoever wants to make it express more finds nothing, finds that it expresses nothing."[13]

"That it is"—this is all the work can "say." And in this saying is the affirmative expression of nothing, that is, of O. But in this essential state of the work's being, *whence* this O? Whence does it *really* originate? We must turn then to the second matter, the question of origin. Blanchot never speaks directly of the O as such. When he speaks of the circle, he speaks in terms of a certain hermeneutical circle, picking up, no doubt, from Heidegger. The writer, he says, is "one whose power to write comes from an anticipated relation with death." Invoking again Kafka, he continues:

> *Write to be able to die—Die to be able to write.* These words close us into their circular demand; they oblige us to start from what we want to find, to seek nothing but the point of departure, and thus to make this point something we approach only by quitting it. But they also authorize this hope: the hope, where the interminable emerges, of grasping the term, of bringing it forth.[14]

So how do we isolate this point of departure? This is a similar question we asked of Heidegger: How do we come into the circle in the right way? What is our point of departure or origin? Where, ultimately, do we place the beginning of O?

For Blanchot, this place is what he calls the "'Outside' (*Dehors*)," a benighted place where possibility and impossibility meet. Without any light, one is largely incapable of describing where this place is, or what it looks like. But art opens up its space. Blanchot, according to Hart, "sees in art a veiling and unveiling of the Outside from which human beings have tried to shield themselves by religion and philosophy. Neither subjective nor objective, the Outside precedes this distinction, though Blanchot does not specify its mode of priority."[15] We might say that its mode is in "death," but not the phenomenal death of the body. It is in the death of "I." It is in the outside of being, who, when outside of itself, can finally understand that this death, this being able *not* to be, this *possibility* for nothingness, is precisely the power that it holds: "That I am nothing certainly implies that 'I hold myself back from within nothingness,' and this is black and agonizing, but it also implies this marvel: that nothingness is my power, and that I *can* not be. Hence man's liberty, his mastery, and his future."[16] *Here* is the fullest figuration of the O and its power in Blanchot: humans' power (*creative* power, Blake would insist, along with Nietzsche) that only comes when nothingness is fully consummated within.

And hence our origin too: "[W]hen nothingness becomes power, man is fully historical."[17] This is among Blanchot's profoundest of statements, with much Hegelian overtone. What Blanchot means by "historical" here is not, however, something we can say is fixed to a specified place in time (or time in place). "The past that interests Blanchot is not historical; it is the origin of the work that he identifies with the Outside."[18] In the power of nothingness, we are brought "back" to (but we could also say "forward" to, "toward") our origin, which is not in any way temporal, nor even ontological, but is that which allows being and time to emerge in the first instance. This is precisely what we have been arguing for the O. When we try to place O historically, that is, within a linear history, we end up going around in circles. And yet, even Blanchot admits that any work of art, as a manifestation of O, emerges at a specific historical juncture. But this "history" is not what defines its most original beginning. That beginning lies elsewhere, in the Outside, and thus in the *inside* of what we have been figuring as O, the Wholly Other within the mirror, the void at the center of our figuring, and which allows emergence its possibility.

> And yet the work is history; it is an event, *the* event of history itself, and this is because its most steadfast claim is to give to the word *beginning* all its force. . . . Always it says, in one guise or another: beginning. It is thus that history belongs to it and that nevertheless it escapes history. . . .
>
> The work says this word, beginning, and what it claims to give to history is initiative, the possibility of a point of departure.[19]

To be "fully historical" means, then, to be able to initiate history, to be "always original and at all moments a beginning."[20] (A vicious circle, or eternal return, since the return is also and already the starting point.) This is how Blanchot begins to end his book. And this is why Auden writes *The Sea and the Mirror*: the staginess of art can only bring us to a beginning, which is a death: the death of thinking and believing that the work can *direct* history from *within* history; and the death of the "I" that sees history as One, a unity of action and a unified economy of value. At best, art can only create history anew. Yet such a history will signify nothing but its own "insubstantial stuff." All the rest is silence.

So, an unlikely pairing though they may appear, given the disparate worlds they inhabited—the one French, Continental, reclusive, and deeply philosophical, the other Anglo-American, public, a paragon of the literati— we can read Blanchot's 1955 text as the principle theoretical gloss on *The Sea and the Mirror*. Is there a better summation of this poem, and of Auden's own thinking from the early 1940s onward, than Blanchot's words at the end of the second section "Approaching Literature's Space"?

> Writing begins only when it is the approach to that point where nothing reveals itself, where, at the heart of dissimulation, speaking is still but the shadow of speech, a language which is still only its image, an imaginary and a language of the imaginary, the one nobody speaks, the murmur of the incessant and the interminable which one has to *silence* if one wants, at last, to be heard.[21]

Conjoining Blanchot here with Auden has a double effect. On the one hand, it says something about the history of ideas we have been constructing throughout. As contemporaries, something transpires in the middle of their century that allows them to bring the O onto center stage, as it were, the one informing the other, if only after their time. And yet it also tells us that the O itself will tend to hollow out any such history, and leave us back at a certain beginning point that defies historical origins. The void of the O has brought a paradoxical day of reckoning, then. The work of art is no longer about framing the real world through mimetic play, or holding a mirror up to nature. And neither is it about locating us more deeply within our history to effect change upon that history. With the recession of the One, with the dissolution of the "I," the work of art has been forced to come to terms with the fact that both reality and our historical understanding of that reality have succumbed to a dislocating O.[22] Art, along with religion and philosophy, can no longer claim an inviolable authority, either human or divine, based on unity and coherence, for ordering us in *History*. There is a certain "end of History" being announced here. "The time of art is the time before time."[23] And yet, despite this, and within the paradox of the O, that "end of History" will always allow itself to be construed historically, to be historically "figured," if figured anew. To be both given to a history while at the same time rent from that history, starting with the history of one's own "I," is what has made the artist of the last century, in his or her specific (Western) historical situation, so anxious, so marked by fracture, lack, and despair. "The time of distress," as

Blanchot calls it.[24] The "age of anxiety," as Auden calls it. Or, we might say, the crisis of O's history.

HISTORICIZING O

History before the twentieth century has obviously not been without its crises of negativity, and Western literature before the twentieth century has certainly not been without its negating Os. As far back as Homer, we have seen the O at play against the One. Odysseus escapes the clutches of the Cyclops—paramount myopia—by the cunning negation of his own being: "Nobody" is the name he gives for himself, to elude capture by the one-eyed beasts. (This self-negation is also at play, as Horkheimer and Adorno remind us, in the Siren episode, when Odysseus must bind himself to the mast in order to counter his most primal passions evoked by the Sirens' song.)[25]

There is the Book of Job, that great Hebrew contemplation and circular interrogation on divine justice. The O here manifests itself not as the middle dialogue with the three friends, which famously leads nowhere, nor as the imposing voice of Yahweh that issues forth from the storm at the end, but as the *ha satan* figure of the prologue, who sets the plight of Job off on its course, and who disappears as a character soon thereafter. This disappearance is the very enactment of the negating O, only to surface again, if it surfaces at all, as the storm itself, the harsh Lear-like vehicle for divine reprisal and human concession, before restoration returns in the epilogue.

The Gospel of Mark also enacts the O in its circular structure, if we take the oldest version (or the *original* version, if we follow Blanchot properly) as the most definitive. Here, with its shorter ending, an empty and hollow tomb silences the women in fear and trembling (16.8), and our only recourse is to go back with them to the beginning, back to Galilee, back to "the Gospel of Jesus Christ, Son of God," whose identity is affirmed from on high in the waters of baptism. This identity carries us again to the middle apex, the transfiguration (9.2–9), the repeated affirmation from on high, about which secrecy and silence are demanded, until the "Son of Man has risen from the dead," that final moment when, instead of great triumph and consummation, we must encounter the empty vessel yet again.

These are random selections, and we can think of many others more recently: Rabelais, and what Bakhtin called the "positive negation" throughout his scandalizing work. Or Shakespeare himself, whose seemingly innocuous Os, uttered by various voices within the circle of the Globe, lead to the great O of *The Tempest*, Caliban. Or Laurence Sterne's anti-novel *Tristram Shandy*—can we think of a better emblem of the O Auden had isolated and delineated than the blank pages at the center of the final volume of that wonderfully iconoclastic "autobiography"?[26] We cannot overestimate the importance of Blake, of course, in thinking about the confluence of positive and negative creative forces, as we have already alluded to. We've discussed Coleridge's "Kubla Khan" and Wilde's *The Picture of Dorian Gray*. We could have added any number of Kafka's stories, testimonies to the oppressive presence of the forever unrealized. And we could add the others in Blanchot's purview—Hölderlin, Mallarmé, Rilke. These and many more, inside and outside of literature, reveal that the O has never been merely a late import into our history, a late modern origination. But has it before provoked a general crisis?

There is something about the twentieth century that gives rise to an unforeseen and unprecedented concentration upon the nature of the O itself. It is no longer that the O slipped in, disguised in one or another form, amid the unities and coherences of agreed systems, paradigms, and orthodoxies. It is that the O became the exclamation of a new "reality," a new way of seeing the world, or how it might be constructed. It was as if there was a final concession, a distinct "so be it," to what had been culminating since the turn of the century (if not earlier), and now was an undeniable *fait accompli*: the One had given way to its secret foe, now wholly unsecreted. And this was indeed now a crisis of an almost unbearable nature, not only because the One and the "I" had lost their sovereignty, finally and irretrievably, but because in the void left behind was a fundamental paradox: O's point of entry into this history was itself a dissolution of that history, at least as previously conceived, unless in some never fully understood Hegelian sense of an "end of History" and, coterminously, an "end of Art."

Is there a crux to this crisis, a crossing of the two lines of the paradox at a distinct juncture? It has become standard, within the many fabrications we have now come to call "a history of ideas," to view the end of a century as the defining point of cultural crisis. Certainly, the last two centuries have been understood in this way, and we have not been able to see the twentieth century as anything but that defined by the *fin de siècle* ushered in with, foremost among others, Nietzsche's death-of-God madman, and ushered out by an apocalypticism most publicly marked by that impending technological disaster, which never materialized, as the year 2000 approached. The outer ends have been our moments of reckoning, we have felt, perhaps because we have come upon our self-made measures, and never have quite known if these measures, as boundaries, are real life or reified illusions marking out very little, if anything at all. Or perhaps it is because the centennial measure as a numerical figure is the one time in a hundred years when zeros will outnumber cardinals. The millennial measure would thus only multiply this perturbation in our cultural psyche. Whatever the case may be, the end has always been feared more than the middle.

But what if, under the influence of our long exegesis of Auden's *The Sea and the Mirror,* and of Blanchot's complementarity, we were to see the middle as the most indicative? What if, under the poem/commentary's intricate symmetry and concentric structure, and Blanchot's Outside, the original movement that originates, necessarily, inside (and inside a circle, the empty space of literature), we think of the center as the most critical? At the middle point of the middle section of *The Sea and the Mirror*, Alonso, the good traditional king about to expire, sets up two sides: the siren's song and the demon's void (Ariel and Caliban). Antonio, the dominant voice of the middle section as a whole, shows us that both sides are caught in the same circle, and that if there is a middle way between them, as Alonso had preached, it is a middle that encompasses, by necessity, both ends: the illusory song is no different, and nothing other, than the brilliant void. Caliban, this demon turned siren in the third chapter, has his own middle void in the center section of his three-part speech: he himself, the "indifferent zero." Perhaps these troubling middles, surrounded by two kinds of respiratory reactions, the frightened exclamation ("O!") and the retiring sigh ("I"), are really for us the location of our most expressed, and expressive, condition.

ALTERNATE Os OF THE MIDDLE

We continue to have difficulty marking the middle of the twentieth century in our Western intellectual conceptions and theorizations. From the period of, say, 1940 to 1960 (and how convenient we can be with our rounded figures, until we peer into them too deeply), a horrific global war gave way to a disorienting period of restoration, and then to the entrenchment of yet another binary system, in which communism and liberal democracy were held precariously over the void of total atomic annihilation. No one quite knew how to respond to the Holocaust, nor, in America especially, to the following economic boom, and the cold war escalation only succeeded through an absurd logic of "zeroing out" the other's capabilities by upping one's own, the ultimate zero sum game. The height of modernism had passed, the onslaught of postmodernism had not yet hit. The middle period was, if we label it at all, something we have only called a vague and untheorizable period of transition.[27]

"Modernism" and "postmodernism" have become our dominant theoretical markers, and this especially for our cultural output. The figure of Auden, whose most important work was written in these middle decades, has always struggled in the academy, his reputed "greatness" notwithstanding, and this because he fits into neither of these two categories (or stratagems) neatly or decisively.[28] But Auden is among a list of literary figures, and *The Sea and the Mirror* among a list of literary works, that force us to reconsider the nature of this transitional period as something other than a state of confusion or an invisible change of the tide. There was, we might say, an emergence of writers or works whose very theme, in one way or another, was the O as positive negation as we have been trying to trace out thus far.

James Joyce

On the front end of this period, we would have to begin with that most circular of all books, *Finnegans Wake* (published in 1939). What does one do after "the book to end all books" has been written, which few if any were willing or able to read, and few still are? This book is the ultimate circulating text not in general circulation, a text that encircles itself—the "beginning" of the opening sentence is in fact the last line of the book—while at the same time breaks open language in the most open-ended manner possible. It is the overflow of paradox: the polyglottic text that only a precious few can read; the authorial "I" dissolved into a sea of vocal artifice and multiplicity that at the same time pushes "author-ness" to its most radically pronounced; the breakdown of all conventions of artifice to produce artifice in its extreme; the transhistorical story that operates out of the specificities of history, and is the supreme "book of its time" (modernist experimentation, Freudian theory, between the wars, etc.). Joyce not only invokes Vico's notion of history repeating itself, the "commodius vicus of recirculation" of the opening line, but he repeats throughout the text the archetypal Western story of origin, The Garden of Eden, and its Fall, *the* beginning point which keeps beginning. What was one to do with this brazen performance of insistent paradox? How was one to even think of it (never mind read it)? The early Joyce was certainly a model of modernist experimentation, but the *Wake* seems to have surpassed even that desig-nation, in its absolute reinscription of the possibilities of what language could, and should, offer or enable. This was a watershed of a different kind, beckoning a different and hitherto unforeseen era. And if, upon the publication of literature's most anarchical text, yet another global war was to break out, scattering aesthetic focus even further, how does one (and here we return to the generic "one" deliberately) recover? How does art recover? How does thinking recover? This text, we could say, inaugurates a middle period of the twentieth century indicative of an all-important loss of recoverability, figured in the O that recovers, repeatedly, only its beginning point as lost origin (the Fall). The *Wake* is the "end of art" as Hegel might have conceived it, except that it is also a wholly new begin-ning—not recovered, but generated for the first time. And whether fellow artists, or those who came directly after, fully understood this or not, they seemed to have intuited the essence of this inauguration.

T. S. Eliot

As early as the 1920s, in the writing of *The Waste Land,* T. S. Eliot had
anticipated what the *Wake,* in all its later radicality, had obliquely suggested
through the notion of the Fall: the idea or concept of negation. Yet for all
its anarchy, the *Wake,* as *Ulysses* before it, is a deeply affirming, yea-saying
text, since its negation is a regenerative negation. Eliot, in the early years of
The Waste Land, unable to see much in the way of regeneration or affirmation, was more interested in the vacuous spaces left by the undoing of the
modern project, the "empty cisterns," the "empty men." In the middle of
the second section, "A Game of Chess," he gives us a vivid picture of the
emerging O as nothing, as it had made its way into the reality of Europe
just after the Great War.

> "What is that noise?"
> The wind under the door.
> "What is that noise now? What is the wind doing?"
> Nothing again nothing.
> "Do
> "You know nothing? Do you see nothing? Do you remember
> "Nothing?"[29]

The nothing emerges here first in repetition of itself, as the nothing
that cannot be suppressed, and then in the interrogative structure by which
knowledge, perception, and memory are each put into question. In this
exchange between one voice and another (the strained couple in the bar),
the first seeks to hold onto its "I" through those marks of spoken presence,
the inverted commas ("'I never know what you are thinking'"), while the
second broods within, uncommunicative, lost inside the "I" that is dying
("I think we are in rats' valley / Where the dead men lost their bones").
So when the first tries to break through this moribund state—"'Are you
alive or not? Is there nothing in your head?'"—the answer of the second
must again repeat nothing:

> O O O O that Shakespeherian Rag—
> It's so elegant
> So intelligent . . .[30]

Hamlet's and Lear's dying Os (those of Folio and Quarto respectively—
and how significant that we do not know what to do with the transliteration of death, whether it should remain or not—a phenomenon Blanchot
himself repeatedly addressed) are now coupled with the "elegance" of a
popular song, a specific musical fashion, ragtime, with its brief heyday. For

the early Eliot, as for the later Auden, the nothing, repeated again and again, affects both the serious and the frivolous, the high and the low, the universal and the ephemeral.

But *The Waste Land,* however much it captures the times of an early century, is, in relation to the powerful nothingness of O, only anticipatory. What it anticipates is the later *Four Quartets* ("Burnt Norton" [1936]; "East Coker" [1940]; "The Dry Salvages" [1941]; "Little Gidding" [1942]). "What we call the beginning is often the end / And to make an end is to make a beginning. The end is where we start from." The final poem, whose writing overlaps with that of *The Sea and the Mirror,* ends famously with this circular refrain. Earlier it had asked, "Where is the summer, the unimaginable / Zero summer?"[31] Whatever we say the *Four Quartets* is about—and it is doing much more than giving us a glimpse into the crisis of the times, whether this "more" be a deeply Christian appropriation of certain Eastern ideas, or an elemental study of the poetic paradoxes of mortality—we have here the acknowledgment of a fundamental negation at work in our conception of reality, what Eliot called in "East Coker" the "vacant interstellar spaces," when the mind "is conscious but conscious of nothing."[32] This is now more than simply painting the canvas black. Eliot, we sense here, is trying to harness a power that, if before a measure of pervading malaise, might now offer some new way to conceive of a path through our situation. "There is no end, but addition," he says in "The Dry Salvages," as if the nothing, rather than marking a terminal crisis, might actually now have something to contribute, through an extension of creation.[33] "It seems, as one becomes older, / That the past has another pattern . . . ," a past more cyclical in nature, where, like Mark's Gospel and *Finnegans Wake,*

> . . . the end of all our exploring
> Will be to arrive where we started
> And know the place for the first time.[34]

Eliot pursued these figurations of the O with typical erudite seriousness. This seriousness, even in such matters as the frivolous "Rag," is a far cry from Auden's "frivolity." The negation emerges in Eliot from the grounds of a deep religious conservatism. This is not Creation's O, in which we find an origin for play, but a high-minded, even godly O, one much closer to Giotto's, and one crucial to Eliot's understanding of the divine/human relationship in all its traditional, even if reconfigured, formulations and "dispensations."

Samuel Beckett

One far less serious in tone, but even more serious about nothing, is Samuel Beckett. Even more than his close friend and compatriot Joyce, Beckett has been called a precursor to the postmodern. But he is also still linked to the modernist agenda, even if he takes that agenda to its most logical, and most illogical, conclusion. Beckett understood the importance of an "ending" that is just a beginning. He eventually gravitated to theatre, we might say, because it is on the living stage where life—the life of the play—has its repeated endings and beginnings. And so he wrote *Endgame* (1957) as a living out of the interiority of that which we call a "play," outside of which is nothing. And yet the very substance of that interiority is itself the acknowledgment of that nothing, the acknowledgment that both outside and inside the O's perimeter are marked by absence, by the end of things to say, by nothing. In the following episode, the outside of the play's circle is penetrated be means of a telescope:

> CLOV: Things are livening up.
>
> (*He gets up on ladder, raises the telescope, lets it fall.*)
>
> I did it on purpose.
>
> (*He gets down, picks up the telescope, turns it on auditorium.*)
>
> I see . . . a multitude . . . in transports . . . of joy.
>
> (*Pause. He lowers telescope, looks at it.*)
>
> That's what I call a magnifier.
>
> (*He turns toward Hamm.*)
>
> Well? Don't we laugh?
>
> HAMM (*after reflection*): I don't.
>
> CLOV (*after reflection*): Nor I.
>
> (*He gets up on ladder, turns the telescope on the without.*)
>
> Let's see.
>
> (*He looks, moving the telescope.*)
>
> Zero . . .
>
> (*he looks*)
>
> . . . zero . . .
>
> (*he looks*)
>
> . . . and zero.
>
> HAMM: Nothing stirs. All is—

CLOV: Zer—

HAMM (violently): Wait till you're spoken to!

(Normal voice.)

All is . . . all is . . . all is what?

(Violently.)

All is what?

CLOV: What all is? In a word? Is that what you want to know? Just a moment.

(He turns the telescope on the without, looks, lowers the telescope, turns towards Hamm.)

Corpsed.

(Pause.)

Well? Content?[35]

In a way, the "ham" actor is content. For the end, the dead, the life-less—and Hamm points to all of these—are always a new beginning, and like Joyce, and in his way Eliot, the play begins with an ending—"Finished, it's finished, nearly finished, it must be nearly finished."[36] And yet it ends with a beginning:

HAMM: . . .

(He takes out the handkerchief.)

Since that's the way we're playing it . . .

(he unfolds handkerchief)

. . . let's play it that way . . .

(he unfolds)

. . . and speak no more about it . . .

(he finishes unfolding)

. . . speak no more.

(He holds handkerchief spread out before him.)

Old stancher!

(Pause.)

You . . . remain.

(*Pause. He covers his face with handkerchief, lowers his arms to armrests, remains motionless.*)

(*Brief tableau.*)

Curtain[37]

In between—"remaining" to play it again, to start all over—this circularity is continued as the circularity of movement itself:

HAMM: Take me for a little turn.

(*Clov goes behind the chair and pushes it forward.*)

Not too fast!

(*Clov pushes chair.*)

Right round the world!

(*Clov pushes chair.*)

Hug the walls, then back to the center again.

(*Clov pushes chair.*)

I was right in the center, wasn't I?[38]

The actor must remain at dead center, even if there is little more to say:

NAGG: One for me and one for—

HAMM: One! Silence!

(*Pause.*)

Where was I?

(*Pause. Gloomily.*)

It's finished, we're finished.

(*Pause.*)

Nearly finished.

(*Pause.*)

There'll be no more speech.

(*Pause.*)[39]

So it goes throughout the dialogue, until "Moments for nothing, now as always, time was never and time was over, reckoning closed and story ended."[40]

To speak the silence at the dead center—this seems the supreme task of the Beckettian "I," who is always dissolving within the silence of its O. And this is no more evident than in the earlier novel *The Unnamable* (*L'Innomable*, 1953; English translation, 1958), where the paradox of silent speaking (or speaking silence), of static movement (or moving stasis), is all-pervasive. Is there a better epigram, a better rubric, to this "unnamable" (as "I," or place, or knowledge), or to Beckett's *oeuvre*, or to this middle period as a whole, than these words of the novel?

The search for the means to put an end to things, an end to speech, is what enables the discourse to continue.[41]

And continue it does:

For to go on means going from here, means finding me, losing me, vanishing and beginning again, a stranger first, then little by little the same as always, in another place, where I shall say I have always been, of which I shall know nothing, being incapable of seeing, moving, thinking, speaking, but of which little by little in spite of these handicaps, I shall begin to know something, just enough for it to turn out to be the same place as always . . .[42]

Even the prose circles here, moving forward only to end up at the same place:

It is not mine, I have none, I have no voice and must speak, that is all I know, *its round that I must revolve, of that I must speak,* with this voice that is not mine, but can only be mine . . .[43]

And so in the subsequent and more directly titled *Texts for Nothing* (*Nouvelles et Textes pour rien*, 1955; English translation, 1967), nothing begets nothing, and yet, out of that nothing, that begetting, something continues to survive, the music and the speech that is predicated on the silence in between:

Ah, to know for sure, to know that this thing has no end, this thing, this thing, this farrago of silence and words, of silence that is not silence and barely murmured words. Or to know it's still life, a form of life, ordained to the end, as others ended and will end, till life ends in all its forms.[44]

This is a stripping down of artifice, in order to delineate the O at the center of one's being. It is in direct opposition to Auden's Caliban, where artifice is padded on to extreme. But the void around which they both revolve is the same. In Beckett the movement is always an aporia, where the "I" can never move forward or backward, but only in circles around its nothingness. Nevertheless, the very energy of its circling prose dictates a wilful motion—"you must go on, I can't go on, I'll go on," ends *The Unnamable*;[45] or as the thirteenth and last *Texts for Nothing* finishes: "still all would be silent and empty and dark, as now, as soon now, when all will be ended, all said, it says, it murmurs."[46] In the present tense, in conflation of past and future, it murmurs the "sounded note" of Caliban, or the "evaporating sigh" of Ariel. "Play and lose and have done with losing," concludes Hamm.[47]

This *play*, as insistent strategy or endgame, is neither the Babel-play of Joyce's yea-saying, nor the "frivolity" of Auden's self-conscious and heightened dissimulation. It is more what J. M. Coetzee has called "philosophical comedy,"[48] the denuded and placeless existential self in its dark comedy of O.

Luis Borges

Taking O's playful nature in a much different, one might even risk "lighter," vein is someone with whom Beckett shared the *Prix Formentor* (International Publisher's Prize) in 1961, Jorge Luis Borges. Borges's collective *Ficciones* were published in 1944. Amid the labyrinths, the libraries, the mirrors, the forking paths, all the fabular stories and "artifices" in which time, history, and writing circle back upon themselves, stands out "The Circular Ruins." In this "artifice" the circle encloses the most primitive of religion and belief, the magician and his power to engender new life. A man from upriver enters the ruins of an ancient circular temple. He sleeps in its enclave and envisions an ultimate fulfillment: to dream another person into being and insert them into reality. Through successive tries, and with the power of the multiple god Fire, he manages to give oneiric birth to a son, and then, miraculously, to release that son from his dreams into the living world of reality. Once separated, the son establishes a magician's life of his own in another circular temple. Only then can the father relinquish his life to an oncoming fire that consumes his own ruined circle. But standing amid the flames, he is not consumed: he himself is a phantom, a mere appearance dreamed up by another.[49] Here, the O is creation as eternal recurrence in all the contradictory splendor of *homo faber*, which blurs once again the line between what we can trust as our own fiction (or fictions) and what we can trust as our own reality (or realities). This is the point of the short parable "Borges and I," where the writer does not know which one (the historical person called "Borges" or the narrator of the parable, "I") has written the page. In the parabolic "Everything and Nothing," Borges presents a pure cipher of a figure, about whom the opening line states, "There was no one in him . . . a dream dreamt by no one."[50] Invoking the Book of Job, and with striking resemblance to the Prospero of *The Sea and the Mirror,* the story ends:

> History adds that before or after dying he found himself in the pres-ence of God and told Him: "I who have been so many men in vain and want to be one and myself." The voice of the Lord answered from a whirlwind: "Neither am I anyone; I have dreamt the world as you dreamt your work, my Shakespeare, and among the forms in my dream are you, who like myself are many and no one."[51]

Borge's O reverses Eliot's, whereby the O does not act to mark out the divine, but rather the divine acts to mark out the O. The O is both all and nothing in Borges. At the end of "The God's Script," the narrator has a mystical vision of a union between divinity and the universe, which takes the form of a high Wheel made of both water and fire. From this infinite Wheel he is granted understanding of the universe's intricate designs, includ-ing "the faceless god concealed behind the other gods," neither strictly one God nor many gods. He concludes:

> Whoever has seen the universe, whoever beheld the fiery designs of the universe, cannot think in terms of one man, of that man's trivial fortunes or misfortunes, though he be that very man. That man *has been* he and now matters no more to him. What is the life of that other to him, the nation of that other to him, if he, now, is no one. This is why . . . lying here in the darkness, I let the days obliterate me.[52]

The "I" in Borges always disappears in the universe's infinite textual-ity, imagined not as the result of a speaking Divine, the eternal Word, but as the divine Library of Babel that is both unlimited and cyclical: "If an eternal traveller were to cross it in any direction, after centuries he would see that the same volumes are repeated in the same disorder (which, thus, repeated, would be an order: the Order)."[53] This would be Borges's eternal recurrence of the same, in which all "I"s must be consumed, because "I" is the supreme textual nothing from which all texts emerge.

Paul Celan

In stark contrast to the late modernists and Borges is the poetry of Paul Celan. Emerging first in the 1950s, Celan's fertile darkness and negation was, along with Nelly Sachs, the first sustained attempt at responding aesthetically to the horrors of Auschwitz, and certainly the most important response in the German language. The figure of O is never explicitly rendered in his early poems, though its positive negating power is pervasive nonetheless, and perhaps finds its greatest symbolic manifestation in the most dominant and recurring image throughout all of his work: the eye. The eye for Celan is both blind and mirroring, both dry and tearful, both presenting and absenting. It is often a human eye, an eye of an unnamed "you" especially: "I looked for your eye when you opened it, no one was looking at you"; "You opened your eyes—I saw my darkness live"; "Your eye, as blind as the stone." But it is also "our eye," "Time's eye," "another eye, / a strange one," "Eyes, world-blind, in the fissure of dying," "Aching depth of the eyeball," etc.[54] This eye, which sees into the paradox as paradox itself, is closely associated with the word. The word both speaks and is silent, both harvests and destroys meaning, is both caged and free. "Our eyes and our mouths are so open and empty, Lord," says the prayerful as they bend down to "the crater" at the center of "Tenebrae."[55] This "crater" becomes the more explicitly named Nothing in the middle poems, especially in *Die Niemandsrose* (1963), where the "O" is brought directly into the poetry:

> O einer, o keiner, o niemand, o du:
> Wohin gings, da's nirgendhin ging?
> O du gräbst und ich grab, und ich grab mich dir zu,
> Und am Finger erwacht uns der Ring.

> [O one, o none, o no one, o you:
> Where did the way lead when it led nowhere?
> O you dig and I dig, and I dig towards you,
> And on our finger the ring awakes.][56]

Here in these poems the absence of the one God, as One, is most revealed. The empty heavens and silent stars shine blindly, and the cosmos has lost all center and all meaning. Yet this, for Celan, *contra* Pascal, is a place of reawakening: in the middle of "On Either Hand," "where your eye is" becomes "O this wandering empty / hospitable midst." The One, as Self, is cut off from this midst, as the last stanza expresses in its chopped manner:

> Das
> Selbe
> hat uns
> verloren, das
> Selbe
> hat uns

vergessen, das
Selbe
hat uns—

[One
and the same
has
lost us, one
and the same
has
forgotten us, one
and the same
has—][57]

This absence recurs in "Psalm" (again with "nothing" at its middle, before it ends with an "O over / the thorn"), in "Radix, Matrix" ("No one's / root—O / ours"), and in "Mandorla" ("Your eye, on Nothing it dwells").[58] Yet as the image of the *Niemandsrose* ("nobody's rose") suggests, it is not simply the loss of One that defines our situation—the O as nothing carries the possibility for reflowering. The fertile soil, though it "gapes" as a chasm, or perhaps *because* it gapes as a chasm, still allows growth. Celan's O, though dark and empty, though blackened by the ashes of the worst in human atrocity, and even perhaps by Celan's own final despair, is still a generative O. "Flower," he says, is "a blind man's word."[59]

Georges Bataille

The combination of generative power and death is played out on a very different register in the works of eroticism that came out of France during this period. The earliest and most striking of these is that of Georges Bataille, whose *Story of the Eye*, first written under the pseudonym of Lord Auch in the audaciously early 1928, showed a seminal fascination with the round object as a place of perverse negation. But it is in his novella *Madame Edwarda*, written in the late '30s but first published pseudonymously (Pierre Angélique) in the early '40s, where this negation takes its most concentrated form. Unlike the German response after the second great war, Bataille's writing explored the nature of desire, a desire that is always, at some level, destructive. This desire becomes the O that we have been figuring, not merely as it leads toward a sexual climax, but as it provides space to go *beyond*, in the absence that has been carved out by the encroachment of Nothing. Ecstasy is a central notion for Bataille—the going beyond or outside of oneself, in a manner very different from Borges's vision. The beyond is precisely where Bataille's eroticism intends to take us, even if beyond our normal conceptions of sexuality. It is not a question of titil-lation—about pornography designed for this purpose Bataille had nothing good to say—but of negation of what we thought ourselves to be, what world we thought we lived in. This negation obviously includes the negation of self, and the prostitute Madame Edwarda represents the ultimate loss of self in this regard. So in coupling with her, the narrator is himself lost to an infinite chasm: "[T]he mirrors which covered the walls, and of which the ceiling itself was made, multiplied the animal image of a coupling: at the slightest movement, our broken hearts opened up to the void into which the infinity of our reflections finished losing us."[60] But it also included the beyond of God, the monotheistic God of orthodox religion, and of Chris-tianity especially, so that as the prostitute opens herself in absolute blank surrender, she exclaims, "I am God."[61] Here, the ecstasy reaches perverse levels, and the inverse of rapturous delight becomes a certain repulsion at the opening the narrator encounters before him, the O that is physical, psychological, and spiritual all at once.

For Bataille, death and ecstasy become intermingled, where the loss at the center of negation is the beyond that transforms us beyond even nihil-ism itself. What we do at this "beyond" is beyond what we can say, beyond any meaning we could find for it. But it is in this ultimate excess where we reach our "final culmination." Bataille's O is an inverted religious desire that takes us outside anything we could call religion, while remaining true to the passion(s) that have escorted us, in their own way, through religion.

Dominique Aury/Anne Desclos

If Bataille's eroticism set a precedence, its most celebrated offspring (if such a term is here appropriate) is *The Story of O,* the erotic novel published in 1954 by Pauline Réage (pseudonym of Dominique Aury, who was in fact born Anne Desclos, as it later emerged). Once again total sexual surrender or submission leads to complete loss of self, as the name "O" suggests. But now the protagonist is not a prewar prostitute, who functions in spiritual oblivion, but a postwar fashion photographer, whose sexual escapades, even if at the behest of men, represents the fantasies of possibility. Despite succes-sive tortuous treatment, which worsens as the novel progresses, O becomes more serene, more accepting, more resigned, in what Susan Sontag has famously called "an ascent through degradation."[62] This is because love com-pels her, love for the man who first introduced her to this sacrificial pattern of self-annihilation. Unlike Bataille's parody of Christian self-sacrifice, *The Story of O* can be read very much as a straight allegory of the Christian passion story, this time with a woman as the lamb led to slaughter. It need not be, of course, and with the novel losing its initial erotic energy, and ending not so much with closure as with discontinuation, we can read it simply as the nothing of O that, with each successive orgasmic experience, is hollowed out even further, until, for better or worse, it reaches a purity of the lost, negated self. (Even the longtime double pseudonymity of its authorship lends itself to this loss.) In *The Story of O* we have the opening up of the erotic self as an attempt to counter the ineffaceable violence that the twentieth century, by its middle period, had come to embody. O's O represents the erotic possibility of that violence, turned now toward human self-giving.

Italo Calvino

But perhaps the most significant portrayal of O as Eros during this period does not come from France at all, but Italy. Italo Calvino's story *The Non-Existent Knight,* published in 1959, at first does not seem a story of sexual fantasy, but a fable of medieval chivalry. In fact, it seems so consciously fabular that the question of sex, cloaked in the raiment of chivalric love, appears as no more than something we might find in an expurgated version of a Chaucerian tale. A knight in shining white armor excels in the army of Charlemagne during battles with the Saracens. But what really sets him apart from all others is that beneath his impervious armor there is absolutely nothing inside. Fantastically, all the other knights, including the king himself, acknowledge this: the knight does not actually exist, despite the most elaborate of names—"Agilulf Emo Bertrandin of the Guildivern . . . ," etc., the absurd length of which betrays its inability to hold a "proper" name, and thus a "proper" being. And yet he carries on his knightly duties—organizing, arranging, fighting—in a manner superior to all the other knights, and with their total acceptance. This picture of an armored body, executing the required tasks and functions with a fastidious precision, and yet completely empty inside, becomes perhaps the perfect "coat of arms," as it were, for the O we have been trying to describe throughout. It even carries the figure zero from which the need of numbering gains its necessity:

> But if the world around was melting instead into the vague and ambiguous, he would feel himself drowning in that morbid half-light, incapable of allowing any clear though or act of decision or punctilio to flower in that void. In such moments he felt bad, faint, and sometime only at the cost of an extreme effort did he feel himself avoid melting away completely. It was then he began to count; trees, leaves, stones, lances, pine cones, anything in front of him . . .[63]

This nothing, counting in order to maintain an existence in spite of himself, could alone be the quintessential symbol of our mid-century O—loss functioning as gain, emptiness leading toward fulfillment, zero exercising cardinality. But there is more to this parable.

The knight is pursued by the only female in the composite army, a certain Bradamante (a name directly opposing the ephemerality of the knight), whose wanton ways are tossed aside in a desire (of Bataille-like vigor) for the one thing she had yet to possess, nonexistence itself. When the knight's title is drawn into question—he had gained his knighthood by rescuing a virgin from marauders, only to find the virgin's chastity now later being challenged—he sets off on a quest to find the virgin and clear his name, the name that, besides his white armor, is the only "subsistence" he can claim. Here, self-identity is connected to sexual purity, or to the lack of consummation. Bradamante follows after the knight in his quest because, having experienced sexual consummation with virtually the entire army, she now wants to know herself the consummation of pure nonexistence, the one sexual fantasy, or ecstasy (in Bataille's sense) that eludes her. She thus shuns the advances of all others, especially a young new warrior who has fallen fatuously in love with her, while he tries to model himself on the nonexistent knight.

In the course of his quest, the knight encounters Priscilla, a Siren-figure who lures men into her castle of women and, after consummation, reduces them to wastrels. Despite advance warning, the knight joins in the ritual of Priscilla's seduction. But his perfections in the art of courtly love—as O, he executes all codes of practice with meticulous success— soon gain the upper hand, and the Siren is led from one deferment to the next, each gesture inciting more desire than the next, until dawn breaks, and the knight, still armored in white, departs, leaving his seducee short of the consummation in which the entire ritual is designed to culminate. But Priscilla is strangely fulfilled. Her maidens have had the direct opposite experience with the knight's squire, "a subject who exists but doesn't realise he does," and who therefore takes on the identity of whatever is immediately before him, with a sexual compulsion of animal ferocity. But they are not fulfilled, these maidens; their consummations are reached quickly and with indifference. They want to know what true consummation is like with the white knight, and they entreat Priscilla to recount her experience. Yet she, in raptures, has nothing to say:

"But what did he *do*? What did he *do*?

"How can one tell that? Oh, lovely, how lovely it was . . ."

"But has he got everything? Yet . . . Do tell . . ."

"I simply wouldn't know how . . . So much . . ."[64]

The ultimate consummation—"so much"—is no consummation, and this is the nature of the O at work in its perfection.

So the O is naturally tied to the erotic, and to desire in all its post-Freudian permutations. What Calvino is portraying here is the mechanism of desire in a world after the One has receded: the moment consummation is reached, desire is lost; but if the possibility of consummation, as the singular end point or completion, whether sexual, historical, economic, religious, etc., is always deferred, desire becomes the remaining force that rules being. Thus, the consummation of desire, *as desire,* must be no consummation at all, just an ongoing deferment, carried forward by the desiring impulse in its increasing intensity, until the object departs altogether, and the desire is converted to memory (the memory of desire). Thus, in the end when the knight thinks he has failed in his quest, driven by his own desire to seek out virginity (the direct inverse of erotic desire), he disappears into thin air, and all that is left is his abandoned armor, strewn in pieces. And when the young aspiring knight puts on this armor, and uses it to seduce the female knight Bradamante, she is deeply disappointed at the moment of consummation, and retreats to a convent in a vow of chastity. Only at the end, when, through her writing of the tale (she is the narrator, we now find out), she has reinvoked the memory of desire, can she desire again, and pursue the existent knight who has come back to find her. But in pursuing that knight, and leaving the convent, she must break off her tale, so that consummation once again becomes impossible—the end of the story itself ensures that any union, or reunion, can only be in the realm of desire (for narrator, character, and reader alike). In this way Calvino's O becomes a greater harbinger for the postmodernity that is to follow this period, greater than *Madame Edwarda* and *The Story of the O,* whose repeated consummations plunge us into the black hole at the center of what we thought was an accomplished wholeness, but do not express the fundamental desire that outlines that hole, and that, like the white armor that gives nonexistence its form, allows us to pursue it willingly.

THE O OF AUDEN

Each of these above writers, and many more could be found (Céline, Stevens et al.)—the selection is representative, not comprehensive—shows the unusual literary prevalence, as well as diversity, of O during these

middle years. Their geographical spread also shows that this was a thoroughly Western fixation: Irish (displaced in Europe), British (via America),
Argentinian, German, French, and Italian. Collectively, they are indicative of a crucial change. But we have used Auden (the British poet who
moved to America and then spent half the year on an island in Italy) as
most representative because in his *The Sea and the Mirror* we find each
of the above Os opening and operating at some level. As a supposedly
"Christian conception of Art," it shares with Eliot the weight of religious
understanding required to grasp fully what Art (in its still capitalized form)
is trying to do or seek or express. In this sense the commentary is as earnest
as Eliot's poetry. But it shares with Beckett and Borges the self-reflexive
playfulness with which we must set out upon the task (in art or out), and
in this sense it counters earnestness with a necessary frivolity or a serious
sense of gaming.[65] Written during the 1939–1945 war, it also shares with
Celan a certain gravitas of human failure to avert atrocity, especially as
suggested by Antonio, and of human loss or destruction, especially in those
existential moments, prevalent throughout the poem, when one must learn
to live with one's death, whether imposed from outside or impelled from
within. And with Calvino it shares the sense of extravagant artifice, in
which a willing suspension of disbelief is made especially requisite, now in
a highly self-conscious manner.

What, upon first sight, *The Sea and the Mirror* does not seem to possess
is the eroticism that the O came to represent during this period in works by
Bataille, Réage (Aury/Desclos), and Calvino. And yet present scholarship
on Auden seems obsessed with reading Auden's work precisely through the
lens of an (auto)biographical eroticism. In John Fuller's large *Commentary* on
Auden's major works, "an autobiographical thrust" characterizes all the long
poems of the 1940s, we are told,[66] and *The Sea and the Mirror* is contextual-
ized by Auden's ill-fated relationship with Chester Kallman, what Auden
had called "l'affaire C." So, in reference to Prospero's poem, Fuller writes:

> The sexual ambience within which this truth [Art's function] may
> be glimpsed is interesting here. Auden revealed himself to Ansen
> as a "oncer," frightened of any deeper relationship than a one-night
> stand, hurt by Chester Kallman's defection. The holiness of his love
> for Kallman prompts complicated metaphors of Rome facing the
> barbarians and Andromeda chained for the dragon. The oblique-
> ness of Prospero's songs may be due to their originating in part in
> "l'affaire C," as "Prosper to Ariel" in general certainly did. As Auden
> admitted to Isherwood: "It's OK to say that Ariel is Chester, but
> Chester is also Caliban . . ."[67]

Fuller suggests the final poem, "Ariel to Prospero," "is perhaps cast as an aria as a tribute to Kallman, who could well recognize the opera's urge to transcend the passions it exploits, just as Auden could ruefully acknowledge that poetry could still be made out of sexual unhappiness (the body's lameness casts its shadow, the ideal that it can never be)."[68] This reading certainly accords with Calvino's nonexistent knight, and suggests that the ultimate O in the poem (the Ariel/Caliban fusion) is in fact a loss at the center of the consuming desire Auden had for his love.

Edward Mendelson, in his psychologically driven *Later Auden*, follows a similar line, especially in relation to Caliban's speech. Of the general period after the 1930s, when disillusionment with politics and social change reached its height, and Auden began writing *The Sea and the Mirror*, Mendelson remarks:

> The mind has no ultimate centre of meaning to which all other meanings refer or from which they are derived: Auden's exemption from the [war] draft and his revulsion against his efforts to reshape Kallman's personality combined to give a recurring pattern of thought and feeling a private erotic tinge that it had not had earlier and that, for many reasons, it would not have again.[69]

Mendelson does not explain this particular "erotic tinge" further, though he leaves us to think there is something in Auden's own middle period for which the O, as defined by Eros, is central in understanding what drives Auden's poetic task.

Richard Bozorth has written most specifically about Auden's homosexuality and this poetic task. In his *Auden's Games of Knowledge: Poetry and the Meanings of Homosexuality*, he suggests "Auden viewed poetry as a fictional but primal erotic encounter with the reader":[70]

> Auden is, I suggest, the modernist heir to Byron and Wilde, for his career constitutes a staging of public and private selves through a range of codings of queer desire. That Auden is preoccupied with the relation between public and private, the personal and the political, is hardly news. But I argue that his ongoing grapplings with these fraught binaries reflect in large measure this negotiation of the constraints on speakability traditionally faced by gay, lesbian, and queer writers.[71]

Thus: "Auden should be seen as central to a tradition of gay poetics of indeterminacy." Or, "Indeed, it is precisely Auden's perception of homosexuality *as a difference* that energizes his concerns with how poetry addresses others collectively and individually."[72]

And Arthur Kirsch, in his commentary on *The Sea and the Mirror*, also links Kallman's betrayal directly to the poem: "'The Crisis' in 'l'affaire C,' as Auden later called it, directly underlies Prospero's lyrics in Chapter I of 'The Sea and the Mirror': *'Inform my hot heart straight away / Its treasure loves another.'* But Auden's relation to Kallman also affects the representation of Caliban and Ariel in *The Sea and the Mirror*, and indeed the whole conception of art that Auden develops." He adds, "[H]is identification of Chester with the *lebendigste,* but ungovernably phallic, Caliban as well as with Ariel, who represented the Muse to Shakespeare as well as to him, also suggests that he saw an intersection between his vocation as a poet and his own sexual nature."[73]

So *The Sea and the Mirror* might be far more than an *Ars Poetica,* as Auden had once called it; when seen through the biographical life that is Auden's own sexual struggle, it seems to have become an *Ars Erotica.* Two years before he began this work, Auden wrote an epithalamium in honor of his "marriage" to Kallman. The poem, "In Sickness and in Health" (1940),[74] is in some ways an anticipation of *The Sea and the Mirror,* with the principal topic of Art exchanged for Love. And yet like the later work, the poem sets up two divisions, two ways of conceiving the phenomenon: animal, carnal desire on the one hand, and spiritual, divinized Love on the other. One might even say these correspond to the sickness and health of the title. Mediating these two realms is society (just as the Anglican Church mediates holy matrimony, from whose rite the title is taken). Society was in the grip of "murderous year" in 1940, and the image of this time in the opening stanza is that of a "Black / Dog" leaping upon the individual's back in a ferociously copulative gesture. "Inert," "corrupt," with "New Machiavellis flying through the air," this society, having now politicized Eros ("nature in unnature ends," rejecting the "disobedient phallus for the sword"), can only see the healthy side with "metaphysical despair," the sick side with murder as "their last voluptuous sensation." The passion needed for either side, carnal or spiritual love, has been reduced to "one passionate negation." "How warped the mirrors where are worlds are made," sighs the poet.

And yet, as Auden does not simply give over to either Caliban or Ariel, either the sea or the mirror, so here too he does not simply reject the carnal sickness for divine health, whatever inadequacies society may hold in either respect. As the title suggests, both sides need to remain integral to the lovers' relationship. In the first half, where the dangers of wrong and wronged love are set out in admonition, he tells his love: "O promise nothing, nothing, till you know / The kingdom offered by the love-lorn eyes /

A land of condors, sick cattle and dead flies." There is an acknowledgment of a necessary fallibility in our relationships; "we are always in the wrong," and love must be constantly aware of its "selfish loves." But despite this, in the second half, there is a call to "Rejoice." This call is first introduced in the poem's middle stanza,[75] emanating from the "tohu-bohu" of our lives. "Tohu-bohu" is the transliteration of the Hebrew found in Genesis 1:2, which the Authorized Version translates as "without form and void"; both terms point to emptiness and vacuity. And Auden soon after links this phrase with the circle:

> Rejoice, dear love, in Love's peremptory word;
> All chance, all love, all logic, you and I,
> Exist by grace of the Absurd,
> And without conscious artifice we die:
> O, lest we manufacture in our flesh
> The lie of our divinity afresh,
> Describe round our chaotic malice now,
> The arbitrary circle of a vow.

Emergent in this stanza are all the themes of the later long poem: existence by virtue of the Absurd, the self-conscious construction of artifice that is our "real" life, the dispossession of self's sovereignty (the "lie of our divinity"), the encircling chaos and malice, and the artificer's circle to protect us from these, here an "arbitrary" yet necessary avowal of a social construct (a marriage vow) that somehow keeps to the peremptory nature of a greater Love. As in the end of Caliban's speech, the divine Word issues forth, but it takes several forms in this poem besides the Kierkegaardian "Absurd": "O Essence of creation," "O Fate," "O Felix Osculum" ("happy kiss"). The interjecting "O" accompanies each deliberately, for this divine is less the loving Word of the New Testament than it is the creating Elohim of the Old Testament and Hebrew Scriptures, who creates out of the void and empty space. "Remain nocturnal and mysterious," he says to these Os in the final lines, with their function of marrying opposites. The "Essence of creation" must force desire to seek it within "Thy substances"; "Fate" must "hold us to the voluntary way"; the Felix Osculum, invoking the Felix Culpa, must teach us to "love soberly"—the sensuous kiss combining positively with divine embrace, as the manufacturing of our flesh combined negatively with the fabrications of our divinity.[76] Thus, whatever conception of the divine we might construe out of our "tohu-bohu," it is never divorced from the postlapsarian Eros of our being. And so in the penultimate stanza he inscribes the O into the very endangered sphere of love that always must exist between two humans wedded in passion:

> That this round O of faithfulness we swear
> May never wither to an empty nought
> Nor petrify into a square,
>   . . . permit
> Temptations always to endanger it.

The metaphysical conceit, the "round O" (as the marriage ring, the construct of the marriage vow, the divine Love to whom we are ultimately faithful), is also a necessary invitation to temptation, to the disruption of that faithfulness, to the desire of Eros directed elsewhere, the essence of the Fall (to which of course Kallman eventually succumbed). And thus it is in this tension that the "empty nought" (with pun on "knot") is, against the "I" of the poem's very intention, already operative.

There is a further irony: the poem eroticizes the O within the artifice of the metaphysical poets. (The poem is modeled on the grand style of these poets, Donne's "The Litanie" especially, with its hallowed subject and lofty tone.)[77] But it does more than treat "sex as a sort of church ritual," as has been argued;[78] it also marks out the O that is at the center of desire, both sexual and spiritual, to suggest a kind of Bataille-like and Calvino-like convergence of both realms. It does this, like both Bataille and Calvino, within the constructs and embellishments of literature. Going farther than the metaphysical conceit of Donne's era ("Deliver us for thy descent / Into the Virgin, whose wombe has a place / Of middle kind . . ."),[79] it becomes the orgasm in Bataille's erotic world that takes one Beyond, into the night and mystery, where all self is lost.

> But all of being, ready and open—for death, joy, or torment—unreservedly open and dying, painful and happy, is there already with its shadowed light, and this light is divine: and the cry that being—vainly?—tries to utter from a twisted mouth is an immense *alleluia*, lost in endless silence.

So ends Bataille's "A Preface to 'Madame Edwarda,'" written in 1957.[80] Auden's earlier poem is both a celebration and lament of this insight, an attempt to rejoice in the face of "suffering [love] too little or too long," to find something divine in love's inevitable pain. And inevitable it was for Auden, as "l'affaire C" proved a year or so later.

THE EROTICS OF O

But why this fascination with reading Auden through his sexual biography? Why now even our own reading of it, here in this one poem chosen among numerous possibilities? Is it because, like the Kierkegaard who so influenced him during this middle period, his romantic relations are fraught with such life-altering disunion that his writings become transparent coverings over the pathology of the self? Is it because his homosexuality turned the O into something that frustrated further his ability to stabilize his inner being, under the wary acceptance of society and Church, and thus that hollowed out even more the place where his "I" might dwell? And yet we've been arguing that the O displaces the historical biography of any one author.

In answer we might say that an erotics of O functions on several fronts. First, it collapses that age-old distinction between body and spirit, a dualism we saw actually predicated on Oneness. But now the body is not merely the material substance of our corporeal self, but all its attendant drives and desires, those that operate in the subterranean channels of our being. The eroticization of the spiritual is not something new to the West—it is as old at least as Teresa of Avila of the sixteenth century, and a lot older if we consider the ancient Greeks. But here, in the twentieth century, it becomes part of a widening imaginary in which the sexualization of the supposedly liberated self no longer contends with its spiritual longing, since either the one is the sublimation of the other (the first half of the century, as informed by Freud), or both are under the compulsion of the same symbolic desire (the second half of the century, as informed by Lacan).[81] For Auden in the middle ("In Sickness and in Health"), sublimation is the "sin of the high-minded," because it "damns the soul by praising it": reason, that is, forces sexuality into the safer realm of the noncorporeal. Instead, our corporeal bodies ("Thine opaque enigmas") need to seek out in desire the substances of creation's Essence. The *Felix Osculum* becomes the arch-image of this fusing desire: the kiss that rescues the original sin of the Garden by undamning, as it were, its passionate tides, and allowing them to move across the human/divine gulf.

Secondly, in its erasure of this dualism, the O allows the history of the body to be made present. We should perhaps say made present *again*, that is, represented, in a history that can never be original, except in the sense of being originated (anew). In that representation, the body is already compromised in its purity of presence. It is such compromise that Auden was trying to "represent" in his epithalamium, a poem of love's ultimate compromise, where the O of faithfulness must remain forever endangered, where conscious artifice is necessary for survival, where nature inevitably ends "in unnature." We can speak of "Auden" then because his own "nature," his biographical and autobiographical elements and features, arise out of an Eros that must always keep the body in view, even if it is a body reshaped—unnatured—by Eros's own poetic devices. Auden was continually fascinated by the inability of poetry to retrieve the original feeling or experience that first motivated the poem, as we saw earlier in his Ferdinand poem of *The Sea and the Mirror*, and later in his prose poem "Dichtung und Wahrheit," the most elaborate and expressive of this dilemma.[82] The erotic moves us (as a forwarding impulse) toward the Audenian "I" that is always compromised by its own guilt of not being the purely natural self (Calvino's Knight).[83] But it is that very guilt (an "erotic" guilt where the object of desire is always something other than what it appears, even in the Lacanian sense of the *objet petit a*, which remains inextricable with the ego) that generates the writing, that allows the history its starting point, and that allows us to reconstruct an "Auden" from the "I" that is always not there—"The I Without a Self," as he says of Kafka's writing. The reconstruction is always "literary": the superlative contrivance that is Caliban's speech shows us this. But it is also "negative": it is not about reconstructing a singular portrait of truth regarding any one person, but about allowing, through the ambiguities of writing's devices and fissures, the self to emerge from a lack, a lack that, like Cordelia's nothing, nevertheless signifies something important, something even "honest," we might say. So Auden writes of Kafka:

> In the case of the ordinary novelist or playwright, a knowledge of his personal life and character contributes almost nothing to one's understanding of his work, but in the case of a writer of parables like Kafka, biographical information is, I believe, a great help, at least in a negative way, by preventing one from making false readings. (The "true" readings are always many.)[84]

The erotic always lends itself to parable (Bataille, Aury/Desclos, Calvino, and, below, Brecht) because, unlike pornography, the consummation, as meaning, is always, if not deferred, then lost in dispossession or abandonment or multiplicity. The parable never states exactly what it means. So a biographical reading of Auden does not bring us to some essential Auden, whatever that would be, any more than Klossowski's reading of Nietzsche's letters brings us to an essential Nietzsche. Rather, it brings us to a multiplicity of readings, none of which are any truer than the other, because in the middle of them all is an O that stares out blankly for some reconfiguration. In "One Circumlocution," the final stanzas press the issue:

> One circumlocution as used as any
> Depends, it seems, upon the joke of rhyme
> For the pure joy; else why should so many
>
> Poems which make us cry direct us to
> Ourselves at our least apt, least kind, least true,
> Where a blank I loves blankly a blank You?[85]

The last line here embodies the "one circumlocution" as the O's eroticization of I, the blank that keeps returning, through love (carnal and spiritual), to the blankness of both "I" and "Other."

Thirdly, then, the erotics of O instantiates this blankness as a fundamental abandonment. "One" is not only passively abandoned by its own self, but One actively abandons itself to the nothing that is, ultimately, its own death. Bataille is our foremost and fiercest spokesman for this erotic death.

> We receive being in an intolerable transcendence of being, no less intolerable than death. And since in death it is given and taken away at the same time we must seek it in the feeling of death, in those unbearable instants where we seem to be dying because the being within us is only there through excess, when the fullness of horror and joy coincide.[86]

This kind of ecstasy, where the self is self-abandoned (or self-transcended), is for Bataille coextensive with death: the erotic O is always the extremities of both intensified life and intensified death, the "I" always given up, exceeded, in a fullness that is simultaneous emptiness. This simultaneity plays itself out on all parties involved.

SIMONE DE BEAUVOIR

And so this death can be gendered as well. But apart from Aury/Desclos, who draws a picture of the ultimately submissive female, where are the women writers in this story of O? Can the death of being in Bataille be neutered in such a way that gender has no bearing on the kind of death being experienced? Simone de Beauvoir, in her classic text of these middle decades, *Le Deuxieme Sexe* (*The Second Sex*, 1949), shows us that it cannot. She writes about women's experience in love, and the kind of self-abandonment they undergo. Men, even "in their most violent of transports," will "never abdicate completely; even on their knees before a mistress, what they still want is to take possession of her."[87] She calls men the "sovereign subject (*sujet souverain*)," a wonderfully paradoxical phrase suggesting a sovereign subjectivity undercut by being subject to its own desires. But women are wholly servile subjects: in love they exist for the sake of the sovereign male only, in profound and comprehensive self-abandonment.

> Shut up in the sphere of the relative, destined to the male from childhood, habituated to seeing in him a superb being whom she cannot possibly equal, the woman who has not repressed her claim to humanity will dream of transcending her being toward one of these superior beings, of amalgamating herself with the sovereign

subject. There is no other way out for her than to lose herself, body and soul, in him who is represented to her as the absolute, the essential.[88]

What de Beauvoir was able to chart in her groundbreaking study of this middle period, which comes *before* Bataille's *Eroticism* (even if after Sartre's *Being and Nothingness*), was the way men had arrogated the One and the "I" for themselves, absolutizing its material embodiment through abstraction and divine right. What she was able to invoke, even in this laconic phrase "sovereign subject," was the untenability of this hold on power, the internal division and paradox that it ultimately possessed. And what she was able to inaugurate, in her own history of women as the "second sex," was a way for women to rescue their own eroticism from a dominating male imagination. Like Bataille, her language here is decidedly religious, in her employment of such terms as *immanence* and *transcendence*. Love, before and under the male sovereign subject, "becomes for her a religion." She will "humble herself to nothingness before him."[89] But this religion is a purely immanent one, and a purely negative one, bound to the male sovereign in self-annihilation, and "shrouded in darkness: darkness of the flesh, of the womb, of the grave."[90] She can transcend this darkness, this negative (or negating) religion, in a kind of mystical ecstasy, but one still very much dependent upon the male and his religious discourse, upon, that is, his absolutization of his relation to her, or of her relation to him, in which he assimilates her into his own sovereign One. At this point, "abandon becomes sacred ecstasy,"[91] and the mystic dream seems fulfilled: the absolute dream of losing oneself in the other, of ecstatic union, of a kind of Neoplatonic consummation. Except that this dream of transcendence—and here Bataille would agree with her—is in fact not fulfilled: "She abandons herself to love first of all to *save herself*; but the paradox of idolatrous love is that in trying to save herself she *denies herself* utterly in the end."[92] Or as she concludes her chapter on the mystics:

> But in themselves these attempts at individual salvation are bound to meet with failure; either woman puts herself into relation with an unreality: her double, or God; or she creates an unreal relation with a real being. In both cases she lacks any grasp on the world; she does not escape her subjectivity; her liberty remains frustrated.[93]

De Beauvoir, contra Bataille, calls instead for "positive action." And indeed what her "history," as an "originating" history, enabled in the latter half of the twentieth century was for women to begin to realize their liberty through various positive actions, the creativity of literature being among the most important of these. But the embracing of the O remains part of this "history," since it operates to strip the "sovereign subject" of its sovereignty, releasing both men and women from their own subjected desires, whether toward possession (men) or dispossession (women), and toward a desire, an "eroticism," in which the abandonment of self is part now of a mutual acknowledgment, a leveling of all being through the nothing of its innermost center. As Judith Butler will later say, "Desire can thus be said to reveal negation as constitutive of experience itself"—regardless of gender.[94] We will see next chapter how this has been theorized in other, later feminist thinkers around the concept of the O directly.

This gendering of O's erotics is significant here because it undercuts gender sovereignty as much as One's sovereignty. Or perhaps better, it undercuts One's sovereignty *as* gendered sovereignty. And in this light it accords with Auden's homosexuality, for the sovereignty of sexual identity is also undermined in the same gesture. Auden was generally reticent about his sexual orientation. He never disavowed his own homosexuality, or that in others, but by the same token he never championed it as a right. If pushed, he saw it as a psychic maladjustment, but one that ought to be worked out on a personal level, not a social level. And, as is increasingly being argued, his poetry was, ironically, part of that personal level. But the shift to the middle period, from his move to America onward, showed that the "personal" was forever being rewritten, that whatever "adjustments" were needing to be made could only come through an artificiality that, by necessity, distanced both author and reader alike from any original being. This was not a deliberate obscuring of the self through literary trickery, as we might find in Borges. Nor was it an existential deconstruction of the self through imagined character, as we could find in Beckett's novel trilogy (*Molloy*, *Malone*, and finally *The Unnamable*). Auden's "I" was genuinely "self"—the "I" upon whose arm lay that sleeping head in 1937 could say in full genuineness: "Let the living creature lie, / Mortal, guilty, but to me / The entirely beautiful."[95] And yet in the middle period that "self" would become increasingly caught up in an intensification of baroque conceit, while its genuineness increasingly lost to a silence. Auden's personal erotic struggle falls to this similar division of conceit and silence. But it is in this very division that we can see *all* sexual identity caught. We rewrite our identity over and over, whether in confirmation of societal expectations, or, if we embrace the O, in the contradictions of self-abandonment. What is at the core of our desire is a nothing that requires the greatest of conceits to "enact." This is the lesson of Calvino's parable of the nonexistent Knight. In the "enactment," all self-sovereignty is lost, including sexual sovereignty (Priscilla the seducer becomes herself seduced by the enactment of nothing), and we all find ourselves falling silent before our preconceptions and our expectations. Perhaps we might say that Auden's homosexuality is significant because it is a basis for neither pathology nor ethics, for neither reform nor doctrine. Its significance is in a reticence that engulfs all sexual orientation, since love's desire is forever toward a fundamental blankness that erases all distinction, even if elaborated through the artifices of our constructed selves. As Auden would write later in 1953, in a poem whose title is already under erasure—"'The Truest Poetry is the Most Feigning'":

> What but tall tales, the luck of verbal playing,
> Can trick his lying nature into saying
> That love, or truth in any serious sense,
> Like orthodoxy, is a reticence?[96]

What makes both questions of gender and sexual orientation found in de Beauvoir and Auden of the 1940s and '50s here more than a token acknowledgment of present-day emancipatory discourses is their connection of O's erotics to religion. Auden's shift to Christianity coincides with his most important love "affair"—a marriage, a divorce, a longing for restitution, an acknowledgment of love's inherent faithlessness. This coincidence makes for an understanding of religious love that is always informed by the flesh. As Bozorth says, for Auden, "the interrelation of Eros and Agape was an abiding concern,," the two ultimately seeming "to merge in his views of poetry."[97]

If "In Sickness and in Health" treated this coincidence from the principle vantage of the flesh (the marriage of flesh being worked out in terms of religion), then the long works of the 1940s, especially *For the Time Being* (1941–42), but also *The Age of Anxiety* (1944–46), saw it from the principle vantage of the spirit (religion being worked out in terms of the flesh). Either way, it is the *co-incidence* that matters. Likewise for de Beauvoir, her emphasis on the mystics in the final chapters of her magnum opus is in anticipation of the final part, "Towards Liberation." Mystical ecstasy is an important step in taking women beyond the purely negative immanence of religion, which remains under the authority of the male, and in allowing for a transcendence, even if that of their own very self. But it is crucial to see that this transcendence alone cannot suffice: it must be reintegrated back into human society, it must allow women to reinsert themselves back into *their situation* within that society, in order for women to find authentic liberty. (Here we see the influence of Sartre's philosophy, though Hegel's fundamentally.) If we employ the (mystical) language of religion it must be for the purposes of grounding women in the lived realities they materially experience and of encouraging a genuine reciprocity of gender relations and human love. So, "Christianity gave eroticism its savor of sin and legend when it endowed the human female with a soul; if society restores her sovereign individuality to woman, it will not thereby destroy the power of love's embrace to move the heart." On the contrary, "when we abolish the slavery of half of humanity, together with the whole system of hypocrisy that it implies, then the 'division' of humanity will reveal its genuine significance and the human couple will find its true form."[98]

De Beauvoir never wrote a theology. Nor did Auden as such, though his Christianity increasingly informed his writing from the middle period,[99] out of which one might construct a theological poetics.[100] What both allowed is a figuration of O's erotic nature that takes us to a place beyond all sovereignties, and toward a trans-sovereign understanding of both the human and the divine. This figuration will find a broadening in both philosophy and religion as the twentieth century progresses through the second half. But as we have already seen with Blanchot and Bataille, and as we will see with others, that broadening becomes inclusive of art, even necessitates art. In our final section we will see a return to philosophy and to religion that, under the circumscription of the O, involves necessarily a poetics, a poetics of negation.

PART THREE

LOOKING AFTER O

SIX

THE REMAKING OF PHILOSOPHY

AND RELIGION

So I break off here, provisionally, the reading of *The Origin*. The encirclement of the circle was dragging us into the abyss. But like all *production*, that of the abyss came to saturate what it hollows out.

—Jacques Derrida, *The Truth in Painting*

There is a clearing, a lighting. Thought of in reference to what is, to beings, this clearing is in a greater degree than are beings. This open center is therefore not surrounded by what is; rather, the lighting center itself encircles all that is, like the Nothing which we scarcely know.

—Martin Heidegger, "The Origin of the Work of Art"

PHILOSOPHY AND RELIGION: INSIDE THE PERIMETER

We began with a history in which philosophy and religion, as proprietors of the One, with its long and fruitful reign in Western constructions of reality, held a distinct advantage over art in ordering how we conceptualize the cosmos (or later, the *universe*) and our human position within it. Theories of art were largely held to a mimetic role: the work of art was to imitate, or reflect back to us, the truth of the world in its unified structure. Mimesis in fact only worked within such a structure: it depends on the binaries of imitation/imitated, reflection/reflected, image/reality, where the first term is grounded in the second as the veritable location of Truth in its divinely singular form. This is how the *Imago Dei* had customarily been understood—humans are an image of the creator God, and therefore human creations

199

are the image of the created realm. Western religion, especially in its most comprehensive stages when theology and philosophy had no categorical distinction (the stages when mimetic theory was at its height, and the One had catholic sovereignty), had controlling power in assuring the One its supreme place, and thus in holding art to its subservient place, because the One is a *conceptual* notion, even the arch-conceptual notion. The One does not survive outside of philosophy/religion. The ancient Greeks under-stood this best when they made mathematics and geometry synonymous with philosophy and religion, and, as with Euclid, conceived of One beyond numbering, and as the basis of numbering.

But what of the O? It too is conceptual, but it is also anticonceptual. Better, the O is the place that allows the conceptual first to emerge. It is therefore the place of creative genesis, the nothing as the origin, the gen-erative locus of beginning, the *tohu-bohu*. How then does it operate within philosophy and religion, if its presence is a countervailing force to unity and unification? *Can* it operate—or was Parmenides right, that nothing should be precluded completely from all our thought and speech?

If philosophy and religion are to admit the O, or penetrate the O, they are not simply to admit the concept of nothing, as a concept (the nothing *as* something, e.g.—"nothing *is*"; or an apophaticism).[1] They must also admit something (or nothing) preconceptual, the nature of O in its function as a generative mode before conceptuality. That is, they must admit creation, or *poesis,* unveiled in Part II of our discussion. In the language of the creative, they must admit Caliban, or Caliban as Ariel. Yet despite Western philosophy and religion's general insistence upon the conceptual as their foundation, they have always admitted this Caliban, if unwittingly, onto their islands of reason. More disturbingly, they have been forced to acknowledge Caliban's original residency there. Such is the case in our Western religious traditions the moment they introduce "the sacred text," and such is the case of our earliest Western philosophers such as Parmenides, who could only disclose the Truth through *mythos* ("didactic" perhaps, but a poem nevertheless), or Plato, for whom *mythoi* were a continual and nec-essary encroachment into the dialogues of *logoi,* or later Lucretius, whose materialist poem *De Rerum Natura* is predicated ultimately upon the Void.

If we traced One's drawn-out reign and eventual abdication of the throne in chapter 1—albeit in the dangerously sketchy and meager form of a selective history of ideas—we now must trace out briefly the rise of the replacement to that throne in the form of O's insubordinate residence within the philosophical and, in the latter half of the twentieth century, religious/ theological domains. Here we shall see art no longer the handmaiden in a mimetic relationship of hierarchical power. Art, as *mythos,* is brought into the innermost chambers of conceptuality as co-resident. There, with its unruly powers of passion, it seduces reason into audacious submission toward the negative. But how can reason accept, willingly, the embrace of negativity, without abandoning itself altogether, and for good?

NEGATION'S TRIUMVIRATE: HEGEL, NIETZSCHE, HEIDEGGER

In chapter 1 we saw the modern One, in appropriating all the inherited paradigms of One into an unsustainable unity of newness, succumb to a competing multiplicity and inevitable relinquishment of rule. Our tracing there was all too faint, but in part because the introduction of the modern, we saw, also coincides with the introduction of a fundamental diremption at the heart of Lutheran and Cartesian subjectivity. The O, we said in chapter 0, helps to define "modernity." And now we are in a position to say more firmly that it does so precisely because the "modus," the here and now quality of the newness marking the modern turn, is constituted modally by a generative power to bring in the new. Modernity before the twentieth century is thus made up of a tacit power struggle between a One trying to function within competing paradigms of the new, and an O that allows that very new its newness. The *newly* One simply does not hold to the end. It is de-constructive at its core. (Perhaps this is why the theology of ongoing creation—*creatio continua*—has never sat comfortably within orthodoxy.) Thus, it was only a matter of time before explicit and sustained attention was given to that de-constructive condition (as *deconstruction*) within a philosophical context.

In his early analysis on Freud and philosophy, Paul Ricoeur famously proposed "three masters of suspicion" for our critical heritage: Marx, Nietzsche, and Freud.[2] Under this illumination, we propose in turn, using Blanchot as our Sybil, "three masters of negation": Hegel, Nietzsche, and Heidegger. That Nietzsche should share in both rolls of honor should not surprise us, since suspicion and critique, and the corresponding question of interpretation in which Ricoeur first cast his three masters, are correlative with the nature of the O. And though Hegel and Heidegger have never been traditionally understood as starting from positions of suspicion as such, their philosophies begin by suspecting something *other* about the true nature of "Spirit" (*Geist*) and "Being" (*Dasein*) respectively. We could go farther and say that their analyses of negation, like Nietzsche's, are inherently those of "suspecting" the positive negation of O, bearing in mind that the Latin *suspicio*, from which we derive our "suspicion," cuts both ways: the literal "look up" (*sub-spicio*) can in Latin be rendered "look up *to*," in admiration, as much as "look at furtively," in mistrust. Let us then quickly sketch a triptych of mastery on O's paradoxical existence within our conspectus of modern reality.

Hegel

No modern philosopher has explored negation more seriously, and more comprehensively, than Hegel in the beginning years of the nineteenth century. Leibniz had equated negation with evil in his theodical attempts (*"nihil est sine ratione"*). Kant had had his antinomies, but they were apparent contradictions operating as a result of the limitations that the phenomena/ noumena split necessarily presented, a result of overstepping our rational boundaries: in the realm of the infinite or the unconditional, the principle of reason can only be regulative, but not constitutive.[3] Schelling was the first to expose truly the Godhead to its own necessary internal negation with his notion of indifference in the non-ground [*Ungrund*] or not-Being [*Nicht-sein*].[4] But Hegel, following Schelling, was the first to elaborate negation as something more than the result of a limitation or indifference: conversely, it operates in the very essence of who or what we are as being *actively*. We have already alluded to Hegel as a producer of split decisions: to some, Hegel's system is the apotheosis of the One in its most absolutized form, a One, we have said, approaching a perfect unity of materiality and spirit; yet to others, more recent Continental theorists, Hegel's understanding of nega-tion is the very marker of our times, undermining every notion of system, including Hegel's own dialectical System in its most advanced form. Hegel then becomes the absolute fulcrum on which, philosophically, the fall and rise of the One and the O make their pivot.

How do we summarize such a complex understanding in a philosopher so accustomed to contrary interpretations, and in the limited space we can only allow ourselves here? Perhaps we can approach the matter this way. Philosophy and religion have always been obsessed with trying to determine the fundamental force that generates into being. This is why most all reli-gions offer creation accounts, or cosmogonies, and why philosophies have tried to find alternative names for the power or motive force that stands at the basis of our ontology, if that name is not ultimately "God" (and hence ontotheology). This is not merely a matter of playing God ourselves—the "Frankenstein syndrome"—but of trying to determine what is the ultimate relation between creation and freedom, or, we could say, between the deter-minable and the indeterminable, the material and the spirit. Every religion, every philosophy, tries to explain how generative powers of creativity (in or as God/gods, in or as ourselves) relate to the question of freedom (Are we free or determined? Is the universe open-ended or prescribed? Is real-ity a place for making or merely describing? Is our self-identity brought about through activity or passivity?—and so on). The concept of One has remained so powerful and effective because it neatly provides a paradigm to treat both sides: there is one ultimate source of creation, and therefore there is one way of best acting in accordance with that source (whether it be toward freedom or away from it). Stoicism offers a perfect "resolve" here: there is one cosmic design or plan, and it is up to us to act in accordance with it or not. The inherent diremption within modernity is a result, we could say, of losing such a resolve, insofar as the subjectivity that stands over against objectivity now has no way of assuring its connection, or reconnection, to that objectivity. Its unity with the whole, whether freely granted or freely obtained, is fundamentally renounced. Hegel's philosophy, of course, offered a new resolve to this dilemma by collapsing the two, creation and freedom, determinability and indeterminability, subjectivity and objectivity, into an absolute "one." But that "one," as "One," had already abdicated its own unity—and there is the rub.

The generative force that makes creation and freedom possible is negation. This is Hegel's great contribution to the history of nothing, his great insight into the O. What *initiates*, what *drives*, what *compels*, what *furnishes possibility* for all these motive forces, is in fact the power of negation. We can understand why it took so long for modern thought to understand this crucial point (in Hegel or out), since very little in our Western conceptual history would ever allow for such contradictory thinking. And yet Hegel builds it into the very foundation of his "system." We can catch a glimpse of this negation in the early tour de force *Phenomenology of Spirit*, where he employs different terms to develop the notion: *difference, pure opposite, antithesis, contradiction, self-sundering, division,* and *negation* itself. In the Preface he refers to "the tremendous power of the negative; it is the energy of thought, of the pure 'I,' and famously says that 'tarrying with the negative' is a 'magical power' that converts Spirit into being."[5] But it is the subsequent *Science of Logic* (1812) where negation comes into its own, as it were, out of the nothing that is co-constitutive of being. There is being (something), and there is nonbeing (nothing), and in their respective purities the two become identical. For pure being, without any differentiation or determination, would in fact be engulfed by its absence of determination, and therefore would be *nothing*. Pure nothing, as thoroughgoing equality with itself, would likewise be without any determination, and in its absence be the same as pure being. If these two are in fact the same, how can we speak of them differently, especially as pure opposites? For Hegel, the two pass over into each other constantly and simultaneously, but they remain distinct through *becoming*, that third term which introduces the force of *movement*. In becoming, being and nothing coexist, because both are coming-to-be and ceasing-to-be, both arising and vanishing, at all times throughout their movement. Just when we can say one is distinguished, its distinguished character is extinguished, and extinguished in the other. That vanishing then *becomes* the other, the arising. Such is the very basis of the dialectical movement: one can only come into existence through the negating of the other. Determination, then, comes about because two sames (a fundamental paradox) are differentiated through their mutual negation of the other. Thus it is that negation *allows* for being to arise: "this, to be the negation of nothing, constitutes being." We get a sense of the difficulty involved here in the following passage from the *Science of Logic*:

> Being only *is* as the movement of nothing to nothing, and as such is its essence; and the latter does not *have* this movement *within it*, but is this movement as a being that is itself absolutely illusory, pure negativity, outside of which there is nothing for it to negate but which negates its own negative, which latter *is* only in this negating.[6]

If this is impenetrable philosophizing, it is so partly because it is trying to conceptualize that which ultimately evades conceptualization. A less inscrutable description of the same point comes a little later under the section "Contradiction":

> Something moves, not because at one moment it is here and at another there, but because at one and the same moment it is here and not here, because in this "here," it at once is and is not. The ancient dialecticians [e.g., Zeno] must be granted the contradictions that they point out in motion; but it does not follow that therefore there is no motion, but on the contrary, that motion is *existent* contradiction itself.[7]

Such thinking then allows the bold claim: "contradiction is the root of all movement and vitality; it is only in so far as something has contradiction within it that it moves, has an urge and activity."[8] And, "Something is therefore alive only in so far as it contains contradiction within it, and moreover is this power to hold and endure the contradiction within it."[9] Or, in direct reference to the generative force that makes creation and freedom possible: "Only when manifold terms have been driven to the point of contradiction do they become active and lively towards one another, receiving in contradiction the negativity which is the indwelling pulsation of self-movement and spontaneous activity [*Lebendigkeit*]."[10] All this has been rendered as the classic Hegelian dialectic, which propels history forward only on the basis of an antithesis set against a thesis, the sublation of which (synthesis) will require a further antithesis to keep it moving.[11]

At work through this movement, then, is the "System," as Kierkegaard would pejoratively call it. But what keeps Hegel himself alive in our contemporary thinking is not his "System" as such. Hegelianism, as an absolute philosophical program, whether in its right manifestation (idealism) or left manisfestation (historical materialism), has not held up to the forces of twentieth-century history. What keeps Hegel's thinking alive is the root of that "System," the movement of negation, which even undermines the "System" itself.

In the later systematic outworking of the Hegelian dialectic as it develops through history, art gives way to religion, which in turn gives way to philosophy. Each stage is important, historically, but each stage is also "surpassed." The original artistic (creative) impulse, once it reaches self-reflection, becomes "aesthetics," and after aesthetics there is nowhere for art to go but to give way to a higher reflection. So in his introduction to the *Lectures on Aesthetics,* Hegel famously claims that art is a "thing of the past."[12] Religion too, once it has manifested itself in self-consciousness, finds that it must give way to the highest form of reflection, philosophy, where philosophy becomes, as he says at the end of his *Lectures on the Philosophy of Religion,* "the reconciliation of God with himself and with nature."[13] This pinnacle was the "absolute knowing" of the earlier *Phenomenology.*

But what if we held back art from reaching aesthetics (the conceptualization of art in self-reflection) and returned to that impulse which stands behind all creative activity, the "indwelling pulsation of self-movement" above? If we take this impulse as fundamentally "art," the very ability for the work to come into being, as art—and is this not the primary focus of so much art since Shakespeare's Prospero first turned his attentions on his craft, and such as we find with the Romantics (Coleridge's "Kubla Khan")?— then "art" is always complicit with negation and even, in Hegelian terms, constitutive of negation, and therefore art is only ever "a thing of the past," only ever "surpassed," in its motivating role as a negating power that, in its own sublation, negates or surpasses *itself.* And if this is true, then it is not only "art" that falls to this negation, or self-surpassing, but also *religion and philosophy.* For by the nature of its own internal contradictions, religion and philosophy too are motivated by negation, and therefore must face their own countervailment, their own Calibans, at the very core of their conceptual existence. And Hegelianism is not spared. What keeps Hegel so alive, so crucial in our history of the O, is his own self-motivated contradiction, which launches a mastery of negation that is at the same time a complete self-sundering and renunciation of that mastery. Hegel's O, in spite of Hegel himself, in spite of what Derrida called Hegel's 'ontotheological circle,'[14] is philosophy's absolute *suspicion* of itself.

Nietzsche

Nietzsche, suspicious by nature, directed his suspicions repeatedly at the history of metaphysics, and thus at the One that stood behind it, especially in its Platonic-Christian guise. We have already evoked, through Klossowski, Nietzsche's O in the form of eternal return of the same, where *history*, as much as the history of *metaphysics*, is called into profound question, as well as the history of the "I" that claims to know either. Two further features of his thinking now emerge within this O, and both relate to Hegel's own "mastery": the question of nihilism, and the creativity of interpretation. Let us briefly look at each.

Nietzsche's understanding of nihilism—and how many different versions of nihilism there are[15]—is connected to the question of morality and values. We know from his intended book *Revaluation of All Values* that Book II was to be called "The Free Spirit: Critique of Philosophy as a Nihilistic Movement," and his fragmentary thoughts on the matter, as later compiled in the first part of *The Will to Power*, bear out Nietzsche's belief that Western philosophical thinking had painted itself into a corner in which one had no choice but to accept the valuelessness and meaninglessness of life.[16] Of course, this culminates in the cry of the madman: not only is God dead, but *we have killed Him*. It is not just God's absence, however, that now brings a nihilistic state of mind ("a psychological state," as Nietzsche saw it), but that absence's attendant loss of purpose, unity, and truth. Nietzsche summarizes:

> What has happened, at bottom? The feeling of valuelessness was reached with the realization that the overall character of existence may not be interpreted by means of the concept of "aim," the concept of "unity," or the concept of "truth." Existence has no goal or end; any comprehensive unity in the plurality of events is lacking: the character of existence is not "true," is *false*. One simply lacks any reason for convincing oneself that there is a *true* world. Briefly: categories "aim," "unity," "being" which we used to project some value into the world—we *pull out* again; so the world looks valueless.[17]

This "valueless" aspect, then, would figure as Nietzsche's O, his zeroed out valuation (0), which is here equated with nihilism as a necessary culmination of the Western project of moral reasoning and metaphysics. But beyond the "event" of nihilism as a historical emergence, there are for Nietzsche two other kinds of nihilism.[18] One is "passive": it resigns itself to the eventuality into which this history of nihilism has brought us, and therefore it withers the spirit's power to effect any change. The other is "active": it understands that to see values come to an end does not mean a decimation of spirit at all, but on the contrary makes possible an "increased power of the spirit," the power to effect something—but not more values—in the void that is left behind.[19] We know that, for however much

Nietzsche might be seen as the "philosopher with the hammer," he was in the end no naysayer. Despite his apparent *ressentiment* or pessimism, he was always affirmative of what he understood as the "spirit," the power to effect.[20] Therefore, though dismissive of the former nihilism, he very much inclined toward the latter, the "pessimism of active energy," as he saw it: "In sum, that we have a goal for which one does not hesitate to offer human sacrifices, to risk every danger, to take upon oneself whatever is bad and worst: the *great passion*."[21] It is this active, creative passion that Nietzsche's Zarathustra keeps preaching:

> Creation—that is the great redemption from suffering, and life's grow-ing light. But that the creator may be, suffering is needed and much change. Indeed, there must be much bitter dying in your life, you creators. Thus you are advocates and justifiers of all impermanence. To be the child who is newly born, the creator must also want to be the mother who gives birth and the pangs of the birth-giver.[22]

The active nihilistic passion, then, is a combined measure of both destruction and creation, but with the destruction always *in the service of* creation, and this throughout Nietzsche's writings, everywhere (the Dio-nysian force, as "tragic joy," from its earliest stages). Thus, the nihilism that activates the spirit is a nihilism that seeks to offer something new in place of the old system of values—not a new system of values, but a new way of conceiving valuation altogether, beyond value. This new activating nihilism will be manifested in the will to power, a power that, much like Hegel's generative force of negation, *overcomes* but in doing so also necessar-ily overcomes *itself* (Zarathustra and his *Übermensch*). The symmetry of such "power overcoming power," where the two powers are both self-promoting and self-cancelling, is the very essence of Nietzsche's O, even as it can be understood in the eternal recurrence of the same. For the "power overcom-ing," that active force which creates (adds power) through its overcoming, is also the same as the "overcoming power," that zeroing force which negates (cancels power). It therefore always "returns" back upon itself in an over-coming that sublates both strength and weakness:

> Nihilism as a normal phenomenon can be a symptom of increasing *strength* or of increasing *weakness*: partly, because the strength to create, to will, has so increased that it no longer requires these total interpretations and introductions of meanings . . . partly because even the creative strength to create meaning has declined and disappointment becomes the dominant condition. The incapability of believing in a "meaning," "unbelief."[23]

These two opposing forces meet in a *becoming*, where the strength and
weakness, being and nonbeing, as in Hegel, coexist: "Becoming as invention, willing, self-denial, overcoming of oneself: no subject but an action,
a positing, creative . . ." Or, "To impose upon becoming the character of
being—that is the supreme will to power."[24]

This will to power, seen now as a silhouette of Hegel's O above—
"*Overcoming of philosophers* through the destruction of the world of being"[25]—
brings us to the second feature, the creativity of interpretation. For the
activating nihilism, as manifested in the will to power, finds its mode
through interpretation, and interpreting the world anew. (Here Heidegger
owes Nietzsche a great debt.) But as we saw earlier in chapter 2 with the
notion of eternal return, a feature of this interpretation is its multiplicity, for
it is not merely one interpretation that will to power makes possible, but an
indefinite number. "Inertia needs unity (monism); plurality of interpretations
a sign of strength."[26] Taking Hegel farther, Nietzsche sees the multiplicity
inherent in becoming as the true motive power, for the moment that becoming, or interpretation, "stops," it solidifies into an inert unity, one incapable
of generating anything but its own internalized and self-imploding system
(metaphysics). What is radical about the will to power in Nietzsche's conception is not that it breeds a kind of arch-ego or totalitarian bravado, but
precisely the opposite—it is forever trumping itself with a certain open-ended vector of power, which ultimately, and despite its multiplicity, ends up
back where it started, *the place of beginning as becoming*.[27] This is the basis
of Nietzsche's hermeneutic, where interpretation is not an exercise in relativity (everyone has their own interpretation) nor an exercise in absurdity
(meaning is futile) but an outstripping of the old interpretations to open us
up (again, in becoming) to new horizons of interpretation hitherto unseen
or unimagined, even if we remain divested of our authority to claim them,
and they are, in a sense, exactly where we started. Nietzsche articulates this
hermeneutic in the following summary fragment:

> That the value of the world lies in our interpretation (—that other
> interpretations than merely human ones are perhaps somewhere
> possible—); that previous interpretations have been perspective
> valuations by virtue of which we can survive in life, i.e., in the
> will to power, for the growth of power; that every elevation of man
> brings with it the overcoming of narrower interpretations; that every
> strengthening and increase of power opens up new perspectives and
> means believing in new horizons—this idea permeates my writings.
> The world with which we are concerned is false, i.e., is not a fact
> but a fable and approximation on the basis of a meagre sum of
> observations; it is "in flux," as something in a state of becoming,

as a falsehood always changing but never getting near the truth: for—there is no "truth."[28]

The "in flux" of interpretation is the always beginning *poesis* of the active nihilism above, the creator who must be a destroyer, and the destroyer a creator, in always beginning again. It is precisely the "mode" that we see Nietzsche adopting to convey this idea: fragments that keep beginning again, with no view of linear or unified chronology, fragments that can be rearranged, or reinterpreted through their differing arrangements, into continual looping or returning ideas. Within this mode we lose all sense of the authoritative philosopher and his sovereign ideas, even though we continue, ironically, to gesture in this way ("Nietzsche claims . . . ," "Nietzsche sees . . . ," "Nietzsche summarizes . . ."). Instead, we are forced, like Klossowski, to construct a "Nietzsche" who himself is in flux, who is forever becoming. This is ultimately the O of Nietzsche, or Nietzsche as O. (That we still have only one English version of *The Will to Power* [Kaufmann] is mystifying, and untenable, as it runs contrary to the fragments themselves. In a similar respect, if there is one philosopher who deserves to be put on the stage, as character, yet who rightly frightens even the artist as playwright—perhaps because he is too close—it is Nietzsche.)[29]

Art, then, for Nietzsche has nothing to do with aesthetics. Art remains constitutive of the generative impulse—Nietzsche will never follow Hegel's path and conceptualize art at the end of the road. He will stay true to Hegel's original origination. Heidegger will offer the phrase "the will to power as art."[30] This phrase effectively negates any totalizing interpretations we might have of "will to power." Power is an art, willing is an art, interpretation is an art, and all are caught up in the ambiguities and multiplicities that are art. We might add our own interpolation: will to power as interpretation, or even, simply, will to art.[31] But of course the "willer" in all these variations is something itself ambiguous. So Nietzsche carries us most emphatically from one's sovereignty (as author, as self, as unity, as God) to the *poesis* of an O that remains forever open to interpretation. Klossowski, the artist/philosopher, was right to try to capture this openness in the figure of eternal recurrence. But it is even better captured in the doing of art itself. So Nietzsche would return to his book on the beginnings of an art, *The Birth of Tragedy*, and say, in (re-)interpreting his own authorial intention:

> [T]his book is even anti-pessimistic: that is, in the sense that it teaches something that is stronger than pessimism, "more divine" than truth: *art*. Nobody, it seems, would more seriously propose a radical negation of life, a really *active* negation even more than merely *saying* No to life, than the author of this book. Except he

knows—he has experience of it, perhaps has experience of nothing
else!—that art is *worth more* than truth.[32]

And this is perhaps why Nietzsche's writings are always in themselves a
form of a work of art, the "unwritten" *Will to Power* perhaps most of all.

Heidegger

Hegel and Nietzsche were forerunners in the philosophy of negation who
themselves were misinterpreted as a matter of course. (But what can this
mean now, "misinterpreted"? Only that, they were interpreted within a certain history of metaphysics that understood, logically, a particular outcome:
Hegel—absolute idealism; Nietzsche—radical critique and consequential
insanity.) It was Heidegger who was first able to "interpret" them in relation to, primarily, the negation that we have been figuring. In his lectures
on Nietzsche given from 1936–1940 at the University of Freiburg, he had
pointed to German Idealism, Schelling and Hegel in particular, as the philosophy that "dared to think the negative as proper to Being." He then
quotes from the *Phenomenology of Spirit*: "But the life of Spirit is not one
that shies from death and merely preserves itself from corruption; it is rather
the life that endures death and maintains itself in death . . . it looks the
negative in the eye and lingers with it."[33] And from here Heidegger will
build a case—his own case, that is, a case proper to himself—that looks
at will, power, art, eternal recurrence, and nihilism as necessarily negating
features of Being.

　　Heidegger, as early as 1918–19, had been thinking about negation in
a constitutive way—in notes about mysticism, he wrote: "A constituting
moment: comportment towards the world (negative—repulsive?)."[34] Seven
or so years later the parenthesis and question mark would be erased assuredly,
for in *Sein und Zeit* that comportment would carry with it the constituting
nothing of death. Perhaps this is the most singular basis for Heidegger's reputation among those who have little or no direct engagement with him: his
existentialism, as it is seen, makes death not an endpoint in front of which
we stand in preferential avoidance, but a necessary feature of what it means
to *be* in the world "here and now." Death is a *modus*, a *modus operandi*,
by which, paradoxically, we have our being and its existence—"Death is a
way to be, which Dasein takes over as soon as it is"[35]—and thus in some
sense it stands *before*, not after, our life. This "standing before" is also the
comportment that is worked out in the Dasein of *Sein und Zeit*. Having
determined the nature of Dasein in the first part (the *Sein* of the title) as
being-in-the-world, that comportment [*Verhältnis*] that embeds Being inexorably within the world at hand, and then interprets itself as a profound and

anxious care [*Sorge*] in the face of that world (Being qua interpretation qua care, a care for something that is nevertheless "nothing and nowhere"—a care ultimately for/about nothing),[36] he then immediately begins the second part, Dasein's relation to temporality (the *Zeit* of the title), with the now famous *Being toward death* [*Sein zum Tode*]. Instead of historicizing the origin of Being, Being comes into "time," or "time" into Being, on the basis of its nothing, which stands *before* (in all senses)—the nothing is not just anticipated as a possibility, but is made the very character of Being's emergence through care—its "thrownness"—into the world of ontic (factical) being and time. Thus, the two parts of the title are, within the structural body of the work, connected with a care engendered by death (or nullity), and engendered in a way that makes death both its subject and object (the care *of* death). The title's "and" [*und*] therefore both adds and takes away: between being and time stands a nothing that both opens up in possibility and nihilates in anxiety—the central feature of the O as nothing (and now the modern here-and-now "I" as nothing).[37]

This nothing will populate much of Heidegger's writings after the magnum opus of 1927, finding its most famous distillation in that phrase *Nichts nichtet* (nothing nothings or nihilates) of "What is Metaphysics" (1929), his perhaps most condensed analysis of the nothing (*das Nichts*). There, Heidegger was able to agree with Hegel's claim in the *Science of Logic*—"Pure Being and pure Nothing are therefore the same"—but not because both "agree in their indeterminateness and immediacy, but rather because being itself is essentially finite and manifests itself only in the transcendence of a Dasein that is held out into the nothing." Thus, Heidegger was able to aver that "the question of nothing pervades the whole of metaphysics," and so with Nietzsche herald a nihilism that escorts Western philosophy through to its modern "end."[38] But it is in the Nietzsche lectures themselves where we begin to see this "end" give way to an "art" that would characterize so much of Heidegger's later work, and invoke a shift from philosophy as an exclusive domain of ratiocination to one where the poet and the painter speak as prominently, if not more prominently ("The Thinker as Poet," "The Origin of the Work of Art," ". . . Poetically Man Dwells . . . ," etc.). This later work will sometimes lose sight of *das Nichts* to presence, or presencing—and here is where Heidegger has some of his fiercest critics, even among so-called Heideggereans.[39] So let us return to Heidegger on Nietzsche as he expounded him in the lead-up to the middle of the century, that period, we have seen, which becomes the ferment of artists on nothing.

Nietzschean art, we said for Heidegger, is "a configuration of the will to power."[40] That is to say, there is a force of empowerment, the will, which motivates creation of the new, even if this means a (self-)overcoming of the very will that creates it. Art here, as we were trying to argue for Hegel

above, is pre-aesthetic: it is not a question of the conceptualization of the
created object or the contemplation of beauty, but of the *creating* itself, as
a primordial generative impulse. But because this creation also necessitates
destruction, it inheres in a certain nihilism. Yet that nihilism is *active* insofar
as it allows nothing to act as an *origin* for the new. Hence, for Heidegger,
its "inner richness."[41] This origin is never fixed, but is always *becoming*, and
so has a cyclical nature, for to become again always brings us back to an
ongoing beginning. This cyclicality is what invokes the eternal recurrence,
as much as the hermeneutical circle. As Heidegger explains:

> Now, because all being as will to power—that is, as incessant
> self-overcoming—must be a *continual "becoming,"* and because such
> "becoming" cannot move "towards an end" *outside* its own "farther
> and farther," but is ceaselessly caught up in the cyclical increase
> in power to which it reverts, then being as a whole too, as this
> power-confirming becoming, must itself always recur again and
> bring back the same.[42]

This world of becoming is, for Heidegger, the real world of the here
and now, as self-interpreted by Being. It does not incline to history, beyond
the here and now, except by allowing history the capacity to come into being
(now in Heidegger's sense, "come into Being"). When Nietzsche talks of the
history of nihilism, he talks of history as nihilism, that is, of the metaphysical constructs that allow history to take initial shape. Thus, the history of
metaphysics is nihilism, or "Nihilism *is* history," or "Nihilism determines the
historicity of this history."[43] But that determination is caught in a circle, for
it can only stand *outside* history by history becoming its own origin again and
again within the finitude of its being. This is what Blanchot was trying to get
at only several years later in attempting to mark out the space of literature.

From this will to power as art, this nihilism as history and eternal
recurrence, Heidegger will give flesh, as it were, to Being. If Being remains
unthought in metaphysics, obscured by "the glare of concepts,"[44] it is only
through the end of metaphysics, or through the nihilating force that carries
us forward beyond metaphysics, after its end, that Being can properly come
out into the open. The nothing, then, allows Being to come into openness,
an openness that nevertheless is itself characterized by nothingness. For if
Being is to be "seen" fully outside of the cloaking metaphysical apparatus
we have built for its existence (as manifested in both categories of *existentia*
and *essentia*), it must make itself homeless (*unheimlich*) in the nothing that is
this outside (Blanchot's Outside). To make Being so radically homeless and
bare in this way requires a stripping down or stripping off, in the manner of

Lear, of the conceptual sovereignty, or of sovereign conceptuality, that has concealed it for so long ("What need one?"). Only in this open, homeless, nihilated heath can Being emerge properly—now as unconcealment. It is in the power of art, as Heidegger would later come to understand it, that such unconcealment becomes manifest. Here, in the Nietzsche lectures, it is in the active power of nihilism, as the foremost expression of a will to art that overcomes the inertia of historical nihilism, that leads us to such unconcealment. Either way, what we see is an O emerging with creativity at its center. Heidegger's O opens up out of the nothing that becomes unconcealed by O. Heidegger's O is Nietzsche's O reappropriated in the service of Being out on the heath, properly situated in pure homelessness and, concomitantly, in the leave-taking of one's (One's) senses. Of course, the senses return, but only in the full sense of one's (One's) death. This is Being's ripeness, its all.

We cannot possibly go into all the interstices of Heidegger's thought on Being and the nothing as it develops from this and surrounding texts, without being consumed by the task others have so ably executed at much greater length.[45] What interests us here is the way Heidegger's O represents a philosopher trying to philosophize his tradition out of its previous state toward a newer incarnation in which the sense of art is made present through a very particular absence. A detailed study of Heidegger's 1942–43 lecture on Parmenides could bear this out, as it begins with the nature of Truth as both goddess and poem (*mythos*), takes us through the character of unconcealment as *a-leithea* (the Greek truth as constructed privatively: *un*-concealing), and ends with an analysis of poetry in the form of Rilke's eighth *Duino Elegy*.[46] Leaving aside any such study, or the later material on the work of art (its origin, its dwelling, its language, etc.), we stress the continuity between the three masters of negation (where "negation" now becomes a deficient term, unable to capture all the nuances unveiled by these masters) who, in turning their attention to nothing, in rewriting and reinterpreting each others' Os, have brought modern philosophy to a necessary recovery of the generative nature that expends itself in and through art. The previous expenditure of metaphysics gives way to a reconception of *poesis*, now necessitated within the circumference of O's structuring around nothing. As difficult as these thinkers may be to follow in their analysis of this dark middle, collectively they show why the One had to relinquish its hold on the crown, at least within the realm of philosophy, and why the twentieth century invites a new "history" of nothing, especially from its middle decades, through figuring and shaping O as a work of art. By Heidegger's middle period, philosophy and art had begun anew, together.

BEFORE THE POSTMODERN: SARTRE

By first appearances, Jean-Paul Sartre, the self-appointed spokesman of French existentialism, would seem a paragon of twentieth-century negation: a philosopher whose magnum opus, *Being and Nothingness* (*L'Être et le Néant* [1943]) adjusted Heidegger's own great text, but who also wrote novels, plays, screenplays, etc., as a necessary outworking of his "phenomenology." Why then, it must be asked, is not Sartre included with the masters above, to form a quadrumvirate of modern negation? Is not Sartre's work, and his mid-century position, a perfect summation of the philosophical O as it had been launched by Hegel, and by that account the perfect entry into the French radicals of theory who were soon to follow?

By no means can we say Sartre is insignificant in any philosophical history of the nothing we might construe. How could he be, with Nothingness replacing Time in his very title? And yet that title, it might be fair to say, runs the same risk of misleading the reader as that of Gadamer's *Truth and Method,* where the coupling "and" is often said to be more appropriate in the function of an "or." Being *or* Nothingness, one might argue, but only after some serious qualification.

In the opening Introduction, Sartre makes it very clear that his understanding of being in all its existential glory necessitates that, as being in-itself (*en-soi*), it remains as "is." The "is" here is not copulative, in the sense of adjoining. It is plenitudinary, in the sense of a solidity or fullness. It neither comes into being, as becoming, nor is it necessitated by some other factor. It simply *is.* Being *is.* And in that *is,* it is wholly positive, not admitting anything of the negative or negation. So Sartre states: "It [being as being-in-itself] is what it is. This means that by itself it can not even be what it is not; we have seen indeed that it can encompass no negation. It is full positivity."[47] Being, in the purity of an existential tautology, *is what it is.* As he reiterates a little later: "Negation can not touch the nucleus of being of Being, which is absolute plenitude and entire positivity."[48] So why talk of nothingness (*néant*) at all? Why should nothingness appear as central to the question of being, as the title implies?

Sartre seems intent on maintaining nothingness not simply because it belongs to an irrevocable Hegelian tradition or because Heidegger had worked it so inextricably into his concept of the *Dasein* (Sartre virtually ignores Nietzsche in this, his longest, work), but because Sartre was aware that, by the middle of the twentieth century, the question of nothing, of negation, was now far more than a philosophical dilemma. It pervaded the very nature of human identity. It was an inescapable modern existential "problem." As he famously comes to say, "nothingness *haunts* being."[49] By this he wants to say not that being could somehow be fused, or confused, with nothing—

being is pure positivity—but that being is nevertheless pursued by the spectral darkness of nothing as a negating force. Non-being is always a threat. Unlike for Hegel, Nietzsche, and Heidegger, negation is not constitutive of being in any way—"Non-being is denied at the heart of Being." Nor is it coextensive or coinstantaneous with being—"nothingness is logically subsequent to it." Thus, "[W]e must be careful never to posit nothingness as an original abyss from which being arose."[50] And yet, nothingness always encroaches within the existential reality of being. That is, nothingness arises *from* being. This *from* retains a precedence for being, and indeed makes nothingness parasitic upon being: nothingness gets its "being from being," and "is encountered only within the limits of being," so that "the total disappearance of being would not be the advent of the reign of non-being, but on the contrary the concomitant disappearance of nothingness." Thus, *"Non-being exists only on the surface of being."*[51] But still, this nothingness lurks. If it is fundamentally extrinsic to the nucleus of being, it is nevertheless in profound association with being, even somehow ingrained with being.

The opening chapters of *Being and Nothingness* struggle with the location of nothingness in a manner that is indicative of the problematic nature of the O itself. It can neither be outside nor inside, constitutive nor marginal. It is always both/and *and* neither/nor. So Sartre will say it only exists on the surface of being, and then, just a few pages later, will say it "lies coiled in the heart of being—like a worm."[52] Or conversely, he will say nothingness cannot be conceived outside of being, and then immediately reverse this and say being "lacks all relation with it."[53] He admits at the outset that there is something in being that must relate to nothingness— the "non" or "not" continually pursues us—but he sets as his problem the exact determination of what this something, as nothing, is, and where its location, or "origin," lies.

We said above, in connection to Hegel, that philosophy, alongside religion, has always been preoccupied with the question of origination—the coming into being of existing things. Sartre's ontology deliberately shuns becoming, since being only is *what it is*, in all its existing plenitude. Possibility and necessity are not part of its features, nor is coming-into-being, or coming-to-be, or in Heidegger's terms, unconcealment.[54] And yet the opening of Sartre's phenomenological ontology is mired in the question of origination, even if it is the origination of nothingness. He repeatedly asks the question, From whence? It is as if, in the plenitude of being's self-subsisting non-becoming, being must still be haunted with the question of origination, even if only the origination of a nothingness that somehow (contradictorily, Sartre implies) inheres within it. And though, as Sartre concludes, "Man is the being through whom nothingness comes to the world," this still begs the question, "What must man be in his being in order that through him nothingness may come to being?"[55] What Sartre will not admit is what the masters of negation above all admit: that *the question of origination is precisely the question of negation,* or the question of the abyssal nature of nothing. And this, ultimately, is what separates him from his predecessors. Being, for Sartre, must preclude nothing's originating abyss. Where Sartre will try to situate the question of being's nothingness is at a different location: the question of human freedom.

In order to resolve the contradictories of negation, Sartre first must split being into two. We have already referred to being *in-itself* (*en-soi*). This, we saw, is pure plenitude and positivity, allowing no negation. It is also preconscious, or prereflective. But the moment this being becomes conscious, or self-reflective—for Sartre, the moment it becomes *human*—it invites a different kind of self-dynamic. This Sartre calls, borrowing further from Hegel, being *for-itself* (*pour-soi*), and here is where negation finds its foothold. For the moment we speak of consciousness, we speak of the possibility of negation: of denying, of misapprehending, of questioning, of misrepresenting, of deceiving, of lying, of enacting "bad faith," of absenting, or being something other than pure plenitude. Where do all these possibilities of negation come from? They are all negative attitudes not available to being in-itself as pure positivity, and therefore must come from the being *for-itself.* The pure positivity of *in-itself* is negated, or "nihilated," by *for-itself* the moment the latter imposes consciousness upon the former. Sartre uses the example of a friend casting a glance at him. The friend is situated in the world as a certain fact, but the moment the glance is cast, Sartre must accept it as something other than fact, since it has a certain ambiguity or indeterminateness to it. What can the glance mean? In other words, though Sartre will never use this terminology, the one looked at must *interpret* the look and the looker, and this immediately suggests we have left the realm of pure positivity. Something is absent that must be found (a meaning), or must be replaced. So being conscious of someone else or something other, the object, invites a nihilation of that object's positivity. Thus, Sartre will say, "*Consciousness of the Other is what it is not.*" And this even goes for one's own consciousness (self-consciousness), and consciousness in general: "*consciousness is not what it is.*"[56] Consciousness takes leave of pure positivity because the object of consciousness, in consciousness, is always something *other* than *what it is.* In the interpretive ambiguity, in this leeway or gap between what consciousness holds (in what Sartre calls a "transcendence") and the fact of the other's (or one's own) pure positivity of being (in what Sartre, following Heidegger, calls a "facticity"), negation is fundamentally at work. Our transcending powers are always nihilating the facts of our situation. And in this separation or gap between the two, between being in-itself and for-itself, *freedom* resides.

Unlike Heidegger, Sartre never employs hermeneutical language to describe the freedom of the human subject, or its ownmost possibility. His language is more Kantian, in that we have not merely the capacity but the constant necessity of choice in our consciousness of the world around us. Heidegger's hermeneutical circle is therefore not at play. For Sartre, the freedom that consciousness imposes in being for-itself does not catch us in a bind of where to begin, or in a question of preunderstanding and interpretation. Consciousness acts always in a diremptive capacity, separating us from the conditions of pure positivity, invoking a no-thing in the face of the thing, and in this sense negation always comes *after*. Where Heidegger's ontological circle problematizes the before and after in the very heart of *Dasein*, and thus inheres negation, Sartre's ontological structures keep the after, or the future, outside of being's nucleus. Being simply *is*. But this said, the nucleus in its human form is never not being erased or "surpassed" by the consciousness of that "is." Consciousness imposes a surpassing freedom for that "is" to be something "other," a freedom that is both a blessing and a curse. Freedom always implies possibility, and possibility always implies something other. But to be other means to nihilate the pure "is-ness" of one's being. Freedom and negation then are inextricable, and to be free means to "condition the appearance of nothingness."[57] Freedom's condemnation in this nothingness is also freedom's possibility and responsibility for what one conditions. To be truly free means to make conditions possible, even if it is on the grounds of a nothingness of being.

Such conditioning, as a fundamental human reality, carries over into the activities of the imagination. And this is where Sartre remains most significant for the disclosure of O during the twentieth century. The realm of consciousness's freedom is also the realm of art, or literature—the creative manifestation of one's freedom as it is situated in the world or the text (the world and the text being one and the same here). This is not about the work of art manifesting a truth by unconcealing Being, as it would become for Heidegger, but of the work showing the human dilemma of its own nothingness at work in its various situations, since to be situated is to be separated out of one's pure positivity in the world through consciousness. All of Sartre's fictional works, then, beginning with *La Nausée* of 1938, bear out this dilemma, and in fact act as specific manifestations of the freedom Sartre is trying to theorize in his more philosophical work: the freedom of imagination to make choices that place upon the human a responsibility of and for one's own nothingness.

Sartre is in accord, then, with his philosophical predecessors in trying to flesh out the nothing that somehow shadows the self in its identity and being. And he is most in accord when he understands the power of negation to be part of the powers of imagination. Nothingness, he says,

"is made-to-be," or is being in-itself "making itself other," which betrays
the generative nature of Sartre's *néant*.[58] Here, he is closer to Hegel than
Kant: imagination is about generating through separating, rupturing, or
sundering, not through uniting—separating us from the positivity that is
our being in its existential primacy. But he is least in accord with the above
masters when he understands imagination and its nihilating capacity as a
component only of self-reflective consciousness, and therefore as something
that comes *after* the pure positivity and plenitude of that primacy.[59] In
the latter understanding, he remains a metaphysician, even if he reverses
the usual order and puts existence before essence. As Heidegger has said
in regard to Sartre here, "But the reversal of a metaphysical statement
remains a metaphysical statement."[60] And although admitting separation,
fracture, and nihilation into the very structure of self and being, Sartre in
the end upholds a fundamental ontology of being as *unity*, even a metaphysical unity. The two sides of being are ultimately in "*a priori* unity," he
concludes, a "synthetic organization of the in-itself and the for-itself."[61] He
will qualify this synthesis by vacillating between integration and disintegration, between totalizing and detotalizing, with some attempt at finding
a compromise: "disintegrated ensemble," or "detotalized totality."[62] And
these compromises will betray the difficult nature of the O, which he is
attempting, we could say, to contain. But it is clear that, slippery as a
"point of view on the totality" might be, he desires it, even presumes it,
as foundational: "[A]ctually we exist on the foundation of this totality and
as engaged in it."[63] And he therefore resorts, in the end, to the notion of
a "Gestalt form" between what appears continually as two incommensurable realities, the paradoxical character of the totality.[64] It is this ultimate
desire for unity and totality that keeps Sartrean nothingness distinct from
Nietzsche especially, and likely why he bars Nietzsche from the pages of
Being and Nothingness, while distancing himself from any sense of nihilism.
Quite the contrary, as is now generally accepted, Sartre was a humanist in
a long line of humanisms, his existentialism a celebration of humankind,
his ontology what Derrida would later call a "philosophical anthropology"
grounded upon a long tradition of metaphysics.[65]

It is also this desire for unity that makes Sartre's views on literature so
different from the Anglo-American Auden. Sartre saw literature not merely
as utilitarian, but, in good Marxian fashion, as capable of effecting historical change.[66] By contrast, his contemporary Auden, the disaffected Marxist,
came to see literature as figuring an O that negated its effective historical or
world-changing influence and problematized the nature of historicity itself.
In this sense Auden anticipates more directly the postmodernism that was
to come.

Likewise, it is also this desire for unity and totality that, ironically, or some might say justifiably and inevitably, makes Sartre's long-time companion and assistant Simone de Beauvoir perhaps more important in the history of the O. De Beauvoir saw keenly how unity and totality were part of the patriarchal domain, producing the "sovereign subject" whose point of reference had always been male. And despite her celebrated tussle with living in (or as) Sartre's shadow—or precisely because of it—the "other" in Sartre's ontology is translated from consciousness's nihilation of being in-itself to, instead, women as a whole, who have been "nihilated" as subjects in their own right. De Beauvoir's work becomes a point of departure for twentieth-century women and feminist theory, made more evident soon below, precisely because she understands the question of gender as, in Judith Butler's words, "a kind of becoming or activity," an "incessant and repeated action."[67] Sartre's work, on the other hand, is often seen now as an endpoint of a certain metaphysical and (hence) patriarchal tradition, where human possibilities work, ultimately, toward a totalizing "project" characterized by the unifying of being's dyadic components and by "the appropriation of the world as a totality of being-in-itself, in the form of a fundamental quality."[68] Sartre's nothingness, in other words, does nothing in relation to the future of gender, or ultimately the future of self-identity. In fact, it does little in relation to forward thinking at all, if Foucault's now famous charge is to be believed: that Sartre was a man of the nineteenth century attempting to think in the twentieth century.[69] De Beauvoir, on the other hand, was a woman of the twentieth century attempting to think in the twenty-first.

There is a growing amount of scholarship that tries now to rectify the somewhat easy dismissal that Foucault's words about his compatriot suggest, and relate Sartre to the poststructuralism and postmodernism that followed the mid-century.[70] I have dealt with Sartre for as much as I have here because I think he represents a kind of peculiar turnstile concerning the question of nothing. As arguably *the* philosophical figure of the mid-twentieth century—his public fame in and out of France certainly well eclipsed that of virtually all his philosophical contemporaries, Heidegger included—he allows a passage back to the tradition of nothing that stems from Hegel, even if his debt to that tradition also ties him to the metaphysics that Heidegger claimed, rightly or wrongly, to overcome. In this sense of genealogy, Foucault will call Sartre the "last Hegelian."[71] But his efforts to determine the nothing at the heart of being in such an extended manner also allow passage forward to the postmodernism that dominates the latter half of that century, with its emphasis on the self's disintegration and internal nihilations. The stile turns both ways, that is. And his literary output further shows the shift that philosophy—Continental philosophy, at any rate—will take toward the creative and the fictive. I do not think Sartre can be rightly labeled a "master" of negation, given the uncertain and enigmatic nature of his ambidextral movement. But that very nature itself betrays a quintessential feature of the O in operation, as it frustrates the attempt to stabilize an author within a definitive position or direction. By cavorting with the O, even if never naming it as such, one risks authorial self-fracture. Sartre, philosophically and artistically, becomes such a split figure, even against his own desire. He becomes de Beauvoir's sovereign subject, turned by its own devices into a subjected sovereign. And we see even this kind of sovereign left well behind as we move through the century's latter half.

THROUGH THE POSTMODERN: DERRIDA, IRIGARAY

We have now reached that point which is in fact counterpoint to that reached in modernity under the history of One's sovereignty. In chapter 1 we saw, in the development of the modern era, that the competing conceptions of One were so many and so diffuse that it became virtually impossible to draw out a historical trajectory with any kind of clarity or containment. We face the same problem now as we turn to that "era" that has, for better or for worse, been designated the postmodern. The O has become so rampant, so widely diffused or dispersed, so, we might even say, taken for granted, that it becomes impossible to contain it within any tidy history of ideas or even genealogical description. Within philosophy and art, within intellectual and cultural modes of manifold variation operating at multiple levels, we have lived with the O as an everyday phenomenon, so that it seems almost fruitless to try to give it delineation. Where could we begin?

Perhaps it is best now to capitulate the variegated features or figurations of the O we have been tracing throughout the preceding chapters of our discussion, to see how they might have been theoretically appropriated or assumed throughout the last fifty years. There is first the question of origination, where origin arrives in the interrogative and not the indicative: origin is not a stable beginning point reached by working back along a linear path of chronology, a foundational starting point or genesis, but a repeated beginning as newly originated each and every time, and left open as question to its emergent possibilities outside of any *telos*. This sense of creating anew, in the "here and now" that continues to make up the modern experience, leads to a circularity of return, where linearity is broken by a folding back upon itself (the origin is always wholly new), and progression is halted by its own internal disruption. This originating function, as mode, leads in turn to the problematizing of history and historicity. If origination is a repetitious activity—a *creatio continua*—that confines us to an endless recycling of beginning—a *circulus vitiosus*—it places in difficulty the location of any prime beginning and the subsequent historical unfolding that issues from it, and it places in difficulty any access to the past as a reliable source of cause, of answers, or of values. History becomes one more construct, including the history of one's self, the (auto-)biography. And hence the question of self, like all history, becomes a question of artifice. We make what we are, and more, we make anew what we have been.

Artifice is at the heart of O's operation, but so too the dark or blank spots that accompany all artifice. The O, as the creative mode of origination, that which allows origination its possibility, is also revelatory of the abyss that stands deeply at the center of that origination. With every Ariel there is a Caliban. This is not merely creation ex nihilo; this is now creation qua nihilo. And in this transformation, the binaries between the creator and created, between original and copy, and the opposition between making and destroying, begin to come undone. For if creation has an inescapable "nihilating" dimension, to use Sartre's terminology, then in our artifices we must come to terms with our absences, and our creative journey will always be a journey back to where we began as nothing. The nothing will nothing, to draw out Heidegger. The O simply highlights this active journey of negation, as it first negates the binaries that have kept negation to the peripheries of unitary presence. But, ironically, it can only do this through continued reliance upon certain binaries: the binary between O and I, for example, or between center and periphery. The binaries then become victim of their own irony, highly destabilized.

This destabilizing nature of artifice is also captured in the ciphering function of O. The cipher, as a catalytic operative, carries no inherent value. Rather, it allows value to be placed within the context of a given schema. But in doing so, it shows the origin of value to be always under question, since value will always and only take on a provisional role within the schema to which it contributes. The constructed nature of value will, in affirmation of Nietzsche, forever require revaluation. And thus the cipher will lead to the revaluation of some of our most valued "realities," whether they be instantiated conceptually (e.g., One), culturally (e.g., race, gender), or textually (e.g., author, meaning).

In rephrasing the O's operations in this manner, we can see easily how postmodern theory, especially through its French inception, has acted the chief theoretical purveyor of its various figurations. Lacan's seminars on the ruptured psyche that constitutes the self; Foucault's genealogies of power structures and his questioning of our bases of self, knowledge, and history; Derrida's entire deconstructive enterprise; Lyotard's dissolution of the master narrative; Barthes's death of the author; Levinas's Other; Deleuze's multiplicities; Baudrillard's simulacrum; Irigaray's speculum; Kristeva's abjection; Cixous's coming to writing, Nancy's being singular plural—all this, as but a selection, and in addition to the Bataille and Blanchot we have already explored, shows the French have been instrumental in theorizing the O with an unabashed, at times heady, domination. But they have hardly been alone: Rorty, Said, Jameson, Eagleton, Guattari, Vattimo, Agamben, Žižek et al. are part of what is now an industry of writers and theorists who have contributed or continue to contribute to the pervasive, even if still con-tested, world that, up until 2001 at least, had been labeled "postmodernism" (or in the case of Agamben, Žižek, Badiou, etc., "post-postmodernism"). The French theorists, as representative of what those in literary circles had called High Theory, have since had their day, as most will now claim, even outside of literary circles. That is to say, their influence is no longer ruling the agenda of the Humanities departments within the academy. But this is not to say their influence does not continue to run deep, if now in a more tacit manner, or in a continually dispersed capacity. The broad extension of this theory beyond the Francophone celebrities has always been testimony to its abiding potency. What postmodern theory represents, we might now say, is the O finally asserting itself patently and without disguise in the long open corridors where the One once held intellectual sovereignty. What postmodernism became, as an *ism*, is simply the self-conscious and, at its most insistent, doctrinaire expression of an O that had finally come to term beyond reason's doubt. If the middle period of the twentieth century tried to write its way creatively through the O, the latter period stopped it theoreti-cally mid-passage. It is as if Caliban tried the old trick of Goethe's Mephisto, and donned the professor's cap and gown, not now in mock pedantry, but with every intention of confirming philosophically or disputatiously the O as the ineluctable *modus operandi* of our times.

We will dwell briefly on just two recent French figures who are par-ticularly representative of the O, not because more necessarily needs to be written on their understanding of nothing, but because their own *modus operandi* as theorists exemplifies what we have been stressing from the mid-dle of the twentieth century—a shift to thinking philosophically through creative means, or a move from One to O. Nietzsche, of course, is our modern archetype. And Sartre becomes a certain watershed figure for the twentieth century, with his literary output matching his philosophical works. But Sartre's approach was still largely through segregation: his philosophical disquisitions were written discursively (*Being and Nothingness* is subtitled an "essay"), while his art took traditional forms (the play, the novel, etc.). The literary works were certainly philosophical in their way, embodying fully the existentialism of the theoretical analyses. And the nature of that embodiment said something significant about the genus of philosophy that would become so influential. But Western literature embodying distinct philosophical positions is nothing new, not only in the French tradition

(Camus, Mallarmé, Proust, Diderot, Rousseau, Voltaire, etc.) but elsewhere (Mann, Dostoyevsky, Melville, Emerson, the German Romantics—an interminable list going back to the Greeks, and beginning, we might say, with Parmenides). The phenomenon of Western philosophy adopting distinct literary approaches—eschewing ratiocination for creative expression, or better, understanding *logos as mythos*—is quite another matter, and even Sartre did not adopt this line of approach. It took a newer generation of French intellectuals to embrace fully what Nietzsche had so boldly and iconoclastically set out as the precedent.

Derrida

What can we now say about this figure that has not already been said? How do we avoid speaking repetitiously? Jacques Derrida has been the subject of so much commentary and analysis—affirming, critiquing, disparaging—he has now become something of a cliché. This is a terrible indictment against one who, in all his writings, abundant in every respect, set about to undo the textual cliché thoroughly and radically. Yet it is undeniable, and now coarsely ironic, that the term *deconstruction* has become one of the greatest lexical and cultural clichés of the day, misused and misunderstood at almost every turn. It is also undeniable that Derrida is seen as the chief representative of the postmodern excess and cultural vandalism associated with this term, that "Derrida" has become a philosophical conceit that, like all of Nietzsche's, went well beyond serious proposition and good measure. His name has become the watchword for intellectual misadventure, the cliché of French extravagance.

We might think all this now pains him in his grave, but Derrida, being Derrida, would, if he were still among us, turn his attention upon this term "cliché," note its derivation, and, with a genuine if ludic seriousness, subvert its contemporary usage. The original cliché comes from the world of typography, he would explain. It is the French term for the "dab" or the "stereotype," a device made as a second cast from an original form, and used for printing in multiples thereafter. The original cliché was never original, he would say; it took its form from an original, and reproduced that original, but only ever as a secondary and/or repeated event. The "click" of the *cliquer*, first made, according to the *OED*, "by letting a matrix fall face downward upon a surface of molten metal on the point of cooling," is indicative of a state in-between, the metal neither solid nor liquid. And it is only in this between state, or *passage*, that the impression can be made. So too, Derrida would say, my work has operated at this point of in-between, where the two surfaces meet, the die and thermoplastic, the original and the impression, in the passage of becoming (not yet solid, no longer liquid). At the click is the matrix of something newly formed that is not original. If I am that click, that *cliché*, it is because I have sought to sound out that moment when the original is lost in a becoming that, once solidified, can only ever be a refiguration. The click as the echo of a signification split in two (and much more). The click as the bell's toll I wrote about in *Glas*, a text itself split in two (and much more). "The *glas's*, such as we shall have heard them, toll the end of signification, of sense, and of the signifier."[72] *Glas* is my tolling *cliché* for the end of the book as a cliché, that all-too-easily-read repository of transparent signification. If I am a cliché, I am also that *cliché* we French call the photographic negative, the inverse of that original, which must be inverted back again in order to *re-present* that origin, now as a fictive other, all transparency lost, the *glas* obscured. An enabling moment in the process between original and copy.

And so it might go, stereotypically. Derrida's "negative" is well documented, both within literary circles and within philosophical circles.[73] If he has left a "negative impression" in either, it is in both the best and the worst sense of the phrase. Such is the case with all Calibans, all rogues, of the world. And we could spend much time bringing to the foreground all the ways this negative manifests itself textually throughout his work, from the early essays, to the middle "experiments" such as *Glas*, to the later writings that increasingly turned to the questions of politics and religion. But again we would be retracing others' steps.[74] What has received less attention is the nature of this philosophical negative as creative text, or as creative space, or as creative spacing.

What is *Glas*, for example, if not a re-spacing of the text—typographically and logocentrically? For in the middle of this text, in the middle of each page, is always a blank margin, the crossing of which we have no idea how to negotiate, no guide or decipherment provided by either side (Hegel on the left, Genet on the right), a gap that is a disturbing nonpresence of the *logos* we expect to bind our reading together in unity and coherence (like the spine of two pages in any bound book). This is prima facie a traditional gap, separating philosophy (Hegel, the philosopher of both the negative and the Absolute) and literature (Genet, the outlaw writer of—we take special note—the mid-twentieth century, exonerated before the law by his art). But if, coupled on the same page, we have no precedence, no directions on how to read both of the sides together, neither do we have much precedence, much direction on how to read on either side alone. Individually, separately, each text unfolds vertically in an unconventional, discursively altered manner, treating its subject, its texts, its authors with a cut-and-paste logic that reflects the dissymmetry of the horizontal axis. The text(s) must be pieced back together by us the readers, as if typesetters ourselves, or typographic artisans reinscribing or reinventing how to read (this text). But even if we attempt to do this by restricting ourselves to one side or the other (and ignoring all the other embedded texts and quotes), we can never block out that other side, that twin column, from our vision, or worse, from our thought: "Two unequal columns, they say distyle {dissent-ils}, each of which—envelop(e)(s) or sheath(es), incalculably reverses, turns inside out, replaces, remarks, overlaps {recoupe} the other." Philosophy and art continually remarking each other (after any remarking *on*) in an "infinite circulation of general equivalence" we can never quite grasp, except by creating from nothing a passage across the blank middle.[75] Spirit and nature conjoined via nothing, as in Hegel himself. But this text, closest in all of Derrida's corpus to the enactment of Joyce, is not to be seen merely as creative, an imaginary rendering of two worlds united in dissymmetry, though with an *Aufhebung* (sublation) left hanging (unsublated) over the middle margin. It is also *performative*: a performing of philosophy and art (spirit and nature, *logos* and *mythos*, reason and imagination) across the divide that has traditionally separated them, and that now, in the blank space of a central margin, unites them: "*Glas* must be read as a 'singular plural' . . ."[76]

The performative merger of philosophy and art, in the gap of nothing's open center, is a feature of all Derrida's monographs particularly during the decade of the 1970s, beginning with *Dissemination* (1972), and following with *Glas* (1974), *The Truth in Painting* (1978), *Spurs: Nietzsche's Style* (1978), and *The Post Card: from Socrates to Freud and Beyond* (1980). "[E]conomize on the abyss," he says at the beginning of *The Truth in Painting* in reference to the parergon, that term denoting something beside (next to, other than) the work, in a text about re-spacing the relationship between philosophy and art made precedent by Kant, Hegel, and Heidegger (whose philosophies on art are, Derrida says, "ringed together by a circle").[77] Yet despite these longer performances, Derrida was, one could argue, principally an essayist, a "man of letters" in the highest sense of the term. Even the monographs can be seen as stitched together reflections and arguments and explorations and innovations ("I write four times here, *around* painting" [*The Truth in Painting*]).[78] In these single works, he experimented with form in a manner that problematized the unity traditionally accompanying the *mono*graphic thesis. Derrida rarely proposed theses as such. He read texts. He closely read texts. He closely unread texts. And the texts he dissected, or vivisected, with such meticulous, some would say exaggerated, detail, were both philosophic *and* literary. Sometimes together at the same time. "The text is clustered," he wrote in (of) *Glas*.[79]

His attention to literature made Derrida probably the first philosopher to be *properly* accepted and embraced by literary critics—that is, as one of their own. Thus he was paraded, in America especially, during the 1970s,

when his own texts were literary constructions of the most unashamedly
exorbitant kind. Such was the nature of this new understanding of textual-
ity: the "text" shook off all sovereign rights, and principally those held in
place by philosophy. The text became multiple, and thus "literary" in its
most basic sense of the word—full of letters, arranged less according to unified, purposeful argument and more according to open-ended, imaginative
possibility. It slipped free of all proprietary claims. And yet the hard lesson
for literary critics was that it slipped free even of the claim made for it by
literary criticism. So Derrida later distanced himself from the literary critical
world (of the '70s Yale especially). Consciously aware of himself as text, he
was not to let himself be turned into a program. "Derrida" too slipped free
of proprietary claims. This did not mean he stopped writing about literature,
or in a literary way. It meant the activity of literature was as much about
philosophy as the activity of philosophy was about literature: both mutually formative of the other. It also meant Derrida was aware of Blanchot's
(if not Auden's) vision of the author: to write is to disavow oneself as a
sovereign author and authority. To give up the power of a right or a claim.
Disavowal constitutes literature. The name of "Derrida" was only ever a
cipher for this disavowal (or disavowel—*différance*). The decipherment of
which leads toward the abyss constitutive of all creation (even if only by
way of a satire of that abyss,[80] or by way, now, of a cliché.)

     If Derrida as "Derrida" remains significant for our times, as a significant
cliché, it is because in bringing together philosophy and art/literature in the
manner that he does, unlike any before save Nietzsche, and yet different
again (we will address religion below), he was the first to attempt to impress
a name upon the modern figurations of the O, or impress names upon the
modern figuration of O (singular and plural here in conflation). For this is
what philosophy does: it names—traditionally the given, now the giving.
Derrida remains the philosopher, ultimately. (This is how he only ever saw
himself, professionally.) But now a philosopher totally appropriated in or by
the O. And so the various attempts of naming, of circumscribing, of tracing, the O: *différance*, deconstruction, *il n'y a pas de hors-texte*, aporia, the
khōra, *dénégation*, the secret, the gift (of death), *Unheimlichkeit*, *tout autre*,
and others we might isolate, even *the name*.

     The name of the O is the name. The circularity of this phrase, in its
apparent pure symmetry, in which the O acts as speculum, reciprocating
identity that is carried by the name, of course carries the typical Derridean hole at its center. There is always much more, and much less, in a
name. In an essay of 1986 entitled "L'aphorisme à contretemps" ("Aphorism
Countertime"),[81] Derrida gives his reading of *Romeo and Juliet*, and in particular the famous balcony scene. Derrida, the literary philosopher, reading
Shakespeare, and the consummate tragic pair. But he reads the play apho-

ristically, that is, through that form, the aphorism, perfected by that other great literary philosopher, Nietzsche. "Aphorism is the name," begins the first aphorism (form and content mirroring themselves in identical play). By using the aphorism, Derrida wishes to show, once again, how reading the text is always out of step, or out of time, with what we think normal discourse ought to deliver: the logically unfolding narrative of unity, the teleology of the story or the argument. Aphorism disrupts unity, by inserting a break, continual discontinuity, into the flow of reason. So too the name: the name disrupts the flow of nature by individuating something as separate. Appellation as disjunction. And of course this is what Juliet ruminates on as she questions the existence of Romeo, the name she cannot countenance: "O Romeo, Romeo, wherefore art thou Romeo?" She seems, notes Derrida, "to call him beyond his name":[82]

> She wants the death of Romeo. She will have it. The death of his name ("'Tis but thy name that is my enemy"), certainly, the death of "Romeo," but they will not be able to get free from their name, they know this without knowing it [sans le savoir]. She declares war on "Romeo," on his name, in his name, she will win this war only on the death of Romeo himself. Himself? Who? Romeo. But "Romeo" is not Romeo. Precisely. She wants the death of "Romeo." Romeo dies, "Romeo" lives on. She keeps him dead in his name. Who? Juliet, Romeo.[83]

This is Aphorism 21. (Named 21, as a mark of separation, a distinction from the preceding and succeeding. But of course by numbering successively, continuity is maintained. A series of aphorisms, with a continuous break.) Aphorism 22:

> Aphorism: separation in language and, in it, through the name which closes the horizon. Aphorism is at once necessary and impossible. Romeo is radically separated from his name. He, his living self, living and singular desire, he is not "Romeo," but the separation, the aphorism of the name remains impossible. He dies without his name but he dies also because he has not been able to set himself free from his name, or from his father, even less to renounce him, to respond to Juliet's request ("Deny thy father and refuse thy name").[84]

So the name, for Derrida, approximates that death at the center of "O," the name for something that is nothing (death, O). Romeo becomes "Romeo," and therefore lives on, but only through death. The Romeo effect. Derrida does not name this O directly, as Juliet's O ("O Romeo, Romeo . . ."). But he is deeply aware that it circles around the entire dialogue, and play. "The circle of all these names in o: *words, Romeo, rose, love.*"[85] Thus, it generates in the play as the play, the play with the name *Romeo and Juliet*, which is played again and again, repeatedly, successively, but distinct each time—the return of the play as an elliptical essence.[86] And thus the "irony of the proper name," the play, *Romeo and Juliet*, which names names that are, in time and out of time, no-thing, death, "some other name": "The absolute aphorism: a proper name. Without genealogy, without the least copula. End of drama. Curtain."[87]

And thus the irony of the name "O," never named by Derrida, but repeatedly addressed by Derrida. Like the aphorism, the O cuts across time, out of sync with both the traditional discourses of *logos* (philosophy, discursive reasoning, thesis, etc.) and the traditional narratives of *mythos* (story, play, dialogue, etc.). The O is apostrophic: it turns away from the ruling line of address, and addresses an absence; it signifies an omission, an ellipsis ("— . . .": the opening paragraph of Derrida's "Sauf le nom (Postscriptum)");[88] and it signifies the genitive, the case of possession. O is always someone's O, even if that someone is absent, dispossessed. No one owns O, but it always belongs to somebody, always carries a name, is named, is name, as the embodiment of nothing (the name of death). Juliet's O. Romeo's O. Lear's O. Caliban's O. Shakespeare's O. Hegel's O. Nietzsche's O. Auden's O.

Derrida's O encircles writing by the end of the twentieth century, and becomes a cliché, by virtue of Derrida's multiple attempts at naming the O, *sauf le* "O." His style, his *modus operandi*, becomes emblematic, even imitated, not only because the academy cannot avoid speaking in clichés, but also because he himself invited himself to be reworked again and again. Like Joyce. The height of hubris, say his detractors. The sublation of the master by his servants, say the Derrideans. The losing of One's self at its origin, says his unspoken O. This "Derrida" that is not one, always something other.[89]

Irigaray

"*Khōra* reaches us, and as the name. And when a name comes, it immediately says more than the name: the other of the name and quite simply the other, whose irruption the name announces." Derrida originally wrote these words in 1987.[90] *Khōra*, as it appears in Plato's *Timaeus*, has no easy translation—which is precisely why Derrida seizes upon it—but it has been variously understood as a receptacle, a maternal womb, an interval space, or even an "imprint-bearer"[91] (as in the making of the cliché) that generates the becoming (of the cosmos, of signification, of meaning, etc.). In 1974, Julia Kristeva had written on the same term in the context of linguistics and psychoanalysis, though with a different transliteration: "Our discourse—all discourse—moves within and against the *chora* in the sense that it simultaneously depends upon and refuses it. Although the *chora* can be designated and regulated, it can never be definitely posited, as a result, one can situate the *chora* and, if necessary, lend it a topology, but one can never give it axiomatic form." Thus, neither "model nor copy, the *chora* precedes and underlies figuration and thus specularization."[92] Also in 1974, Luce Irigaray chose a related Platonic image—*hystera*—in connection to the famous *mythos* of the cave in *The Republic,* to address a similar space. She begins her essay in *Speculum of the Other Woman:*

> The myth of the cave, for example or as an example, is a good place to start. Read it this time as a metaphor of the inner space, of the den, the womb or *hystera,* sometimes of the earth—though we shall see that the text inscribes the metaphor as, strictly speaking, impossible. Here is an attempt at making metaphor, at trying out detours, which not only is a silent prescription for Western metaphysics but also, more explicitly, proclaims (itself as) everything publicly designated as metaphysics, its fulfilment, and its interpretation.[93]

Derrida associates this spatial image with the name, Kristeva with a prelinguistic process, Irigaray with a specifically female interiority, the womb. Of all the theoretical names or designations we might give the O, these French theorists have captured something crucial with their focus on the highly ambiguous and untranslatable region of the *khōra/chora* or on the metaphorics of *hystera*: its generative nature that prefigures figuration by allowing the possibility for figuration. As Irigaray says of the specular nature of this womb-like region: "The *hystera,* faceless, unseen, will never be presented, represented as such. But the representational scheme and sketch for the *hystera*—which can never be fulfilled—sub-tends, englobes, encircles, connotes, overdetermines every sight, every sighting, face, feature, figure, form, presentification, presence. Blindly."[94] And we could make much more of these similarities—between writers, between images, between metaphors—by means of protracted analyses of their respective writings. What the chosen images do not stress, however, is a negating aspect, even if they do have an abyssal nature to their features. Here, other Derridean terms would need to supplement, while Kristeva's notion of abjection would offer more of "those articulations of negativity."[95] Irigaray's "blindly" ("the blind spot of an old dream," as the first essay is entitled) begins to hint at a specular feature lost to negation.

But the question here at this point, outside of what theoretical name of the O suits best, is more this: Who is imitating whom? If Derrida, as

"Derrida," became the arch-postmodern stylist, the cliché as the second cast that allows repetitive copying or acting, how is it he, and not several women writing on the same subject, at the same time, or in some instances earlier, and with as much textual innovation, if not the same textual bravado—how is it that he came to this distinction? Here, Irigaray's treatment of gender enters most emphatically the orbit of the O each have tried to circumscribe. For Derrida's *khōra* had already been "traced" by women, which suggests that "Derrida," and its singular reputation—the male who arrogates the name, and naming—falls prey to its own O.

Irigaray's *Speculum of the Other Woman* would serve as a rich and fathomless source for understanding further, and in the context of late modernity, the O as mirror, a figuration we have retraced often throughout our discussion. In fact, Irigaray further inscribes Auden's images of sea and mirror, and explicitly combines them in addressing, like de Beauvoir, a female mysticism whose "center" may have "always been of glass/ice": "Mirror made of matter so fluid, so ethereal that it had already entered and mingled everywhere," even "in the depths of the abyss of the soul" where "I have become your image in this nothingness that I am, and you gaze upon mine in your absence of being."[96] And in "Plato's *Hystera*," she sees the Platonic cave, where all humans "are living in one, same, place," much as the dramatic stages of Shakespeare and Auden: "all stay there in the same spot—same place, same time—in the same *circle*, or circus ring, the theatrical arena of that representation"[97]—the source of metaphysics itself becoming a staged ring of artifice and specularization. We could go on, indefinitely, drawing out correlations from this text.

But for purposes of space, let me focus on the first two short works of her later collection *This Sex Which is Not One* (orig. *Ce Sexe qui n'en est pas un*, 1977),[98] which condenses, or reinscribes, much of that dealt with in the earlier *Speculum* volume. In the opening piece, "The Looking Glass, from the Other Side"[99] (orig. "Le miroir, de l'autre côté," [1973]), Irigaray offers a highly imaginative reflection on the nature of (female) subjectivity. It begins with a quote from Dodgson's *Through the Looking Glass*, when Alice, having returned from beyond the mirror, asks "And now, who am I?" but cannot, despite her efforts, recall. *She? She who? Who's she?* We don't quite know. *Yet there has to be a sequel.* The story never fully ends. *Now is the time for her to come on stage herself.* We immediately sense we are in Auden territory. A story of self's dispossession, in a creative account of what happens after the original story, a poetic commentary on the original, or origin, re-scened after the original as a finale, a finale to the original finale. *You've begun to notice that it is always in/on another stage that things are brought to their conclusion.* A copy, a reflection, the mirror acting as the plane separating imitation from its source, but the source, like Alice and Prospero, getting lost in the crossing vectors of reflection, the imitation never being the same as its source, the conclusion never being finalized. Because *Through the Looking Glass* is already a reflection, a sequel to *Alice in Wonderland*, the "original" reflected in the inverted image of the looking glass, the "other side" of the title is never quite locatable. From the other side of Dodgson's novel(s), as conceived by Irigaray (as from the other side of Shakespeare's *The Tempest,* as conceived by Auden)? From *this* side of Dodgson, the other side to us as readers? From the back of the mirror, the nonreflecting side? We are never sure where we stand, either within the story or without. *Only if I keep on pushing through to the other side, if I'm always beyond, because on this side of the screen of their projections, on this plane of their representations, I can't live. I'm stuck, paralyzed by all those images, words, fantasies.* By the end, we learn we are caught up in another mirror-image: the film of Michel Soutter, *Les arpenteurs* (*The Surveyors* [1972]), whose characters and unconventional narrative/storyline inform the "after" story of Alice being told by Irigaray. So we are completely disoriented, as in a house of mirrors, and have no idea where the beyond might lie, since all images seem to be crossing each other and entangling our sight. Unlike in Plato's cave, we do not look simply in one direction at the screen of projection. We see in all directions. *Behind the screen of projection.* But is "behind" beyond or other? How do we get outside? Out of the cinema, out of the theatre? Out in the sun? In the garden? Outside ourselves? *The out-of-doors is an extraordinary refuge.*

We are not given this refuge in the story. Ultimately, this would be a refuge of subjectivity as one, the subject as, in de Beauvoir's term, the sovereign subject. The sovereignty of subjectivity is precisely what is being de-authorized here, the subjection of sovereignty to that which is more than one. *Duplicating, doubling, dividing: of sequences, images, utterances, "subjects."* So when we read, we are lost not only in a splintered plotline, with no clearly discernible direction (chronologically or episodically), but also in a narrative refraction, with no clearly discernible subject guiding any one utterance. Monologue, dialogue, trialogue, polylogue . . . *One blends into the other.* Confusion *again becomes* legitimate. *The looking glass dissolves, already broken.* What Irigaray is trying to inscribe, by bringing Alice back from Wonderland, is yet another land of displacement, a textual surreality, in which the subject is lost in a circulation, or circumlocution, of voices, of images, of thoughts, of actions. *Where are we? How far along are we? Everything is whirling. Everyone is dancing.* And the subject has no "place" to inhabit, to take refuge. No room of one's own. *Where is one to go? If the house and the garden are open to all comers.* Displacing, dislocating, dispersing, in a story that refracts subjects, subjectivity, subjective unity onto no specific surface except off each other as always other, and never any more one. *Representations of the projects of the one. Which he/she brings to light by displacing them.*

The space of literature that Irigaray here is trying encircle, as a broken speculum, is also very much the artificer's circle, and very much that
of Prospero's finale. The story *is coming to its end. Turning, returning, in a
closed space,* an enclosure *that is not to be violated, at least not while the story
unfolds: the space of a few private properties.* But this is Auden's Prospero: the
private sovereign who looks in the mirror, and sees not the grand artificer,
the master magician, the One who claims ownership of the round property
on/in which he stands, but the split selves, rent open to reveal the O under
foot. A *unity divided in halves. More, or less. Identifiable, or not.* So even the
writing itself requires a split narrative, a split form. But how to situate this
artificial circle, which is both binding and broken, both sealed and split?
We would have needed, at least, *two genres. And more. To bring them into
articulation. Into conjunction. But at what moment?* In what place? *And won't
this second one be just the* other side *of the first? Perhaps more often its complement?* "The Looking Glass, from the Other Side," as a text, is set up as the
"other side," the complement. But to what? There is no singular "this side,"
and therefore there is nothing fulfilled or completed in this story, which, in
continually coming to its end, always seems to be starting again. ". . . she
suddenly began again," it begins. There is nothing except the fullness of a
broken circle (ellipse/ellipsis).

The One, as male, and the Other, as female, are certainly not fulfilled
as complements here. The story, as much as we can piece it together, is a
story of infidelity, broken relations, sexual violation, misinterpretation. *A
highway is to cut through the village.* The One, as sovereign subject, however
much he may reach out for predication, has no fulfillment in the other
as object, as accusative, while the Other, as woman, has no subject to be
nominative. *Since they are not the sum of two units, where can one pass between
them?* The question of gender becomes a dividing point, but confused by the
lack of subjectivity on either side. *Neither one nor the other. Neither one of the
two. Nor the two, either, together or separately.* But this, ultimately (though
where can the ultimate be placed, ultimately?), is Alice's story, the Alice
who tries to come back from the other side, and reside in a name that is
hers from several sources—*except that "she" never has a proper name, that "she"
is at best "from wonderland," even if "she" has no right to a public existence
except in the protective custody of the name of Mister* X [Carroll, Dodgson,
Soutter]—*then, so that she may be taken, or left, unnamed, forgotten without
even having been identified, "i"—who?—will remain uncapitalized.*

If we have tried to capitalize, perhaps unwisely, on Irigaray's own het-
erotopic approach to the story of the authored and gendered subject here—
for what do the above italics represent if not a dispossession or requisition
of authorship, even at the risk of academic impropriety?—it is because she
shows us another dimension to the question of imitation or mimetic reflec-

tion in "philosophical" thinking. Where Derrida's style, as "Derrida," invites, and even necessitates, its own deconstruction, Irigaray's storytelling invites its own reconstruction of gender between One and Other. The highway project in Soutter's film will require the characters not merely to relocate but to rebuild. And this invitation is made more theoretically explicit in the essay to follow, "This Sex Which is Not One."

The title alone invites multiple readings: "this sex" ("*ce sexe*"), which is now the female sex, is not "one" in multiple senses: it is not the male One, it is not a "sex" per se, and it is something other than singular (multiple, or nothing). "Female sexuality has always been conceptualised on the basis of masculine parameters," it begins. Or, "woman's erogenous zones never amount to anything but a clitoris-sex that is not comparable to the noble phallic organ, or a hole-envelope that serves to sheathe and massage the penis in intercourse: a non-sex, or a masculine organ turned back upon itself, self-embracing."[100] Or further, "Woman 'touches herself' all the time . . . for her genitals are formed of two lips in continuous contact. Thus, within herself, she is already two—but not divisible into one(s)."[101] Or, again explicitly, "While her body thus finds itself thus eroticized, and called to a double moment of exhibition and of chaste retreat in order to stimulate the drives of the 'subject,' her sexual organ represents *the horror of nothing*. . . . Woman's genitals are simply absent, masked, sewn back up inside their 'crack.'" So that finally, "Rigorously speaking, she cannot be identified as one person, or two. She resists all adequate definition. Further, she has no 'proper' name. And her sexual organ, which is not *one* organ, is counted as *none*."[102]

In Irigaray's erotics of O, woman, as the female sex, which has been seen as a non-sex by the phallocentric One that has unnamed it (*awoman*, as she herself names it later, with Lacan in mind),[103] figures the O not only by virtue of a metaphorics of absence, which owes its ongoing currency to psychoanalytic theory, but also by virtue of the female body and its "construction" of tactile multiplicity. "*Woman has sex organs more or less everywhere*."[104] And this construction is not merely anatomical, physiological, or somatic; it is also—though undifferentiated—linguistic, semantic, hermeneutical:

> For in what she says, too, at least when she dares, woman is constantly touching herself. She steps ever so slightly aside from herself with a murmur, an exclamation, a whisper, a sentence left unfinished. . . . When she returns, it is to set off again from elsewhere. From another point of pleasure, or of pain. One would have to listen with another ear, as if hearing *an "other meaning" always in the progress of weaving itself, of embracing itself with words, but*

*also of getting rid of words in order not to become fixed, congealed in
them.* For if "she" says something, it is not, it is already no longer,
identical with what she means. What she says is never identical
with anything, moreover; rather, it is contiguous. *It touches (upon).*
And when it strays too far from that proximity, she breaks off and
starts over at "zero": her body-sex.[105]

The opening story of Alice is one stylization of this kind of hermeneutical "touching" that is constantly zeroing itself out to begin anew. ". . . she
suddenly began again." The circle back leads nowhere, and everywhere.
"Nothing. Everything."[106] If we (men—but society as a whole, as driven
by the male point of view, which still predominates women's perceptions)
cannot fathom this nothing and this everything, it is not because it is
irrational and hysterical—the *hystera* is a place *pre*-rational—but because
"it really involves a different economy more than anything else, one that
upsets the linearity of a project [beginning in Plato's cave], undermines the
goal-object of a desire, diffuses the polarization towards a single pleasure,
disconcerts fidelity to a single discourse."[107] Alice's stories disconcert in their
multiplicity. And so she is uncapitalized by the capital powers. Irigaray, by
rewriting Alice, enacts the O that is Alice's mode for reasserting herself.
"(Re-)discovering herself, for a woman, thus could only signify the possibility of sacrificing no one of her pleasures to another, of identifying herself
with none of them in particular, *of never being simply one.*"[108] Multiple Os.
Going even beyond, now, Auden's O, since hetero-sexuality takes on new
meaning beyond the homo-sexuality of male conjugation: "But if women
are to preserve and expand their autoeroticism, their homo-sexuality, might
not the renunciation of heterosexual pleasure correspond once again to
that disconnection from power that is traditionally theirs?"[109] So a homosexuality *as* heterosexuality, or neither one nor the other, but both, and
more. Multiple Os. And this is where Irigaray outperforms "Derrida." She
does not complement Derridean thought by extending it to the female. If
anything, "Derrida" is already caught up in the female, in the fulfilment
of her writing, as the one who cannot be, any longer, the imitated one,
but only the cliché, the name for the postmodern stereotype.[110] We do not
write "Irigaray," who cannot be clichéd, since her subject is not one, and
never has been one. Only her "non-sex," her non-O, if that could make
any sense—the "fake orgasm" of her culturally determined, commercially
provoked, insatiably pornographized, sex.

Irigaray obviously owes much to de Beauvoir, even though she has
expressed differences with her compatriot.[111] For the sovereign subject of
One is fully undone by Irigaray as the next generation of feminists—and
no longer by historical exposition, or by giving "an account of her own

life while backing it up scientifically,"[112] but by a literary enactment (we cannot, after "Derrida," say a "style") that reworks philosophy from neither the inside nor the outside. Irigaray's Os show a very different kind of erotics at work, a fully gendered a-topological sexual dynamic, one that is not one, but simultaneously multiple and nought, and which emerges out of a re-inscripting of the pairings of male and female, of reality and mirror, of philosophy and art, a re-speculation that leads beyond the one and the other together.

OUT OF THE POSTMODERN: BADIOU

Before we leave philosophy proper, or, through Irigaray, having just left philosophy *propre*, the philosophy that one can rightly call one's own, we must consider one last French contemporary, Alain Badiou, keeping in mind that the return to the male here must be continually problematized by the sovereign subject of "one's own." We have already seen Badiou in the context of Pauline thinking on universalism.[113] But Badiou is significant here and now for several further reasons: he acts as Sartre's complementary bookend to textbook postmodernism, he places himself in the modern ontological tradition of nothing that goes back through Sartre and Heidegger, and, more than any other philosopher since Frege, he has dealt directly with the "concept" (or anti-concept) of zero and its extension into the void. We can only be brief in our considerations here, but each of these reasons is worth parsing further as a measure of how the most recent philosophical scene stages the O.

   If Sartre looked both ways, backward from and forward to postmodern thought, Badiou looks backward through and forward from postmodern thought. He has often been compared to Sartre, and he himself has openly expressed Sartre as a major influence, particularly in regard to his literary works.[114] Badiou's novels and plays have never received the same attention or critical acceptance as those of his predecessor—as the undisguised Marxist, philosophizing through his plays, he is unlikely to endear himself to present-day audiences, and least of all to feminist appropriation, since his approach to these works is in the same segregated manner as Sartre's: novels in traditional form, plays as traditional theatre, philosophy as traditional discursive analyses. His stories and drama, all steeped in the French lineage, are heavily weighted with philosophy, undeniably, but they do not try to merge the creative with the conceptual as, say, both Derrida and Irigaray have innovated, each in their way. Rather, through traditional forms, they have, *contra* Auden, direct political intent. In fact, in his "Rhapsody for the Theatre: A Short Philosophical Treatise," he talks of a "theatre-politics isomorphism," though not in the customary understanding of the world of politics being essentially theatrical, but the reverse: "it is theatre, in the circle of its provisional repetition, that figures the knotted components of politics." "Theatre," in its now-capitalized form (as distinguished from bad "theatre," or that which does not ultimately concern itself with the "state of the State") becomes "the figurative reknotting of politics, and this regardless of its subject matter."[115] And so like Sartre, theatre must be grounded in this world and in this time, the material conditions of reality in the Marxian political sense; and yet, at the same time, theatre "must possess the powerful simplicity of the atemporal, it must bespeak a *generic* humanity."[116] For most philosophers, all this will appear as "bastard philosophy."[117] But for Badiou, like Sartre, philosophy, along with politics, must necessarily see art as a form of the same gesture toward truth, even if that form cannot be draped with the same garments as the philosophical argument. And truth, again as with Sartre, will carry a negation at its core.

In an earlier essay of 1992, "Philosophy and Art," Badiou had expounded upon the historically fraught relationship between philosophy and art. He admitted that all "philosophy uses fictive incarnations in the texture of its exposition" (image, comparison, rhythm, narrative, fable, the parable, etc.),[118] but that the philosopher ought not to usurp the role of the poet. We philosophers, he says, must "leave to the poets the care of the future of poetry beyond all that the hermeneutic concern of the philosopher pressed upon it. Our singular task is rather to rethink, from the point of philosophy, its liaison or its un-liaison with the poem, in terms that can be neither those of the Platonic banishment, nor those of the Heideggerean suture, nor even those of the classificatory care of an Aristotle or a Hegel."[119] Philosophy divests itself of all those non-principled features of poetry ("aura," "trembling," "pathos") in order to grasp "*truth's proving of itself* as such." But in its proving it cannot escape those moments when it comes up against a certain negativity of meaning, an ab-sense, "the radical underside of sense, the void of all possible presentation, the hollowing of truth as a hole *without borders.*" And at the place of this void the work of art (the poem, etc.) arises *within* philosophy's universalizing gestures:

> The poem occurs in philosophy when the latter [philosophy], in its will to universal address, in its vocation to make the place that it erects inhabited by all, falls under the imperative of having to propose to sense and to interpretation the latent void that sutures all truth to the being of that of which it is truth. This presentation of the unpresentable void requires the deployment within language of the latter's literary resources; but under the condition that it occur at this very point; thus under the general jurisdiction of an entirely different style, that of argumentation, of conceptual liaison, or of the Idea.[120]

So philosophy proceeds with a literary rupture always threatening to emerge, and emerge where "the relation of a truth to sense is a defective or void relation. It is this defection that exposes philosophy to the imperative of a localized fiction."[121] The O begins to take shape in Badiou, then, at an originary point, like so many before him—the point where truth is *produced*, but produced necessarily from or with or within a void or a negation. As he says by way of the essay's conclusion: "The poem marks the moment of the empty page in which the argument proceeds, proceeded, will proceed."[122]

So Badiou is always soliciting the poets in his philosophy, when not being the "poet" himself (however eclipsed, with justification, his literary output has become by his philosophical output). But why is truth or truth's being "sutured" to a void (or a void "sutured" to this being truth)? What is Badiou's understanding of truth and, more significantly, of being that distinguishes him from Sartre, and, by his own intention, from postmodernism?

Badiou's employment of the term *truth*, even "axiomatically," has suggested to many something beyond the general view of postmodern theory, which, if it could speak of "truth," could only do so under erasure or in the plural. But a first look at Badiou's own definitions suggests he remains firmly in the postmodern camp: "All the categories by which the essence of a truth can be submitted to thought are negative: undecidability, indiscernibility, the generic not-all (*pas-tout*), and the unnameable."[123] Or, "A truth is, first of all, something new."[124] And yet these definitions operate within a different kind of ontological derivation than virtually of Badiou's philosophical forebears and indeed even his postmodern contemporaries.

Badiou's first volume of his *magnum opus*, *L'être et l'événement* (*Being and Event*), is clearly in the tradition of those immediate forebears, Sartre and Heidegger, while the structure of the text, a series of thirty-seven meditations, points directly to Descartes (and Husserl). The question of being is still paramount, but as the title indicates "time" and "nothingness" have given way to "event." ("Nothingness gone, the castle of purity remains," ends the entire volume.)[125] But ontology, the question of being, is, for Badiou, not a question to be pursued in the first instance by inherited philosophical categories and concepts. Here, he is Heideggerean. It is to be pursued as a *mathematics*, and thus the now famous claim of the text: "*mathematics is ontology*." Here, he is assuredly not Heideggerean. The simple unpackaging of this claim is this: rather than seeing being substantially (classical) or existentially (Heidegger or Sartre), being is seen in terms of set theory (Cantor et al.), which posits being as multiples or multiplicity operating by way of structuring and procedural conditions. A *proper* unpackaging of this claim would require another book-length analysis, which obviously goes well outside our aim at this late stage of our discussion. Without going into all the *arcana* of set theory mathematics and its nomenclature, let me try to provide some framework to this thought and draw a few salient points germane to our development of the O and its deportment in late modernity.

Let us return first to the condition of modernity that I have previously elaborated, the here-and-now *modus*, which perpetuates the *novum* by de-Latinizing it into (at first) the "nouveau." I have said repeatedly, and elsewhere,[126] that what marks modernity as "modern" is the aggrandizing of the ever-new, this forward-looking modal vision that repeals the past as outmoded, or nonmodal. In inheriting the One, modernity felt compelled to fashion it anew, while at the same time continuing to rely upon it for its subjectivity—the new "One" as autonomous sovereign subject. But a "new One" is an inherent contradiction, if by "new" we understand an always originating beginning, and if by "One" we understand an always originated beginning. Hence the fundamental problematic that haunts modernity from its "inception"—the unity (of the new One, and, eventually, the new *Ones*) cannot hold. An O marks its center. This problematic begins with the question of the subject (Descartes's *nouveau* subject), which will remain a problematic throughout all of modernity's phases: how can the sovereign subject keep its sovereignty (as One) while being subject to an eternally renewing beginning (the O)? This question modulates into all the difficulties of modern subjectivity encountered since Descartes, whether in the form of the subject's relation to the object (as put forward consummately by Kant and Hegel), or of the subject's relation to itself (as manifested by the modernists, psychoanalysis, and postmodernists), or of the subject in relation to gender (as revealed by the many feminisms from de Beauvoir onward). It also initiates Badiou's own philosophy: *Théorie du sujet* (1982) is one of his earliest philosophical investigations, as he tries to lay the ground for a modern doctrine of the subject that overcomes modernity's inherent self-division. (Badiou has "reworked" this text in *Being and Event's* second volume: *Logics of Worlds* [2009; orig. French 2006]).

What allows Badiou to move through and beyond this division, to resolve the paradox of the "new One" as a unity that cannot hold, an endless multiplicity of singularities, is the mathematical context of set theory. In set theory, everything is a multiple of a multiple, and no one set (despite calling it "one" set) can be reduced to a singular unit or One, since all the elements making up that set are themselves multiples of other elements (there being no overriding Set of sets). If we speak of "one," or "One," it is only as "an operational result" of the presented multiplicity (or "regime of presentation").[127] One can count something as one, but this counting-as-one is not One in any strict absolute or transcendental sense, only in an operational sense: "there is no one, only the count-as-one."[128] There is, therefore, no ground to these operational moves, the "count-as-ones," nor to their sets of multiples, only a procedurality that is always, and only ever, a "presentation of a presentation" (multiples and their elements, however they are presented in sets, being only ever the same thing, in a constant nominal or re-presentational loop; that is, One is never an origin or a cause, but only ever an effect).[129]

Now "being" is caught up in this endless accruing of presentations, for being is none other than the "situation" of certain accrued or structured presentations. Being has no ultimate structure or hypostatic substance, in the old ontological sense of the "qua" in "being qua being," but only a *structuring*—i.e., situational, operational, procedural—multiplicity. *The ontological reality of this being is that it is irreducibly multiple.* And the corollary of such a being is that the subject too has no structure or substance. The individualized subject in this theory of sets and "setting" (situation, presentation, procedure all being operative terms) is, we learn later on, neither a substance nor an origin nor an "invariable of presentation." It is not self-identical nor self-reflective nor transcendental. It is not anything we have ever understood as the subject in the modern sense. The subject, like being, has no single point, no One, on which to ground itself, and yet neither is it a void point nor, like the One, merely a result. It is "subjectivization"—the subject turned into operational function or term. This subject is not a given in any sense: a subject may arise out of a situation, as "a *local* status of a procedure, a configuration in excess of the situation,"[130] but it also may not. Every individual is not necessarily a subject, therefore. The subject retains the notion of singularity, without ever being reduced to it, but only in connection to an "event." "It could be said that subjectivization is a *special count*, distinct from the count-as-one, which orders presentation, just as it is from the state's reduplication. What subjectivization counts is whatever is faithfully connected to the name of the event."[131] But just what is this "event," this second half of the title linked so prominently to being?

An event is an especial gathering of multiplicities that somehow breaks with the normal gathering of multiplicities. It is an "ultra-one" that emerges from the accruing of certain presentations (as count-as-one situations) to stand outside its mere accrual, and disrupt the general situation. This emergence is possible only from an "evental site," or an "entirely abnormal multiple" made abnormal by virtue of its not revealing its elements, which somehow lie hidden "beneath."[132] This process might be seen as a sophisticated version of "the whole is greater than the sum of its parts": the event, by virtue of its disruption, appears or presents itself as greater than the sum of its individual parts or elements (that sum being the "evental site," which does not reveal its abnormal elements, only the abnormal sum), except that the appearance or presentation, taken as "ultra," is nothing other than its assemblage, now counted or nominated as one in an amplified way. The French Revolution is Badiou's oft-repeated example: "[A]s event it must be said that it both presents the infinite multiple of the sequence of facts situated between 1789 and 1798, and, *moreover,* that it presents itself as an immanent résumé and one-mark of its own multiple."[133] In more technical terms, "the event is a one-multiple made up of, on the one hand, all the multiples which belong to its site, and on the other hand, the event itself."[134] Or in more simplified terms, the French Revolution was a series of occurrences that did not fit in with the established norm, but whose elements remained hidden from view (*"on the edge of the void"*), with no ultimate ground or cause other than a contingency within their coincidence and "setting." This contingency stands apart as an event only by its nomination as such—ultra presentation of presentation—and the subject arises by being in fidelity to that nomination, "in excess" of the normal situation. The subject becomes a process of subjectivization that "intervenes" in the situation (through *"interpretative intervention,"* which suggests a lingering hermeneutic, if not a nominalism)[135] to help give the event its nomination as event, the "interventional nomination *from the standpoint of the situation."* Such, for example, is Paul in the emergence of the Christian Church, and of the corresponding universalism.[136] (The subject in praxis, we could say, invoking Sartre again.) The coupling of "being and event" then becomes the nomination of being caught up in (its own) multiplicity and retaining a "One" only in the sense of an "ultra-one," a rupturing event, which itself has no ultimate ground, and therefore is more than one, a "one-multiple," and to which being has no ontological connection except through its own negation as one, "that-which-is-not-being-qua-being."[137]

How, finally, does the void fit in all of this? We said above that being was sutured to the void that is its truth. What does this now mean? If all being is multiple, because multiplicity marks all sets and their constituent elements, then being can never be presented as being qua being. Being is only a situation (as ontology is only a situation). This situation is present in the count-as-one (*a* situation), but as soon as we try to unveil what stands behind this count-as-one, we encounter multiplicity. This is the departure point of Badiou's entire project (and set theory), and thus the title of Meditation One—"The One and the Multiple: *a priori* conditions of any possible ontology."[138] We cannot present multiplicity except through *a* situation, which is counted as one; beyond this "one" of the count nothing is presentable. We cannot present pure multiplicity, or infinity, for this, we know from Hegel and others, would amount to nondifferentiated nothing: "[I]t is necessary, from the standpoint of immanence to the situation, that the pure multiple, absolutely unpresentable according to the count, be *nothing.*"[139] All we can present is the count of the one, as counted; any "subtraction from the count" would be a non-one, "scattered all over, nowhere and everywhere," leading to nothing, "the name of the unpresentation in presentation."[140] The void becomes this nothing as named. It is "sutured to being," or being is "sutured to its void," by virtue of just such a situation (which is all situations) that opens us up to unpresentation, even if denying us access: "The void is the name of the being . . . according to a situation, inasmuch as presentation gives us therein an unpresentable access, thus non-access, to this access, in the mode of what is not-one nor composable of ones; thus what is qualifiable within the situation solely as the errancy of nothing."[141] The void, in other words, is the proper name of being. *Void and Event.* Or, "the null sovereign of interference."[142] Or, as he states elsewhere, "Zero is being qua being thought as Number, from within ontology."[143]

We can see it becomes impossible to enter Badiou's ontological world without recourse to its technical jargon and specialized calculus. And a seeming far cry it is from the literary *esprit* of his postmodern and feminist compatriots. The set theory context presents itself as the very antithesis of the poetry Badiou tries to interpolate (Mallarmé and Hölderlin in *Being and Event,* among others). It threatens to alienate even the committed reader who does not possess sufficient mathematical acumen (the majority of us, I suspect). This is a problem even Badiou admits, and in Meditation 11 sets nature within the context of *both* the poem and the matheme, even if the latter, as mathematical ontology, interrupted the former through the "Greek event" (beginning with Parmenides).[144] We might assist Badiou in his own attempt here by summarizing the entirety of *Being and Event,* if not imparting some relief, with a poetic quote:

> Before our eyes, thing seems to limit thing,
> Air bounds the hills, and forests the trees,
> Earth sea, sea earth, but add them up, and nothing
> Limits the sum.

These words are from Lucretius, that other philosophical champion of thoroughgoing materialism, whose *De Rerum Natura* is composed as one vast poem.[145] The sum of all things is unlimited multiplicity; and nothing, as Void, defines this sum. This in turn sums up both Lucretius's and Badiou's positions: Badiou's mathematical ontology may be seen as a modified, discursively articulated Lucretianism, exchanging atomism for set theory and Epicurean activism for political (Marxist) activism. So it is not surprising that the final pages of Badiou's essay on "Philosophy and Art" end with a discussion of this poem. There, Badiou sees his Roman predecessor as first and foremost a poet, over against the philosopher; *Being and Event,* and its follow-up *Logics of Worlds,* might be seen as a philosophizing of that poet's truth, over against the poet (a philosophical orientation that "thinks being subtractively in the mode of an ideal or axiomatic thought").[146] And yet for Badiou, both he and the poet are still *making* truths, not finding them. For truth, or *a* truth, does not correspond to or verify knowledge; on the contrary, truth, through the event, "bores a hole in knowledge."[147]

The O makes its mark here by boring a hole, philosophically if not poetically, into our inherited conceptions of being and reality, of the One over against the Many, and of the something over against the nothing. In some sense—or in the sense of a predictable pun or trope that runs the risk of triteness—Badiou returns us full circle, via Sartre and Heidegger, back to our opening figurations in Chapter 0 (whose numbering I have borrowed from Badiou) of 1 and 0, and to the numerology spawned from the symbology predicated upon the straight line and the curve/circle. The question of number, of quantity, is the substratum of Badiou's thinking, with its axiomatics in the theory of the pure multiple, reducible to one clarification: *all is multiple.* Here, using the copula in its singular form, the "one-multiple" emerges from its essential backdrop, that which exceeds numbering altogether, infinity, or the void as nothing. So our initial questions of One and Zero have been reintroduced anew by Badiou's ontological reprogramming of set theory, and brought into our philosophical agenda from the cultural and technological realms of present-day binary code. For Badiou this would constitute a "second modernity," what we have been calling a late modernity:

> The passage to a second modernity of the thinking of number obliges thought to *return* to zero, to the infinite, and to the One. A total dissipation of the One, an ontological decision as to the being of the void and that which marks it, a lavishing without measure of infinities: such are the parameters of such a passage. Unbinding from the One delivers us to the unicity of the void and to the dissemination of the infinite.[148]

There is no passage in all of modernity (first, second, early, late) that captures better the present situation of our modern "history." Zero, as a profound anti-concept, "neither positive nor negative,"[149] finally makes its full appearance within the conceptual frames of our reality, both to affirm and to deny (conceptually). It may still retain a mathematical context—the zero as the null or empty set, marked by "an old Scandinavian letter, Ø, emblem of the void, zero affected by the barring of sense"[150]—but it is now operative within ontology as the very possibility of being, and of the *concept* of being (or the concept of *anything*):

> "Zero exists" is inevitably a *first* assertion; the very one that fixes an existence from which all others will proceed. . . . Number comes first here: it is that *point of being* upon which the exercise of

the concept depends. Number as the number of nothing, or zero, sutures every text to its latent being. The void is not a production of thought, because it is from its existence that thought proceeds, in as much as "it is the same thing to think and to be" [Parmenides]. In this sense, it is the concept that comes from number, and not the other way around.[151]

By the end of his book *Number and Numbers*, Badiou will refer to "Number" in the same way he does to "Theatre," in capitalized form, opposing it to "numbers," and denoting "*a form of Being*,"[152] something ultimately "supernumerary . . . from which a truth originates,"[153] but something sutured to the Void, from which itself as being originates. For Badiou, something will come of nothing, an event, a truth, Number, but only as a multiple type of being (and only in four specific realms: art, politics, science, and love). And its very multiplicity will always keep it "sutured" to its negative source. So his translator will say of him in his Preface to *Being and Event*: "Badiou is the King Lear of philosophy, but a Lear who retains a part, a part to which one may return after voyaging through diverse realms opened up by new artistic, political, scientific and amorous procedures." In these procedures, never escaping their procedurality, "Philosophy is thus dethroned, and it wanders over the heath, open to storms of evental reworking."[154] Whether Badiou can ultimately keep to his own axiomatic procedures, or to his own strict materialism, having opened himself to the O, is the question of many. Is Badiou his own event, or in fidelity to his own event? Or does Badiou's O, rendered Ø, inhere in its own negation, through a mode that counters axiomatic procedure? Or we might pose the question as a theologian might: Could not the O swallow the material conditions of the event as well?

GOD—POSTMORTEM THEOLOGY

In *Being and Event*, Badiou relates the term "death of God" to the Church in *disconnection* to the Christ-event universalized by Paul.[155] He further implies that this term has had a history prior to Nietzsche, besides the theological history of *connection* to the Christ-event (in the theology of the cross). We certainly know that apophaticism has an extended history within and without the Church,[156] that the *via negativa* has been a distinct if narrow path available to religious adherents in all three religions of the Book, and of course a central pathway for many outside the Abrahamic tradition, in Mahayana Buddhism especially. But it is one thing to attempt to give speech to the ineffable, to say the unsayable, to name anonymity, or to empty a name, a concept, an existence through language; it is quite another to declare that God is truly *no more*, erased from the horizon, dead in every conceivable sense. Nietzsche's clarion call is surely a gateway to a new way of thinking, even if it was already prefigured in Schelling and pre-announced in Hegel. For it is not simply the old metaphysical God of Christianity that is eradicated from our reality, but all that attended to this God in the name of the One. Apophaticism, as we saw with Plotinus, can and often does operate within the One. The death of God, as Nietzsche saw it, meant a wholly new way of understanding the *universe*, and of revaluing our existence in it. If there was any precedence to this revaluing in the modern world, it would have come from Kierkegaard, that inverted Hegelian, whose Abraham in *Fear and Trembling* did not merely fall silent before the God who dared to demand his son's sacrifice, but *couldn't speak* upon trying.[157] Kierkegaard himself never stopped trying, of course, though his own *modus* was through an indirection made manifest in the pseudonymic, ironic, and parabolic nature of his variously creative texts. If Nietzsche is our modern archetype in thinking philosophically through creative means (even if his philosophy is deeply obsessed with theology), Kierkegaard is our modern archetype in thinking theologically through creative means (even if his theology is deeply obsessed with philosophy). The Schelling-Hegel-Kierkegaard axis thus provides a preparatory ground for the emergence of the O in modern religion—not now as *via negativa*, but as *negativa per se*.

But any preparatory ground, whether from this axis or from Nietzsche, sat long in the waiting. For very understandable reasons, traced out above, religion, and in particular the monotheism of the West, was the last bastion to relinquish its hold on the One, and let its ground be breached by the O. Karl Barth of the *Der Romerbrief*, steeped as he was in Kierkegaard, certainly did much to loosen the crust of the soil, as did Bonhoeffer and Tillich after him. And we know this was precisely Kafka's understanding of the role of literature. So too other religious writers of the early-to-mid-century: Eliot—or Auden, whose return to orthodox religion, via Kierkegaard, was, unlike Eliot's, unorthodox precisely at the point of the making of the O. But each of these twentieth-century harbingers, Auden included, pulled back from taking fully Nietzsche's madman at his word, as Kierkegaard himself had pulled back, proleptically and, in the end, emphatically. It was not until that Western cultural ferment of the 1960s that the O truly came to inhabit the fortress of religion in what is now, historically, called the "death of God" movement.

Postmodern theory, which first began to gain traction in the decade of the '60s, even if not labeled as such, certainly provided lethal blows to the idea of the transcendent God, through means philosophical, psychoanalytical, political, cultural, and literary. The implications for God as sovereign One were unmistakable under the sustained attack that put metaphysics, the Subject, the State, History, the Author, or the Grand Narrative under serious question and, for all intents and purposes, under burial ground. The death of God thus seemed, within Continental and largely French thinking, a *fait accompli* by the time postmodern theory had reached North American shores a decade later (primarily through literary channels). In this move, Nietzsche finally appeared the consummate anti-Christ he claimed he was, and his madman's cry the cry of triumph. But then, philosophy, psycho-analysis, and literary criticism (as routed through New Criticism) had, for all intents and purposes, long left religion behind in any effective sense. It was not as if postmodernism was announcing some antireligious enlightenment. It was more that it was providing the theoretical *coup de grâce*, and now for all the masses to see. And by the time the masses were able to appropriate postmodern theory in their own cultural terms, it was no longer a question of their co-conspiracy with God's death but of their identification of the corpse after the crime. Postmodernism thus became synonymous with athe-ism—in-your-face atheism—carrying the ironically unequivocal message that it was time for a true wake, if not in pure Joycean style, then in something approximating its radical abandon.

Of course, the story can no longer be written this way, not least because, whatever the masses understood, and whatever the intelligentsia had tried to promulgate, religion had never really gone away. As Lacan had alluded to as early as 1959, postmodernism would not provide the death knell for religion, nor even the death knell for the monotheistic God.[158] With an irony only possible under the celebrated terms of postmodern-ism's self-acclaimed *modus ironicus*, postmodern theory would simply give religion the means to speak of its God now in terms of the O instead of an all-abiding Universal. That is, it would allow religion to try to refigure itself by incorporating negation directly into its hallowed space, as a kind of substitutionary act in the death of the One. This would by no means render religion obsolete or impossible, even if statistically, in Europe at least, it was in its most moribund state since the Caesars. It would not even render theology impossible. On the contrary, a "postmodern theology" would emerge, one that has now become a well-worked concept, grounded upon those very names who were first seen as the pallbearers in theism's supposed late great twentieth-century funeral.

So the move of Derrida—whose turn to religion in the latter part of his career, upon the claim of philosophy's own "return to religion," alien-ated many in critical circles who once laid claim to his name within their ranks. Derrida's attention to negative theology finally allowed "Derrida," the name of the one who fathered deconstruction, to be released into a sphere of unnaming, of de-denomination. And thus in "Sauf le nom" he backs away from averring what the name consists in—the name of "negative theology" in the first instance, but also his own name, and that of "God":

— However much one says, then, that beyond the theorem and constative description, the discourse of negative theology "consists" in exceeding essence and language, by testifying it *remains*.

— What does "remain" mean here? Is it a modality of "being"?

— I don't know. Perhaps this, precisely, that this theology would be nothing . . .[159]

"God" as unknowable, except in name, names only a "bottomless collapse,"[160] and theology by necessity must remain in the negative, even if as remainder to that negative. Derrida's name, by turn, names an O that can only be figured, ultimately, in "I don't know," in "Perhaps . . . precisely . . . nothing."[161]

Upon this "perhaps . . . precisely" follows a procession of Derrideans. Mark C. Taylor, for example, introduces the term *a-theology* into English-speaking theological discourse, predicated on a thorough engagement with Derrida's work of deconstruction.[162] In *nOts*, published in the same year as "Sauf le nom," that predication reaches its most pronounced in relation to the nothing. (Its second chapter, "nO nOt nO," was actually first written for a volume on Derrida and negative theology, to which Derrida's "Sauf le nom" was the "Post-scriptum" as response.)[163] Here, Taylor was the first to connect, in any explicit sense, Derrida's name to the O, not only as the main title and chapter titles indicate, but also by correlating it to Derrida's relation to autobiography (chapter 2) and to his own autobiography (chapter 8), in a style wholly modeled upon, indeed even traced over, Derrida. So ends the second chapter:

> This *tout autre* might imply the denegation . . . that Derrida's quasi-"autobiographical" atheological text performs. Perhaps. Perhaps not.
>
> O
> O
> O[164]

In similar formation is the work of John Caputo, whose *Prayers and Tears of Jacques Derrida: Religion without Religion*, owing much to Taylor, even in its homographs and homophones ("tears," "nots," etc.), shows a hagiographic reverence for Derrida as "Derrida," even to the point, however wryly, of renaming him "Saint Jacques."[165] Here, the affirmative religious passion of Derrida is sung again and again, as Derrida says *Oui* to a *tout autre* that is yet to come, and that can never come, except in the future. This is, as the subtitle tells us, religion without religion, a faith operating outside the traditional structures or even the formal conditions of religion, a faith in a *passion* (the word for Caputo is always deeply freighted religiously) that is always called forth—*viens, viens*—in the manner of an a-theistic Augustine, a saint whose theism cannot take the form of an expressible sacral language, doctrine or ritual, but only the inexpressible gesture of an apophatics, a muted but nevertheless holy desire, a sacred secret, which, as in the Gospel of Mark, must be repeatedly told not to be passed on. Caputo's notion of a "weak theology" is an extension of such Derridean ideas.[166]

These processions now form a long enough train in select religious and theological circles. But Derrida's is hardly the lone cortege, we know. Edmund Jabès, Emmanuel Levinas, Jean-Luc Marion, Michel de Certeau, Julia Kristeva, Jean-Yves Lacoste are among many within the French tradition who have their following, along with others we have already mentioned (Bataille, Blanchot, Irigaray). And there are numerous outside France giving (or having given) voice in various (non-Derridean) ways: Gianni Vattimo, Slavoj Žižek, Hent de Vries, Don Cupitt, Edith Wyschogrod, Charles Winquist, Graham Ward, Grace Jantzen, Rebecca Chopp, Stephen Moore—this hall within academia stretches an internationally long and variegated mile now.

But the originators of the death of God movement, however diverse a path their followers may now take, were not exclusively French, nor even Continental. Equally as prominent in the 1960s was the American "death of God" uprising, unique because it did not first arise from French theory of the day, nor within philosophical or cultural critical circles, but directly within *theology* itself. Gabriel Vahanian, Harvey Cox, William Hamilton, Paul van Buren, and Thomas Altizer were Protestant theologians (Vahanian French-born, but largely working in the States) who took seriously Nietzsche's call from a distinctly *theological* perspective, and dared to carry the logic of that call through to its most radical, but always theological, end. They were inheritors of the philosophical masters of negation, but they always understood this negation as a centerpiece of modern—now late modern—Christianity (or in the case of Richard Rubenstein, Judaism). Since its now iconic media attention in *Time Magazine* (an article in 1965, and then a feature cover in 1966),[167] this version of the movement has received scholarship or press by turns laudatory and execratory, the latter more by virtue of its indigenous social and cultural context where religion, and Protestant Christianity especially, counters the general Western trend with a statistically vibrant adherence to conservative religious traditions and values. As a result of such context, the movement might have been as short-lived as so many of the cultural movements of the febrile '60s in America, had it not been for its natural confluence with the French and Continental version above, and, not unrelated, and as significant, for its most fervent, prolific, and deep-rooted adherent, Thomas J. J. Altizer.

Since his early and audaciously titled book *The Gospel of Christian Atheism* (1966), Altizer has placed the "death of God" into a new register of theological importance, through numerous books, essays, letters, and more recently an autobiography.[168] We might even say, as many have, this is a prophetic register, even if for others his work constitutes the endpoint of theology itself, sometimes captured in the neologism "theothanatology." However construed, his embrace of Nietzsche's madman has been tenacious and unrelenting, as read through a distinct pantheon of artists and thinkers who form a litany within his writings, including Augustine, Dante, Milton, Spinoza, Blake, Hegel, Kierkegaard, Melville, Dostoyevsky, Barth, Joyce, and Heidegger. But Blake, Hegel, Nietzsche, and Joyce hold the most hallowed positions, returning again and again throughout his pages. Altizer's theological position, which he describes himself as unabashedly Hegelian, may be formulated in the following abbreviature:

> The death of God is an inexorable advent within the logics of modernity that marks a complete and radical end for any transcendent, metaphysical theistic One; this advent is wholly apocalyptic in nature, revealing a pure nihilism or nothing as the new "origin" on which all new thinking and believing must be founded; this advent comes about through a comprehensive and consummate *coincidentia oppositorum*, in which God and Evil (Satan), life and death, genesis and apocalypse, self and non-self, yea-saying and nay-saying, etc., exist in a purely selfsame relation and identity; this advent, as *nihilo*, opens up all possibility for new beginning, in a positivity of a pure immanence, as best embodied in the Christian West's greatest literary epics: Dante's *Commedia*, Milton's *Paradise Lost*, and, above all for late modernity, Joyce's *Finnegans Wake*.

All this must be seen first and foremost as *theological*: theology continues anew, and must *only* continue anew, from this "apocalyptic advent," or this "advental apocalypse"—the death, birth and return of God forever reconstituting our horizon in a pure simultaneity of incarnation, kenosis, and resurrection. Altizer will elaborate this abbreviature with sophistication and nuance across contexts philosophical, literary, and theological—or, and in good Hegelian fashion, across all three together. In Badiou's terms, Altizer's advent would be modernity's principle *event*, except that the event is never foreclosed to divine possibility, even in the purity of its abyssal immanence. In our terms, Altizer's advent becomes the full figuration of a religious/

theological O, the solitary halo that lingers behind after divine presence has been wholly occluded or entombed from view.

Altizer's radical theological thinking is only now beginning to gain a wider recognition among those who have, in one way or another, aligned themselves to the Continental manifestation of God's Nietzschean death, namely, postmodern thought in its predominantly French attire. The lateness of this attention may be a result of the '60s legacy, where the term *death of God theology* is consigned to the ephemeralities of fashion. And certainly, in America at least, such consignment has played some role. But I suspect Altizer's idiosyncratic manner of writing has also contributed to its slow acceptance. For Altizer's style is, like Derrida's, both singular and imitable, and yet it is so in a completely un-Derridean way: it does not possess the exuberance of literary invention and profligacy, is not, on the surface, what anyone would call *creative* (and thus has been virtually ignored by those in literary studies). Neither does it appear to deconstruct itself, or self-ironize itself; on the contrary, it employs a language unsparingly apodeictic, a tone homiletically sure of itself, where things are absolutely the case, truly, utterly, and without reserve (and thus it has been virtually ignored by those in feminist studies). Nor is this language supported by the academic apparatus of annotation and reference; it simply speaks itself. More, it is excessively repetitive. Its central position, condensed as above, can be found on virtually every page in some modulation or other, though very often unmodulated, the same notes being struck again and again. What is a likely factor in scholarly reluctance to induct Altizer to the A-list of contemporary thinkers is thus a perceived lack of imaginative writing, made worse by his insistence, in a narrative voice all too resembling the preacher and the prophet, that what one is reading when reading his work is not a-theology but theology *sensu strictissimo*, truly, absolutely, and utterly.

Much has been recently made of Altizer's voice or style.[169] It is so consistent that we can choose an example almost at random, as in the following passage from *Godhead and the Nothing* (2003):

> If the Christian God is the absolute No to the "nothing," the very absoluteness of that No is inseparable from the absoluteness of that "nothing" which it absolutely negates, so that inevitably such absoluteness must be known as being within the Godhead itself. Perhaps this finally occurs in every genuinely Christian theology. This alone could account for a uniquely Christian apprehension of the absolute otherness of the Godhead, and otherness that Christianity alone can know as being within the Godhead, and surely only such an otherness could make possible and real what the Christian alone knows as the Crucified God. While only a

uniquely modern Christianity fully knows and realizes the Cruci-
fied God, this realization calls forth a truly new "otherness" of the
Godhead. Now it can only be an otherness most deeply and most
profoundly directed against itself, so that now God itself can be
known as being in absolute opposition to itself.[170]

Here, most features of the abbreviature appear, and those that do not can be
found in the immediately adjacent paragraphs. What we encounter in this
sample of writing, and in our reading, is a condensed proclamation of an O set
out now in what we could call liturgical terms, that is, in repetition of its continual assertion, which, by virtue of that assertion, repeated again and again,
as in the manner of a rite, is "most profoundly directed against itself" and in
"absolute opposition to itself." The O here reenacts its nothing, repeatedly.
This is the liturgy of eternal return, which ultimately, in its empty circularity, returns us to the sacrality of no thing as a new thing. "Is it not possible
to understand that a nihilistic liturgy is occurring among us, one mediating
a pure nothingness to everyone, a nothingness that *is* our absolutely new
space, but an absolutely new space that is finally an absolute nothingness?"[171]
In returning us to nothing, this liturgical O allows us always to begin again,
and for Altizer, this very allowance is a condition central to the very genesis
of God—the *of* here taken first in its subjective sense, the genesis that God
induces, and then more dramatically, and more here and now, in its objective
sense, the genesis that induces God. This is theology, to be sure, but now
theology fully appropriated by and within the O and its making.

David Jasper, perceptively, has isolated Altizer's own words from *The
Self-Embodiment of God* (1977): "Voice speaks. And when it speaks, and as
it speaks, it embodies itself."[172] Early on, Altizer abandoned any academic
sourcing in his writing, as if to seal his own thought within itself. But
such self-immanence becomes the very enactment, and thus creativity, of
Altizer's proclamatory writing, and of writing his O. That this embodiment
is thoroughly Hegelian shows in its debt to the inducing power of negation.
That it is theological shows in its debt not only to the apophatic but also
to the prophetic tradition. That it is antischolastic shows in its attempt to
rise above the mechanics of rationalized thinking and discursive knowledge.
That it might now be seen, despite initial appearances, as *creative*, even
liturgically so, opening up space through an eternal recurrence of a nothing
that keeps voicing itself, reveals an O forever styling itself beyond itself.

Therein and thereby the hearer is hurled out of every center which
is not present and actual here and now, which is not fully and
immediately present in the horizon of speech. That hearing ends
a center which is everywhere, and ends it by hearing a center

which is wholly here and now, and wholly here and now in an actual and immediate voice whose own self-naming realizes itself as total presence.

That presence could only be the self-negation of eternal and transcendent presence . . .[173]

For some, such as Mark C. Taylor, this remains too theological,[174] or, as Graham Ward claims, remains firmly in the tradition of liberal theology, even as its apotheosis.[175] For others, and certainly the majority of Christians, it is not *theo*-logical enough, since nothing, ultimately, is made of God. For still others, like John Caputo and Gianni Vattimo, the question of "*after* the death of God" must now be mooted.[176] Altizer's work does not promote any "after" in the sense of theology looking to outstrip its present nihilistic conditions. Theology must always be caught in the "here and now" of its abyssal state, and in this regard Altizer's work is thoroughly *modern*, if not perhaps postmodern. If there is an "after" to Altizer's O, it is one that must, necessarily, be encountered in a *before* of its repetitive circulation. Such is his style: the "after/before" is always wholly new, but wholly new in the "here and now" of its own previous and repeated making.

There has been much utilization of the adverb/preposition "after" in recent theological/religious thinking and publication, with its double sense of succession and pursuit. *Religion After Religion, Religion After Metaphysics, God After Metaphysics, After Christianity, After Christianity* (again), *After God, After God* (again), *After God* (yet again), *Life After God, After the Death of God* . . .[177] There is an obvious fascination, even obsession, with "after's" inherent ambivalence, translated as it is from the Latin prefix "post-," which of course marks so much of our present times. This "after," as "post-," betrays a conflicting desire to move beyond religion and theology and a clear inability to let go, even a passion to hold on. The Derridean O will want to remain in this ambivalence, with the secret promise of an "after" that never arrives impassioning the pursuit; the Altizerian O will always remain in pursuit, within a Nothing that completely engulfs the terrain. But both will need their Os to keep navigating their terrain, to keep providing the impulse to motivate themselves across their terrain. Both Os are creative by virtue of originating ways to keep themselves motivated toward the divine, even if that divine remains unavailable.

> . . . but how
> Shall we satisfy when we meet,
> Between Shall-I and I-Will,
> The lion's mouth whose hunger
> No metaphors can fill?

Well, who in his own back yard
Has not opened his heart to the smiling
Secret he cannot quote?[178]

We might now have some answer to how we could satisfy the O, at
least if we allow its paradoxical nature to be fulfilled through emptying, as
the preceding pages have tried somehow, in their select way, to figure (out).
But this leaves the inevitable question: What comes after O? Can anything,
rightly, come after O, if O swallows up even the "after" in an ambivalence
of forward movement?

How do move forward? How can the O continue to assert its paradoxical force in the face now of a world demanding a return to some ethical
basis, some juridical ground on which to broker legal consensus (locally and
globally), some moral stance from which to render "no" as "you shall not"
and "yes" as "I will"? Must all the rest be silence? Can something in any
way follow upon nothing? Does the O have any conceivable *future*, even
as usurper of a once sovereign, and singular, throne? Or must it remain a
paradox unto itself?

SEVEN

THE FUTURE OF O?

Stay wisely in between
Keep near the standard bearer.
The first ones always die
The last ones are also hit
Those in the centre come home.

—Bertolt Brecht, *The Caucasian Chalk Circle*

In the ubiquity of the O, how does one move forward (again)? This is the question that repeats itself upon the horizon of our present world. For if, as I have been contending, the O, in its elliptical trajectory through the twentieth century, a trajectory that is, as we have now seen, a circuit, has reached a certain meridian point, a zenith that is, we have argued, also a nadir, how does one (or even One) find the bearings to proceed along the axis that our contemporary situation has determined for us? If O is now everywhere, not just in the religious and philosophical spheres that once gave rise to the supremacy of One, but throughout the universe that is our cultural imagination, so that its coming to light has obscured its own positioning, and we can only speak of a prevailing that is everywhere and nowhere at once, how do we move forward?

To approach this question, with a view to any kind of answer, if any there be, let us return to a play, and even, again, a play within a play, and now, also, a play within a play within a play (the continuing *mise-en-abîme* of the *mise-en-scène* of this book). A play about sovereignty, to be sure, and a playing about sovereignty—who has the right to play at sovereignty, to play with sovereignty?—but also a quite different kind of play and playing than we have thus far seen. Here we turn to Bertolt Brecht's *The Caucasian Chalk Circle*, and in particular the English version for which Auden wrote the verse translations. Why this play? We ask this in two directions: Why did Auden choose this play, and why do we choose it now? And we can answer: it is not simply Auden's association that makes our choice relevant; but it is also precisely Auden's association, in his appropriation of the nega-tive centrality that is the O, which of course has never been *his* O per se, that opens up to us the force of that relevance.

AUDEN'S BRECHT

There is certainly an early political affinity with Auden and Brecht, as Frederick Buell has long since pointed out: both, as part of an interwar generation, were seeking an "artistic voice for a left-wing polemic," and felt literature can be, and *should* be, socially and politically engaged.[1] Yet we know that by the time both found themselves in America, Auden had long since abandoned this vision, even if he continued to admire Brecht's work. The "prolific" as artist and the "devourer" as politician, he had writ-ten, must be considered, in any practical sense, "enemies."[2]

So *was* Auden, in fact, drawn to Brecht and this play? The biographies paint differing pictures. Auden worked on several translations of Brecht, even with Brecht himself during the latter's exile in America, though he regarded the German writer, in the end, "a most unpleasant man."[3] His work on *The Caucasian Chalk Circle* was in tandem with James and Tania Stern, his close friends in New York; Auden translated the song lyrics. Was this just a personal favor, then, or professional maneuvering, or, as one biographer suggests, unimportant "interludes"?[4] Or was there something about the play that drew Auden in, even despite his unease with the author's manner?

Let us bear in mind that Auden was invited by Brecht, who had only just finished drafting the play in German, to translate the songs in August 1944, just as Auden was finishing up his own *The Sea and the Mirror*. The origins of both works, then, are contemporaneous, as was Auden's eventual involvement. Did Auden thus feel a direct correlation between his "com-mentary" on Shakespeare and his "translation" of Brecht?

Or was it the fact that Brecht's play stood as yet "unfinished," perhaps even in constant need of transformation? This was not because the play-wright lacked finish—Auden never questioned Brecht's immense talent. But the nature of the play's own genesis, and hence its title, seemed to demand a continual reworking of itself in manifold forms, much like the O Auden had envisioned in Shakespeare and which took form in Caliban's speech. For the play is based on an old Chinese parable of the chalk circle, which Brecht had first encountered in dramatic form in 1925, when a compatriot had staged "*The Chalk Circle. A play in five acts from the Chinese*, by Klabund." This, the "Chinese" *Chalk Circle*, gave way to *The Odense Chalk*

Circle, Brecht's own attempt at a play version more than a decade later, when he moved to Denmark in the late 1930s before the outbreak of World War II. This in turn gave way to *The Augsburg Chalk Circle*, a short story version Brecht wrote in 1940 and published a year later. And this, finally, gave way to *The Caucasian Chalk Circle*, the first version written in America in 1944, and translated first by the Sterns/Auden, with a second and third version to follow later that year, and with an alternative English translation (by yet different translators) to follow in 1948 under the new title (twinned with another play) *Two Parables for the Theatre*.[5] Is this continual renaming of the "Circle," these reinventions and permutations, a feature of the O that Auden had intuitively grasped, as manifestations already in his own work? Is the "chalk circle" simply another apparition of the cipher that had become Auden's own O?

Or was it the play's own content that kept Auden involved? Was the infamous Judge of the play's last scenes the very embodiment of what Auden was already coming to espouse, and working out himself in the figure of Caliban: the conflation of the frivolous with the earnest, or a frivolity that can, in all seriousness, evince the truth? Was the fact that it was strewn with contradictions and inversions, and that it made a virtue of these—was this what drew Auden's sensibilities into accord with it? Or was it simply the draw of the O itself, the drawn circle as the place where the truth of art, the truth *as* art, emerges?

If there are historical answers here, they are likely not available. Or, as we have continually seen, the history is available only by naming it something other. Thus, the "chalk circle" here would become Auden's Chalk Circle, as much as we could speak of Brecht's O. But what exactly would Brecht's O be, in light of this long historical trope that has gained the name of Auden? And how does it figure in the making of O's future, its forward movement?

Let us propose the following: that amid all the affinities between Auden and Brecht, it is the parabolic force of the Chalk Circle that is most binding. It is not the original Chinese parable that we refer to, however. Nor is it the parable *of* Brecht's play—the message that the play intended us to receive, parabolically. For Brecht first disavowed any parabolic function: "The 'Caucasian Chalk Circle' is not a parable," he said categorically in his official author's notes.[6] But then those same notes later claim the play is "parable-like";[7] and several years later he had renamed it as one of *Two Parables for the Theatre*. What then is this parable that is not a parable? It relays no parabolic message, and yet it bears a parabolic potency. It is this potency as force—the force of the parable and the movement of the parabola, the curve that cross-sections the form of the circle, the open curve that is on its way to the elliptical circle, but not yet there—that we mean here. It is the Chalk Circle, as a rewritten play The Caucasian Chalk Circle, that becomes a parable of the O as a future possibility, and a possibility that carries an ethical potency, if not (and not ever) an ethical prescription.

In the spirit of Auden's commentary, then, which we now invoke in the form of a hermeneutical strategy—wherein the circle will operate, as it does in all hermeneutics, only and decisively as a problematic—let us offer an interpretation of this parable: a parable of parabolic force, that is to say, a parable of sovereignty unseated within the O, and a parable of the ethical potency of that O.

THE PARABOLIC WITHIN

A story unfolds. A story of a contested valley, decimated by the Nazi army in the early 1940s, and now requiring reconstitution. How does one reconstitute a valley? Two parties claim "rights" for that process: on the one side, goatherders, on the other side, fruit growers. The two parties sit in a circle and debate, while an expert from the city attempts to arbitrate. But the laws of the land have too been decimated, and they also need reconstitution. Thus, the "rights" of either side are no longer in play. We are in a state of anomaly: sovereignties have been uprooted, the land is laid waste, and property no longer obtains. How to restore to the land its right and its fertility? How to restore to the people their life and their livelihood?

The setting of this Prologue is crucial, and Brecht fought against its exclusion on several occasions. It may be Soviet territory, but it is land ravaged by Nazism, Brecht's own people. The anomalous state is thus the state of the West, deracinated by its own internal forces. Rational sovereignty has lost its throne. There can no longer be one guiding principle, any more than there can be one ruling nation, one ruling people. The Prologue sets up the an-archic conditions from which the story to follow, like a parabolic cross-section, will be cut.

The debate remains unresolved, but an irrigation plan is revealed that will side with the fruit growers, and add vineyards to the crops. The goatherders need to concede, but before any decision is to be reached, a play will be performed. In The Tempest, a play within a play is broken at a decisive moment—Prospero interrupts the masque to contend with the foul deeds of Caliban. In Hamlet, the play within the play catches out the conscience of the king. Here, something different takes place—at the decisive moment when there should be resolve, a play within a play breaks out. And of course, the internal play, the parable that is not the parable, becomes the "real" play, the principal play (we never return to the story in the Prologue). In this new territory, in these new times, where sovereignty is homeless, art must now play a decisive role.[8]

And so the story unfolds anew. The same story, we might say—"old and new wisdom mix"[9]—but now towards a moment of resolve. A Governor during times of strife is about to fall to a revolution. He is a sovereign (on behalf of a sovereign) who disregards his suffering subjects for his own gain. And he is a sovereign with a newborn heir, his ultimate gain. Gain gained in the blood. As on Easter. Except that during the Passion, blood is shed. It is Easter Sunday, and as the Governor emerges from the Easter service, between mass and banquet, the enemies strike. Resurrection is followed with insurrection, the new world of inversion. And the sovereign's head is chopped off.

Amid the tumult, the Governor's wife, caught up in her own survival, abandons the infant heir. (A mistake? An oversight? A vanity?) Sovereignty always has a proclivity toward self-preservation. Already the ancient cosmogonies had taught us this: a ruling god must be wary even of his offspring. For sovereignty seems all the stronger when blood drips from the knife of parricide. So too the West's sovereignty of One: its greatest enemy issues from within. But a young servant girl, a kitchen maid, takes up the abandoned child, and flees for safety with the rebels in pursuit.

The heir becomes the new sovereign threat. But there is no longer a throne, no longer a governorship. Insurrection always has the immediate aftermath of anarchy. In this anomic space, the question of legitimacy now arises. Is there succession when there is nothing to succeed to? Is their regal blood in the wake of regicide? And what happens to parental blood when the parent has abandoned the child? Who now can legitimate an heir? Who can de-legitimate one? These are the questions the embittered Edgar had posed, the questions Lear had thrust upon himself, in the wake of his daughter's question: "What need one?"

While in flight, the young girl decides to become the child's mother. How can one "decide" this, outside the bounds of a formal agreement? Blood is never a choice. Only in the extremity of anomalous circumstances can the inversion of the laws—biological, civil—be conceivable. At her moment of decision, the young girl must then risk the crossing of a deep gorge and traverse a broken suspension bridge. How does one, where does one, originate the possibility of new life, of new bonds, of new structures for contrary laws? Only in the abyssal moment, only over the void of the O. Thus, once across, safe from pursuants, a new legitimacy is born.

But this new legitimacy will soon founder. The young girl seeks refuge at her brother's home in the mountains. Soon the brother's wife grows intolerant, and some solution is needed, for a mother without a husband remains illegitimate. A solution presents itself when a young man on his apparent deathbed agrees to wed the girl. The girl, already betrothed to a soldier fighting in the surrounding war, agrees only on the assumption of impending widowhood. It will be marriage only "on paper," insists her brother. The ensuing marriage ceremony becomes a parody itself of legitimacy: with a proper priest too expensive, a doubtful, bibulous monk performs the rites. But union and annulment lie next to each other: "We declare this marriage contracted," says the monk. "Now what about Extreme Unction?"[10]

The legitimacy of the child is also, once again, drawn into question. For whose is this child? If the young girl is the mother and the dying man the father, as the monk and wedding guests are led to believe, then the dubious nature of the nuptial rite brings a dubious nature to the child's legitimacy. So too the legitimacy of the husband, who, having feigned illness to escape soldiery in the war, now finds himself in a marital bond that remains only on paper, as the girl refuses to consummate the marriage. So says the husband: "You're my wife and you're not my wife."[11] The anomic remains across all socio-legal transactions.

In this state, the child becomes an allegory of disenfranchised sovereignty—de Beauvoir's sovereign subject. But his disenfranchisement can operate in two ways—deprivation of a privilege, a right, or a claim, and freedom from political tyranny, from the culpability of power. The child is both disinheritance and exculpation, as long as he remains in the ambiguity of the anomic state, and does not, like Edgar, force the issue.

A children's vignette, as a play within a play within a play, shows the parabolic force of this state—freedom through deprivation. Now old enough to join in children's games, the child partakes in a reenactment of his father's beheading. "Today we're going to play Head's Off."[12] The boy is first given the role of his father. But he too wants to wield a sword and strike a blow, and after some remonstration, he is allowed the first go. In great Oedipal tradition, he strikes off the head of his father. So the heir to sovereignty, abandoning the role of sovereignty, decapitates (his own) sovereignty in the name of . . . what? New sovereignty? Countersovereignty? Anarchy? What is power that is wielded against itself? Is this the inverted power of a possible negation? But this is all yet child's play.

At that precise moment, the young mother's betrothed soldier enters the scene. The war having ended, the Governor's seat of power having been re-legitimized, the soldier now stands across a river and confronts the new reality, a lost possibility. Marriage, a child—the promise appears to him shattered. But the young girl tries to dispel appearances. Nothing has changed, she insists. Nothing stands between us. The young man replies with parabolic force: "How can nothing stand between us and things be changed?"[13] How indeed? How can nothing imply anything? How can change arise from nothing, or nothing give way to change? Here, Lear's words—"Nothing will come of nothing. Speak again"—are reformulated into this new prevailing context of the O.

But the answer to the question, the speaking again, the reckoning, will come only after the child has been remanded by the return of power of the once governing sovereign.

PONTIUS PILATE IN THE CREED

And so we come to the parable that most attaches its name to this work. The work is not a parable, we are told, and yet it clearly contains one—an undeniable parable of a circle, originally a Chinese circle (with Hebrew concentricities). But it is also a parable of our times, and not just the time of Nazi tyranny, but of Western anomie. And so it is a parable of our O, Auden's O, though a parable of parabolic force rather than of any specific moral. How does this parable, as force, now show itself, in all its forms?

It comes by way of the illegitimacy of legitimacy, and the legitimacy of illegitimacy: a judge who is a rogue judge. At the time of insurrection, a scabrous character—not a crook, nor a ruffian, but a clerk—harbors the Grand Duke, the sovereign of the Governor, in disguise as a beggar and on the run from the revolutionaries. But unaware of whom he is hiding, the clerk lets the sovereign go. When he learns of his error (he *is* not a man for sovereignty) he binds himself in chains and turns himself in to the authorities (he is a man of conscience). Self-judgment—"A new age has come."[14] But what are these authorities to whom he has given himself? They are as bereft of power as those they toppled. And the old judge hangs by the rafters behind them as a symbol of the power vacuum they have created, this anomic state. In court, the quick-witted clerk outmaneuvers the system of the judge's reappointment, and is bestowed, half-mockingly, half-seriously, the judge's mantle himself. "The Judge was always a rascal. Now the rascal shall be the Judge."[15] In his course, he preserves the "dignity of the law" by inverting the law: those who have nothing or little are always judged in the right, so they might have more. His reputation grows, and he becomes itinerant, judging cases *in situ*, bringing the new law, the law of illegitimacy, to the people. He always exacts a bribe, but chiefly from the haves, to favor the have-nots. "He broke the laws like bread."[16]

And now several years later, after abiding support from the commoners, the era of disrule and misrule—anomic socialism—is over. The Grand Duke is reinstated, and the tides have turned against our Judge. He is disrobed, beaten, and about to receive the punishment he never meted out himself—death—when a new case is brought before his courts: the Governor's wife, biological mother of our child, seeks the return and custody of her boy, now in authorities' hands. But the Judge presently occupies the space of negated legitimacy: even his illegitimate law no longer stands. As the child, motherless, is brought in, the child already stands, in effect, within the circumference of the O. For there is not only no legitimate judge, but there is no illegitimate judge. And the child himself is neither legitimate nor illegitimate. In the eyes of the law, which is now nugatory, he too is nothing. But by a turn of fate, at that precise moment, a dispatch is received from the Grand Duke: the one who, years earlier, had sheltered him, had granted his escape, is the one who shall now be the new judge. So the one who judges sovereignty a farce, by sovereignty now regains his jurisdiction. Legitimate illegitimacy. And just in time to rule on the child, the nothing that "stands between."

So now the Judge must rule on legitimacy itself, the very question of legitimacy's legitimacy. For what makes a child legitimate? Blood and marriage, argues the Governor's wife. But in this anomalous quasi-juridical space, blood is now no bond. Neither is marriage, for the young girl and the young soldier (who now stands at her side) have no marriage vows between them. No one appears to be legitimate. In such a space, the *law* cannot decide. So states the rogue judge. Only the Judge has "the duty of choosing."[17]

And how to choose? The moment of reckoning is upon us. And so is the ineluctability of the O. For now the O is drawn, and the child is placed in its center, as the metonymic gesture of what the child has always been, and what the judge's court has always enacted. Disenfranchised sovereignty judged by legitimate illegitimacy. Will its deprivation lead to freedom? Can deprivation—negation, the O—*be* freedom? And can it be this in anything other than the Leftist politico-philosophy of a Brecht, a Sartre, a Badiou?

Auden's O, in all its permutations throughout our text, furnishes us with an answer to this parabolic question. The O is the negative space of new creation (artificer's circle, *khora/chora, hystera,* etc.). It is origination, not because it starts from nothing, ex nihilo—for how many "nothings" have we now seen, have we now historically, textually, poetically named?—but because it allows history to begin again, rewritten under the imperatives of its new cultural, social, and political conditions.

Thus, conception is reconceived. Even the conception of law itself: "What there is belongs to those who are good for it."[18] Thus, the parable's "lesson." And by its virtue, the conception of force is reconceived. For in the test that is the chalk circle, force should win the day—the strongest of the mothers will extract the child from the circle. In the old dispensation, force is tied to legitimacy: the legitimate mother, the true mother, will find the force within. But in the new dispensation, the parabolic force that lies within inverts that old show of force, and no force is evinced. Force, in fact, is withdrawn. And it is precisely that withdrawn force, that parabolic force, expressed by not being expressed, that wins the child. The illegitimate move, not playing by the rules, rewrites the rules, and in doing so, makes the space, the space of the O, where truth emerges. And a new life can begin. A new life not based upon a preconceived notion of truth—the Governor's wife is the true mother—but a truth created out of the necessity of the disenfranchisement of negation.

Thus, the rogue judge, "almost just,"[19] judges from out of the center of the O. And into that O he justly disappears, as, in accordance with stage directions, the triumphant parties form a circle around him, and he is seen "less and less as more couples enter and join the dance."[20] This judge, this "cracked Isaiah on the church window,"[21] is, parabolically, the force of the O. He is no saint, he is no hero even. But like Pontius Pilate, he is the only one in the story willing to ask the question, What is truth? The theological conundrum—Why is Pontius Pilate in the Creed?—is here inverted—Why does the law reside within this rogue? The answer, in the penumbra of the O, is that in his illegitimacy, he is *almost just*.

THE OTHER ROGUE

In the summer of 2002, Jacques Derrida was invited to speak at a ten-day conference in Cerisy, France under the general theme "Democracy to Come (Around Jacques Derrida)." This was not yet a year after 9/11, and two years before his own death. The paper he gave, in ten parts, was entitled (as translated) "The Reason of the Strongest (Are There Rogue States?)." This was a long meditation, in typical Derridean fashion, on the nature of sovereignty in late modernity, beyond now the Bataillean sovereignty of his earlier examinations[22]—a post-9/11 sovereignty, and particularly the sovereignty of the democratic nation state. "*Around* Jacques Derrida"—this circling theme Derrida would exploit. For the question at hand starts with revolution (and for Derrida, with the French Revolution), since all revolutions, etymologically, are circular affairs. So Western democracy begins with a revolution, the circular movement of a turn that overturns the previous sovereignty (French, English, etc.). But how does any new sovereignty take up residence in a democracy? The circle becomes an endless turning, since every person has a voice, and thus "the act of sovereignty must and can, by force, put an end in a single, indivisible stroke to endless discussion."[23] In pure democracy, the individual, the *demos*, assumes the power of the law as and for itself. *Auto-nomy*. The law is *self*-generated, and returns to the self in the form of self-representation. The self becomes the new sovereign, therefore, even in a collective arrangement, and in this sense Derrida says that this "sovereignty is a circularity, indeed a sphericity. Sovereignty is round . . . the turn of the re-turn upon the self."[24] For democratic sovereignty is a force that also must uphold *freedom*. The law is set forth in an external realm of governance, but it must circulate back to its origin, the interior realm where it was first generated, in order to ensure individual freedom.[25] That is, this new kind of sovereignty that is democracy—the force (-*cracy*) of the people (*demos*)—is forever zeroing out itself in the name of a freedom: no one can be sovereign over the self except the self itself, and so the law must, *by force* (autocracy), return to its source as non-law, only to be posited again. And thus Derrida can speak of a "strange necessity of the zero, the necessity of a circular annulment of zeroing out in the perfectly round zero."[26]

But we do not reinvoke Derrida here, in the wake of Brecht, to conjure up, in the name of one of philosophy's greatest rogues, yet one more reference to the circular O as zero, now in a decidedly political context. Derrida's "democracy to come" has had enough question and criticism, and not just from the pragmatists, to keep it, for the time being, at bay. But there is a more important reason Derrida returns now, after Brecht's chalk circle. For it is from this question of sovereignty that Derrida leads us to the ethical question of the rogue.

Even pre-9/11, "rogue states" had become part of the political lexicon. But the determination of the "rogue," one who, erratic and unprincipled, deviates from the instituted norm, or more radically, from the ruling paradigm, could only arise over against higher power(s) that sets in place, and enforces, the norm (even if, in Kuhn's quasi-Hegelian schema of scientific history, the rogue in time sets the new norm). In traditional sovereignties, the rogue is the one who divagates from monarchical rule or from the divinely sanctioned laws of the land. But in democratic states, where sovereignty has an infinite dispersal across the *demos,* it is much more difficult to determine deviation. *Impossible* even, says Derrida, since the return to the self as the origin of the power must, necessarily, undo the law as absolute standard—if, that is, the *demos* is to remain free. Thus, every democracy is a system that must, by its very nature, allow for the rogue, the freedom to choose differently from the status quo. But this freedom invites an internal contradiction: if one has the power, in freedom, to choose differently, one can then elect for something antithetical to democracy itself. And we see this happening repeatedly in our world at present: democratic elections that vote in such "enemies" as communist or theocratic parties. Democracies, to remain democracies, must therefore develop a certain autoimmunity: they must, by some force, resist the enemy within, the rogues their very constitution permits. But to do this, they must consolidate sovereignty, make it *unequal* across the people, and thus betray the very essence of democracy. When this happens between nation states, Derrida argues, the one that refuses to share sovereignty, or to share it equally (in the name of democratic preservation), becomes itself a "rogue state." "As soon as there is sovereignty, there is abuse of power and a rogue state. Abuse is the law of use; it is the law itself, the 'logic' of a sovereignty that can reign only by not sharing."[27]

If we think of this problematic in the more customary religio-philo-
sophical terms of alterity, or the "other," the rogue then is the other that
wanders, disruptively, outside the One, whether that be the One of traditional sovereignties (God, the king, etc.), or of modern democracies (the
Self as pure auto-nomy), or of neoliberalism (free-market Capitalism). The
other disrupts the self-contained system, the hermeneutically sealed interpretation, the uniformity of sameness. The other comes to me, as self, from
elsewhere and, in the now familiar terms of Emmanuel Levinas, breaks my
totality, or the totality within which I live and have my being, the totality
of the One.

THE ROGUE WITHIN

But to wander "outside" is also, in the circumambulation of the O, to wander
"within." What we have been trying to show throughout this entire text,
and what Derrida captures with his sense of the rogue, is that the O, as a
power of negation, works from within. And so too in its manifestation as
other—the other *within*. Even in the profoundest depths of our subjectivity, the O erupts as the roguish force that exceeds our oneness. This we
saw in Hegel especially, though of course there are later conceptualizations
(Freud, Lacan, Kristeva, etc.), and later poeticizations—Auden's Prospero
and Caliban, for example. And this is precisely on what the young Derrida
had taken Levinas to task: alterity or otherness that denies or precludes its
own interior residency within the same. For Levinas, the other must remain
wholly and radically other, completely extrinsic to the subjective ego, and
not "subject to" any negation, a subjection that would convert the Other
to the Same, or allow the Same to engender the Other. Only then can the
Other come to us with its call of responsibility, a call that is otherwise than
our own being. But Derrida questions whether such bypassing of negation,
such "anti-Hegelianism," is possible in the finite world in which we have
any such encounter. For negation is what allows the Other its "external"
resistance to the Same in the first place, or the infinite its resistance to the
finite. Negation, we have said, is what makes possible the arising of the
concept, or of such "conceptual operations" as Other-Same, infinite-finite,
etc., and thus without it, "there is no way to conceptualize the encounter."[28]
In the language of the Derrida at the other end of his career: "There are
thus no longer anything but rogue states, and there are no longer any rogues
states."[29] The rogue resides always, and already, within—as a state of being.

Thus, if the O is to allow us any movement forward, it must not
overcome its own roguish behavior, as if it could, but must make it somehow responsible. And here is where the parabolic force of the chalk circle
might now return. For if we retain Levinas's insight, that the Other calls

us to responsibility, but now allow that Other its internal residency as O (following Auden's figuring of Caliban), then we might say the O furnishes us with the possibilities of a response that exceeds the law of violent force. (For all law, Benjamin taught us, hinges on violence.) We draw a circle, and place the possibility of legitimacy within it. In that space, we allow the exertion of force to be overcome by the letting go of force. But in doing so, legitimacy is rewritten, and truth reconceived. For the blood mother may not prevail. And the "good" of the child may now be a certain poverty. But that impoverishment may be the very future of its thriving. This would be its parabolic force: the drawing out of, and from, what is not expressly present. Why is it that our greatest ethical teachers have always taught us through parables? Because they state, positively and convincingly, what is *not* there. And thus all great ethical teachers are in some sense rogues, before they are domesticated back into the normativity of One.

This space of possibility must remain, then, a *poetic* space. It must be a space of continual making, even roguish making, like Shakespeare's Fool.[30] Yet for many ethicists this is the most inimical kind—departure from rationalism leaves the ethical decision open to its greatest abuse. Parables are not the stuff of ethics; at best they only *lead to* ethics. But if the twentieth century has taught us anything, it is that we can no longer see the rational as inoculated from supreme abuse. If ethics is to gain a sovereignty, a legitimacy, here in the twenty-first century, it must be of the kind that understands its own internal poesis. This is the parable of the rogue judge. It must be in some sense *itinerant*—resituating itself in each new context. But more, it must be willing to admit the law cannot always judge, especially in its own courts, under the rubric of its own jurisprudence, without incurring a certain violence. A creative circle must be redrawn, where even the judge does know the outcome, but where there is the possibility of withdrawing the force, and where that withdrawing of force can yield a newness of life.

In this regard, Derrida can speak proactively, at the level of nation-state politics, "of an international juridico-political space that, without doing away with every reference to sovereignty, never stops innovating and inventing new distributions and forms of sharing, new divisions of sovereignty."[31] We need not see this only in terms of something *to come*, however. The innovation of the O is that it prefigures as much as it figures, and figures as much as it prefigures, so that, as in the chalk circle, the legitimacy is always, so to speak, in hand, to hand, even if a letting go is required—a letting go for the purposes of return.[32] This does not mean there is an "end" to the O, as in the finality of an absolute law (how can there be?). But it does mean, in the space of its activity, the artifice of O keeps reinventing the One, now with One's full agreement and full implication. I share my sovereignty, says the One ("We the people"). I share my illegitimacy, says the rogue O ("I'll invite you to my dance, I'll invite you to my feast"). Together, perhaps, this poetic alliance and integration can innovate something we might just call . . . "almost just."

ANOTHER EPICYCLE

THE TRUEST O IS THE MOST FEIGNING

This book could have been written so differently. The O takes many forms by definition, and we could have rendered a very different scenario, a very different story line, a very different set of players and a very different protagonist. We might have reshaped the argument as a phenomenology of O, at which point the consummation of our discussion would have been Hegel, our central reading, say, his *Phenomenology*. We might have worked out a will to O, a deliberation of recurrent nothing, at which point our main focus would have been Nietzsche. We might have presented a being-toward-O, at which point Heidegger. A solely theatrical O would have given Shakespeare titular honours. Other twentieth-century artists, as we have seen, could have taken center stage, and maybe deserved to—e.g., Beckett, Celan. If we had followed Altizer, it would have been, if not Blake's O, then Joyce's O—or better yet, *Finnegans O*. And of course the French have lined up in an elongate queue: Bataille, Blanchot, Derrida, Irigaray, and others less mentioned—Mallarmé, Lacan, Deleuze. But we have chosen a less expected figure, Auden, precisely because he was less expected. The contraction of One's sovereignty was not abrupt, nor was the dilation of O immediate, stimulated by a radical few. Auden was not the insurgent, not the marginal experimenter or prophetic outcast of modern, or modernist, upheaval. An early socialist, a later Christian, a muted homosexual, a poet's poet—a man of tremendous talent and literary breadth, but not an artistic renegade, nor an intellectual extremist, nor any other subversive categories we might enlist (a revolutionary, an anarchist, a nihilist—a rogue, even). He was a public school Englishman who moved to America's artistic and academic circles, leaving us a literary oeuvre expansive yet not definitive, falling between the heightened experimentations of modernism and the lavish disruptions of postmodernism. For that very reason, his figuration of the O seems all that more extraordinary: it announced itself *sotto voce* as if from the sides of the stage, neither spotlight performance, nor audience, nor critic—an *understudy*, we might say, under those before him and those to follow. And yet in this role he made manifest a self-consciousness that had not been seen since Nietzsche, but now in purely poetic terms—the self-consciousness of "Auden's O," a trope, expletive, apostrophe, ellipsis that calls attention to itself only to show its own internal absence and negation. *The truest O is the most feigning.* It feigns to be "Auden," or any other name we might place before it. And in the end this understudy can only lend itself to a false study, a *pseudonym* and a *pseudo-identity*, whose very negated truth leads us, through a refiguration of what it means to bear a name and an existence, to a *negating truth*. Truth by means of nothing. The hard lesson of Lear, Hamlet, and Prospero, the truest studies of the false role. And the hard lesson of Romeo and Juliet, the truest study of the absent role. The truth of nothing.

"SIGNIFYING NOTHING"

But what finally of this hard lesson? We could say that modernity offers us two possibilities: we either rehabilitate the One, and purge it of its total-izing and tyrannical tendencies; or we turn the O into a responsible gesture toward something that might approximate "the just." But the two cannot be mutually exclusive: any rehabilitation of the One must now include its internal O, and any responsibility of the O must rehabilitate the One. For the One will not go away, this is certain. What we cannot do is confuse the role of the O for that of the One.

We began with a king who tried to retain his sovereignty, only to be reduced by his own powers to nothing. We saw the son of a murdered king catch out illicit sovereignty through the play of nothing. We centralized a king who had his sovereignty taken from him, and who regained that sovereignty by his own powers, only to realize it was never his. We moved to an heir for whom disenfranchised sovereignty was the very means of his legitimation. There is now yet another who arrogated sovereignty to himself and became king, through means premeditated and bloody, only to admit that his sad and fatal role signifies nothing. What can Macbeth, in the opprobrium of his dark deeds, possibly leave to us as we finalize the shift in fortunes of the One against the O?

If the O has taught us anything in the course of its modern revelation, it is that we cannot claim a finality for any process, least of all the process of One's diminishment. The One has not expired, and never will. Its fortunes may have shifted, through a recession brought on by the O's accession, but that does not mean its fatality is sealed or its powers eclipsed totally and irreversibly. The One continues to assert itself in various capacities within our world, even if its meridian now lies behind it. Though we have no idea if it can regain its former heights, it never will or can disappear completely from view. A corona of light will always remain, at the very least. Our judicial systems, for one, depend upon it. By the same token, the O will never itself *replace* the One with its own sovereignty. Eclipsing, benight-ing, overshadowing—these are not the same as blazoning forth with a new omnipotent light. If the O burns, it burns in ashes. "Ashes in truth," in Derrida's phrase.[1] The O may now be ubiquitous, but it is not sovereign, and never has been. Nor should it strive for sovereignty, even if it had any hope of attainment. This is the lesson, the hard lesson, of *Macbeth*.

In *Lear*, the heath is self-imposed exile. In *The Tempest*, the island is haven from imposed exile. Both are, ultimately, existential terrain. In *Mac-beth*, the heath on which the witches first appear is wholly different: it is the place Macbeth comes, whether by chance or by design, to make manifest a murderous inclination. If this is a place of coinciding opposites—fair is foul and foul is fair—it is not for the purpose of zeroing out both sides to see clearly in the purity of an all-pervading lack. It is to bring one side of the polarity to the fore. When murder first shows itself already resident in Macbeth's heart, it is "yet but fantastical," though already formed enough to discompose his good fortune. So when he says in the same context, "And nothing is but what is not" (I.iii, 140),[2] this is not the prelude to a coming awareness of a being laid bare against the backdrop of nothingness. It is an admission of a desire for something to be converted from nothing: the real from the imaginary, the realization from the promise, "the King" from "Macbeth, Thane of Cawdor." "If Chance will have me King, why / Chance may crown me / Without my stir," he vacillates in the next lines. But his "nothing" has already overridden his inertia, since no action leads only to what is not. As Lady Macbeth will reason it later:

> Nought's had, all's spent
> Where our desire is got without content.
> 'Tis safer to be that which we destroy
> Than by destruction dwell in doubtful joy. (III.ii, 5–8)

Macbeth is bent upon the deed, even before his Lady's solicitations, by first placing nothing in the service of the nonfantastical, the nonimaginary, of the must-be-attained. Only in the end does Macbeth realize that the future, as attainment, is already nothinged. So in his famous "Tomorrow, and tomorrow" speech, a fatalism blackens his view of human life, and his sovereignty, attained through the foul and diabolical deed, amounts to noth-ing, the banal nothing of mortality's inevitability. The imaginary of murder catches out the sovereign in *Hamlet*; here in *Macbeth*, the nonimaginary of murder, the realization of the soul's disposition toward murder, catches up with the sovereign, and the "realities" of life become petty affairs shuffling toward "dusty death." And so Macbeth can only ever see the stage, the place of repeated origination, as a place of nonrepeated, nihilistic expiration:

> Life's but a walking shadow, a poor player
> That struts and frets his hour upon the stage
> And then is heard no more. It is a tale
> Told by an idiot, full of sound and fury,
> Signifying nothing. (V.v, 24–28)

If O should ever attain sovereignty, it would only throw nothing into the moral turpitude of a Macbeth (or in *Lear*, of an Edgar). It would do exactly what Nietzsche warned against: turn nihilism into one side of a moral polarity, with no hope of allowing nothing to *make* our way out of the mess. The O is not a figuration of sovereignty. The O exists only in the interrogative, and like the mock judge in the *Caucasian Chalk Circle*, at best can ask questions of the sovereignty. But it cannot assume the crown itself, without devastation.

Macbeth's tale remains potent in warning us of our inherent inclinations: to reach for sovereignty against the very nature of being, our O. Lear's tale remains potent in the delineation of a nothing that, in its becoming something, remains crucially nothing. Prospero's tale, and Brecht's "parable," remain ultra-potent in showing us that the creative act has no sovereignty, and in that lack lies its greatest strength, beyond all sovereignties.

The O, in the end, is what we make of it. But that is precisely our responsibility. For all its disruption, for all its roguish behavior, the O is the place from which we must create a worthy response, a response that allows others, even as Other, to keep open and thriving anew, and be the good for what there is to be. This response may always belie our "incorrigible staginess," but this is nothing other than the incorrigible staginess of the O itself. And from the play of its force, we fashion a possibility that keeps the power of sovereignty from its most destructive ends, and converts it, not to "the perfected Work which is not ours,"[3] but maybe at least to the just work that is almost possible. Almost, but not quite. (For, as Walter Benjamin, Brecht's close friend, had said, justice without law is that which we call God.) Auden's O, in all its manifestations, opens up this space, and its strength, and ushers in a new way of making nothing work, for nothing.

And if we ourselves work for nothing, we become free: free to ask, to figure, to labor toward, in hard labor, what it is our nothing, our O, might become.

NOTES

EPICYCLE

1. Lines numbers here and elsewhere below correspond to the Arden Shakespeare's *King Lear*, ed. R. A. Foakes (London: Thomas Nelson and Sons, 1997).

2. Pierre Klossowski, *Nietzsche and the Vicious Circle*, trans. Daniel W. Smith (London: Continuum 2005; orig. 1969), 47–48, 50. The German *Stimmung* (tonality, mood) is related to *Stimme* (voice, register).

3. Ibid., xiii, xv.

4. Ibid., xv.

5. Ibid., xvii.

6. Ibid.

7. Ibid., xiii.

8. W. H. Auden, *Collected Poems*, ed. Edward Mendelson (London: Faber and Faber, 1976), 626. Hereafter cited as *CP*.

CHAPTER O. INTRODUCTION

1. Chapter 6, "The Structure of Artistic Revolutions," in *The End of Modernity*, trans. Jon R. Snyder (Cambridge: Polity Press, 1988), 91.

2. Even if Giotto may have helped to usher realism in.

3. Johannes Kepler, *Gesammelte Werke*, ed. W. Von Dyck, M. Caspar et al. (Munich: Beck, 1938 et seq.), Vol.7, 330, as translated by Fernand Hallyn in *The Poetic Structure of the World: Copernicus and Kepler* (New York: Zone Books, 1990), 213.

4. In "The Second Coming."

5. Jacques Derrida, "Ellipsis," in *Writing and Difference*, trans. Alan Bass (London: Routledge, 1978), 296.

6. As quoted by Derrida, ibid.

7. Ibid., 299. The verb disagreement in the first sentence is clearly, and significantly, deliberate.

8. "For *ellipsis* names not only lack but a curved figure with more than one focus. We are thus already between the 'minus one' and the 'more than one.'" Jacques Derrida, *Rogues: Two Essays on Reason*, trans. Pascale-Anne Brault and Michael Naas (Stanford: Stanford University Press, 2005), 1.

9. G. W. F. Hegel, *Phenomenology of Spirit*, trans. A. V. Miller (Oxford: Oxford University Press, 1977), §706, 427. In the *Zusatz* of the *Philosophy of Nature*, we read a modification of this idea: "The first determination of spatiality is only the straight line, curved lines being in themselves at once in two dimensions. In the

271

circle we have the line raised to the second power"—trans. A. V. Miller (Oxford: Oxford University Press, 1970, 2004), 32.

10. We should say something here about one other possible rudimentary figure, or figural concept, which also plays its role, and has its history—the "point." For without the hub, or the center point, the wheel likewise falls in on itself. Much could be made of the point or the dot beyond the hub, from the spatial notion of the coordinate, to the typographical unit of the period, to the mathematical function of the decimal, to the scientific history of the atom, to the philosophical understanding of the monad, and ultimately to the oxymoron that is the generalized concept of particularity. And from these iterations the point carries its own metaphorics: the metaphorical leap to the postulate (the *point* of the argument) and to purpose (the *point* as raison d'être). (On this last point [*sic*], it is worth nothing that, in the First Quarto of Shakespeare's *Hamlet*, its most famous speech reads: "To be or not to be—ay, there's the point." [*Hamlet*, The Arden Shakespeare, ed. Ann Thompson and Neil Taylor (London: Thomas Nelson and Sons, 2006), 18.] I am indebted to an anonymous reader for this particular insight.) Now ultimately the "point" is a node through which converge the concepts of the simplex and the multiple, as Leibniz had already elucidated in his "Monadology." We shall not develop this "point" any further here, except to say that, in the Western history of the point, its implied multiplicity has always tended (with only a few exceptions—e.g., Epicureanism or contemporary astrophysics) toward oneness and universality, and the end of Leibniz's treatise on Monadology is perhaps our paramount example: all monads, in the end, and as their name already implies, form the omniscience that is God's absolute point of view, and thus in their totality make up the "City of God," the "truly universal monarchy." G. W. Leibniz, *Philosophical Texts*, trans. and ed. R. S. Woolhouse and Richard Francks (Oxford: Oxford University Press, 1998), 280.

11. Martin Davis, *The Universal Computer: The Road from Leibniz to Turing* (New York: W. W. Norton, 2000), 16. Brian Rotman, in his *Signifying Nothing: The Semiotics of Zero* (Basingstoke: Macmillan, 1987), describes how Leibniz even "refracted the binary relation between 1 and 0 into an iconic image of the Old Testament account of creation *ex nihilo*, whereby the universe (the infinitude of numbers) is created by God (the unbroken 1) from the void (the cipher 0)" (105–107).

12. Ibid., 32.

13. See Mark C. Taylor's discussion of these two architectural representatives in *Moment of Complexity* (Chicago: University of Chicago Press, 2003), 25–46.

14. *Paradise Lost*, Book II, 1051. *Complete Poems and Major Prose*, ed. Merritt Y. Hughes (Indianapolis: Bobbs-Merrill, 1957), 257.

15. E.g., Frederick Copleston's Gifford Lectures published as *Religion and the One: Philosophies East and West* (London: Continuum, 1982).

16. See Martin Heidegger, *Poetry, Language, Thought*, trans. Albert Hofstadter (New York: Harper and Row, 1971), esp. the essays "Building Dwelling Thinking" and ". . . Poetically Man Dwells. . . ."

17. We might see a kind of triangulation, then, between nothingness, singularity, and plurality. The latter of these three, though not given preferential treatment in this discussion, will be present enough throughout, even if spectrally. Though it has already been manifest in the idea of Eternal Return, we will see it again especially

in the religious and philosophical issues pertaining to the One in chapter 1. And it will perhaps become most forceful in the generative function of nothing we will later expound: the possibilities, endless in their number, that the O originates by virtue of its powers of *poesis*.

18. Thomas S. Kuhn, *The Structure of Scientific Revolutions*, 3rd Ed. (Chicago: University of Chicago Press, 1996), 173.

19. Ibid., 94.

20. Ibid., 176.

21. Philosophically, Derrida has famously addressed this problem of the structure, in relation especially to structuralism, in his essay "Structure, Sign, and Play in the Discourse of the Human Sciences," in *Writing and Difference*, 278–93.

22. D. G. Leahy *Novitas Mundi: Perception of the History of Being* (Albany: State University of New York Press, 1994), 83. Leahy extends this to include the entire *universe*: "What is universally new, absolutely without prior potentiality, what began to be after simply not being, what comes perfectly from God's omnipotent hand is this universe. But *novitas mundi*, this universe's novelty, creation *per se*, is not properly, that is, metaphysically, *caused*. . . . Natural reason is implicitly itself novelty; it is uncaused, or it is its own cause. That is, it takes itself to be a cause for its own purposes; it is itself its own solution to *what is new*." Ibid.

23. As Agamben says, the camp is the ultimate "state of exception" in the modern world, which, we might say, turns ecstasy into its most perverse form. See *Homo Sacer*, trans. Daniel Heller-Roazen (Stanford: Stanford University Press, 1998), Part III, 119ff.

CHAPTER ONE. THE SOVEREIGNTY OF ONE

1. Friedrich Nietzsche, *The Gay Science*, ed. Bernard Williams, trans. Josefine Nauckhoff (Cambridge: Cambridge University Press, 2001), 141 (200). *Schadenfroh* is the adjectival form of *Schadenfreude*.

2. There are of course other "conceptions" of the concept: Deleuze and Guattari's is one of the more notable, for example. See *What is Philosophy?*, trans. Graham Burchell and Hugh Tomlinson (London: Verso, 1994).

3. Thomas Pynchon, *Gravity's Rainbow* (London: Vintage, 2000; orig. 1973), 774, 776.

4. All biblical quotes here and thereafter are taken from the New Revised Standard Version, unless otherwise noted.

5. Of course, as Derrida reminds us, YHWH is also caught up in the self-dispersal, by virtue of the proper name, the tetragrammaton, which here is not only singular and plural, not only spoken and unspoken, but, as "the proper name of God (given by God), is divided enough in the tongue, already, to signify also, confusedly, 'confusion.'" Derrida, "Des Tours de Babel," in *A Derrida Reader: Between the Blinds*, ed. Peggy Kamuf (New York: Columbia University Press, 1991), 249. We will return again in chapter 6 to Derrida's notion of the (divine) name.

6. For a comprehensive analysis of henological thinking, and its hegemonic roots in Greek thinkers, see Reiner Schürmann, *Broken Hegemonies*, trans. Reginald Lilly (Bloomington: Indiana University Press, 2003; orig. 1996), esp. 49–188.

7. As quoted by Plotinus in *The Enneads*, trans. Stephen MacKenna (Burdett, NY: Larson Publications, 1992), IV.8.1, 410.

8. *The Presocratic Philosophers*, 2nd ed., ed. G. S. Kirk, J. E. Raven, and M. Schofield (Cambridge: Cambridge University Press, 1957, 1983), 187.

9. Nietzsche: "First *images*—to explain how images arise in the spirit. Then *words*, applied to images. Finally *concepts*, possible only when there are words—the collecting together of many images in something nonvisible but audible (word). The tiny amount of emotion to which the 'word' gives rise, as we contemplate similar images for which *one* word exists—this weak emotion is the common element, the basis of the concept." *The Will to Power*, ed. Walter Kaufmann, trans. Walter Kaufmann and R. J. Hollingdale (New York: Vintage, 1967), 275, §506.

10. "God cannot here be essentially different from Logos; and the Logos is, among other things, the constituent of things which makes them opposed, and which ensures that change between opposites will be proportional and balanced overall. God, then, is said to be the common connecting element in all extremes, just as fire is the common element of different vapours." Kirk et al., 191. Of course, John's Gospel later appropriates this term for the incarnated Jesus. The "connecting element" of God, fire, human, and nature Gerard Manley Hopkins captures elegantly in his famous phrase, "I am all at once what Christ is . . . immortal diamond." *Poems and Prose*, ed. W. H. Gardner (London: Penguin, 1953; rpt. 1988), 66.

11. Kirk et al., 192. Translation altered.

12. "Thus the unity of God contains one power within it, which is accordingly the absolute power. Every externality, every sensible configuration and sensible image, is sublated in it. For this reason God here [in the Jewish Religion] subsists without shape—he subsists not for sensible representation but only for thought." Hegel, *Lectures on the Philosophy of Religion*, trans. R. F. Brown et al., ed. Peter C. Hodgson (Berkeley: University of California Press, 1988), 359. Of course, Hegel would also admit that conceptualization is no sure barrier against divine provocation, or even divine right.

13. Kirk et al., 187.

14. A later quote from Sextus states that the Pythagoreans "are accustomed sometimes to say 'All things are like number,' and sometimes to swear this most potent oath: 'Nay, by him that gave the *tetractys*, which contains the fount and root of ever-flowing nature.' By 'him that gave' they meant Pythagoras (for they deified him); and by 'the *tetractys*' a number which, being composed of the four primary numbers, produces the most perfect number, as for example ten, (for one and two and three and four make ten). This number is the first *tetractys*, and it is called 'fount of ever-flowing nature' inasmuch as the whole universe is arranged according to attunement, and the attunement is a system of three concords, the fourth, the fifth and the octave, and of these three concords the proportions are found in the four numbers just mentioned—in one, two, three and four." Ibid., 233–34.

15. Aristotle, *Metaphysics*, trans. Richard Hope (Ann Arbor: University of Michigan Press, 1960), 16 (986a).

16. Alain Badiou, *Number and Numbers*, trans. Robin Mackay (Cambridge: Polity, 2008), 7.

17. Plato, *Philebus*, 15a, in Plato, *Complete Works*, ed. John M. Cooper, trans. (*Philebus*) Dorothy Frede (Indianapolis: Hackett, 1997), 403.

18. *Parmenides*, 166c, in Plato, *Complete Works*, trans. Mary Louise Gill and Paul Ryan, 397.

19. Deleuze and Guattari: "The *Parmenides* shows the extent to which Plato is master of the concept" (29).

20. *The Presocratic Philosophers*, 248. For more on Parmenides's thought, see Alexander P. D. Mourelatos, *The Route of Parmenides* (Las Vegas: Parmenides Publishing, 2008; orig. 1970); Schürmann, *Broken Hegemonies*, 55–136; and of course Martin Heidegger, *Parmenides*, trans. André Schuwer and Richard Rojcewicz (Bloomington: Indiana University Press, 1992).

21. What is this theory, exactly? In many ways the Forms are like universal paradigms, as Socrates describes them: "[T]hese forms are like patterns set in nature, and other things resemble them and are likenesses; and this partaking of the forms is, for the other things, simply being modeled on them" (*Parmenides*, 132d, *Complete Works*, 366–67). The Forms are those universal paradigms that, unchanging, allow all things to have their being grounded in something permanent, fixed, and absolute. For every single river there is a Form called River, which absolutizes all the properties we associate with rivers, and from which all rivers draw their essential being. And the most supreme Forms are those that reside in the mind—Reason, the Beautiful, the Good, the Just, etc.

22. *Parmenides*, 136c, *Complete Works*, 371.

23. Ibid.

24. See for example F. M. Cornford, *Plato and Parmenides* (London: Routledge and Kegan Paul, 1939); Mitchell H. Miller, *Plato's Parmenides: The Conversion of the Soul* (Princeton: Princeton University Press, 1986); Constance C. Meinwald, *Plato's Parmenides* (Oxford: Oxford University Press, 1991); Samuel Scolnicov, *Plato's Parmenides* (Berkeley: University of California Press, 2003), and, most recently, and in relation specifically to Nothing, Slavoj Žižek, *Less Than Nothing* (London: Verso, 2012), 39–67.

25. *Parmenides*, 166c, *Complete Works*, 397; italics added.

26. This is how J. N. Findlay reads it in his *Plato: The Written and Unwritten Doctrines* (New York: Humanities Press, 1974), for example. See also Heidegger's rendering in *Parmenides*.

27. And for Plato, at least according to the *Timaeus* (e.g., 69c, 70c-d), the immortal soul was seated in the head, or the marrow of the brain.

28. Heidegger, *Parmenides*, 70.

29. All following quotes taken from Aristotle, *Metaphysics*, op. cit.

30. "Our One-First is not a body: nothing simplex can be a body and, as a thing of process cannot be a First, the source cannot be a thing of generation; only a principle outside of body, and utterly untouched by multiplicity, could be The First." Subsequent unification can thus never be rid of admixture: "Any unity, then, later than The First must be no longer simplex; it can be no more than a unity in a diversity." Plotinus, *Enneads*, V.4.1, 460. All subsequent quotations are from this edition.

31. "It is precisely because there is nothing within the One that all things are from it." Ibid., V.2.1, 436.

32. This accords with later Jewish mysticism in the Kabbalah, where the ineffable One *is* Nothing, and vice versa. Hegel also will appropriate this understanding for his ontology of being and nonbeing, particularly in *The Science of Logic*—see further chapter 6 below.

33. Conor Cunningham, in his *Genealogy of Nihilism* (London: Routledge, 2002), is among those who employ the term *meontology* to describe the position here of Plotinus (3–9).

34. *Enneads*, V.2.1, 436.

35. Ibid., VI.8.16, 691–92.

36. A point often missed by the commentators. See for example John Bussanich, "The Metaphysics of the One," in *The Cambridge Companion to Plotinus*, ed. Lloyd P. Gerson (Cambridge: Cambridge University Press, 1996), 38–65.

37. The entire *Enneads* ends with the phrase "the passing of the solitary to solitary" (VI.9.11), or as it has been elsewhere rendered, "the flight of the alone to the Alone" (Copleston, 30, 124). On this final phrase, and its erroneous readings, which suggest a subjectivism, self-absorption, or narcissism at the root of Plotinian mysticism, see Kevin Corrigan's nuanced counterargument in " 'Solitary' Mysticism in Plotinus, Proclus, Gregory of Nyssa, and Pseudo-Dionysius," *Journal of Religion* 76, no. 1 (Jan. 1996): 28–42.

38. *Enneads*, V.3.13, 452.

39. Ibid., V.5.6, 469–70.

40. See Copleston, esp. 123–25 on Plotinus.

41. Plotinus will claim (in V.1.8) that Plato's *Timaeus* had anticipated the distinction between the One and the Intellectual-Principle.

42. *Enneads*, V.5.3, 466.

43. Ibid., VI.2.6, 543.

44. Ibid., VI.4.2, 589.

45. Ibid., II.9.17, 169.

46. Ibid., IV.4.32, 361.

47. Schürmann, 141.

48. The Neoplatonists have a term to denote the Soul's generation of the physical world through the actualizing of its own thoughts—*logoi spermatikoi*—in which *phusis* becomes the living image of the One and its Intellect. This is not dissimilar to the idea Paul the "babbler" (*spermologos*) is claiming here for the Unknown God, the God of Jesus Christ.

49. On the body metaphor, see also Rm. 12.4–5; 1 Cor. 6.17; Eph. 3.6; 4.4, 25; Col. 3.15.

50. Alain Badiou, *Saint Paul: The Foundation of Universalism*, trans. Ray Brassier (Stanford: Stanford University Press, 2003), 108.

51. Ibid., 76.

52. Ibid., 111.

53. Badiou's concept of "subjectivation" is not yet this maximal personal force, but simply "fidelity to the Christ-event." For Badiou, "[L]ove is under the authority of the event and its subjectivation in faith, since only the event allows the subject to be something other than a dead Self, which it is impossible to love" (90), and not the other way around, as Christian theology generally has it: the authority of the event is under God's love, since it is God who first so loved the world.

54. For more on the relation of Paul to love, see especially Werner Jeanrond, *A Theology of Love* (London: T and T Clark, 2010).

55. We could, for example, claim *the One as numerical*, following upon Pythagorean thought, in which reality is seen as number, and number one is seen as primary for all numbers, therefore primary in defining reality. However, as a paradigm, this understanding has had too limited an effect—limited only to a few esoteric movements and, perhaps, certain isolated theories of mathematics and physics. We therefore exclude it from our list.

56. Copleston, 129. See in general 125–30.

57. Thomas Aquinas, "Commentary on *Sentences* I," in *Selected Writings*, ed. and trans. Ralph McInerny (London: Penguin, 1998), 58; italics added.

58. Martin Luther, *Christian Liberty*, ed. Harold J. Grimm (Philadelphia: Fortress Press, 1957), 12.

59. As in the writings of Jean-Luc Nancy, Giorgio Agamben, and Slavoj Žižek, for example. See more below, chapter 6.

60. Hegel, *The Science of Logic*, trans. A. V. Miller (New York: Humanity Books, 1969), 601.

61. *Hyperion*, Volume 1, Book 1, in Friedrich Hölderlin, Hyperion *and Selected Poems* (*The German Library, Vol. 22*), ed. Eric L. Santner (New York: Continuum, 1990), 3.

62. Friedrich Schleiermacher, *On Religion: Speeches to its Cultured Despisers*, trans. John Oman (New York: Harper and Row, 1958, 1986), 48–49.

63. Ibid., 49–50.

64. Charles Taylor, *Sources of the Self* (Cambridge: Harvard University Press, 1989), 374.

65. Hölderlin, Hyperion *and Selected Poems*, 138. [*Einig zu seyn, ist göttlich und gut; woher ist die Sucht denn / Unter den Menschen, daß nur Einer and Eines nur sie?*] Michael Hamburger (ibid., 139) freely translates this: "Being at one is god-like and good, but human, too human the mania / Which insists there is only the One, one country, one truth and one way."

66. The early Nietzsche of *The Birth of Tragedy* would still talk of an "*Ur-Eine*," a primordial unity brought about through the Dionysian. But the later Nietzsche will speak of the Dionysian unity only as a unity of creation and destruction, in which becoming takes precedence over being. He states: "*My hypothesis:* The subject as multiplicity" (*The Will to Power*, 270).

67. Bertrand Russell, *The Problems of Philosophy* (Oxford: Oxford University Press, 1967), 88.

68. Milan Kundera, *The Joke* (New York: Harper Collins, 1992; orig. 1967), 245.

69. Ibid., 246.

CHAPTER TWO. THE REVOLUTIONS OF O

1. William Shakespeare, *King Richard II*, II, i. All subsequent quotations from Shakespeare, unless otherwise noted, are taken from *The Complete Shakespeare*, ed. Alfred Harbage (New York: Viking, 1969, rpt. 1977).

2. On the enigmatic function of the apostrophe, see Jonathan Culler, *The Pursuit of Signs* (Ithaca: Cornell University Press, 1981), 135–54. Culler admits, "We

know too little about the apostrophe to assert what happens when an apostrophe succeeds . . ." (153). On the apostrophe's relation to negativity, see Sanford Budick, "Tradition in the Space of Negativity," in *Languages of the Unsayable: The Play of Negativity in Literature and Literary Theory*, ed. Sanford Budick and Wolfgang Iser (Stanford: Stanford University Press, 1987), 314–19.

3. Shakespeare, *Romeo and Juliet*, II, ii.

4. Shakespeare, *The Two Gentleman of Verona*, IV, iv.

5. As Brian Rotman describes it: "Instead of literal mimesis, copying a space by a space, one can *depict* an absence through a signifier that contains a gap, a space, an absence in its shape. The most elemental solution, the urmark of absence, is any instance of an iconographic hole; any simple enclosure, ring, circle, ovoid, loop, and the like, which surrounds an absence and divides space into an inside and an outside" (*Signifying Nothing*, 59).

6. For a fuller discussion of this problem, see Charles Seife, *Zero: The Biography of a Dangerous Idea* (London: Souvenir Press, 2000), 56–57.

7. See also Rotman, 60–63.

8. Seife, 8–9.

9. I am indebted here to both Seife and Robert Kaplan, *The Nothing That Is: A Natural History of O* (London: Oxford University Press, 1999). See especially Kaplan, 93–95, for the manifold etymological sources that played into the concept of zero. For an even fuller descriptive history of the zero, through its Egyptian, Babylonian, Mayan, and Indian incarnations, see John D. Barrow, *The Book of Nothing* (London: Vintage, 2001), ch. 1, 13–52. All three authors—Seife, Kaplan, and Barrow—published their books within two or so years of each other (1999–2001—across the threshold of the new millennium), and, notably, come from the world of mathematics.

10. Hans Waldenfels also informs us that the etymology of *sunya* comes from *svi*, which means "to swell," and the "idea of swelling was then further tied up with that of hollowness," that which is swollen being hollow inside. "This relationship is made still clearer by the fact that the mathematical symbol for zero was originally none other than the symbol for *sunyata* [emptiness]." *Absolute Nothingness: Foundations for Buddhist-Christian Dialogue* (New York: Paulist Press, 1980), 19.

11. E. M. Forster, *A Passage to India* (Harmondsworth: Penguin, 1924, rpt. 1986), 158–59.

12. Ibid., 138, 139.

13. See Kaplan, 36–49, for a detailed account of its emergence in India as the figure O.

14. Even if, ironically, they helped to bring Aristotle to the medieval Western world.

15. Rotman, 8.

16. See Seife, 71–74.

17. Ibid., 83. See also Rotman, 7–14.

18. Seife, 95, and Barrow, 126–27.

19. Blaise Pascal, *Pensées de Pascal: Publiées dans leur texte authentique avec un commentaire suivi par Ernest Havet* (Boston: Adamant Media Corporation, 2001), 499.

20. Blaise Pascal, *The Mind on Fire: An Anthology of the Writings of Blaise Pascal*, ed. James M. Houston (Portland: Multnomah Press, 1989), 139. See further

Barrow, 109–17, and the entire book (*The Book of Nothing*) for an excellent and complete discussion on the problematic nature of vacuums in cosmological, scientific, and cultural thinking in general throughout history.

21. Seife, 83.

22. ". . . and that they are so in their very being, in different ways; although both are located, by virtue of this fact, on the shores of a Nothingness." Alain Badiou, *Number and Numbers*, 51.

23. Shakespeare, *King Henry VI, Part II*, IV.i.

24. Editorial, "The Vanishing Arts at Ground Zero," *The New York Times*, March 29, 2007. The Memorial site now contains a museum, in which is an "Artists Registry," a "gathering place and virtual gallery for art created in response to the events of 9/11" (http://registry.national911memorial.org/—last accessed October 8, 2011).

25. Another *New York Times* article of September 8, 2011, "Omitting Clergy at 9/11 Ceremony Prompts Protests" (Laurie Goodstein), shows the continuing controversy and disagreement, and the persistent effects of zero displacement. Alan Wolfe, director of the Boisi Center for Religion and American Public at Boston College, was quoted as saying, "9/11 was this moment that [sic] we came together, and it lasted about three-and-a-half minutes. The country went from a brief moment of something like unity, to complete Balkanization, and now we're seeing it in religion and in politics, like in everything else."

26. Shakespeare, *King Richard II*, VI, i.

27. Shakespeare, *King Henry VI, Part II*, V.i.

28. Did the architects of the two fountains at Manhattan's 9/11 Memorial site inherently understand this, when they built large reflecting pools, at the center of which lie black holes leading into what appear to be bottomless abysses? One reads what they will into the reflecting pool; but one cannot escape the black holes, into which those reflections drain. That these pools are square, and not circular, suggests a pulling back from zero's most abyssal implications. (The base of capitalism may be square, but it is still an empty hole.)

29. *Timaeus*, 45b–46a.

30. Rodolphe Gasché's *The Tain of the Mirror: Derrida and the Philosophy of Reflection* (Cambridge: Harvard University Press, 1986) is still a seminal text in tracing the history of reflection to its fractured point in the deconstruction of Derrida.

31. Ellie Ragland-Sullivan, *Jacques Lacan and the Philosophy of Psychoanalysis* (London: Croom Helm, 1986), 25.

32. Ibid., 41.

33. Gilles Deleuze and Félix Guattari, *Anti-Oedipus: Capitalism and Schizophrenia*, trans. Robert Hurley et al. (London: Athlone Press, 1984), 55.

34. Trans. Geoff Bennington and Ian McLeod (Chicago: University of Chicago Press, 1987).

35. Following the Arden edition, Third Series, ed. Ann Thompson and Neil Taylor (London: Thomson Learning, 2006).

36. Ingram Bywater's preferable translation in the volume *Introduction to Aristotle*, ed. Richard McKeon (New York: Modern Library, 1947), 635 (1451^a, lns. 36–38) and 661 (1460^a, lns. 26–27).

37. Shakespeare, *Love's Labour's Lost*, V, ii.

38. For the text of this 1816 Preface, see *The Collected Works of Samuel Taylor Coleridge: Vol. 16 (Poetical Works I: Poems [Reading Text])*, ed. J. C. C. Mays (Princeton: Princeton University Press, 2001), 511–12.

39. In actuality, Samuel Purchas's *Purchas in Pilgrimage* (1613).

40. Coleridge, 512.

41. As suggested by, among many others, the poet Stevie Smith in and through her poem "Thoughts about the Person from Porlock," in *Selected Poems*, ed. James MacGibbon (London: Penguin, 1975, 1978), 230–32.

42. Percy Bysshe Shelley, "Prometheus Unbound" (IV, lns. 382–84), in *The Major Works*, ed. Zachary Leader and Michaeol O'Neill (Oxford: Oxford University Press, 2003), 307.

43. Or as Rotman describes it in relation to the sign and signification of zero: "zero . . . though it demolishes the anteriority inherent in the idea of an absolute and transcendental origin, is nevertheless itself *nothing other than an origin*" (104–105).

44. Shakespeare, *Love's Labour's Lost*, IV, iii.

45. John D. Caputo, *Radical Hermeneutics* (Bloomington: Indiana University Press, 1987), 72.

46. Martin Heidegger, *Being and Time*, trans. John Macquarrie and Edward Robinson (Oxford: Blackwell, 1962), 194.

47. *The Taming of the Shrew*, II.i.

48. Maurice Blanchot, "Literature and the Right to Death," in *The Work of Fire*, trans. Charlotte Mandell (Stanford: Stanford University Press, 1995), 303–304. The quote from Hegel is from *The Phenomenology of Spirit*, Chapter V, Section Ia.

49. *King Richard II*, III, ii.

50. Klossowski, *Nietzsche and the Vicious Circle*, xvii.

51. As Blanchot exhorts us, "we must listen to Jaspers: when we think we see Nietzsche, he says, he is not this but something else. And, at the same time, this Other seems each time to escape us." ("On Nietzsche's Side," in *The Work of Fire*, 298–99).

52. Klossowski, 45. Or similarly, 140: "The other utterance, the *death of God*, concerned Nietzsche's relationship with the guarantor of the *ego's* identity: namely, the abolition, not of the divine itself, which is inseparable from *Chaos*, but of an identical and once-and-for-all individuality." Interestingly here, the divine for Nietzsche, according to Klossowski, is transferred from the One to the manifold, i.e., *Chaos*.

53. Ibid., 50.

54. Ibid., 167.

55. Ibid., 131.

56. Walter Kaufmann, *Nietzsche: Philosopher, Psychologist, Antichrist*, 4th Ed. (Princeton: Princeton University Press, 1974), 321.

57. Klossowski, xiii.

CHAPTER THREE. SHAKESPEARE'S EYE OF THE STORM

1. Rotman, in his own strong and insightful reading of *Lear's* nothing and "O" (78–86), highlights this phrase, "What need one?" as indicative of the language of modern mercantile arithmetic, with its now invasive 0, used as "the vehicle and image

of the destruction of Lear's self and of natural love. Both, by being converted into number signs, are emptied, neutered, stripped of human content" (83). See also 87.

2. Rotman reads this paradigm shift also as a one toward a new economic reality: "Lear registers, he acts out, he is, the rupture in the medieval world brought about by the transactions of Renaissance capitalism. Read thus, the play is Shakespeare's encounter with the empty doubleness of 'nothing,' with the spectre that he saw in those transactions; saw not in terms of abstract meta-signs or some grand metaphysical void but as zero, painfully concretised in the buying and selling of kinghood, self and love through numbers" (86).

3. See also Rotman, 84.

4. Northrop Frye, "Introduction to *The Tempest*," in *William Shakespeare—The Complete Works*, ed. Alfred Harbage (New York: Viking Press, 1969, rpt. 1977), 1370.

5. All quotations here and below taken from The Arden Shakespeare's *The Tempest*, ed. Frank Kermode (London: Routledge, 1954; rpt. 1994).

6. Principally, John Dryden and William Davenant's adaption of 1667, fully entitled *The Tempest: Or, The Enchanted Island*. See Alden T. Vaughan and Virginia Mason Vaughan, *Shakespeare's Caliban: A Cultural History* (Cambridge: Cambridge University Press, 1991), 90–93.

7. Even Erich Auerbach, who in his now classic *Mimesis* (trans. Willard R. Trask [Princeton: Princeton University Press, 1953]) treats his subject under the traditional understanding that "reality" is somehow represented in the figurations (*figura*) of great writers—Shakespeare "includes" or "embraces" earthly reality, even though he "goes far beyond the representation of reality in its merely earthly coherence" by including the "presence of ghosts and witches," (e.g., 327)—even Auerbach cannot avoid admitting (perhaps unwittingly) the self-reflective, self-enclosed world that operates at the heart of Shakespearean drama. In describing the difference between Shakespeare's world and that of his Middle Age predecessors, he writes: "Dante's general, clearly delimited figurality, in which everything is resolved in the beyond, in God's ultimate kingdom, and in which all characters attain their full realization only in the beyond, is no more. Tragic characters attain their final completion here below when, heavy with destiny, they become ripe like Hamlet, Macbeth, and Lear. Yet they are not simply caught in the destiny allotted to each of them; they are all connected as players in a play written by the unknown and unfathomable Cosmic Poet; a play on which He is still at work, and the meaning and reality of which is as unknown to them as it is to us" (327). He follows these thoughts with a quote from Prospero's speech in *The Tempest* in which the world is compared to the play just witnessed—to "the baseless fabric of this vision," to "this insubstantial pageant faded" (IV.i, 151, 155).

8. This goes even for the "indeterminacy" movement of the last century, championed particularly in the field of music by John Cage, and now by much performance art, where chance and contingency are given the greatest room to maneuver. But even in such aleatory forms, something must be prearranged—a music score, however unorthodox, or musicians in a room, or a can of paint ready to spill on a canvas, or actors out on a street ready to perform. Chance and random happenings are not in themselves art, for they lack the assemblage of an audience. To assemble an audience for a "random" event is to impose a frame around the event, and to block out thorough contingency.

9. Oscar Wilde, "The Preface," in *The Picture of Dorian Gray*, in *Plays, Prose Writings, and Poems* (London: J. M. Dent and Sons, 1975), 64.

10. From the opening of "Jerusalem," in *Blake—The Complete Writings*, ed. Geoffrey Keynes (Oxford: Oxford University Press, 1959, 1966, 1969, 1971, 1972), 621.

11. Wilde, *Plays, Prose Writings, and Poems*, 234. Wilde's prose poem "The House of Judgment," in which God has accused Man of many evils, and Man has admitted to all of them, concludes:

> And God closed the Book of the Life of Man, and said, "Surely I
>   will send thee into Hell. Even into Hell will I send thee."
> And the Man cried out, "Thou canst not."
> And God said to the Man, "Wherefore can I not send thee to Hell,
>   and for what reason?"
> "Because in Hell have I always lived," answered the Man.
> And there was silence in the House of Judgement.
> And after a space God spake, and said to the Man, "Seeing that I
>   may not send thee into Hell, surely I will send thee unto Heaven.
>   Even unto Heaven will I send thee."
> And the Man cried out, "Thou canst not."
> And God said to the Man, "Wherefore can I not send thee unto
>   Heaven, and for what reason?"
> "Because never, and in no place, have I been able to imagine it,"
>   answered the Man.
> And there was silence in the House of Judgment. (Ibid., 406)

12. The idea of "the prison-house of language" has of course a deep critical history, beginning with Nietzsche, as Fredric Jameson points out in his further use of the phrase in *The Prison-House of Language: A Critical Account of Structuralism and Russian Formalism* (Princeton: Princeton University Press, 1972), i, and continued in such works as Valentine Cunningham's *In the Reading Gaol* (Oxford: Blackwell, 1994). The idea is also implicit in Wittgenstein's famous line: "Die Grenzen meiner Sprache bedeuten die Grenzen meiner Welt" ("*The borders/limits of my language* means the borders/limits of my world"). 5.6, *Tractatus Logico-Philosophicus*, trans. C. K. Ogden (London: Routledge and Kegan Paul, 1922, rpt. 1981), 148.

13. See Vaughan and Mason Vaughan's extensive study, *Shakespeare's Caliban—A Cultural History*, op. cit. One of the most notable literary recreations of Caliban is by Robert Browning, in his "Caliban upon Setebos" (1864).

14. "The Significance of Tragedy" (1802), in *Classic and Romantic German Aesthetics*, ed. J. M. Bernstein (Cambridge: Cambridge University Press, 2003), 193. I am indebted to David Klemm for directing me to this highly relevant quote.

15. Jacques Derrida, *Memoirs of the Blind*, trans. Pascale-Anne Brault and Michael Naas (Chicago: University of Chicago Press, 1993), 65. Derrida, like Hölderlin, suggests the idea of tragedy *as* creation. Inasmuch as Caliban represents an aporia within the creator's creation, an unnegotiable entrapment that Prospero can neither escape from nor ignore, Shakespeare leads us in the direction of a tragedy of *poesis* itself, a flaw in creation that requires a sacrifice of creation to its own abnegation of

the O, Hölderlin's zero sign (0). To speak of tragedy in such terms, one reconstitutes the critical discussion of the *tragic form*, for it is indeed *form* in its formation, over and above entextualized *content*, that carries the brunt of the tragic realization. "The creator of form must suffer formlessness. Even risk dying of it," says Iris Murdoch in *The Black Prince* (London: Penguin, 1973), 414. For a more philosophical treatment of this tragic sense, especially as it arises in German Idealism, see David Farrell Krell's magisterial *The Tragic Absolute: German Idealism and the Languishing of God* (Bloomington: Indiana University Press, 2005).

16. Larry D. Bouchard, "Playing Nothing for Someone: *Lear*, Bottom and Kenotic Integrity," *Literature and Theology* 19, no.2: 159–80 (177).

CHAPTER FOUR. REFLECTIONS OF AUDEN

1. *Letters from Iceland* (with Louis MacNeice) (London: Faber and Faber, 1937; New York: Random House, 1937); *Journey to a War* (with Christopher Isherwood) (London: Faber and Faber, 1939; New York: Random House, 1939).

2. See, e.g., Slavoj Žižek, *The Fragile Absolute* (London: Verso, 2000), 11–21.

3. This despite having gone to Spain, in the wake of other European intellectuals, to lend support to the resistance against Franco. It was this futile experience in Spain that helped catapult Auden back to the Christian beliefs of his upbringing—see Auden's own version of his conversion in *Modern Canterbury Pilgrims*, ed. James A. Pike (London: A. R. Mowbray, 1956), 41.

4. Auden, *The Prolific and the Devourer* (Hopewell, NJ: Ecco Press, 1976, 1981), 26. See also Humphrey Carpenter, *W. H. Auden—A Biography* (London: George Allen and Unwin, 1981), 256. A later and more personal version of the same idea: "I know that all the verse I wrote, all the positions I took in the thirties, didn't save a single Jew" (Carpenter, 413). Earlier in *The Prolific and the Devourer* he had said: "The Prolific and the Devourer: the Artist and the Politician. Let them realise that they are enemies, i.e., that each has a vision of the world which must remain incomprehensible to the other" (23).

5. See, for example, Lucy McDiarmid, *Auden's Apology for Poetry* (Princeton: Princeton University Press, 1990), or Arthur Kirsch, "Introduction," in *The Sea and the Mirror*, ed. Arthur Kirsch (Princeton: Princeton University Press, 2003).

6. Kirsch, "Introduction," xivff.

7. Ibid., xix.

8. Given the commentary's complexity and length, as well as appertaining issues around permissions, reproduction of the text has been kept to a minimal in the exegesis to follow, and the reader would do well to keep a copy of the poem to hand throughout. The text used here is Arthur Kirsch's 2003 edition for Princeton University Press; no line numbers are given.

9. *Collected Poems*, 613.

10. In *The Complete Poems of Emily Jane Brontë*, ed. C. W. Hatfield (New York: Columbia University Press, 1941).

11. Søren Kierkegaard, *Fear and Trembling*, trans. Alastair Hannay (London: Penguin, 1985), 90.

12. The First Folio had added, "O o o o. [*Dyes*]." *Hamlet*, 460, n. 342.

13. Again Kierkegaard: "The tragic hero, the darling of ethics, is a purely human being, and is someone I can understand, someone all of whose undertakings are in the open. If I go further I always run up against a paradox, the divine and the demonic; for silence is both of these. It is the demon's lure, and the more silent one keeps the more terrible the demon becomes; but silence is also divinity's communion with the individual." *Fear and Trembling*, 114–15.

14. For example, John Fuller, *W. H. Auden: A Commentary* (London: Faber and Faber, 1998); Edward Mendelson, *Later Auden* (New York: Farrar, Straus, and Giroux, 1999), 206–15; Kirsch, xviii–xix.

15. In his essay "Balaam and the Ass," in *The Dyer's Hand and Other Essays* (New York: Random House, 1963), 129, as reprinted by Kirsch, 57.

16. Kirsch, xxi.

17. Maurice Blanchot, *The Space of Literature*, trans. Ann Smock (London: University of Nebraska Press, 1982), 165.

18. Maurice Blanchot, *The Instant of My Death*, trans. Elizabeth Rottenberg (Stanford: Stanford University Press, 2000), 11.

19. See ibid., and Derrida's accompanying *Demeure: Fiction and Testimony*, trans. Elizabeth Rottenberg (Stanford: Stanford University Press, 2000), 46.

20. Ibid., 16.

21. McDiarmid, 106.

22. Ibid.

23. Gerald Nelson was one of the first to recognize Prospero and Antonio in artistic opposition, where Prospero, having put aside art in "an attempt to be honest," now faces "life with no power but his own ignorance"; whereas Antonio, having picked up Prospero's magic cloak, now becomes "the actor who has gone mad and believes he is the role." He summed up the two sides: "Prospero, the one-time artist who has begun to recognize the true value of both his art and himself, setting out on his silent quest for truth; and Antonio, the would-be artist, but in a totally negative sense, dependent on the attention of others to save him from really seeing himself." *Changes in Heart: A Study in the Poetry of W. H. Auden* (Berkeley: University of California Press, 1969), 33–34. On this reading, Antonio's folly is not an inability to see the artistic stratagems, but to deny any alliance with them.

24. CP, 663.

25. Nelson, 36.

26. Lucy S. McDiarmid and John McDiarmid, "Artifice and Self-Consciousness in *The Sea and the Mirror*" in *W. H. Auden*, ed. Harold Bloom (New York: Chelsea House, 1986), 78.

27. Cf. Antonio's "sweet brother," Ferdinand's "Dear Other," Stephano's "Dear daughter," Gonzalo's "dear island," and Miranda's "Dear One."

28. Nelson, 37–38. See also Edward Callan, *Auden: A Carnival of Intellect* (Oxford: Oxford University Press, 1983), 196. Auden writes, "The sea . . . is the symbol of primitive potential power as contrasted with the desert of actualized triviality, of living barbarism versus lifeless decadence." *The Enchafèd Flood: or the Romantic Iconography of the Sea* (London: Faber and Faber, 1951), 27. See also Mendelson, 240 (or Kirsch, xvi), for a schematic drawn by Auden in which "sea" as a primary symbol is put under "Hell of the Pure Deed, Power Without Purpose," and "desert" is put under "Hell of the Pure Word, Knowledge Without Power."

29. Cf. Auden's later poem "Memorial For the City" (1949), which substitutes the image of the tightrope for that of the barbed wire.

30. This belief is one Auden believes Shakespeare himself held. In *The Enchafèd Flood* he writes: "In the last plays, *Pericles*, *The Winter's Tale*, *The Tempest* . . . not only do the sea and the sea voyage play a much more important role, but also a different one [than the earlier plays]. The sea becomes a place of purgatorial suffering: through separation and apparent loss, the characters disordered by passion are brought to their senses and the world of music and marriage is made possible" (20).

31. Or from childhood into adulthood. See Kirsch's analysis in connection to Freud, xxvi–xxvii.

32. McDiarmid, 107.

33. As quoted by Carpenter, 328.

34. Fuller, 367.

35. Carpenter, 325.

36. In an essay entitled "Music in Shakespeare," Auden wrote: "Ariel is neither a singer, that is to say, a human being whose vocal gifts provide him with a social function, nor a nonmusical person who in certain moods feels like singing. Ariel *is* song; when he is truly himself, he sings. . . . Yet Ariel . . . cannot express any human feelings because he has none. The kind of voice he requires is exactly the kind that opera does not want, a voice which is as lacking in the personal and erotic and as like an instrument as possible." *Dyer's Hand*, 524–25.

CHAPTER FIVE. THE EMPTY MIDDLE

1. Maurice Blanchot, *The Space of Literature*, 219.

2. *Thomas the Obscure*, trans. Robert Lamberton (New York: Station Hill Press, 1973, 1988), 99–100.

3. Ibid., 101–102. "I lean over you, your equal, offering you a mirror for your perfect nothingness, for your shadows which are neither light nor absence of light, for this void which contemplates" (108).

4. But perhaps Kafka is their crucial point of literary overlap. See, for example, Auden's "The I Without a Self," in *Dyer's Hand*, 159–67; "K's Quest," in *The Kafka Problem*, ed. Angel Flores (New York: Octagon, 1963), 47–52.

5. Blanchot writes, in a significant passage: "Death, in the human perspective, is not a given, it must be achieved. It is a task, one which we take up actively, one which becomes the source of our activity and mastery. Man dies, that is nothing. But man *is*, starting from his death. He ties himself tight to his death with a tie of which he is the judge. He makes his death; he makes himself mortal and in this way gives himself the power of a maker and gives to what he makes its meaning and its truth. The decision to be without being is possibility itself: the possibility of death. Three systems of thought—Hegel's, Nietzsche's, Heidegger's—which attempt to account for this decision and which therefore seem, however much they may oppose each other, to shed the greatest light on the destiny of modern man, are all attempts at making death possible." *The Space of Literature*, 96.

6. As quoted in Kevin Hart, *The Dark Gaze* (Chicago: University of Chicago Press, 2004), 90.

7. *The Space of Literature*, 26. See also below, chapter 6.

8. Ibid., 93–94.

9. As quoted in Edward Mendelson, *Later Auden* (New York: Farrar, Straus, and Giroux, 1999), 361.

10. *The Space of Literature*, 28.

11. Ibid., 55. On separation, see also 252. Cf. Auden, "Words and the Word," in *Secondary Worlds* (London: Faber and Faber, 1968), 106–109.

12. Hart, 117.

13. *The Space of Literature*, 22.

14. Ibid., 94.

15. Hart, 203. Julia Kristeva will later figure this Outside as "abjection"—see her *The Powers of Horror: An Essay on Abjection*, trans. Leon S. Roudiez (New York: Columbia University Press, 1982).

16. *The Space of Literature*, 252.

17. Ibid.

18. Hart, 202. See also *The Space of Literature*, 204–207.

19. *The Space of Literature*, 228.

20. Ibid., 229.

21. Ibid., 48. Auden's own prose, as in the later collection of lectures *Secondary Worlds*, cannot match the philosophical insight here. His closest possible approximation is the following: "One might say that for Truth the word 'silence' is the least inadequate metaphor, and that words can bear witness to silence only as shadows bear witness to light. Sooner or later every poet discovers the truth of Max Picard's remark: 'The language of the child is silence transformed into sound: the language of the adult is sound that seeks for silence'" (119).

22. This against Alain Badiou's later claim, drawn from Vitez, and made still very much under a Marxist banner of historical materialism, "that the real function of theatre consists in *orienting us in time*, in telling us *where* we are in history." Alain Badiou, "Rhapsody for the Theatre: A Short Philosophical Treatise," trans. Bruno Bosteels, *Theatre Survey* 49, no. 2 (November 2008): 229.

23. *The Space of Literature*, 246.

24. Ibid.

25. See *Dialectic of Enlightenment*, trans. John Cumming (New York: Continuum, 1999), 32–34. "The strain of holding the I together adheres to the I in all the stages; and the temptation to lose it has always been there with the blind determination to maintain it" (33).

26. Volume IX, chapters XVII and XIX.

27. Is it not curious that a book such as Hardt and Negri's *Empire* (London: Harvard University Press, 2000), which has been one of the more celebrated histories of ideas to be written since the turn of the millennium (published on the very threshold of that millennium), does not give any noticeable attention to this period?

28. This despite Rainer Emrig's book *W. H. Auden: Towards a Postmodern Poetics* (New York: Palgrave MacMillan, 2000), one of the few to see Auden's anticipation of postmodern concerns.

29. T. S. Eliot, *The Complete Poems and Plays, 1909–1950* (London: Harcourt Brace Jovanovich, 1952, 1971), 40–41.

30. Ibid.

31. Ibid., 138, 144.

32. Ibid., 126.

33. Ibid., 131.

34. Ibid., 145.

35. Samuel Beckett, "Endgame," in *The Complete Dramatic Works* (London: Faber and Faber, 1986), 106.

36. Ibid., 93. Echoing, of course, Jesus's final words on the cross.

37. Ibid., 133–34.

38. Ibid., 104.

39. Ibid., 116.

40. Ibid., 133.

41. Samuel Beckett, *The Unnamable*, in *Samuel Beckett: The Grove Centenary Edition, Volume II: Novels* (New York: Grove Press, 2006), 293.

42. Ibid., 296.

43. Ibid., 301; italics added.

44. Samuel Beckett, "Texts for Nothing," in *Samuel Beckett: The Grove Centenary Edition, Volume IV: Poems, Short Fiction, Criticism* (New York: Grove Press, 2006), 315.

45. *The Unnamable*, 407.

46. "Texts for Nothing," 339.

47. "Endgame," 132.

48. "Introduction," in *Samuel Beckett: The Grove Centenary Edition, Volume IV*, xiii.

49. Jorge Luis Borges, *Labyrinths: Selected Stories and Other Writings*, ed. Donald A. Yates and James E. Irby (New York: New Directions, 1962, 1964), 45–50.

50. Ibid., 248.

51. Ibid., 249.

52. Ibid., 173.

53. Ibid., 58.

54. From *Poems of Paul Celan*, trans. Michael Hamburger (New York: Persea, 1972, 1985, 1988, 1995), 77–137.

55. Ibid., 115.

56. Ibid., 157.

57. Ibid., 167.

58. Ibid., 179, 191, 193.

59. Ibid., 117. For another view of Celan's negating poetry, see Conor Cunningham's *Genealogy of Nihilism*, 142–49.

60. This is Leslie Anne Boldt's translation offered in her Introduction to Georges Bataille, *Inner Experience*, trans. Leslie Anne Boldt (Albany: State University of New York Press, 1988), xx.

61. "Madame Edwarda," in *The Bataille Reader*, ed. Fred Botting and Steve Wilson (Oxford: Blackwell Publishers, 1997), 229. And thus Austryn Wainhouse's translation of the end of the previous lines we just quoted from Boldt: ". . . but, at each least movement, our bursting hearts would strain wide-open to welcome 'the emptiness of heaven'" (230).

62. Susan Sontag, *Styles of Radical Will* (New York: Picador, 2002), 55.

63. Italo Calvino, "The Non-Existent Knight," in *Our Ancestors*, trans. Archibald Colquhoun (London: Vintage, 1998), 298–99.

64. Ibid., 356.

65. Auden: "What no critic seems to see in my work are its comic undertones. Only through comedy can one be serious." As quoted in Charles Osborne, *W. H. Auden: The Life of a Poet* (New York: M. Evans, 1979, 1995), 339. And this is likely informed by Kierkegaard: "The comic is always a sign of maturity, and then the essential thing is only that a new shoot emerges in this maturity, that the *vis comica* [comic force] does not suffocate pathos but merely indicates that a new pathos is beginning"—*Unscientific Postscript, Vol. 1*, ed. and trans. Howard V. Hong and Edna H. Hong (Princeton: Princeton University Press, 1992), 281.

66. Fuller, 356.

67. Ibid., 358.

68. Ibid., 367–68.

69. Mendelson, *Later Auden*, 221. See also 202–203, 206, 226.

70. Richard R. Bozorth, *Auden's Games of Knowledge: Poetry and the Meanings of Homosexuality* (New York: Columbia University Press, 2001), back cover.

71. Ibid., 3–4.

72. Ibid., 4, 11.

73. Kirsch, xviii–xix. The German *lebendigste* ("the one most alive") is a reference to the homosexual loved one in Hölderlin's poem "Sokrates und Alkibiades." See also Kirsch's *Auden and Christianity* (New Haven: Yale University Press, 2005).

74. All following references to this poem are from *Selected Poems*, ed. Edward Mendelson (New York: Vintage, 1979), 111–15.

75. At least in the pre-1966 version, when there were fifteen original stanzas. (Auden returned to some of his most reputable earlier poems in 1966 and amended them according to a new moral sensibility. He dropped the eleventh stanza from this poem, for reasons unclear to most.)

76. ". . . Evil miracles are done / Through the medium of a kiss," Auden wrote a year later, after the relationship with Kallman had soured. *CP*, 270.

77. See Mendelson, *Later Auden*, 153.

78. Fuller, 393.

79. Donne, "The Litanie," XVIII.

80. Georges Bataille, *Eroticism*, trans. Mary Dalwood (London: Penguin, 1962), 271.

81. E.g.: "The function of the phallic signifier touches here on its most profound relation: that in which the Ancients embodied the Νοῦς and the Λόγος." Jacques Lacan, "The signification of the phallus," in *Écrits: A Selection*, trans. Alan Sheridan (New York: W. W. Norton, 1977), 291.

82. We'll see another explicit example below: "The Truest Poetry is the Most Feigning" (1953).

83. Cf. also Bataille, from *Le Coupable* (1944): "Human existence is guilty: it *is* this to the degree it opposes nature." *The Bataille Reader*, 55.

84. *Dyer's Hand*, 160.

85. *CP*, 626.

86. Bataille, *Eroticism*, 268.

87. Simone de Beauvoir, *The Second Sex*, trans. and ed. H. M. Parshley (New York: Viking Books, 1989), 642.

88. Ibid., 643.

89. Ibid.

90. Ibid., 648.

91. Ibid., 649.

92. Ibid., 650. She adds later, in relation to this mystical impulse of women towards the Other: "Human love and love divine commingle, not because the latter is a sublimation of the former, but because the first is a reaching out toward a transcendent, an absolute. In both cases it is a matter of the salvation of the loving woman's contingent existence through her union with the Whole embodied in a supreme Person" (670)—with the One, we might add.

93. Ibid., 678. For more on de Beauvoir's relationship to female mysticism, especially vis-à-vis Bataille, see Amy Hollywood's *Sensible Ecstasy: Mysticism, Sexual Difference, and the Demands of History* (Chicago: University of Chicago Press, 2002), 120–45.

94. Judith Butler, *Subjects of Desire: Hegelian Reflections in Twentieth-Century France* (New York: Columbia University Press, 1987; Preface 1999), 35.

95. *CP*, 157.

96. Ibid., 621.

97. Richard Bozorth, "Auden: Love, Sexuality, and Desire," in *The Cambridge Companion to W. H. Auden*, ed. Stan Smith (Cambridge, Cambridge University Press, 2004), 175, 185.

98. de Beauvoir, 731.

99. See Kirsch, *Auden and Christianity*.

100. See, for a start, my own earlier essay "The Nostalgia of Adieux," in *Self/ Same/Other: Revisiting the Subject in Literature and Theology*, ed. Heather Walton and Andrew W. Hass (Sheffield: Sheffield Academic Press, 2000), 34–44.

CHAPTER SIX. THE REMAKING OF PHILOSOPHY AND RELIGION

1. Nothing as a concept, nothing as something, is the basis of Cunningham's "genealogy" in *A Genealogy of Nihilism*. For an excellent anthology of apophaticism, see William Franke's two-volume *On What Cannot Be Said: Apophatic Discourses in Philosophy, Religion, Literature, and the Arts* (Notre Dame: University of Notre Dame Press, 2007), especially *Volume 1: Classic Formulations*.

2. Paul Ricoeur, *Freud and Philosophy*, trans. Denis Savage (New Haven: Yale University Press, 1970), 32ff.

3. Immanuel Kant, *Critique of Pure Reason*, trans. Norman Kemp Smith (London: Macmillan, 1929; rpt. 1990), 384–484, esp. 450. Kant does deal with the concept of nothing in this foundational text, and, as Hegel saw (*The Encyclopaedia Logic*, §44), admits it into his categories, but only in terms of concepts and their objects, and as conditions of their impossibility or emptiness: nothing is either an

empty concept, or an empty object, or an empty intuition. It is not the absence or negation of these things *as such*. See 294–96 (B346–49).

4. F. W. J. Schelling, *Philosophical Investigations into the Essence of Human Freedom*, trans. Jeff Love and Johannes Schmidt (Albany: State University of New York Press, 2006), 68–69.

5. *Phenomenology of Spirit*, 19.

6. *Science of Logic*, 400.

7. Ibid., 440.

8. Ibid., 439.

9. Ibid., 440.

10. Ibid., 442.

11. Which is why, earlier, even *becoming* is sublated as the third term to being and nothing. See 106–108. This "classical" view of the dialectic generally retains a "higher" result, a teleological consummation in an advanced positive state. But such a characterization, prevalent as it still remains, neglects the unremitting movement of negation as a diremptive force, which disturbs the security of any so-called higher state, and in fact sends it back to its divided origins.

12. *Hegel's Aesthetics: Lectures on Fine Art, Vol. 1*, trans. T. M. Knox (Oxford: Oxford University Press, 1975), 11.

13. *Lectures on the Philosophy of Religion*, 489.

14. Jacques Derrida, "Tympan," in *Margins of Philosophy*, trans. Alan Bass (London: Harvester Wheatsheaf, 1982), xx.

15. See for example Heidegger's *Nietzsche Vol. IV: Nihilism*, trans. Frank A. Capuzzi, ed. David Farrell Krell (San Francisco: Harper Collins, 1982). Cf. also Conor Cunningham's *Genealogy of Nihilism*, which, perplexingly, leaves Nietzsche out of the general picture. The term *nihilism* was purportedly introduced in 1799 by Jacobi, Hegel's contemporary, a fact not without significance.

16. Kaufmann, *Nietzsche*, 113.

17. *The Will to Power*, §12 (A), 13.

18. Heidegger will say even more—*Nietzsche, Vol. IV: Nihilism*, 56.

19. *The Will to Power*, §22, 17.

20. "We others, we immoralists, have, conversely, made room in our hearts for every kind of understanding, comprehending, and *approving*. We do not easily negate; we make it a point of honour to be *affirmers*." *Twilight of the Idols*, in *The Portable Nietzsche*, trans. and ed. Walter Kaufmann (New York: Viking Penguin, 1982), 491.

21. *The Will to Power*, §26, 19.

22. *Thus Spoke Zarathustra, Second Part*, in *The Portable Nietzsche*, 199.

23. *The Will to Power*, §585 (B), 319.

24. Ibid., §617 (B), 330–31.

25. Ibid., §585 (A), 319.

26. Ibid., §600, 326.

27. "That *everything recurs* is the closest *approximation of a world of becoming to a world of being*:—high point of the meditation." Ibid., §617, 330.

28. Ibid., §616, 330. For Nietzsche's understanding of "truth," see my *Poetics of Critique* (Aldershot: Ashgate, 2003), ch. 5.

29. Again, see *Poetics of Critique*, "Interlude."

30. Martin Heidegger, *Nietzsche Vol. I: The Will to Power as Art*, trans. and ed. David Farrell Krell (San Francisco: Harper Collins, 1979).

31. Cf. Heidegger on Nietzsche: "Art is the condition posited in the essence of the will to power for the will's being able, as the will that it is, to ascend to power and to enhance that power." "The Word of Nietzsche: 'God is Dead,'" in *The Question Concerning Technology and Other Essays*, trans. William Lovitt (New York: Harper and Row, 1977), 86.

32. *The Will to Power*, §853 (IV), 453.

33. Heidegger, *Nietzsche Vol. I: The Will to Power as Art*, 61–62.

34. Martin Heidegger, *The Phenomenology of Religious Life*, trans. Matthias Fritsch and Jennifer Anna Gosetti-Ferencei (Bloomington: Indiana University Press, 2004), 234.

35. Heidegger, *Being and Time*, 289.

36. Ibid., 231–33.

37. Significantly, the book ends with Hegel, as Heidegger tries to situate himself against Hegel's interpretation of the connection between Time and Spirit on the grounds of "a negation of a negation." Whereas Hegel tried to achieve the concretion of the spirit through its fall into time, Heidegger "starts with the 'concretion' of factically thrown existence itself in order to unveil temporality as that which primordially makes such existence possible" (468). See further David Krell, "Analysis," in *Nietzsche Vol. IV: Nihilism*, 277–79, for the role of the nothing in *Being and Time*.

38. Martin Heidegger, "What is Metaphysics?," in *Pathmarks*, ed. William McNiell (Cambridge: Cambridge University Press, 1998), 94–95.

39. See here, for example, George Pattison, *The Later Heidegger* (London: Routledge, 2000), 193.

40. *Nietzsche Vol. I: The Will to Power as Art*, 122.

41. *Nietzsche Vol. IV: Nihilism*, 44.

42. Ibid., 7.

43. Ibid., 53.

44. Ibid., 213.

45. See again, for example, Krell's "Analysis," in *Nietzsche Vol. IV: Nihilism*, 276–94.

46. Heidegger, *Parmenides*.

47. Jean-Paul Sartre, *Being and Nothingness*, trans. Hazel E. Barnes (London: Routledge, 1958, 2003), 22.

48. Ibid, 39.

49. Ibid., 35, 40.

50. Ibid., 39.

51. Ibid., 40.

52. Ibid., 45.

53. Ibid., 46.

54. Sartre admits in the Conclusion (639) that "questions on the origin of being or on the origin of the world are either devoid of meaning or receive a reply within the actual province of ontology," a reply he himself will not furnish.

55. Ibid., 48.

56. Ibid., 85.

57. Ibid., 49.

58. Ibid., 638.

59. Foucault says something similar of Sartre, though using the language of authenticity, rather than of self-reflective consciousness: "I think that the only acceptable practical consequences of what Sartre has said is to link this theoretical insight to the practice of creativity—and not that of authenticity. From the idea that the self is not given to us, I think there is only one practical consequence: we have to create ourselves as a work of art. In his analyses of Baudelaire, Flaubert, and so on, it is interesting to see that Sartre refers the work of creation to a certain relation to oneself—the author to himself—which has the form of authenticity or inauthenticity. I would like to say exactly the contrary: we should not have to refer the creative activity of somebody to the kind of relation he has to himself, but should relate the kind of relation one has to oneself to a creative activity." Michel Foucault, *Essential Works of Foucault 1954–1984, Volume 1: Ethics*, ed. Paul Rabinow (London: Penguin, 2000), 262.

60. Heidegger, "Letter on 'Humanism,'" in *Pathmarks*, 250.

61. *Being and Nothingness*, 641–42.

62. Ibid., 643.

63. Ibid., 644.

64. Ibid., 644, 645.

65. See Derrida's essay "The Ends of Man," in *Margins of Philosophy*, trans. Alan Bass (London: Harvester Wheatsheaf, 1982), 115–16.

66. See Sartre's essay of 1947 "What is Literature," in *What is Literature? And Other Essays*, trans. Bernard Frechtman et al. (Cambridge: Harvard University Press, 1988).

67. Judith Butler, *Gender Trouble* (London: Routledge, 1990, 1999), 143.

68. *Being and Nothingness*, 643.

69. Foucault in a 1966 interview with C. Bonnefoy, as quoted by Thomas Flynn in *Sartre, Foucault, and Historical Reason, Volume One: Toward an Existentialist Theory of History* (Chicago: University of Chicago Press, 1997), 237.

70. See for example the work of Thomas Flynn (e.g., ibid.); Nik Farrell Fox, *The New Sartre: Explorations in Postmodernism* (London: Continuum, 2003); or Steve Marinot, *Forms in the Abyss: A Philosophical Bridge between Sartre and Derrida* (Philadelphia: Temple University Press, 2006).

71. Flynn, 237.

72. Jacques Derrida, *Glas*, trans. John P. Leavey Jr. and Richard Rand (Lincoln: University of Nebraska Press, 1986), 31.

73. The list is now too long even to highlight. Some on that list remain important as volumes where Derrida's own writing on negation first appears in English—*Languages of the Unsayable: The Play of Negativity in Literature and Literary Theory*, as but one example, in which "How to Avoid Speaking: Denials" first appeared in translation.

74. One of the last texts, *Rogues*, will come back into play in chapter 7. But under a different configuration.

75. *Glas*, 1.

76. Ibid., 150.

77. *The Truth in Painting*, 37, 9.

78. Ibid., 9.

79. *Glas*, 216.

80. *The Truth in Painting*, 17.

81. As it was translated by Nicholas Royle, in *Acts of Literature*, ed. Derek Attridge (New York: Routledge, 1992), 414–33.

82. Ibid., 425.

83. Ibid., 426.

84. Ibid.

85. Ibid., 429.

86. Derrida writes in "Ellipsis": "[T]he return of the book is of an *elliptical* essence . . . *the origin has played*. Something is missing that would make the circle perfect" (*Writing and Difference*, 296).

87. *Acts of Literature*, 433.

88. Translated as "Save/Except the name"—found in *On the Name*, ed. Thomas Dutoit, trans. John P. Leavey Jr. (Stanford: Stanford University Press, 1995).

89. *Reb Derissa*, for instance, the rabbinic signature ending "Ellipsis," in *Writing and Difference*, 300. See John Caputo's *The Prayers and Tears of Jacques Derrida: Religion without Religion* (Bloomington: Indiana University Press, 1997) for more on how the name of "Derrida" becomes a text that is other (than the man himself) (e.g., 110, or 281ff).

90. *"Khōra,"* in *Poikilia: Études offertes à Jean-Pierre Vernant* (Paris: École des Hautes Études en Sciences Sociales, 1987), and revised for the English translation in *On the Name*, 89.

91. See *On the Name*, 93, 126 for Plato's use of this metaphorical term.

92. Julia Kristeva, *Revolution in Poetic Language*, trans. Margaret Waller (New York: Columbia University Press, 1984), 26.

93. Luce Irigaray, *Speculum of the Other Woman*, trans. Gillian C. Gill (Ithaca: Cornell University Press, 1985), 243.

94. Ibid., 245.

95. Kristeva, *The Powers of Horror*, 7. In *Revolution in Poetic Language*, Kristeva directly address Hegelian negativity, specifically as the "fourth term" of the dialectical movement, a "term" which is more of an excess, which she claims is operative in the prelinguistic process she explores across two other key terms, "semiotic" and "symbolic." See Part II, "Negativity: Rejection," 109–164, and esp. 109–26.

96. *Speculum of the Other Woman*, "La Mystérique," 196–97.

97. Ibid., 243, 245.

98. Trans. Catherine Porter, Carolyn Burke (Ithaca: Cornell University Press, 1985).

99. Ibid., 9–22. The sentences below in italics are quotes taken variously from these pages.

100. Ibid., 23.

101. Ibid., 24.

102. Ibid., 26.

103. Ibid., "The 'Mechanics' of Fluids," 113; "Questions," 169.

104. Ibid., 28.

105. Ibid., 29.

106. Ibid.

107. Ibid., 29–30.

108. Ibid., 30–31.

109. Ibid., 32.

110. All "Derrida" can do, writing a year after *This Sex Which is Not One,* is quote Nietzsche in the context of the female as a *style*: "Thank goodness I am not willing to let myself be torn to pieces! the perfect women tears you to pieces when she loves you," to which Derrida adds himself, in a manner (or "style") that *gives him away*: "The question of the woman suspends the decidable opposition of true and non-true and inaugurates the epochal regime of quotation marks which is to be enforced for every concept belonging to the system of philosophical decidability. The hermeneutic project which postulates a true sense of the text is disqualified under this regime. Reading is freed from the horizon of the meaning or truth of being, liberated from the values of the product's production or the present's presence. Whereupon the question of style is immediately unloosed as a question of writing. The question posed by the spurring-operation (*opération-éperonnante*) is more powerful than any content, thesis or meaning. The stylate spur (*éperon style*) rips through the veil." In *Spurs Nietzsche's Styles / Éperons Les Styles de Nietzsche,* trans. Barbara Harlow (Chicago: University of Chicago Press, 1979), 107.

111. As she admits, for example, in the aptly titled "A Personal Note: Equal or Different?" *Je, tu, nous: Toward a Culture of Difference,* trans. Alison Martin (New York: Routledge, 1993), 9–14. For how the third of the French "trinity" of female theorists, Hélène Cixous, might figure in this lineage, see my final chapter in *Poetics of Critique,* 167ff.

112. Ibid., 9.

113. See chapter 1 above.

114. In a question and answer session during the first English reading of his play *Incident at Antioch,* February 13, 2009, University of Glasgow, part of a two-day conference entitled "Paul, Political Fidelity, and the Philosophy of Badiou: a Discussion of *Incident at Antioch*."

115. "Rhapsody for the Theatre," 193.

116. Ibid., 227.

117. Ibid. Cf. "Theses on Theatre," in *Handbook of Inaesthetics,* trans. Alberto Toscano (Stanford: Stanford University Press, 2005), 72–77.

118. Badiou, "Philosophy and Art," translated and reproduced in *Infinite Thought,* ed. and trans. Oliver Feltham and Justin Clemens (London: Continuum, 2003), 103.

119. Ibid., 100. Odd that Badiou the philosopher would not himself heed his own words here. Cf. a similar essay "Art and Philosophy," in *Handbook of Inaesthetics,* where Badiou claims that "art is always already there, addressing the thinker with the mute and scintillating question of its identity while through constant invention and metamorphosis it declares its disappointment about everything the philosopher may have to say about it" (1–2).

120. Ibid., 104. Cf. "What Is a Poem? Or, Philosophy and Poetry at the Point of the Unnamable," in *Handbook of Inaesthetics*, 16–27.

121. Ibid., 105.

122. Ibid., 107.

123. "Philosophy and Truth," in ibid., 58.

124. Ibid., 61.

125. *Being and Event*, trans. Oliver Feltham (London: Continuum, 2006), 435.

126. See *Poetics of Critique*, 147ff.

127. *Being and Event*, 24.

128. Ibid.

129. Ibid., 25.

130. Ibid., 392.

131. Ibid., 393.

132. Ibid., 175.

133. Ibid., 180.

134. Ibid., 179.

135. Ibid., 181.

136. Ibid., 393.

137. Ibid., 189–90.

138. Ibid., 23.

139. Ibid., 53.

140. Ibid., 55.

141. Ibid., 56.

142. Ibid., 10.

143. *Number and Numbers*, 158.

144. *Being and Event*, 123–29. For a more lay understanding of set theory and its relation to nothing (the empty set), see Barrow's *The Book of Nothing*, 164–75.

145. Book One, *The Way Things Are: The* De Rerum Natura *of Titus Lucretius Carus*, trans. Rolfe Humphries (Bloomington: Indiana University Press, 1968), 48.

146. *Being and Event*, 126. This is opposed to Nietzsche, who, "in the guise of the suture to the poem," had tried to seal "the jointly anti-matheme and anti-truth destiny of a century" (*Manifesto for Philosophy*, trans. Norman Madarasz [Albany: State University of New York Press, 1999], 101). This shows Badiou separating himself from the lineage of Nietzsche, and thus from the postmodern thought so indebted to Nietzsche. "Today the Nietzschean diagnosis must be toppled" (ibid.).

147. *Being and Event*, 525. In the Author's Preface of 2005, Badiou claims: "However, if I use mathematics and accord it a fundamental role, as a number of American rationalists do, I also use, to the same extent, the resources of the poem, as a number of my continental colleagues do" (xiv).

148. *Number and Numbers*, 14–15.

149. Ibid., 158.

150. *Being and Event*, 69.

151. *Number and Numbers*, 22–23.

152. Ibid., 211.

153. Ibid., 214.

154. Oliver Feltham, "Translator's Preface," *Being and Event*, xxiii.

155. Ibid., 392.

156. See again William Franke's excellent collection of readings in the aphophatic tradition, *On What Cannot be Said: Apophatic Discourses in Philosophy, Religion, Literature, and the Arts*, Vols. 1&2.

157. Problemata III, in *Fear and Trembling*, 137.

158. See "The Death of God," in *The Seminars of Jacques Lacan, Book VII*, trans. Dennis Porter (London: Routledge, 1992), 167–78, and reproduced, with a worthy introduction by Cleo McNelly Kearns, in *The Postmodern God: A Theological Reader*, ed. Graham Ward (Oxford: Blackwell, 1997), 32–44.

159. *On the Name*, 54–55.

160. Ibid., 55.

161. The essay opens with equal diffidence: "Sorry, but more than one, it is always necessary to be more than one in order to speak, several voices are necessary for that . . ." (35).

162. Mark C. Taylor, *Erring: A Postmodern A/theology* (Chicago: University of Chicago Press, 1984).

163. *Derrida and Negative Theology*, ed. Harold Coward and Toby Foshay (Albany: State University of New York Press, 1992).

164. Mark C. Taylor, *nOts* (Chicago: University of Chicago Press, 1993), 54. See also Taylor's contribution "Nothing Ending Nothing," in *Theology at the End of the Century: A Dialogue on the Postmodern with Thomas J. J. Altizer, Mark. C. Taylor, Charles E. Winquist, and Robert P. Scharlemann*, ed. Robert P. Scharlemann (Charlottesville: University Press of Virginia, 1990), 41–75.

165. E.g., Caputo, *Prayers and Tears of Jacques Derrida*, 134–51.

166. See especially *The Weakness of God* (Bloomington: Indiana University Press, 2006).

167. See now http://www.time.com/time/magazine/article/0,9171,941410,00.html, and http://www.time.com/time/magazine/article/0,9171,835309,00.html, respectively.

168. A comprehensive list of his writing, up until 2004, is compiled at the end of *Thinking Through the Death of God*, ed. Lissa McCullough and Brian Schroeder (Albany: State University of New York Press, 2004), 231–44. On Altizer as a prophet, see for example David Jasper's review of his autobiography *Living the Death of God: A Theological Memoir* (Albany: State University of New York Press, 2006) in *Conversations in Religion and Theology* 5, no. 2 (2007): 160–62, or more obliquely, Daniel Price, "God Turns a Blind Eye: Terrifying Angels Before the Apocalypse," *Literature and Theology* 21 no. 4 (December 2007): 362–80.

169. See for example Jasper, or, in a more extended analysis, Petra Carlsson's article "A Deleuzian Analysis of Thomas Altizer's Style," *Literature and Theology* 23, no. 2 (June 2009): 207–209.

170. *Godhead and the Nothing* (Albany: State University of New York Press, 2003), 67–68.

171. Altizer, "An Absolutely New Space," *Literature and Theology* 21 no. 4 (December 2007): 357.

172. "In the Wasteland: Apocalypse, Theology and the Poets," in *Thinking Through the Death of God*, 185.

173. Thomas Altizer, "The Beginning and Ending of Revelation," in *Theology at the End of the Century*, 80.

174. See his contribution "Betraying Altizer," in *Thinking Through the Death of God*, 11–28.

175. Graham Ward, "Introduction, or, A Guide to Theological Thinking in Cyberspace," in *The Postmodern God*, xl–xli. See also Ward's "Postmodern Theology," in *The Modern Theologians*, ed. David F. Ford (Oxford: Blackwell, 1997), 588–91.

176. *After the Death of God*, ed. Jeffrey W. Robbins (New York: Columbia University Press, 2007). Here, Caputo calls death of God theologies "thinly disguised *grand récits*," and refers to "the metaphysical residues that cling to Altizer's patently metaphysical version of the death of God" (68–69).

177. Steven M. Wasserstrom, *Religion after Religion: Gershom Scholem, Mircea Eliade, and Henry Corbin at Eranos* (Princeton: Princeton University Press, 1999); *Religion After Metaphysics*, ed. Mark A. Wrathall (Cambridge: Cambridge University Press, 2003); John Panteleimon Manoussakis, *God After Metaphysics: A Theological Aesthetic* (Bloomington: Indiana University Press, 2007); Daphne Hampson, *After Christianity* (London: SCM Press, 2002; orig. 1996); Gianni Vattimo, *After Christianity*, trans. Luca D'Isanto (New York: Columbia University Press, 2002); Don Cupitt, *After God: The Future of Religion* (New York: Basic Books, 1997); *After God: Richard Kearney and the Religious Turn in Continental Philosophy*, ed. John Panteleimon Manoussakis (New York: Fordham University Press, 2006); Mark C. Taylor, *After God* (Chicago: Chicago University Press, 2007); Douglas Coupland, *Life After God* (London: Simon and Schuster, 1994); John Caputo and Gianni Vattimo, *After the Death of God*; and, with some sense of reversal, Richard Kearney, *Anatheism: Returning to God After God* (New York: Columbia University Press, 2010).

178. Auden, *The Sea and the Mirror*, 4.

CHAPTER SEVEN. THE FUTURE OF O?

1. Frederick Buell, *W. H. Auden as a Social Poet* (Ithaca: Cornell University Press, 1973), 90ff.

2. See above, chapter 4, fn. 4.

3. Osborne, p. 258. See also revelations in Brecht's letters, only discovered lately, as reported by the *Guardian*—http://www.guardian.co.uk/world/2006/apr/03/research.germany; last accessed 01/02/12. Auden worked off and on with Brecht from 1943 on an adaptation of Webster's *The Duchess of Malfi*. Brecht had abandoned his association by the time it was mounted on Broadway in 1946, perhaps for good reason—the production met with little success. Auden later worked on translations of Brecht's *Die sieben Todsünden* and *Mahagonny* with Chester Kallman.

4. Richard Davenport-Hines, *Auden* (London: Heinemann, 1995), 232.

5. For this complicated history, I am following the "Editorial Note" of John Willet and Ralph Manheim in *The Caucasian Chalk Circle*, trans. James and Tania Stern with W. H. Auden, ed. John Willet and Ralph Manheim (London: Methuen

Modern Plays, 1988), 108–15. Auden himself was to participate in a revision of his original translation decades later.

6. Ibid., 100.

7. Ibid., 104.

8. An art that is also in some sense "homeless": the play, *The Caucasian Chalk Circle*, is written in a land (America) as a work that is very clearly not *of* that land (as the later charges of communism exposed). It is neither strictly a German play nor an American play.

9. *The Caucasian Chalk Circle*, 8.

10. Ibid., 50.

11. Ibid., 56.

12. Ibid.

13. Ibid., 58.

14. Ibid., 64.

15. Ibid., 72.

16. Ibid., 80.

17. Ibid., 94.

18. Ibid., 96.

19. Ibid.

20. Ibid.

21. Ibid., 92.

22. See in particular "From Restricted to General Economy: A Hegelianism without Reserve" (*Writing and Difference*, 251–77), where the working out of sovereignty—the "sovereign silence"—is done chiefly in relation to writing and meaning, and not law and politics.

23. Derrida, *Rogues*, 10.

24. Ibid., 13.

25. Of such freedom, Derrida writes (with Hegel in mind) of a "double *circulation*": "on the one hand, the circulation of the circle provisionally transfers power from one to the other before returning in turn to the first, the governed becoming in his turn governing, the represented in his turn representing, and vice versa; on the other hand, the circulation of the circle, through the return of this 'by turns,' makes the final and supreme power come back *to itself, to the itself of self, to the same as itself*. The same circle, the circle itself, would have to ensure the returning to come but also the return—or returns—of the final power to its origin or its cause, to its for-itself" (ibid., 24).

26. Ibid., 12–13.

27. Ibid., 102. "[T]hose states that are able or are in a state to denounce or accuse some 'rogue state' of violating the law, of failing to live up to the law, of being guilty of some perversion or deviation, those states that claim to uphold international law and that take the initiative of war, of police or peacekeeping operations because they have the force to do so, these states, namely, the United States and its allied states in these actions, are themselves, as sovereign, the first rogues states" (ibid.). This is Derrida's modulation of Carl Schmitt, and later Giorgio Agamben's reading of Schmitt, where sovereignty is defined as the power to instate the exception, to effect a suspension of the law. Agamben's *State of Exception*, in

which he modulates Derrida's own phrase, "force-of-~~law~~," had not yet been written (2003; trans. Kevin Attell in 2005 for University of Chicago Press). But Derrida puts "logic" into inverted commas here to draw attention both to the inverted nature of this logic, and to Agamben's first chapter "The Logic of Sovereignty," in *Homo Sacer* (orig. 1995). Derrida's significant essay "Force of Law: The Mystical Foundation of Authority" can be found in the volume *Acts of Religion*, ed. Gil Anidjar (New York: Routledge, 2002), 230–98.

28. See Derrida, "Violence and Metaphysics," in *Writing and Difference*, 94–95 in particular.

29. Derrida, *Rogues*, 106.

30. In Brecht's author's notes, he says, in relation to the casting of the Judge, that this character "is utterly upright, a disappointed revolutionary posing as a human wreck, like Shakespeare's wise men who act the fool. Without this the judgement of the chalk circle would lose all its authority" (*The Caucasian Chalk Circle*, 102).

31. *Rogues*, 87.

32. This is the similar, if perhaps not identical, "letting go" gesture that is at work in the Akedah, Abraham's sacrifice of Isaac (Gen. 22), that other great "parable" of giving up the heir and of its return, which provoked such a response in Kierkegaard (*Fear and Trembling*), and an elaboration in Derrida (*Gift of Death*). (There are numerous modern versions as well: one recalls, for example, the character of Sarah in Graham Greene's *The End of the Affair*.) Of course in the parable of the chalk circle, the heirdom is truly sacrificed.

ANOTHER EPICYCLE

1. Said in reference to Celan's poetry. In "Shibboleth: For Paul Celan," the full version translated by Joshua Wilner in Jacques Derrida, *Sovereignties in Question: The Poetics of Paul Celan*, ed. Thomas Dutoit and Outi Pasanen (New York: Fordham University Press, 2005), 47.

2. All quotes taken from *Macbeth*, The Arden Shakespeare, ed. Kenneth Muir (London: Methuen, 1951, 1964, 1984).

3. Auden, *The Sea and the Mirror*, 52.

BIBLIOGRAPHY OF CITED WORKS

Agamben, Giorgio. *Homo Sacer: Sovereign Power and Bare Life*. Trans. Daniel Heller-Roazen. Stanford: Stanford University Press, 1998.

———. *State of Exception*. Trans. Kevin Attell. Chicago: University of Chicago Press, 2005.

Altizer, Thomas J. J. *The Self-Embodiment of God*. New York: Harper and Row, 1977.

———. "The Beginning and Ending of Revelation." In *Theology at the End of the Century: A Dialogue on the Postmodern with Thomas J.J. Altizer, Mark. C. Taylor, Charles E. Winquist, and Robert P. Scharlemann*, ed. Robert P. Scharlemann. Charlottesville: University Press of Virginia, 1990.

———. *Godhead and the Nothing*. Albany: State University of New York Press, 2003.

———. *Living the Death of God: A Theological Memoir*. Albany: State University of New York Press, 2006.

———. "An Absolutely New Space." *Literature and Theology* 21, no. 4 (December 2007).

Aquinas, Thomas. *Selected Writings*. Ed. and trans. Ralph McInerny. London: Penguin, 1998.

Aristotle. "Poetics." Trans. Ingram Bywater. In *Introduction to Aristotle*, ed. Richard McKeon. New York: Modern Library, 1947.

———. *Metaphysics*. Trans. Richard Hope. Ann Arbor: University of Michigan Press, 1960.

Auden, W. H. *Letters from Iceland* (with Louis MacNeice). London: Faber and Faber, 1937; New York: Random House, 1937.

———. *Journey to a War* (with Christopher Isherwood). London: Faber and Faber, 1939; New York: Random House, 1939.

———. *The Enchafèd Flood: or the Romantic Iconography of the Sea*. London: Faber and Faber, 1951.

———. "W. H. Auden." In *Modern Canterbury Pilgrims*, ed. James A. Pike. London: A. R. Mowbray, 1956.

———. "K's Quest." In *The Kafka Problem*, ed. Angel Flores. New York: Octagon, 1963.

———. *The Dyer's Hand and Other Essays*. London: Faber and Faber, 1963.

———. *Secondary Worlds*. London: Faber and Faber, 1968.

———. *Collected Poems*. Ed. Edward Mendelson. London: Faber and Faber, 1976.

———. *The Prolific and the Devourer*. Hopewell, NJ: Ecco Press, 1976, 1981.

———. *Selected Poems*. Ed. Edward Mendelson. New York: Vintage, 1979.

———. *The Sea and the Mirror*. Ed. Arthur Kirsch. Princeton: Princeton University Press, 2003.

Auerbach, Erich. *Mimesis*. Trans. Willard R. Trask. Princeton: Princeton University Press, 1953.

Badiou, Alain. *Manifesto for Philosophy*. Trans. Norman Madarasz. Albany: State University of New York Press, 1999.

———. *Infinite Thought*. Ed. and trans. Oliver Feltham and Justin Clemens. London: Continuum, 2003.

———. *Saint Paul: The Foundation of Universalism*. Trans. Ray Brassier. Stanford: Stanford University Press, 2003.

———. *Handbook of Inaesthetics*. Trans. Alberto Toscano. Stanford: Stanford University Press, 2005.

———. *Being and Event*. Trans. Oliver Feltham. London: Continuum, 2006.

———. *Number and Numbers*. Trans. Robin Mackay. Cambridge: Polity, 2008.

———. "Rhapsody for the Theatre: A Short Philosophical Treatise." Trans. Bruno Bosteels. *Theatre Survey* 49 no. 2 (November 2008).

Barrow, John D. *The Book of Nothing*. London: Vintage, 2001.

Bataille, Georges. *Eroticism*. Trans. Mary Dalwood. London: Penguin, 1962.

———. "Madame Edwarda." In *The Bataille Reader*, ed. Fred Botting and Steve Wilson. Oxford: Blackwell Publishers, 1997.

Beauvoir, Simone de. *The Second Sex*. Trans. and ed. H. M. Parshley. New York: Viking Books, 1989.

Beckett, Samuel. *The Complete Dramatic Works*. London: Faber and Faber, 1986.

———. *Samuel Beckett: The Grove Centenary Edition, Volume II: Novels*. New York: Grove Press, 2006.

———. *Samuel Beckett: The Grove Centenary Edition, Volume IV: Poems, Short Fiction, Criticism*. New York: Grove Press, 2006.

Blake, William. *The Complete Writings*. Ed. Geoffrey Keynes. Oxford: Oxford University Press, 1959, 1966, 1969, 1971, 1972.

Blanchot, Maurice. *Thomas the Obscure*. Trans. Robert Lamberton. New York: Station Hill Press, 1973, 1988.

———. *The Space of Literature*. Trans. Ann Smock. London: University of Nebraska Press, 1982.

———. *The Work of Fire*. Trans. Charlotte Mandell. Stanford: Stanford University Press, 1995.

———. *Writing of the Disaster*. Trans. Ann Smock. London: University of Nebraska Press, 1995.

———. *The Instant of My Death*. Trans. Elizabeth Rottenberg. Stanford: Stanford University Press, 2000.

Borges, Jorge Luis. *Labyrinths: Selected Stories and Other Writings*. Ed. Donald A. Yates and James E. Irby. New York: New Directions, 1962, 1964.

Bouchard, Larry D. "Playing Nothing for Someone: *Lear*, Bottom, and Kenotic Integrity." *Literature and Theology* 19, no.2.

Bozorth, Richard R. *Auden's Games of Knowledge: Poetry and the Meanings of Homosexuality*. New York: Columbia University Press, 2001.

———. "Auden: Love, Sexuality, and Desire." In *The Cambridge Companion to W. H. Auden*, ed. Stan Smith. Cambridge, Cambridge University Press, 2004.

Brecht, Bertolt. *The Caucasian Chalk Circle*. Trans. James and Tania Stern with W. H. Auden. Ed. John Willet and Ralph Manheim. London: Methuen Modern Plays, 1988.

Brontë, Emily Jane. *The Complete Poems of Emily Jane Brontë*. Ed. C. W. Hatfield. New York, Columbia University Press, 1941.

Budick, Sanford, and Wolfgang Iser, eds. *Negativity in Literature and Literary Theory*. Stanford: Stanford University Press, 1987.

Buell, Frederick. *W. H. Auden as a Social Poet*. Ithaca: Cornell University Press, 1973.

Bussanich, John. "The Metaphysics of the One." In *The Cambridge Companion to Plotinus*, ed. Lloyd P. Gerson. Cambridge: Cambridge University Press, 1996.

Butler, Judith. *Subjects of Desire: Hegelian Reflections in Twentieth-Century France*. New York: Columbia University Press, 1987.

———. *Gender Trouble*. London: Routledge, 1990, 1999.

Callan, Edward. *Auden: A Carnival of Intellect*. Oxford: Oxford University Press, 1983.

Calvino, Italo. "The Non-Existent Knight." In *Our Ancestors*. Trans. Archibald Colquhoun. London: Vintage, 1998.

Caputo, John D. *Radical Hermeneutics*. Bloomington: Indiana University Press, 1987.

———. *The Prayers and Tears of Jacques Derrida: Religion without Religion*. Bloomington: Indiana University Press, 1997.

———. *The Weakness of God*. Bloomington: Indiana University Press, 2006.

———, and Gianni Vattimo. *After the Death of God*. Ed. Jeffrey W. Robbins. New York: Columbia University Press, 2007.

Carlsson, Petra. "A Deleuzian Analysis of Thomas Altizer's Style." *Literature and Theology* 23, no. 2 (June 2009).

Carpenter, Humphrey. *W. H. Auden—A Biography*. London: George Allen and Unwin, 1981.

Celan, Paul. *Poems of Paul Celan*. Trans. Michael Hamburger. New York, Persea, 1972, 1985, 1988, 1995.

Coleridge, Samuel Taylor. *The Collected Works of Samuel Taylor Coleridge: Vol. 16 (Poetical Works I: Poems [Reading Text])*. Ed. J. C. C. Mays. Princeton: Princeton University Press, 2001.

Copleston, Frederick. *Religion and the One: Philosophies East and West*. London: Continuum, 1982.

Cornford, F. M. *Plato and Parmenides*. London: Routledge and Kegan Paul, 1939.

Corrigan, Kevin. "'Solitary' Mysticism in Plotinus, Proclus, Gregory of Nyssa, and Pseudo-Dionysius." *Journal of Religion* 76, no. 1 (January 1996).

Coupland, Douglas. *Life After God*. London: Simon and Schuster, 1994.

Coward, Harold, and Toby Foshay, eds. *Derrida and Negative Theology*. Albany: State University of New York Press, 1992.

Culler, Jonathan. *The Pursuit of Signs*. Ithaca: Cornell University Press, 1981.

Cunningham, Conor. *Genealogy of Nihilism*. London: Routledge, 2002.

Cunningham, Valentine. *In the Reading Gaol*. Oxford: Blackwell, 1994.

Cupitt, Don. *After God: The Future of Religion*. New York: Basic Books, 1997.

Davenport-Hines, Richard. *Auden*. London: Heinemann, 1995.

Davis, Martin. *The Universal Computer: The Road from Leibniz to Turing*. New York: W. W. Norton, 2000.

Deleuze, Gilles, and Felix Guattari. *Anti-Oedipus: Capitalism and Schizophrenia*. Trans. Robert Hurley et al. London: Athlone Press, 1984.

———. *What is Philosophy?* Trans. Graham Burchell and Hugh Tomlinson. London: Verso, 1994.

Derrida, Jacques. *Writing and Difference*. Trans. Alan Bass. London: Routledge, 1978.

———. *Spurs Nietzsche's Styles / Éperons Les Styles de Nietzsche*. Trans. Barbara Harlow. Chicago: University of Chicago Press, 1979.

———. *Glas*. Trans. John P. Leavey Jr. and Richard Rand. Lincoln: University of Nebraska Press, 1986.

———. *The Truth in Painting*. Trans. Geoff Bennington and Ian McLeod. Chicago: University of Chicago Press, 1987.

———. *A Derrida Reader: Between the Blinds*. Ed. Peggy Kamuf. New York: Columbia University Press, 1991.

———. *Acts of Literature*. Ed. Derek Attridge. New York: Routledge, 1992.

———. *Memoirs of the Blind*. Trans. Pascale-Anne Brault and Michael Naas. Chicago: University of Chicago Press, 1993.

———. *Gift of Death*. Trans. David Wills. London: University of Chicago Press, 1995.

———. *On the Name*. Ed. Thomas Dutoit. Trans. John P. Leavey Jr. Stanford: Stanford University Press, 1995.

———. *Demeure: Fiction and Testimony*. Trans. Elizabeth Rottenberg. Stanford: Stanford University Press, 2000.

———. *Acts of Religion*. Ed. Gil Anidjar. New York: Routledge, 2002.

———. *Rogues: Two Essays on Reason*. Trans. Pascale-Anne Brault and Michael Naas. Stanford: Stanford University Press, 2005.

———. *Sovereignties in Question: The Poetics of Paul Celan*. Ed. Thomas Dutoit and Outi Pasanen. New York: Fordham University Press, 2005.

Eliot, T. S. *The Complete Poems and Plays, 1909–1950*. London: Harcourt Brace Jovanovich, 1952, 1971.

Emrig, Rainer. *W. H. Auden: Towards a Postmodern Poetics*. New York: Palgrave MacMillan, 2000.

Findlay, J. N. *Plato: The Written and Unwritten Doctrines*. New York: Humanities Press, 1974.

Flynn, Thomas. *Sartre, Foucault, and Historical Reason, Volume One: Toward an Existentialist Theory of History*. Chicago: University of Chicago Press, 1997.

Forster, E. M. *A Passage to India*. Harmondsworth: Penguin, 1924, rpt. 1986.

Foucault, Michel. *Essential Works of Foucault 1954–1984, Volume 1: Ethics*. Ed. Paul Rabinow. London: Penguin, 2000.

Fox, Nik Farrell. *The New Sartre: Explorations in Postmodernism*. London: Continuum, 2003.

Franke, William. *On What Cannot Be Said: Apophatic Discourses in Philosophy, Religion, Literature, and the Arts*. Vols. I and II. Notre Dame: University of Notre Dame Press, 2007.

Fuller, John. *W. H. Auden: A Commentary*. London: Faber and Faber, 1998.

Gasché, Rodolphe. *The Tain of the Mirror: Derrida and the Philosophy of Reflection.* Cambridge: Harvard University Press, 1986.

Hallyn, Fernand. *The Poetic Structure of the World: Copernicus and Kepler.* New York: Zone Books, 1990.

Hampson, Daphne. *After Christianity.* London: SCM Press, 2002; orig. 1996.

Hardt, Michael, and Antonio Negri. *Empire.* London: Harvard University Press, 2000.

Hart, Kevin. *The Dark Gaze.* Chicago: University of Chicago Press, 2004.

Hass, Andrew W. "The Nostalgia of Adieux." In *Self/Same/Other: Revisiting the Subject in Literature and Theology*, ed. Heather Walton and Andrew W. Hass. Sheffield: Sheffield Academic Press, 2000.

———. *Poetics of Critique.* Aldershot: Ashgate, 2003.

Hegel, G. W. F. *Phenomenology of Spirit.* Trans. A. V. Miller. Oxford: Oxford University Press, 1977.

———. *The Science of Logic.* Trans. A. V. Miller. New York: Humanity Books, 1969.

———. *Philosophy of Nature.* Trans. A. V. Miller. Oxford: Oxford University Press, 1970, 2004.

———. *Hegel's Aesthetics: Lectures on Fine Art, Vol. 1.* Trans. T. M. Knox. Oxford: Oxford University Press, 1975.

———. *Lectures on the Philosophy of Religion.* Trans. R. F. Brown et al. Ed. Peter C. Hodgson. Berkeley: University of California Press, 1988.

Heidegger, Martin. *Being and Time.* Trans. John Macquarrie and Edward Robinson. Oxford: Blackwell, 1962.

———. *Poetry, Language, Thought.* Trans. Albert Hofstadter. New York: Harper and Row, 1971.

———. *The Question Concerning Technology and Other Essays.* Trans. William Lovitt. New York: Harper and Row, 1977.

———. *Nietzsche Vol. I: The Will to Power as Art.* Trans. and ed. David Farrell Krell. San Francisco: HarperCollins, 1979.

———. *Nietzsche Vol. IV: Nihilism.* Trans. Frank A. Capuzzi. Ed. David Farrell Krell. San Francisco: HarperCollins, 1982.

———. *Parmenides.* Trans. André Schuwer and Richard Rojcewicz. Bloomington: Indiana University Press, 1992.

———. *Pathmarks.* Ed. William McNiell. Cambridge: Cambridge University Press, 1998.

———. *The Phenomenology of Religious Life.* Trans. Matthias Fritsch and Jennifer Anna Gosetti-Ferencei. Bloomington: Indiana University Press, 2004.

Hölderlin, Friedrich. *Hyperion and Selected Poems (The German Library, Vol. 22).* Ed. Eric L. Santner. New York: Continuum, 1990.

———. "The Significance of Tragedy." In *Classic and Romantic German Aesthetics*, ed. J. M. Bernstein. Cambridge University Press, 2003.

Hollywood, Amy. *Sensible Ecstasy: Mysticism, Sexual Difference, and the Demands of History.* Chicago: University of Chicago Press, 2002.

Hopkins, Gerard Manley. *Poems and Prose.* Ed. W. H. Gardner. London: Penguin, 1953; rpt. 1988.

Horkheimer, Max, and Theodor W. Adorno. *Dialectic of Enlightenment.* Trans. John Cumming. New York: Continuum, 1999.

Irigaray, Luce. *Speculum of the Other Woman.* Trans. Gillian C. Gill. Ithaca: Cornell University Press, 1985.

———. *This Sex Which is Not One.* Trans. Catherine Porter and Carolyn Burke. Ithaca: Cornell University Press, 1985.

———. *Je, tu, nous: Toward a Culture of Difference.* Trans. Alison Martin. New York: Routledge, 1993.

Jameson, Fredric. *The Prison-House of Language: A Critical Account of Structuralism and Russian Formalism.* Princeton: Princeton University Press, 1972.

Jasper, David. "In the Wasteland: Apocalypse, Theology and the Poets." In *Thinking Through the Death of God,* ed. Lissa McCullough and Brian Schroeder. Albany: State University of New York Press, 2004.

———. "Review of *Living the Death of God: A Theological Memoir.*" *Conversations in Religion and Theology* 5, no. 2 (2007).

Jeanrond, Werner. *A Theology of Love.* London: T and T Clark, 2010.

Kant, Immanuel. *Critique of Pure Reason.* Trans. Norman Kemp Smith. London: Macmillan, 1929; rpt. 1990.

Kaplan, Robert. *The Nothing That Is: A Natural History of O.* London: Oxford University Press, 1999.

Kaufmann, Walter. *Nietzsche: Philosopher, Psychologist, Antichrist.* 4th Ed. Princeton: Princeton University Press, 1974.

Kearney, Richard. *Anatheism: Returning to God After God.* New York: Columbia, 2010.

Kierkegaard, Søren. *Fear and Trembling.* Trans. Alastair Hannay. London: Penguin, 1985.

———. *Unscientific Postscript, Vol. 1.* Ed. and trans. Howard V. Hong and Edna H. Hong. Princeton: Princeton University Press, 1992.

Kirk, G. S., J. E. Raven, and M. Schofield, eds. *The Presocratic Philosophers.* 2nd Ed. Cambridge: Cambridge University Press, 1957, 1983.

Kirsch, Arthur. *Auden and Christianity.* New Haven: Yale University Press, 2005.

Klossowski, Pierre. *Nietzsche and the Vicious Circle.* Trans. Daniel W. Smith. London: Continuum 2005; orig. 1969.

Krell, David Farrell. *The Tragic Absolute: German Idealism and the Languishing of God.* Bloomington: Indiana University Press, 2005.

Kristeva, Julia. *The Powers of Horror: An Essay on Abjection.* Trans. Leon S. Roudiez. New York: Columbia University Press, 1982.

———. *Revolution in Poetic Language.* Trans. Margaret Waller. New York: Columbia University Press, 1984.

Kuhn, Thomas S. *The Structure of Scientific Revolutions.* 3rd Ed. Chicago: University of Chicago Press, 1996.

Kundera, Milan. *The Joke.* New York: HarperCollins, 1992.

Lacan, Jacques. *Écrits: A Selection.* Trans. Alan Sheridan. New York: W. W. Norton, 1977.

———. *The Seminars of Jacques Lacan, Book VII.* Trans. Dennis Porter. London: Routledge, 1992.

Leahy, D. G. *Novitas Mundi: Perception of The History of Being.* Albany: State University of New York Press, 1994.

Lucretius. *The Way Things Are: The* De Rerum Natura *of Titus Lucretius Carus*. Trans. Rolfe Humphries. Bloomington: Indiana University Press, 1968.

Luther, Martin. *Christian Liberty*. Ed. Harold J. Grimm. Philadelphia: Fortress Press, 1957.

Manoussakis, John Panteleimon, ed. *After God: Richard Kearney and the Religious Turn in Continental Philosophy*. New York: Fordham University Press, 2006.

———. *God After Metaphysics: A Theological Aesthetic*. Bloomington: Indiana University Press, 2007.

Marinot, Steve. *Forms in the Abyss: A Philosophical Bridge between Sartre and Derrida*. Philadelphia: Temple University Press, 2006.

McCullough, Lissa, and Brian Schroeder, eds. *Thinking Through the Death of God*. Albany: State University of New York Press, 2004.

McDiarmid, Lucy. *Auden's Apology for Poetry*. Princeton: Princeton University Press, 1990.

McDiarmid, Lucy S., and John McDiarmid. "Artifice and Self-Consciousness in *The Sea and the Mirror*." In *W. H. Auden*, ed. Harold Bloom. New York: Chelsea House, 1986.

Meinwald, Constance C. *Plato's Parmenides*. Oxford: Oxford University Press, 1991.

Mendelson, Edward. *Later Auden*. New York: Farrar, Straus, and Giroux, 1999.

Milton, John. *Complete Poems and Major Prose*. Ed. Merritt Y. Hughes. Indianapolis: Bobbs-Merrill, 1957.

Miller, Mitchell H. *Plato's Parmenides: The Conversion of the Soul*. Princeton: Princeton University Press, 1986.

Mourelatos, Alexander P. D. *The Route of Parmenides*. Las Vegas: Parmenides Publishing, 2008.

Murdoch, Iris. *The Black Prince*. London: Penguin, 1973.

Nelson, Gerard. *Changes in Heart: A Study in the Poetry of W. H. Auden*. Berkeley: University of California Press, 1969.

Nietzsche, Friedrich. *The Will to Power*. Ed. Walter Kaufmann. Trans. Walter Kaufmann and R. J. Hollingdale. New York: Vintage, 1967.

———. *Thus Spoke Zarathustra*. In *The Portable Nietzsche*. Trans. and ed. Walter Kaufmann. New York: Viking Penguin, 1982.

———. *Twilight of the Idols*. In *The Portable Nietzsche*. Trans. and ed. Walter Kaufmann. New York: Viking Penguin, 1982.

———. *The Gay Science*. Ed. Bernard Williams. Trans. Josefine Nauckhoff. Cambridge: Cambridge University Press, 2001.

Osborne, Charles. *W. H. Auden: The Life of a Poet*. New York: M. Evans, 1979, 1995.

Pascal, Blaise. *The Mind on Fire: An Anthology of the Writings of Blaise Pascal*. Ed. James M. Houston. Portland: Multnomah Press, 1989.

———. *Pensées de Pascal: Publiées dans leur texte authentique avec un commentaire suivi par Ernest Havet*. Boston: Adamant Media Corporation, 2001.

Pattison, George. *The Later Heidegger*. London: Routledge, 2000.

Plato. *Complete Works*. Ed. John M. Cooper. Indianapolis: Hackett, 1997.

Plotinus. *The Enneads*. Trans. Stephen MacKenna. Burdett, NY: Larson Publications, 1992.

Price, Daniel. "God Turns a Blind Eye: Terrifying Angels Before the Apocalypse." *Literature and Theology* 21, no. 4 (December 2007).

Pynchon, Thomas. *Gravity's Rainbow*. London: Vintage, 2000.

Ragland-Sullivan, Ellie. *Jacques Lacan and the Philosophy of Psychoanalysis*. London: Croom Helm, 1986.

Ricoeur, Paul. *Freud and Philosophy*. Trans. Denis Savage. New Haven: Yale University Press, 1970.

Rotman, Brian. *Signifying Nothing: The Semiotics of Zero*. Basingstoke: Macmillan Press, 1987.

Russell, Bertrand. *The Problems of Philosophy*. Oxford: Oxford University Press, 1967.

Sartre, Jean-Paul. *What is Literature? And Other Essays*. Trans. Bernard Frechtman et al. Cambridge: Harvard University Press, 1988.

———. *Being and Nothingness*. Trans. Hazel E. Barnes. London: Routledge, 1958, 2003.

Scharlemann, Robert P. ed. *Theology at the End of the Century: A Dialogue on the Postmodern with Thomas J. J. Altizer, Mark. C. Taylor, Charles E. Winquist, and Robert P. Scharlemann*. Charlottesville: University Press of Virginia, 1990.

Schelling, F. W. J. *Philosophical Investigations into the Essence of Human Freedom*. Trans. Jeff Love and Johannes Schmidt. Albany: State University of New York Press, 2006.

Schleiermacher, Friedrich. *On Religion: Speeches to its Cultured Despisers*. Trans. John Oman. New York: Harper and Row, 1958, 1986.

Schürmann, Reiner. *Broken Hegemonies*. Trans. Reginald Lilly. Bloomington: Indiana University Press, 2003.

Scolnicov, Samuel. *Plato's Parmenides*. Berkeley: University of California Press, 2003.

Seife, Charles. *Zero: The Biography of a Dangerous Idea*. London: Souvenir Press, 2000.

Shakespeare, William. *The Complete Shakespeare*. Ed. Alfred Harbage. New York: Viking, 1969.

———. *Macbeth*. The Arden Shakespeare. Ed. Kenneth Muir. London: Methuen, 1951, 1964, 1984.

———. *The Tempest*. The Arden Shakespeare. Ed. Frank Kermode. London: Routledge, 1954; rpt. 1994.

———. *King Lear*. The Arden Shakespeare. Ed. R. A. Foakes. London: Thomas Nelson and Sons, 1997.

———. *Hamlet*. The Arden Shakespeare. Ed. Ann Thompson and Neil Taylor. London: Thomas Nelson and Sons, 2006.

Shelley, Percy Bysshe. "Prometheus Unbound." In *The Major Works*, ed. Zachary Leader and Michaeol O'Neill. Oxford: Oxford University Press, 2003.

Smith, Stevie. *Selected Poems*. Ed. James MacGibbon. London: Penguin, 1975, 1978.

Sontag, Susan. *Styles of Radical Will*. New York: Picador, 2002.

Taylor, Charles. *Sources of the Self*. Cambridge: Harvard University Press, 1989.

Taylor, Mark C. *Erring: A Postmodern A/theology*. Chicago: University of Chicago Press, 1984.

———. *nOts*. Chicago: University of Chicago Press, 1993.

———. *Moment of Complexity*. Chicago: University of Chicago Press, 2003.

————. "Betraying Altizer." In *Thinking Through the Death of God*, ed. Lissa McCullough and Brian Schroeder. Albany: State University of New York Press, 2004.

————. *After God*. Chicago: University of Chicago Press, 2007.

Vattimo, Gianni. *The End of Modernity*. Trans. Jon R. Snyder. Cambridge: Polity Press, 1988.

————. *After Christianity*. Trans. Luca D'Isanto. New York: Columbia University Press, 2002.

Vaughan, Alden T., and Virginia Mason Vaughan. *Shakespeare's Caliban: A Cultural History*. Cambridge: Cambridge University Press, 1991.

Waldenfels, Hans. *Absolute Nothingness: Foundations for Buddhist-Christian Dialogue*. New York: Paulist Press, 1980.

Ward, Graham. "Introduction, or, A Guide to Theological Thinking in Cyberspace." In *The Postmodern God: A Theological Reader*. Oxford: Blackwell, 1997.

————. "Postmodern Theology." In *The Modern Theologians*, ed. David F. Ford. Oxford: Blackwell, 1997.

Wasserstrom, Steven M. *Religion after Religion: Gershom Scholem, Mircea Eliade, and Henry Corbin at Eranos*. Princeton: Princeton University Press, 1999.

Wilde, Oscar. *Plays, Prose Writings, and Poems*. London: J. M. Dent & Sons, 1975.

Wittgenstein, Ludwig. *Tractatus Logico-Philosophicus*. Trans. C. K. Ogden. London: Routledge and Kegan Paul, 1922, rpt. 1981.

Wrathall Mark A., ed. *Religion After Metaphysics*. Cambridge: Cambridge University Press, 2003.

Žižek, Slavoj. *The Fragile Absolute*. London: Verso, 2000.

INDEX

abjection (*see also* Kristeva), 221, 229, 285n15

Abram, Abraham, 29, 30, 31, 52, 129, 243, 244, 299n32

absence, 3, 67–69, 80, 109, 143, 156, 160, 163, 172, 178–179, 203, 206, 213, 216, 221, 228, 230, 233, 268, 278n5, 290n3

ab-sense, 236

absurdity, the Absurd, 137, 187, 208

abyss, 118, 131, 139, 143, 146, 155, 156, 199, 215, 216, 221, 225, 226, 229, 230, 248, 251, 257, 279n28

account, accounting, 7, 14, 17, 33, 35, 36, 39, 40, 42, 44, 48, 53, 54, 58, 68, 70–71, 74

actuality (*see also* potentiality), 42–45

Adam, 31

Adorno, Theodor, 65, 166

advent, 215, 248

Aeschylus, 58

aesthetics, aestheticism, xii, 1, 2, 13, 19, 81, 96, 118, 122, 129, 130, 132, 133, 135–137, 143, 147, 151, 169, 178, 205, 209, 212

Agamben, Giorgio, 222, 273n23, 277n59, 298–299n27

Al-Ghazali, 46

allegory, xii, 258

Altizer, Thomas, 247–251, 267

Altizer's O, 251

Anaxagoras, 35

Anaximander, 32

Anaximenes, 32

anarchy, 256, 257, 258, 267

anomaly, anomie, anomic, 256–259

anthropology, 66, 218

anxiety, 10, 14, 73, 131, 147, 149, 153, 165–166

aphorism, 32, 148, 226–228

apocalypse, apocalypticism, 167, 248

apophatics, apophaticism, 38, 46, 143, 200, 243–244, 247, 250

aporia, 20, 38, 39, 40–41, 93, 155, 176, 226, 282n15

apostrophe, 67, 228, 268, 277n2

Aquinas, Thomas (Thomism), 59

Aristotle, xi, 9, 25, 35, 36, 38, 41–43, 46, 48, 52, 59, 81, 99, 236, 278n14

   Metaphysics, 41–43, 44; *Poetics*, 81; Peripatetic philosophy (Aristotelianism), 48, 72, 81, 140

artifice, xv, 23, 83, 109, 111–113, 113, 118, 123, 127–128, 133, 135, 142, 144–145, 146, 148, 150, 157, 161, 169, 176, 184, 187, 188, 189, 193–194, 221, 230, 232, 264

artificer, 82–83, 118, 137, 145, 155, 160, 232; artificer's circle, 82–88, 112, 113–114, 124, 127, 128, 143, 155, 158, 187, 232, 260

"as if," 128

astronomy, 7–8, 60

atheism, 245, 247

atom, atomics, Atomists, 35, 73, 74; atomic age, 75

Auden, W.H., 10, 11–12, 13, 19, 20, 46, 95–96, 111, 121–126, 128–132, 133–136, 138, 143–146, 151, 156, 159–161, 164, 166, 168, 171, 176, 184–190, 193–195, 218, 226, 230, 231, 232, 235, 244, 253–256, 267–268, 297n3

Auden, W.H. (continued)
  Auden's O, xiii, xv–xvi, 10, 13, 19,
    95, 123, 129, 159–160, 183, 228,
    234, 255, 259, 260, 267, 270;
    Auden Group, 122; "l'affaire C,"
    184, 186, 188, 194; The Age of
    Anxiety, 194; The Caucasian Chalk
    Circle, 253–261, 270, 298n8;
    "Dichtung and Wahrheit," 136,
    143, 190; The Dyer's Hand and
    Other Essays, 284n15, 285n36,
    285n4, 288n84; The Enchafèd
    Flood, 138, 284n28, 285n30; For
    the Time Being, 194; "Homage
    to Clio," 125; "In Sickness and
    in Health," 186–187, 189, 194;
    Journey to a War, 122; The Kafka
    Problem, 285n4; "Lay your sleeping
    head my love," 122; Letters from
    Iceland, 122; "Memorial For the
    City," 285n29; Modern Canterbury
    Pilgrims, 283n3; On the Frontier,
    122; "One Circumlocution," xv,
    190–191; The Prolific and the
    Devourer, 160, 282n4; Secondary
    Worlds, 286n11, 286n21; "The
    Sea and the Mirror," 10, 123–158,
    160, 162, 164, 165, 167–168, 170,
    176, 177, 184, 185, 186, 190, 205,
    232, 254, 263, 264, 270; "Spain,"
    122; " 'The Truest Poetry is the
    Most Feigning,' " 194, 288n82
Auerbach, Erich, 281n7
Augustine, 58–59, 60–61, 95, 247, 284
Aury, Dominique, (Pauline Réage—see
    also Desclos), 180–181, 183, 184,
    190, 191
authenticity, 47, 94–95
autobiography, 58, 82, 99, 101, 109,
    130, 166, 184, 189, 220, 246, 248
autonomy, 116, 238, 261, 263

Babel, Tower of, 30–31, 34, 50, 66,
    176; Library of Babel, 177
Badiou, Alain, 35, 51–52, 73, 222,
    235–243, 248, 260, 286n22

Bakhtin, Mikhail, 166
Barrow, John D., 278n9, 278n18,
    278–279n20, 295n144
Barth, Karl, 244, 248
Barthes, Roland, 221
Bataille, Georges, 105, 179–180, 182,
    183, 184, 188, 190, 191, 192,
    195, 222, 247, 261, 267, 288n83,
    289n93
Baudelaire, Charles, 292n57
Baudrillard, Jean, 221
beauty, 2, 47
Beauvoir, Simone de, 12, 191–193,
    195, 219–220, 230, 231, 234, 238,
    258, 289n93
Beckett, Samuel, 65, 171–176, 184,
    193, 267
  Endgame, 172–175, 176; The
    Unnamable, 175–176, 193; Texts
    for Nothing, 175–176
becoming, 203, 208–209, 212, 214,
    219, 223–224, 228, 290n11,
    290n27
being, Being (see also ontology), xiii,
    xv, 3, 4, 20–21, 36, 38, 39, 44,
    45, 46, 51, 52, 56, 65, 73, 79, 87,
    90–91, 99, 119, 122, 125, 141,
    151, 163–164, 166, 176, 181, 183,
    187, 188, 189, 191, 192, 193,
    199, 201, 202, 203–204, 206, 208,
    210–211, 212–219, 221, 230, 236,
    237, 239–243, 246, 263, 267, 269,
    270
  Dasein (see also Heidegger), 201,
    210–211, 214, 217
  "primary being," 42–43, 44, 53
Benjamin, Walter, 264, 270
Bible (see also canon), 57, 60, 187
  Pentateuch, 30; Gospels, 48–50,
    55; Genesis, 29–31, 50, 66, 70,
    72, 187, 299n32; Exodus, 30;
    Deuteronomy, 30; Psalms, 32;
    Proverbs, 32; Ecclesiastes, 32; Job,
    32, 166, 177; Matthew, 49, 115,
    117; Mark, 49, 166, 171, 247;
    Luke, 49; John, 49; Acts, 50, 51;

Romans, 276n49; 1 Corinthians, 50–51, 276n49; Galations, 51; Ephesians, 51, 52, 276n49; Colossians, 276n49
binary, 2–6, 7, 9, 10, 11, 12, 13, 17, 37, 123–124, 145, 148, 151, 152, 154, 158, 168, 185, 199, 221, 272n11
  binary code, 5–6, 242
black hole, 7, 16, 73, 183, 279n28
Blake, William, 115, 119, 135, 164, 166–167, 248
  Blake's O, 267
Blanchot, Maurice, 12, 96–97, 105, 123, 130, 132, 159–166, 167, 170, 195, 201, 212, 222, 226, 247, 267, 280n51
  Thomas l'obscur, 160; *The Space of Literature*, 160–165, 285n18; Outside (*Dehors*), 163, 168, 212, 285n15
blindness, 83, 107, 143, 147, 178, 179, 229
Bonaventure, 46, 59
Bonhoeffer, Dietrich, 244
Boole, George, 5, 6
border, bordering, boundary (*see also* frame, framing and limit, limiting), 21, 32, 33, 34, 80–81, 98, 110–111, 113, 114, 115, 118, 121–122, 123, 126, 127, 129, 145, 146, 148–149, 151, 157, 167, 202, 236
Borges, Luis, 176–177, 180, 184, 193
Bouchard, Larry, 119
Brecht, Bertolt, 190, 253–256, 260, 262, 270, 297n3
  Brecht's O, 255; *Caucasian Chalk Circle*, 20, 114, 253–261, 262, 270 298n8, 299n30
Brontë, Emily, 125–126, 128, 129, 154
Bozorth, Richard, 185, 194
Browning, Robert, 282n13
Buddhism, 71, 243
Budick, Sanford, 278n2

Buell, Frederick, 254
Bussanich, John, 276n36
Butler, Judith, 67, 193, 219
Byron, George Gordon (Lord), 83, 87, 185

Cage, John, 281n8
calculus, 8, 73, 74, 241
Callan, Edward, 284n28
Calvino, Italo, 181–183, 184, 185, 188, 190, 193
Camus, Albert, 130, 223
canon, canonization, canonicity, 55, 57, 59
Cantor, Georg, 237
capitalism, 76, 263, 279n28, 281n2
Caputo, John, 90, 246–247, 251, 293n89, 297n177
cardinality, xiii, 3, 8, 17, 34, 67, 70, 182
Carlsson, Petra, 296n169
Carpenter, Humphrey, 283n4, 285n33, 285n35
Catholicism, 2, 54–59, 60
Celan, Paul, 177–179, 184, 267, 299n1
Céline, Louis Ferdinand, 183
Certeau, Michel de, 247
change, 32–33, 42, 44, 107, 111, 122, 143, 160, 165, 169
  sea-change, 111
chaos, 3, 11, 66, 143, 146, 187, 280n52
chasm, 85–87, 91, 179, 180
Chaucer, Geoffrey, 181
Chopp, Rebecca, 247
Christendom, 58, 59
Christianity, 8, 48–61, 65, 66, 71–72, 73, 155–156, 171, 180–181, 184, 194–195, 206, 240, 244, 247, 248–250, 251
church, Church, 1, 2, 54, 55, 56, 59, 61, 65, 72, 186, 188, 189, 240, 243
cipher, 68–70, 72, 73, 76, 77, 78, 99, 114, 123, 131, 151, 161, 162, 177, 221, 226, 255

circle, circularity, xi, xiii, 1–2, 3, 8, 9–10, 11, 12, 15–16, 21, 31, 48, 66, 79, 82, 84, 86–88, 91, 92, 97, 98–101, 102, 106, 108, 110, 111, 123, 129, 130, 132, 133–135, 137, 142, 143–144, 147–148, 158, 159, 160, 161, 163, 164, 166, 168, 169, 171, 172, 174, 175–176, 187, 199, 205, 212, 217, 220, 225, 226, 228, 230, 231, 232, 234, 236, 242, 250, 251, 255, 256, 259, 261–262, 264, 278n5, 293n86, 298n25
  artificer's circle, 82–88, 112, 113–114, 124, 127, 128, 143, 155, 158, 187, 232, 260; artist's circle (see also Giotto), 147–148, 159; chalk circle, 254–256, 260, 262, 263, 264; hermeneutical circle (see also hermeneutics), 88–94, 96, 100–101, 163, 212, 217, 256; hymeneal ring, 133, 143–144; vicious circle (circulus vitiosus), xiv–xv, 16, 88, 90, 98, 99, 100, 102, 129, 164, 220
circumlocution, xv–xvi, 101, 190–191, 231
circus, circus ring, 127, 128, 141, 158, 230
Cixous, Hélène, 221, 294n111
cliché, 223–224, 226, 228, 229, 234
Coetzee, J.M., 176
coexistence of opposites, coincidentia oppositorum, 33, 37, 39, 45, 48, 80, 248, 269
Coleridge, Samuel Taylor, 64, 87–88, 93
  "Kubla Khan," 83–91, 92, 140, 151, 167, 205
collateral damage, 75–76
comedy, 26–27, 127, 128, 141, 176, 288n65
commentary (see also "The Sea and the Mirror"), 10, 11, 99, 100, 124–126, 127, 129, 133, 139, 144–145, 154, 155, 156, 158, 160, 161, 167–168, 230, 254, 256

computer, computation, 5–6, 71, 98
conceit, 27–28, 188, 193, 223
concept, conceptuality, conception, xi–xii, 5, 10, 12, 13, 14, 17, 20–21, 27–28, 32, 33, 35, 36, 43, 44, 45, 49, 51, 63, 70, 156, 168, 171, 199–200, 203, 204, 212–213, 221, 233, 235, 236, 237, 242–243, 260, 263, 273n2, 274n9, 274n12, 289n3
consciousness, 47, 63, 78, 83, 96–97, 99, 133, 138, 140, 150, 159, 162, 171, 216–219
  self-consciousness (see also self), 3, 63, 78, 79–80, 95, 99, 135, 140, 145, 176, 184, 187, 205, 216, 218, 222, 267–268
Constantine, 55, 56
containment, 3, 16, 69–70, 71, 124, 218, 220
  self-containment, 16, 126, 263
contradiction, 33, 37, 38, 39, 65, 88, 95, 119, 176, 193, 203, 204, 205, 215–216, 238, 255, 262
Copernicus, Nicolaus, 7, 15, 60, 73
Copleston, Frederick, 59, 272n15, 276n37, 276n40
Cornford, F.M., 275n24
Corrigan, Kevin, 276n37
cosmogony, 202, 257
cosmos, cosmology, 7, 18, 39, 32–34, 47, 53, 59, 61, 72, 73, 74, 107, 108, 109, 199, 203, 228
Coupland, Douglas, 297n177
Cox, Harvey, 247
creatio continua, 201, 220
creatio ex nihilo, xii, 77, 88, 221, 260, 272n11
creation's O, 128, 132, 144, 152, 153, 155, 158, 171
creed, the Creed, 55, 56–57, 59, 261
critique, 9, 39, 63, 93, 98, 201, 206, 210
  critical theory, 121
cross, 51, 115, 243, 287n36
crown, xii–xiii, 138, 140, 213, 269, 270
Culler, Jonathan, 277n2

Cunningham, Conor, 276n33, 287n59, 289n1, 290n15
Cunningham, Valentine, 282n12
Cupitt, Don, 247, 297n177
curve, curvature, 3–4, 6–8, 74, 242, 255, 271n9

da Vinci, Leonardo, 2
Dadaism, 136
Dante, Alighieri, 7, 248, 281n7
Davenant, William, 281n6
Davidson, Donald, 65
Davis, Martin, 272n11
Day-Lewis, Cecil, 122
de Vries, Hent, 247
death, 50, 71, 101–102, 107–109, 117, 127–128, 130, 132, 137–140, 142, 151, 156, 158, 160, 161, 162–165, 170, 173, 180, 184, 188, 191, 210–211, 213, 226, 227–228, 245, 248, 257, 259, 269, 285n5
  dance of death, 128, 144, 150; fatalism, 269; fatality, 130, 132, 160, 267; mortality, 83, 128, 131, 149, 150, 153, 157, 171, 193, 269; murder, 186, 269; parricide, 257; regicide, 257
deconstruction (see also Derrida), 19, 193, 200, 221, 223, 233, 245, 246, 249, 279n30
Deleuze, Gilles, 80, 102, 221, 267, 273n2, 275n19
Delphic oracle, 40
Democritus, 35
Derrida, Jacques (see also deconstruction), 2, 81, 119, 129, 132, 199, 205, 218, 220, 221, 223–228, 229–230, 233, 234, 235, 245–247, 249, 261–264, 267, 269, 273n21, 273n5, 279n30, 284n19, 299n32
  Derrida's O, 228, 251
Descartes, René, 17, 18, 19, 61–62, 72–73, 237, 238
  cogito, 17–18, 20, 62, 80, 91, 162; Cartesianism, 17, 18, 62, 73, 91, 201

Desclos, Anne (Pauline Réage—see also Aury), 180–181, 183, 184, 190, 191
desert, 137–139, 284n28
desire, 12, 20, 68, 69, 79, 108, 113, 128, 134, 140–141, 152, 153, 155, 179, 180, 182, 183, 185, 186, 187–189, 190, 191, 193–194, 218–219, 220, 227, 234, 247, 251, 269
despair, 121, 125–126, 153, 154–155, 165, 179, 186
devil (Satan), demon, 129, 135, 248, 284n13
dialectic (see also Hegel), 37–41, 53, 63, 202, 203–205, 290n11, 293n95
Diderot, Denis, 223
Dionysus, 99, 100, 207, 277n66
dissymmetry, asymmetry, 79, 148, 224–225
doctrine, 1, 10, 17, 37, 39, 55–57, 194
Dodgson, Charles (Lewis Carroll), 230–231, 232
Donne, John, 188
Dostoyevsky, Fyodor, 223, 248
doubt, 18, 37, 39, 62, 91, 125–126, 129, 146, 154, 222, 269
Dryden, John, 281n6
dualism, duality, 35, 37, 38–39, 41, 43, 45, 46, 47, 58, 62, 63, 111, 123, 138, 152, 157, 189
dystopia, 137

Eagleton, Terry, 222
Eckhart, Meister, 46, 59
echo, 71–72, 92, 124, 146, 148, 156–158, 224
  Echo, 156
eclipse, 70, 107, 268–269
ecstasy, 12, 13, 16, 100, 179–180, 191, 192, 194, 273n23
ecumenism, 65
ego, Ego (see also "I," self, subjectivity) 79, 95, 99, 135, 136, 142, 280n52
Einstein, Albert, 73
Eleatic philosophers, xi, 36, 38, 41

Eliot, T.S., 65, 170–171, 173, 177, 184, 244
  Waste Land, 170–171; *Four Quartets*, 171
ellipse, 2, 3, 7, 228, 232, 253, 255, 271n8
ellipsis, 2, 228, 232, 268, 271n8
Emerson, Ralph Waldo, 223
Empedocles, 35, 78
empiricism, 62, 65, 74
emptiness, xii, 67, 69, 71–72, 77–78, 79, 80, 106, 108, 119, 126, 139, 140, 144, 152, 156, 159, 166, 168, 170, 178, 181–182, 187, 188, 191, 242, 252, 278n10
Emrig, Rainer, 286n28
Enlightenment, 60, 62, 92
Epicureanism, 48, 50, 241, 272n10
erotics, eroticism (*see also* sex), 12, 20, 140, 179–181, 183, 184–185, 188–193, 233, 235
  Eros, 181, 185, 186, 187–188, 189, 194, 285n36; autoeroticism, 234
eschatology, 31
eternal return, eternal recurrence, xiii–xiv, xv, 3, 25–26, 97–101, 164, 176, 177, 206, 207, 208, 209, 210, 212, 250, 272n17
eternity, 71
ethics, 9, 19–21, 65, 129, 131, 194, 252, 256, 262, 264, 284n13
etiology (aetiology), 53
Euclid, 35, 200
Eve, 31
evil, 31, 72, 117, 132, 138, 202, 248, 282n11
  theodicy, 202
event, 15, 19, 31, 40, 51–52, 54, 164, 206, 223, 237, 239–240, 241, 242, 243, 248, 276n5
  evental site, 239
excess, 14, 26, 40, 75, 180, 191, 223, 239, 240, 249 293n95
Existentialism, the existential, 65, 91, 92–93, 130, 137, 153, 176, 184, 193, 210–218, 222, 237, 269

expletive, 67–69, 82, 128, 139, 268
eye, 11, 77–79, 102, 105, 142–143, 144, 145, 178–179

faith, 30, 49, 51, 52, 54, 55, 57, 60–62, 66, 73, 125–126, 154, 247
  faithfulness, 188, 189; bad faith, 9, 216
fascism, 122
fate, Fate, xiii, 34, 99, 108, 187
Feltham, Oliver, 296n154
feminism, 12, 92, 191–193, 194, 219, 234, 235, 238, 241, 249
figure, figuring, figuration, xii–xiii, xv–xvi, 3, 5, 7, 8, 9–10, 11–12, 13, 16–17, 19, 21, 30, 66, 69, 77, 80, 87, 96, 99, 100, 101, 103, 105, 114, 126, 128, 135, 144, 151, 155, 161, 164, 165, 167, 168, 169, 171, 177, 178, 179, 181, 195, 209, 210, 213, 218, 220, 221, 224, 226, 229, 230, 233, 242, 246, 248252, 264, 267–268, 270, 271n8, 272n10, 281n7, 286n15, 292n74
  transfiguration, 166
film, 122
fin de siècle, 167
Findlay, J.N., 275n26
Flaubert, Gustave, 292n57
Flynn, Thomas, 292n70–71
Forster, E.M., 71–72, 87, 118
Foucault, Michel, 219, 221, 292n57
Fox, Nik Farrell, 292n70
frame, framing (*see also* border, bordering and limit, limiting), 13, 14, 80–81, 82, 87, 110, 112, 113, 115, 117, 118, 119, 122, 126, 142, 143–144, 149, 150, 152, 156, 157, 281n8
Franke, William, 289n1, 296n156
freedom, freeing, liberty, liberation, 20, 60–61, 101, 109, 112–113, 115–118, 135, 146, 153, 164, 192, 194, 202–204, 216–217, 258, 260, 261–262, 270
Frege, Gottlob, 235

Freud, Sigmund, 19, 80, 189, 201, 263,
    285n31
    Freudianism, 169, 183;
    psychoanalysis, 229, 233, 238, 244,
    245
frivolity, 123, 131, 171, 176, 184, 255
Frye, Northrop, 109
Fuller, John, 155–156, 184–185,
    284n14, 288n78

Gadamer, Hans-Georg, 214
Gasché, Rodolphe, 279n30
Gehry, Frank, 7
genealogy, 31, 52, 54, 57, 59, 219, 220,
    221, 228, 289n1
gender, 12, 191–194, 219, 221, 230,
    232, 233, 235, 238
genesis, 84, 89, 146, 200, 220, 248,
    250, 254
Genet, Jean, 224
geometry, 3, 4, 6, 7, 8, 9, 71, 200
gift, 53–54, 119, 153, 226
    giving, self-giving, 52, 53–54, 58–59,
    60, 61, 64, 181, 226
Giotto, di Bondone (O of Giotto), 1,
    2, 21, 25, 134, 135, 144, 148, 155,
    159, 171
Gnosticism, 47, 48, 49, 58
God (see also monotheism, theology),
    7, 8, 18, 29, 31, 43, 49, 52, 55,
    58–62, 66, 73, 74, 125, 177, 180,
    192, 202, 205, 206, 209, 243–246,
    248–250, 263, 270, 282n11
    Absolute Reason, 46; Atman, 71;
    Cosmic Poet, 281n7; Creator, 52,
    115; Crucified God, 249–250;
    Elohim, 29, 52; Father, 49, 52,
    56, 58; Godhead, 202, 249–250;
    Lord, 30, 52, 55, 56, 70, 177,
    178; Prime Mover, 42–43, 44,
    46; Unknown God, 50; Yahweh,
    29–31, 34, 52, 166, 273n5; death
    of God, 19, 65, 98, 100, 122, 167,
    206, 243–245, 247–251, 280n52;
    deus ex machina, 156; Imago Dei,
    199–200

Goethe, Johann Wolfgang von, 222
good, Good, 31, 47, 49, 53, 72, 117, 119
grace, 114, 115–116, 187
Greene, Graham, 299n32
Guattari, Felix, 80, 222, 273n2, 275n19

Hamilton, William, 247
Hampson, Daphne, 297n177
harmony, 7, 33–34, 50, 62, 64–65, 76,
    110, 115, 133
Hardt, Michael, 286n27
Hart, Kevin, 162–163, 285n6
Hass, Andrew W., 289n100, 290n28–
    29, 294n111, 295n126
heaven, heavens, 1, 7–8, 15, 29, 30,
    34, 42, 49, 56, 66, 74, 107, 108,
    115, 125, 142, 153, 157, 178,
    282n11
Hebrews, The (Ancient Israelites),
    29–32, 52, 54, 259
Hegel, G.W.F. (see also dialectic), 4,
    19, 63, 64, 79–80, 95–97, 124,
    161, 164, 169, 194, 201, 202–205,
    206, 207, 208, 209, 210, 211–212,
    214–215, 216, 218, 219, 224, 225,
    236, 238, 240, 244, 248, 250,
    263, 267, 276n32, 289n3, 291n37,
    293n95, 298n25
    Hegelianism, 14, 34, 52, 63, 132,
    164, 167, 204–205, 262, 263;
    Hegel's O, 205, 208, 228; Geist
    (Spirit), 201, 203; Lectures
    on Aesthetics, 205; Lectures on
    the Philosophy of Religion, 205;
    Phenomenology of Spirit, 63, 95,
    203, 205, 210, 267, 280n48;
    Science of Logic, 203–204, 211,
    276n32
Heidegger, Martin (see also being/
    Dasein), 11, 40–41, 76, 90–91,
    129, 161, 163, 199, 201, 208,
    209, 210–213, 214–215, 216–217,
    218, 219, 225, 235, 236, 242, 267,
    275n20, 275n26, 290n15, 290n18,
    291n31
Heidegger's O, 213

Heisenberg, Werner, 74, 93, 94
hell, 282n11, 284n28
henology, 32
Heraclitus, 33–34; 35
Herder, Johann Gottfried von, 64
heresy, 55, 57, 58
hermeneutics, interpretation, 9, 14,
    26–27, 31, 32, 57, 58, 60–61,
    76–77, 87, 88–93, 99–101, 151,
    159, 210, 202, 206, 207–211,
    216–217, 229, 233–234, 236, 240,
    256, 263, 294n110
  hermeneutical circle (see also circle),
    88–94, 96, 100–101, 163, 212,
    217, 256
Hinduism, 71–72
history, historicity, xii–xiii, 9, 10,
    11–12, 15, 17–18, 25, 31–32, 34,
    52, 54, 66, 70, 74, 91, 95, 98,
    100, 107, 123, 159–160, 164–165,
    167, 169, 176, 177, 183, 189, 190,
    192–193, 199, 203, 205, 206, 211,
    212, 213, 218–219, 220–221, 234,
    242, 243, 244, 255, 260, 262,
    286n22
  Heilsgeschichte, 31; history of ideas,
    29, 54, 63, 64, 66, 95, 122, 165,
    167, 200, 220, 286n27; end of
    history, 165, 167
Hölderlin, Friedrich, 11, 64, 118–119,
    160, 167, 241, 282–283n15,
    288n73
hole, 11, 18, 68, 145, 152, 183, 226,
    236, 242, 278n5, 183, 279n28
  black hole, 7, 16, 73, 183, 279n28
Hollywood, Amy, 289n93
Holocaust, 168, 178
Holy Spirit, 50–51, 52, 55, 58
Homer, 33, 166
homograph, 246
homology, 114
homonym, 68, 102
homophone, 246
homosexuality, 12, 184–186, 189,
    193–194, 234, 267, 288n73

hope, 5, 46, 51, 52, 54, 68, 125–126,
    128, 138, 139, 141, 151, 152, 154,
    155, 157, 163
Hopkins, Gerard Manley, 274n10
Horkheimer, Max, 166
humanism, 60, 218
Hume, David, 19
Husserl, Edmund, 237
hypostasis, 46–47, 56
hystera, 229, 234, 260

"I" (see also ego, self, subjectivity), 2–3,
    4–5, 7, 9, 11, 13, 18, 20, 62, 95,
    98–99, 100, 101, 102, 132, 136,
    156, 157–158, 160, 161, 162, 163,
    164, 165, 167, 168, 169, 170,
    175–176, 177, 188, 189, 190, 191,
    192, 193, 206, 211, 232
idealism, 63, 65, 205, 210
  German Idealism, 210, 283n15
identity, xiv, 18, 30, 45, 58, 91–93, 96,
    98–101, 102, 113, 166, 214, 248
  pseudo-identity, 268; self-identity, 29,
    79, 100, 193, 202, 217, 219, 226,
    280n52; sexual identity, 193
illegitimacy, 107, 257, 259–260, 261, 265
illusion, 47, 79, 109, 127–128, 131,
    141, 150, 157, 161, 167–168
  disillusion, 131, 141, 157, 185
imagination, the imaginative, 4, 64, 84,
    86, 96, 124–126, 129, 149, 152,
    154, 192, 217–218, 225, 226, 249,
    253, 269, 282n11
immanence, 47, 48, 51, 192, 194, 240,
    248, 250
incarnation, 55, 156, 213, 236, 248
individualism, 59, 60, 62
  individuality, individuation, 64, 153,
    194, 239, 261, 280n52
ineffability, 48, 53, 119, 180, 243
infinity, the infinite, 7, 13, 44, 64, 71,
    72–73, 74, 100, 101, 180, 202,
    225, 240, 242, 263
inspiration, 59, 83, 125, 142, 147
integrity, 119, 124

interjection, 67
intellect, 46–47, 53, 54, 59, 160, 168, 220, 222, 223, 267, 276n48
Intellectual-Principle, 45–47, 53, 276n41
Irigaray, Luce, 220, 221, 228–235, 247, 267
Irigaray's O, 235
irony, xii, 20, 27, 54, 57, 75, 80, 82, 96, 107, 132, 142, 143, 218, 221, 223, 228, 244, 245, 249
irrationality, 3, 8, 12
irrational numbers, 3
Isherwood, Christopher, 122, 184
Islam, 72, 76
island, 11, 109–115, 118, 119, 126, 130, 139, 143

Jabès, Edmund, 2, 247
Jacobi, F.H., 290n15
James, Henry, 126, 146, 156
Jameson, Fredric, 222, 282n12
Jantzen, Grace, 247
Jasper, David, 250, 296n168–169
Jaspers, Karl, 280n51
Jeanrond, Werner, 277n54
Jesus (Christ), 48–51, 59, 243
the Son, 49–50, 55–56, 58, 166; the Bridegroom, 59; death of Jesus (Christ), 52, 54, 287n36; resurrection of Jesus (Christ), 54, 166
Job, 32
joke, joking, humour, 25–28, 65, 123, 141–142, 190
Joyce, James, 65, 169, 171, 173, 176, 225, 228, 245, 248
Joyce's O, 267; *Finnegans Wake*, 169, 171, 245; Finnegans O, 267; *Ulysses*, 170
justice, justness, 20, 32, 138, 147, 149, 154, 166, 261, 265, 268, 270

Kabbalah, Kabbalarianism, 34, 276n32
Kafka, Franz, 121, 160, 161, 163, 167, 190, 244, 285n4

Kallman, Chester, 130, 184–185, 186, 188, 288n76, 297n3
Kant, Immanuel, 19, 28, 37, 63, 74, 96, 98, 202, 217, 218, 225, 238, 289–290n3
Kaplan, Robert, 278n9, 278n13
Kaufmann, Walter, 209, 290n16
Kearney, Richard, 297n177
Kearns, Cleo McNelly, 296n158
kenosis, 119, 124, 248
Kepler, Johannes, 2, 7
khora, chora, 228–230, 260
Kierkegaard, Søren, 121, 129, 131, 132, 153, 160, 187, 189, 204, 244, 248, 284n13, 288n65, 299n32
Kirsch, Arthur, 123, 130, 186, 283n5, 284n14, 284n28, 285n31, 288n73, 289n99
Klemm, David, 282n14
Klossowski, Pierre, xiii–xiv, 97–98, 99–101, 102, 190, 206, 209
Krell, David Farrell, 283n15, 291n37, 291n45
Kristeva, Julia (*see also* abjection), 221, 228–229, 247, 263, 285n15
Kuhn, Thomas, 1, 13–16, 31, 62, 262
Kundera, Milan, 66, 123

Lacan, Jacques, 19, 79–80, 189, 190, 221, 233, 245, 263, 267
Lacoste, Jean-Yves, 247
language, 4, 5, 6, 10, 19, 27, 30, 33–34, 41, 66, 67, 72, 117, 119, 136, 137, 152, 154, 155, 161, 162, 165, 169, 213, 227, 236, 243, 246, 247, 249, 286n21
pictographic language, 70; prisohouse of language, 117, 282n12
Lao Tzu, 46
laughter, 25–28, 66, 127–128, 141, 158, 172
law, 20, 21, 30, 31, 50, 51, 61, 64, 92, 147, 256, 259–260, 261–262, 264, 270, 298–299n27
Le Corbusier, 7

Leahy, David, 17–18
legitimacy, 21, 91, 107, 231, 257–258,
    259–260, 264, 268
Leibniz, G.W., xi, 5, 6, 52, 62, 202,
    272n10
Leucippus, 35
Levinas, Emmanuel, 17, 20, 221, 247,
    263
literary criticism, 92, 225–226, 245
    New Criticism, 245
Lyotard, Jean-François, 221
liminality, 132
limit, limiting, 3, 15, 21, 35, 38, 63,
    80, 111, 112, 113–115, 122, 135,
    138–139, 151, 202, 215, 241
linguistics, 14, 30, 65, 88, 228–229,
    233
liturgy, 250
logical positivism, 5
logos, Logos, 33–34, 38, 40–41, 42, 49,
    50, 51, 53, 70, 72, 200, 223, 224,
    225, 228, 274n10, 288n81
    logocentricity, 41, 224
love, xii, 49, 51–52, 53–54, 68–69,
    105, 110, 115, 136, 138–140, 141,
    142–143, 147, 153, 156, 157, 180,
    182, 184, 186–188, 190, 191–192,
    194, 227, 243, 276n53
    agape, Agape, 52, 194, 289n92
Lucretius, 200, 241
Luther, Martin, 60–61, 62
    Lutheranism, 201

madness, 102, 106–107, 108, 109
magic, magician, 82, 128, 133–134,
    143–144, 149, 150–151, 155, 176,
    232
Mallarmé, Stéphane, 160, 167, 223,
    241, 267
Manichaeism, 58
Mann, Thomas, 223
Manoussakis, John Panteleimon,
    297n177
many, the many, multiplicity (see also
    plurality), xv, 2, 28, 29–30, 33,
    35, 36–37, 39, 40–41, 42, 44, 45,
    46–47, 49, 50, 52, 55–56, 59, 63,

66, 201, 208, 209, 221, 233–235,
    237, 238–242, 243, 277n66
margin, 156, 157, 215, 224–225
Marinot, Steve, 292n70
Marion, Jean-Luc, 247
Marx, Karl, 19, 201
    Marxism, 122, 218, 235–236, 241,
    286n22
mask, masking, 101
material monism, 32–33, 42, 52
materialism, 108, 200, 241, 243
    historical materialism, 205, 286n22
mathematics, 5, 8, 10, 34, 43, 65, 70,
    71, 72, 73, 74, 151, 200, 237–241,
    242, 278n9–10, 280n1, 295n147
McDiarmid, Lucy, 133, 142, 283n5
McDiarmid, Lucy and John
    McDiarmid, 284n16
Meinwald, Constance C., 275n24
Melissus, 35
Melville, Herman, 223, 248
Mendelson, Edward, 185, 284n14,
    284n28, 286n9, 288n77
mercy, 114–115, 155
meridian, 253, 268
messianism, Messiah, 31, 50
meta-explanation, 52–53, 57, 59, 60,
    62, 63, 66
metaphor, metaphorics, metaphoricity,
    4, 5, 6–8, 9–10, 12, 17, 20–21, 28,
    78, 82, 98, 108, 110, 119, 123, 128,
    133, 146, 148, 152, 155, 156, 184,
    229, 233, 251, 276n49, 286n21
metaphysics, the metaphysical (see also
    Aristotle/Metaphysics), 8, 9, 10,
    18, 35–37, 39, 41, 43–45, 59, 62,
    65, 98, 136, 186, 188, 205–206,
    208, 210, 211, 212, 213, 218, 219,
    229, 230, 244, 248, 251, 273n22,
    276n36, 281n2, 297n176, 297n177
    metaphusis (see also phusis), 36, 37,
    41, 42, 56; metaphysical poets,
    188; post-metaphysical, 92
metonymy, 27, 75
military, 20, 55, 74–75
Miller, Mitchell H., 275n24
Milton, John, 7, 248

mimesis, mimetic theory, 81–82, 112, 125, 165, 199–200, 232, 278n5

mirror, mirroring (*see also* reflection), 11, 67, 77–82, 84, 88, 109–112, 114, 115, 116, 119, 121, 123, 124, 126, 127, 131, 136, 138, 142–146, 148, 150, 152, 154, 155, 157–158, 160, 165, 176, 178, 180, 226, 230–232, 235, 285n3

mirror stage, 79; speculum, 11, 77, 109–111, 119, 124, 143, 145, 221, 226, 230, 232; tain of the mirror, 78, 119

modernity, modernism, 1, 2, 7, 12, 17–20, 32, 57, 58, 60, 63, 64, 65–66, 78, 87, 92, 98, 102, 106, 107, 109, 112, 122, 125, 131, 134, 168, 169, 170, 172, 177, 185, 201, 203, 211, 220, 222, 238, 242, 244, 248, 251, 261, 267, 268, 273n23

late modernity, 4, 5, 6, 20, 124, 167, 230, 238, 247

monad, monadology, 53, 62, 272n10

monism, 35, 36, 37, 48, 52, 62, 208

monotheism (*see also* God), 8, 29–30, 49, 50, 51, 55, 62, 180, 244, 245

Moore, Stephen, 247

morality, morals, 122–123, 147, 206, 252, 259, 270

Moses, 29

Mourelatos, Alexander P.D., 275n20

Munch, Edvard, 159

Murdoch, Iris, 283n15

muse, Muses, 125, 128, 142, 147, 186

music, 34, 123, 130, 170, 175, 281n8, 285n30, 285n36

mysticism, 38, 44, 46, 48, 52, 53, 63, 71, 177, 192, 194, 210, 230, 289n92–93

mystics, 46, 59, 192, 194

myth, mythology, *mythos*, 31, 33, 36, 40–41, 53, 79, 200, 213, 223, 225, 228, 229

Nāgārjuna, 46

name, naming, xiii, xiv, 30, 40, 45, 68–69, 97, 100, 113, 131, 181, 182, 226–228, 229, 232, 233, 241, 243, 245, 251, 255, 262, 268

unnameable, 175, 237

Nancy, Jean-Luc, 221, 277n59

narcissism, 78, 79, 80, 94, 142, 276n37

narrative, narrativity, metanarrative, 31–33, 39–41, 46, 49, 52, 53, 55–61, 162, 221, 227, 228, 231, 232, 236, 244, 249

negation, negativity, nihilation, xiv, 3, 9, 10, 11–12, 19–20, 45, 63, 67, 71, 76, 77, 79, 96, 102, 115, 118, 119, 123, 124, 129, 131, 132, 135, 142, 145–147, 149, 151, 153–154, 156, 158, 161, 162, 166, 170–171, 177–180, 181, 186, 190, 192–193, 194, 195, 201–220, 221, 224, 229, 236–237, 240, 243, 245, 246, 247, 250, 254, 258, 260, 261, 263, 268, 290n11, 292n73, 293n95

negation of God, 19, 202, 244–245; negation of negation, 20, 156; negative image, 155, 224; positive negation, 166, 169, 201; self-negation, 102, 121, 144, 150, 161, 166, 181, 192, 207–208, 211–212, 219, 251

Negri, Antonio, 286n27

Nelson, Gerald, 284n23, 284n25

Neoplatonism (*see also* Plotinus), 9, 38, 41, 43, 44, 47, 48, 49, 52, 54, 56, 61, 63, 153, 192, 276n48

Nicholas of Cusa, 59

Nietzsche, Friedrich, xiii–xiv, xv, 3, 19, 25–26, 65, 97–101, 102, 107, 122, 161, 164, 167, 190, 201, 205–210, 211–213, 214–215, 218, 221, 222, 223, 226, 227, 243, 244–245, 247, 248, 249, 267, 270, 274n19, 277n66, 280n51–52, 282n12, 294n110, 295n146

Nietzsche's O, xiv, 206, 207, 209, 213, 228; *ressentiment*, 207; *Übermensch*, 207; will to power, 107, 206–208, 209, 210, 211–212, 291n31

nihilism, 180, 206–209, 210, 211–213,
  218, 248, 250, 251, 267, 269–270,
  290n15
Noah, 30
nominalism, 240
nonbeing, 36, 38, 39, 45, 202,
  203–204, 208, 215, 285n5
  nonexistence, 118, 129, 130, 158,
  182, 183, 193
nothing, nothingness, nought, nullity,
  xi–xvi, xv, 3, 5, 7, 12, 14, 16–17,
  28, 36, 38, 44, 53, 68, 70–73,
  76–77, 80, 88, 95, 97, 101, 105,
  107–109, 128, 129, 130, 131, 141,
  143, 146, 157, 159–160, 161,
  162–164, 165, 170–172, 175–176,
  177, 178–179, 181–182, 188, 190,
  191, 192, 193, 199, 200, 203–204,
  210–211, 212–213, 214–219, 221,
  222, 225, 227–228, 230, 233, 234,
  235, 237, 240–243, 246, 248,
  249, 250–252, 258, 260, 267–268,
  269–270, 279n22, 281n2, 285n3,
  289–290n3, 291n37, 295n144
noumenon, noumena (see also
  phenomenon), 37, 47, 63, 64, 74,
  146, 202
number, numbers, numbering,
  numerology, 5–6, 8, 11, 12, 16,
  34–35, 42–43, 55–56, 67, 70–73,
  77, 128, 167, 181, 200, 227, 241,
  242–243, 277n55
  even vs. odd, 35; tetractys, 34,
  274n14, 281n1–2

Oedipus (see also Sophocles), 83, 258
one, oneness, One, singularity (see also
  unity), 1–2, 4, 5–6, 8–9, 10, 11,
  13, 14–16, 18–19, 21, 25–66, 67,
  70, 71, 79, 91, 95, 98, 99–100,
  102, 106–107, 109, 110, 122, 123,
  124, 132, 133, 136–137, 142–144,
  146, 147–148, 150, 151, 153, 156,
  158, 164, 165, 166, 167, 169, 174,
  178–179, 183, 189, 191, 192–193,
  199–200, 201, 202–203, 205–206,

213, 220, 221, 222, 225, 226, 228,
  231–235, 238–240, 242, 244, 245,
  248, 252, 253, 257, 263, 264–265,
  267, 268–269, 289n92
ontology (see also being), 34, 37, 42,
  44, 53, 61, 90, 164, 202, 215, 217,
  218, 219, 235, 237, 239, 240–241,
  242, 276n32, 291n54
opera, 154, 185, 285n36; libretto, 122
ordinality, 3, 8, 17, 70
origin, origination, xiii, xv, 2, 5, 6,
  9, 11–12, 29, 87–89, 93, 94, 96,
  98, 118, 119, 124, 126, 148–149,
  151, 154, 159–165, 167, 168, 169,
  171, 192, 199, 200, 209, 211, 212,
  213, 215–216, 220–221, 224, 228,
  230, 237, 238, 239, 243, 248, 251,
  257, 260, 261, 262, 269, 280n43,
  291n54, 293n86
  original, originality, 11, 40, 60, 84,
  87–89, 91, 112, 119, 124, 125,
  127, 154, 157, 158, 159, 189, 193,
  209, 215, 223–224, 230–231
orthodoxy, 48, 55–57, 59, 167, 180,
  194, 201, 244
Osborne, Charles, 288n65
other, Other, otherness, othering,
  alterity, 10, 16–17, 20, 46, 79,
  80, 146, 151, 154, 156, 191, 201,
  216–218, 219, 221, 228, 231,
  232–233, 249–250, 262–264, 270,
  280n51, 293n89
  Wholly Other (tout autre), 17, 46,
  145–146, 155, 156, 164, 226, 246,
  263
Otto, Rudolf, 46

Pascal, Blaise, 72–73, 178
paganism, 55, 61, 83
parable, parabolics, 21, 176, 182, 190,
  236, 244, 254, 255–256, 258, 259,
  260, 261, 263–264, 270, 299n32
paradigm, 1, 12, 21, 25, 36, 37, 39, 48,
  52, 53–57, 58, 59, 62–63, 65–66,
  70, 91, 93, 108, 167, 201, 202,
  262, 275n21

paradigm shift, 13–17, 18, 31, 107, 281n2

paradox, xii, 12, 28, 33, 36, 37, 68, 69–70, 71, 75, 80, 88, 90–91, 99, 102, 118, 133, 141, 142, 146, 156, 157, 158, 165, 167, 169, 171, 175, 178, 191, 192, 201, 204, 210, 218, 238, 252, 284n13

pardon, 114–115

Parmenides, xi, xii, 35, 36–40, 52, 70, 200, 213, 223, 241, 243

patriarchy, 219

Patristics (Church Fathers), 9, 55, 57, 58

Pattison, George, 291n39

Paul (Apostle), 48–52, 54, 60, 235, 240, 243

phallus, phallocentrism, 186, 233, 288n81

phenomenology, 63, 214, 215, 267

phenomenon, phenomena (see also noumenon), 1, 2, 37, 47, 62–63, 74, 76, 78, 202

phusis (see also metaphysics/metaphusis), 36, 37, 41, 42, 44, 47, 56

Pi, 3

Picard, Max, 286n21

Plato, 9, 35–41, 43, 44, 46, 47, 48, 52, 53, 78, 99, 200, 229, 230, 234
    Platonism, 58, 61, 206; Forms, 36–37, 39, 41, 42, 44, 275n21; Parmenides, 35–41, 46, 49, 58; Phaedo, 41; Phaedrus, 41; Republic, 37, 39, 229; Symposium, 41; Timaeus, 228, 275n27, 276n41, 279n29

plenitude, 44–48, 53, 214–216, 218

Plotinus, 44–48, 58, 244, 274n7

plurality (see also many, the many, multiplicity), 13, 29, 31, 37, 45, 47, 55, 60, 100, 206, 208, 237

poesis, 10, 83, 87, 96, 114, 124, 146, 148, 200, 209, 213, 273n17, 282n15

poetics, 12, 81–82, 195

point, 272n10

politics, 9, 14, 19, 31, 43, 51, 55, 56, 60, 65, 107, 122–123, 148, 159, 185, 186, 224, 235–236, 241, 243, 244, 254, 258, 260, 262, 264
    communism, 168, 262; democracy, 20, 261–263; liberal democracy, 168; neoliberalism, 263; theocracy, 262; totalitarianism, 65, 208

polytheism, 50

Pontius Pilate, 259, 261

Porphyry, 44, 58

positivism, 65

postcolonialism, 92

postmodernity, postmodernism, postmodern, 7, 9, 12, 13, 19–20, 64, 121, 131, 168, 172, 183, 214, 218, 219, 220, 221, 222, 223, 230, 234, 235, 237, 238, 241, 244–245, 249, 251, 267, 286n28, 292n70, 295n146, 296n158, 296n162, 296n164, 297n175
    post-postmodernity, 20, 222

poststructuralism, 219

potentiality (see also actuality), 42, 44–45

Presocratics, 9, 32–35, 36, 41, 52, 55, 62, 70, 99

Price, Daniel, 296n168

prison, prison-house, imprisonment (incarceration), 3, 113–117, 124, 146, 150, 157

progress, progression, progressivism, xiv, 3, 9, 14, 18, 31, 70, 138, 220

prosody, 67

Proust, Marcel, 223

pseudonym, pseudonymity, 179, 180–181, 244, 268

psychology, 66, 83, 91, 116, 138, 180, 185, 206

Purchas, Samuel, 280n39

Pynchon, T., 28

pyramid, 71

Pythagoras, Pythagoreans, 16, 34–35, 42, 43, 45, 70, 277n55

quantum mechanics, 74

Rabelais François, 166
Ragland-Sullivan, Ellie, 79
rationality (see also reason), xiv, 5, 8,
    12, 19, 28, 32, 33, 34, 38, 43, 60,
    70, 99, 202, 250, 256, 264
    pre-rationality, 234; rationalism, 264
reason, Reason, reasoning (see also
    rationality), xi, xiii, 17–18, 35, 38,
    40, 41, 53, 63, 106, 125–126, 128,
    129, 189, 200–201, 202, 206, 222,
    225, 228
reflection (see also mirror), 1, 11,
    77–80, 81, 82, 84, 109, 111–113,
    119, 121, 125, 127, 131, 143,
    144–145, 148–149, 150, 154,
    157–158, 164, 180, 186, 199, 205,
    230–231, 232
    self-reflection, 3, 139, 145, 150, 205,
    216, 218, 239
Reformation, Reformers
    (Protestantism), 57, 60, 247
relativity, 73
Renaissance, 60, 72, 122
responsibility, 20–21, 100, 131, 217,
    263–264, 268, 270
resurrection, 50–51, 54, 57, 139, 248,
    257
revelation, xiii, xv, 61, 72, 100, 125,
    268
revolution, 1, 5, 6, 7, 13–15, 18, 20,
    51, 67, 72, 73, 97, 99, 257, 259,
    261, 267
    French Revolution, 239–240, 261
rhetoric, 146, 157
Ricoeur, Paul, 201
Rilke, Rainer Maria, 160, 167, 213
ring (see also circle/hymeneal ring,
    circus ring), 87, 102, 133, 144,
    158, 178, 188, 278n5
rogue, 14, 74, 150, 224, 259, 260, 261,
    262–265, 267, 270; rogue state,
    261, 262, 263, 298n27
Romantics, Romanticism, 63, 87, 126,
    138, 205
    German Romantics, 63–64, 223

Rotman, Brian, 272n11, 278n5, 278n7,
    278n15, 278n17, 280n43, 280n1,
    281n2–3
Rorty, Richard, 65, 222
Rousseau, Jean-Jacques, 223
Rubenstein, Richard, 247
Rumi, 46
Russell, Bertrand, 65

Sachs, Nelly, 177
Said, Edward, 222
Śamkara, 46
Sartre, Jean-Paul, 130, 192, 194,
    214–220, 221, 222, 223, 235–236,
    237, 240, 242, 260
Saussure, Ferdinand de, 3
Schelling, F.W.J., 64, 202, 210, 244
Schlegel, Friedrich von, 64
Schleiermacher, Friedrich, 64
Schmitt, Carl, 298n27
Scholasticism, 59, 61
Schürmann, Reiner, 47, 273n6, 275n20
Scolnicov, Samuel, 275n24
Scotus Eriugena, John, 59
sea, 6, 11, 111, 112, 119, 122, 123–
    124, 130–131, 134–135, 137–140,
    142, 143, 145, 149, 152, 158, 186,
    230, 241, 284n28, 285n30
secret, 47, 77, 128, 129, 149, 166, 167,
    226, 247, 252
Seife, Charles, 72, 278n6, 278n8–9,
    278n16, 278n18, 279n21
self, Self, selfhood, oneself (see also
    consciousness, containment, ego,
    gift/giving, identity, negation,
    reflection, subjectivity), 11, 17, 46,
    54, 57, 58, 59, 61, 62, 63, 78–80,
    87, 88, 90, 93, 94–95, 100, 107,
    110, 111, 121–122, 126, 130–131,
    136, 137, 140, 150, 156, 157, 160,
    162–163, 176, 178, 180, 181, 187,
    188, 189–190, 191, 192, 193, 194,
    209, 217, 218, 221, 226, 227, 228,
    230, 248, 261–262, 263, 276n53,
    277n64, 285n4, 289n100, 292n57,

298n25; for-itself, 80, 216, 217, 218
in-itself, 79, 214, 216, 218, 219; not-self, 79, 131, 156, 248; self-abandonment, 191, 193; self-awareness, 126, 133, 139; self-destruction, 108, 115; self-fracture, 79, 220, 238; self-interpretation, 100, 212; self-knowledge, 79; self-movement, 204, 205; self-originating, 45; self-presence, 45; self-realization, 64, 79, 110; self-sovereignty, 193; self-sundering, 203, 205; self-text, 60; self-understanding, 4
semiotics, semiology, 27, 67
September 11, 2001 (9/11), 19, 75–77, 261, 262, 279n24–25, 279n28
set theory, 237–240, 241, 242, 295n144
sex, sexuality, sexualisation (*see also* erotics), 20, 26, 180–181, 182, 184–186, 188, 189, 193–194, 233–235
non-sex, 233–234; pornography, 180, 190, 234; sexual consummation, 182–183, 190, 258; sexual orgasm (climax, O), 179, 181, 188, 234
Shakespeare, William, 10, 68, 81, 106–119, 124, 126, 129, 130, 145, 146–149, 151, 154, 166, 170, 177, 186, 226, 230, 254, 264, 267, 285n30, 299n30
Shakespeare's O, xiii, 110, 111, 228; Globe theatre, 126, 148, 150, 166; *Hamlet*, 81–82, 111, 112, 114, 116, 118, 129, 141, 148, 170, 256, 268, 269, 272n10, 281n7; *King Henry the Fifth*, 114; *King Henry VI, Part II*, 74 (279n23), 77 (279n26); *King Lear*, xi–xiii, xv, 82, 102, 105–109, 110, 111, 118, 129, 141, 166, 170, 212–213, 243, 257, 258, 268, 269, 270, 281n7; Lear's O, xiii, 108, 228; *King Richard II*, 67 (277n1), 77 (279n26), 97

(280n49); *Love's Labour's Lost*, 82 (279n37), 88 (280n44); *Macbeth*, 114, 268–270, 281n7; *Midsummer Night's Dream*, 82; *Pericles*, 285n30; *Romeo and Juliet*, 67–69, 80, 101–102, 226–228, 268; Juliet's O, 228; Romeo's O, 228; *The Tempest* (Ariel, Prospero, Caliban), 11, 82, 109–119, 124, 126–127, 130, 132, 133, 139, 141, 146, 148, 154, 155, 157–158, 160, 166, 231, 256, 268, 269, 281n7, 285n30; Caliban's O, 152, 158, 228; *The Two Gentleman of Verona*, 69 (278n4); *The Winter's Tale*, 82, 139–140, 285n30
Shelley, Percy Bysshe, 88
Shema Yisrael, 30, 32
silence, 28, 45, 46, 73, 128–129, 130–132, 137, 153, 154–155, 156, 162, 165, 166, 174–175, 178, 193, 244, 252, 282n11, 284n13, 286n21
"sovereign silence," 298n22
Smith, Stevie, 280n41
socialism, 122
sociology, 66
Socrates, xi, 35–37, 39–40, 46, 49
sola scriptura, 57, 60
solipsism, 62
Sontag, Susan, 180
Sophocles (*Oedipus at Colonus*—see also Oedipus), 166
soul, Soul, xiii, xv, 35, 37, 41, 43, 46–47, 61, 62, 71, 99, 100, 125, 154, 155, 189, 192, 194, 230, 269
sovereignty, xi–xiii, 1, 8, 10, 19, 21, 43, 61, 65, 66, 92, 96, 105–107, 109, 110, 119, 122, 135, 136–137, 138, 139–141, 143, 146, 161, 162, 167, 187, 191–193, 194–195, 200, 209, 213 220, 222, 225, 230, 231, 232, 238, 241, 244, 252, 253, 256–260, 261–263, 264–265, 267, 268–270, 298n27
sovereign subject, 191–193, 219, 220, 231, 232, 234, 235, 238, 258

Spender, Stephen, 122
Spinoza, Baruch, 62, 248
stage, staginess, xv, xvi, 65, 82, 106,
    111, 114, 126–127, 133, 137, 145,
    146–147, 154, 155, 164, 165, 172,
    185, 209, 230, 235, 267, 269–270;
    proscenium arch, 145, 149, 155
stage direction, 68, 261
Stern, James and Tania, 254, 255
Sterne, Laurence, 166
Stevens, Wallace, 183
Stoicism, 48, 50, 203
straight line, 3–4, 7–8, 30, 66, 242,
    271n9
Soutter, Michel, 231, 232–233
sublation, Aufhebung (see also Hegel,
    G.W.F.), 204, 205, 207, 225, 228
subjectivity (see also ego, "I," self),
    61–62, 87, 191, 192, 210, 203,
    230–232, 238, 239–240, 263
suicide, 19, 102, 121
Surrealism, Surrealists, the surreal,
    25–26, 27, 231
symmetry, 1, 79, 137, 141, 168, 207,
    224, 226
synthesis, 28, 33, 41, 63, 80, 96, 204,
    218

Tatian, 48
tautology, xi, 15, 16, 214
Taylor, Charles, 64
Taylor, Mark C., 246, 251, 272n13,
    297n177
technology, 60, 74–76, 167, 242
teleology, 9, 43, 53, 99, 220, 227,
    290n11
terrorism, 19, 20, 76
Thales, 32
theology, theologian, 1, 7–8, 9, 10, 13,
    19, 48, 50–52, 59–60, 99, 114,
    119, 155, 156, 161, 195, 200,
    201, 243, 244, 246, 247–251, 261,
    276n53
    a-theology, 246, 249; death of God
    theology, 247–251, 297n176;

liberal theology, 251; negative
    theology, 245–246; ontotheology,
    202, 205; theothanatology, 248;
    weak theology, 247
Theresa of Avila, 46, 189
Tillich, Paul, 244
time, temporality, 31, 42, 54, 97, 135,
    138, 143, 147, 148, 149, 153, 165,
    175, 176, 178, 211, 214, 227, 228,
    237, 286n22, 291n37
    zero time, 74
tonality, xiii, xv, 99–100
totality, 33, 71, 79, 209, 218–219, 251,
    263, 268
tragedy, the tragic, xi–xiii, 87, 101,
    105–109, 118–119, 127, 128, 141,
    207, 226, 281n7, 282–283n15,
    284n13
transfiguration, 166
transcendence, 44–45, 47, 48, 63, 99,
    124, 192, 194, 211, 216, 238, 239,
    244, 251, 289n92
trinity, Trinity, 47, 55–56, 58, 59, 294
trope, xv, 82, 93, 110, 242, 255, 268
truth, Truth, 8, 14, 19, 28, 32, 36,
    37, 39–40, 49, 55, 57, 58, 65,
    97, 99, 132, 149, 154, 184, 190,
    194, 199, 200, 206, 209–210, 213,
    217, 236–237, 240, 241–242, 243,
    255, 260–261, 264, 268, 284n23,
    286n21
typography, 223–224

uncertainty principle, 74, 93, 94
unconsciousness, the unconscious, 79,
    80
unity, unification, union, 1–2, 9, 16,
    28, 30, 33, 35, 37, 40, 41–44, 45,
    46, 48, 49–52, 53, 54–61, 63–64,
    80, 99, 109, 122, 124, 142, 146,
    153, 156, 162, 164, 165, 167,
    177, 192, 199, 200, 201, 202–203,
    206, 208, 209, 218–219, 221, 224,
    225–226, 227, 232, 238, 258,
    277n66, 289n92

universe, 7, 18, 43, 47, 64, 70–71, 73, 74, 177, 199, 202, 244, 253, 273n22
universality, universals, Universal, 8, 9, 10, 19, 33, 40, 47, 49–50, 54, 93, 98, 99, 112, 147, 149, 153, 162, 171, 236, 245
  universalism, 50–51, 235, 240, 243
Upward, Edward, 122
utopia, 1, 110, 137

vacuum, 73, 74, 279n20
Vahanian, Gabriel, 247
van Buren, Paul, 247
Vattimo, Gianni, 1, 222, 247, 251, 297n177
Vaughan, Alden T. and Virginia Mason, 281n6, 282n13
via negativa, 243, 244
Vico, Giambattista, 169
violence, 181, 191, 264
  insurrection, 257, 259
vision, visioning, 2, 46, 77, 83–84, 86–88, 90–91, 106, 109, 110, 125–126, 140, 144, 147, 153, 155, 177, 225, 238, 254
void, 3, 11, 16, 20, 29, 70, 71, 72–74, 77, 86–87, 88, 94–95, 118, 123, 130, 131, 134, 136, 140, 141, 143, 144, 145, 146, 148, 155, 164, 165, 167–168, 176, 180, 181, 187, 200, 206, 235, 236–237, 239, 240–241, 242–243, 257, 278n5, 285n3
  "brilliant void," 138–139, 144, 153, 155, 156, 157, 158, 168, 187;
  Tohu-bohu, 187, 200
Voltaire, 223

Waldenfels, Hans, 278n10
war, warfare, 74, 75–76, 85, 122, 227, 257, 258

Cold War, 14, 75, 168; Spanish Civil War, 122; Thirty Years' War, 62; World War I, 14, 122, 169, 170; World War II, 14, 75, 122, 168, 169, 184, 255, 256
Ward, Graham, 247, 251
Warner, Rex, 122
Wasserstrom, Steven M., 297n177
Webster, John, 297n3
wheel, 4, 8, 108, 177
whisper, whispering, *sotte voce*, 98, 126, 133, 144, 158, 233, 267
Wilde, Oscar, 114, 185, 282n11
  The Picture of Dorian Gray, 114, 115, 167
Winquist, Charles, 247
Wittgenstein, Ludwig, 46, 282n12
womb, 122
Wordsworth, William, 87
Wrathall, Mark A., 297n177
Wyschogrod, Edith, 247

Xenophanes, 35, 42, 43

Yeats, William Butler, 2

Zeno, 35, 36–39, 204
zero, zeroing, xiii, xiv, 3, 5–6, 7, 8, 9, 11, 12, 15–19, 34, 63, 68, 69–77, 78–79, 80, 119, 124, 135, 144, 151, 158, 167, 171, 173–174, 181–182, 234, 235, 241, 242–243, 262, 269, 278n9–10, 280n43, 283n15
  absolute zero, 74; ground zero, 74–77; indifferent zero, 151, 152, 153, 155, 168; zero point, 74–75, 77; zero sum game, 168
Žižek, Slavoj, 122, 222, 247, 277n59, 283n2
Zoroastrianism, 48

6942248R00202

Printed in Great Britain
by Amazon.co.uk, Ltd.,
Marston Gate.